Converso Non-Conformism in Early Modern Spain

"This well-written and thoroughly researched book is an important contribution to our understanding of Spanish social and religious identity in the sixteenth and seventeenth centuries. By means of a lengthy and absorbing series of case studies of individuals, it points up the importance of a Jewish background to understanding many great figures in Spanish life and, as such, has wide, interdisciplinary appeal."
—John Edwards, *University of Oxford, UK*

"This book provides a much-needed reassessment of the impact of the blood-purity obsession on Spanish society. Combining original research into Velázquez's roots with penetrating analyses of the character of Spain's humanist and reform movements, Kevin Ingram's outstanding study reopens debate on the conversos' importance to early modern culture. His examination of race-based discrimination and its social effects also makes the work of great relevance to our own time."
—William Childers, *Brooklyn College, CUNY, USA*

"Kevin Ingram's trenchant, persuasively argued book makes a major contribution to the cultural and social history of early modern Spain, and, needless to say, to the sub-field of what one might call "converso studies" … Although there are many works on conversos, the Spanish Inquisition, and related matters, there is nothing out there that draws on the lives and works of so many New Christians and pulls them all together in a cogent, compelling, and original argument as this does."
—Mark D. Meyerson, *University of Toronto, Canada*

Kevin Ingram

Converso Non-Conformism in Early Modern Spain

Bad Blood and Faith from Alonso de Cartagena to Diego Velázquez

Kevin Ingram
Division of Humanities
Saint Louis University
Madrid, Spain

ISBN 978-3-030-40430-7   ISBN 978-3-319-93236-1 (eBook)
https://doi.org/10.1007/978-3-319-93236-1

Library of Congress Control Number: 2018946529

© The Editor(s) (if applicable) and The Author(s) 2018
This work is subject to copyright. All rights are solely and exclusively licensed by the Publisher, whether the whole or part of the material is concerned, specifically the rights of translation, reprinting, reuse of illustrations, recitation, broadcasting, reproduction on microfilms or in any other physical way, and transmission or information storage and retrieval, electronic adaptation, computer software, or by similar or dissimilar methodology now known or hereafter developed.
The use of general descriptive names, registered names, trademarks, service marks, etc. in this publication does not imply, even in the absence of a specific statement, that such names are exempt from the relevant protective laws and regulations and therefore free for general use.
The publisher, the authors and the editors are safe to assume that the advice and information in this book are believed to be true and accurate at the date of publication. Neither the publisher nor the authors or the editors give a warranty, express or implied, with respect to the material contained herein or for any errors or omissions that may have been made. The publisher remains neutral with regard to jurisdictional claims in published maps and institutional affiliations.

Cover illustration: © classicpaintings / Alamy Stock Photo

This Palgrave Macmillan imprint is published by the registered company Springer Nature Switzerland AG
The registered company address is: Gewerbestrasse 11, 6330 Cham, Switzerland

In memory of my mother Dorothy Ingram with love, gratitude, and admiration.

Preface

Jews may have entered the Iberian Peninsula as early as the eighth century BC, arriving on Phoenician trading ships from the Levant. However, it is unlikely that they established colonies of any importance until 800 years later, under Roman occupation. By the fourth century AD, the Jewish community had grown large enough to pose a problem for Spain's early Christian Church, as witnessed at the Council of Elvira (Granada, circa 324 AD), which decreed that Christians were prohibited from marrying and dining with Jews, or having their crops blessed by rabbis. With the growth of the Catholic Church, the Jews' situation in the Peninsula became increasingly precarious, marked by a series of draconian laws enacted in the seventh century by Visigothic rulers, themselves recent converts to Catholicism. By the end of the century, many Jews had relocated to North Africa, from where, it was claimed, they conspired against the Visigothic king Egica. Several decades later, during the Islamic invasion of 711, Jews were again accused of conspiracy, on this occasion of opening up the gates of the Visigothic capital of Toledo and welcoming the Muslim invaders into the city. These accusations, which have been repeated up to the present day, are not without substance. Certainly the Iberian Jews had much to gain from living under an Islamic regime which respected their right to practice, albeit discreetly, their own religion.

Under Islamic rule, the Iberian Jews prospered as artisans and traders, at least up until the twelfth century, when al-Andalus (Islamic Spain) became governed by Islamic fundamentalists, the Almohads, from North Africa. Faced once again with forced conversion, many Jews traveled east, in search of more tolerant Islamic regimes, or to the north of the Peninsula, where Christian forces were recapturing territory from the Islamic states in what would become known as the *Reconquista*.

By the time the Almohad capital Seville fell to the Christian forces, in 1248, most of the Iberian Peninsula was in the hands of Christian rulers, and the majority of the Jews under Christian law. Once again the Jewish communities survived and prospered, aided by their royal and noble overlords, who relied upon the Jews' business acumen and taxes to maintain their exchequers. However, as the Jewish communities began to expand, they encountered increasing hostility from their Christian neighbors, led by a Church that saw Judaism as a dangerous rival. In a bid to discourage fraternization between Jews and Christians, the Church reminded the faithful of the Jews' deicide. For its part Christian society was disposed to see religious malfeasance in a minority group whose tax collecting and money lending activities had already created social friction. Soon there were rumors that the Jews were mimicking their ancient ancestors by procuring and destroying sacramental hosts (symbolically murdering Christ), and kidnapping and crucifying Christian children. As a result, the Jews' royal and noble protectors came under increasing pressure to eject them from their territories. This situation was not peculiar to Spain. In fact the Spanish Jews initially fared much better than their northern European counterparts, their *Juderias* growing throughout the thirteenth century, long after England's and France's Jewish populations had been expelled.

However, the Spanish Jews' situation deteriorated in the fourteenth century as a concerted proselytizing campaign by the Dominican and Franciscan orders began to destabilize their communities. Then, in 1391, soon after the death of King Juan I, the Christians of Seville rose up against the city's Jewish neighborhoods, killing or forcibly baptizing their inhabitants. These attacks soon spread to other Spanish towns and cities in what would become known as Spain's Jewish pogrom. Between 1391 and 1413, the year in which a group of frightened and demoralized Spanish rabbis were forced to defend their faith in front of the pope in the town of Tortosa, perhaps a third or more of Spain's Jewish population had been baptized into Christianity, the majority under extreme pressure. And thus was born Spain's complex and contentious converso phenomenon.

The conversos, that is to say, the converts from Judaism to Christianity and their heirs (the Old Christian population made no distinction between the original converts and their descendants), tended to thrive in an environment in which they were no longer subject to the restrictions placed on the Jews. This inevitably created tensions between them and their Old

Christian neighbors, who were inclined to believe that the ex-Jews, or even the children of ex-Jews, should act with greater deference and humility, as befitted their neophytic status. In order to remind the conversos of their religious and social inferiority, clerical and secular institutions began, from the mid-fifteenth century onward, to introduce *limpieza de sangre* (pure blood) statutes, prohibiting the entrance of anyone with Jewish ancestors. These statutes did not, however, temper Old Christian animosity toward the converso community, which was continually fanned by the rank-and-file clergy. To placate these critics, the Catholic Monarchs, Isabel and Ferdinand, established an Inquisition in 1478, licensed to investigate and punish converso religious transgressions. Thirteen years later, the same monarchs signed a decree giving Spain's Jews four months to convert to Catholicism or leave the land, ostensibly with the view to taking temptation away from their New Christian subjects. The decree led to another wave of conversions, greater tension among Old and New Christians, and even more prosecutions of converso Judaizers.

The Spanish Inquisition's prosecutions of Spain's crypto Jews has tended to color modern scholarship on the converso phenomenon, at least until quite recently. For nineteenth-century conservatives, led by Marcelino Menéndez Pelayo, the Inquisition was the savior of Catholicism, protecting Spain against alien ideas, including those touted by ex-Jews. For a nineteenth-century liberal camp, on the other hand, it was a baleful religious Cheka, the enforcer of absolutist oppression. In this drama, the main protagonist was the Holy Office itself, the conversos taking secondary roles as typecast villains or victims. Consequently, conversos were only visible as crypto-Jews; those who did not Judaize, it was assumed, blended discreetly into Old Christian society, where they quietly absorbed the mores of a dominant culture that was about to embark on its glorious Golden Age. Even Jewish scholars paid little attention to the converso community outside of its clash with the Inquisition, keen to demonstrate that the New Christians were *anusim* (forced ones) who remained true to their Jewish faith, despite the terrible consequences of this allegiance.

Of course, it was easy for scholars to ignore the conversos' contribution to early modern Christian culture when the protagonists themselves had conspired, so to speak, in their historiographical invisibility, masquerading as Old Christians through false genealogies and protests of honorable, clean (Old Christian) blood. This cover-up was perpetuated by early biographers, who ignored compromising background facts in order to protect their heroes' reputations. Later scholars repeated this misinformation, sometimes out of ignorance, sometimes out of prejudice for an Old Christian Golden Age, overlooking evidence that challenged the established narrative. Thus early modern Spain remained an Old Christian stage, at least up until 1948, when Américo Castro published his highly controversial *España en su historia*.

It was in *España en su historia* and *La realidad historica de España* (1954) that Castro offered a vision of an early modern Spain in which the conversos were *the* intellectual force, a view vigorously rejected by many of his fellow Spanish scholars as both erroneous and unpatriotic (see Chap. 7). Even after evidence emerged supporting Castro's thesis, many scholars, both inside and outside the Francoist academy, continued to pronounce in favor of a Golden Age landscape dominated by eminent Old Christians, rejecting strong circumstantial evidence that challenged the received wisdom. These conflicting views led eventually to a sort of stalemate or tacit truce, still evident today, under the terms of which all parties agreed to acknowledge that a number of conversos made an important contribution to early modern high culture, while generally avoiding claims as to the extent or significance of this contribution. This diplomatic compromise is reflected in Ángel Alcalá's 1994 edited volume, *Judios. Sefarditas. Conversos*, in which Alcalá writes circumspectly, '[T]he fact is that, for whatever the reasons, some of the most eminent writers, humanists, Christian reformers, mystics and saints of the Golden Age had in their veins blood of not remote Jewish origin.' In fact, Alcalá seriously undervalued the contribution of conversos to Golden Age letters. For although background information on Spain's prominent humanists, mystics, and Christian reformers is often sparse, it more often than not alludes to converso ancestries.

The tension between a predominantly converso reform movement and its opponent, a largely Old Christian orthodox moral majority, is one of the most important issues in early modern Spanish society, directly or indirectly influencing many of the great works of Golden Age literature—religious or otherwise. And yet this tense drama still does not figure prominently in early modern Spanish history surveys, where, outside of the Inquisition's attacks on crypto-Jews, the converso remains a somewhat marginal figure. Of course, historians mention that many of Spain's early *alumbrados* and Erasmus apologists were conversos, and they reveal, on occasion, that other heterodox thinkers may have been of Jewish heritage; but this serves only to give the impression that all those humanists, evangelists, and mystics who remain unlabeled are Old Christian. We still lack studies that attempt to collate and synthesize the pockets of scholarship lingering in academic journals to produce a more comprehensive picture of converso non-conformism and its impact across the early modern period.

It seems that many Hispanists still labor under the belief that as the conversos were a minority presence in early modern Spain, they were unlikely to have dominated its intellectual and reform environments. However, while it is true that Spain's converso community represented only a small fraction of the overall population, it made up a much larger proportion of urban society, where middle-sort (proto-bourgeois) conversos often outnumbered their Old Christian counterparts. It was the success of these upwardly mobile conversos that posed a problem for Old Christian society, and it was specifically toward this dynamic, visible entity that the early *limpieza de sangre* and Inquisitorial offensive was directed. Consequently, it was this embattled group of converso merchants, artisans, and, above all, professionals that had most interest in changing the social and religious mores of its society. It is no coincidence that Spain's greatest humanists—Juan Luis Vives, Juan de Vergara, Juan and Alfonso de Valdés, Juan de Ávila, Luis de León, and Benito Arias Montano, were from a converso background. Nor is it a coincidence that two of the three most influential religious movements in sixteenth-century Spain—Juan de Ávila's evangelical movement and Teresa of Ávila's Barefoot Carmelites—were founded by conversos, financed largely by converso money, and, in their fledgling form, dominated by a converso membership. As for Spain's third great religious reform movement, the Jesuits, the founder himself may have been from an Old Christian Basque family (at least on his father's side), but his formative years were spent in the household of the court treasurer, Juan Velázquez de Cuéllar, in an environment, I will argue, dominated by conversos and converso religious disquiet. It was here that the seeds of his own religious awakening were planted, and it was from within this middle-sort converso community that his early support base was established, giving his movement the reputation of being a Jewish conspiracy.

In contrast to Spain's New Christian professionals, its Old Christian middle sort had a more ambiguous view toward reform. As merchants and bureaucrats, they were obviously disposed to challenge the status quo, defined by the nobility and a noble-controlled Church; however, like the rest of Old Christian society, they were swept up by the *limpieza* phenomenon, embracing the conceit that their pure Christian blood conveyed upon them privileged status. They were also aware that this privilege rested on their adherence to the principles of the Catholic Church. To criticize their religion too rigorously was to place themselves in the camp of the impaired conversos, risking accusations that they too were tainted, thus jeopardizing their position in society. The message was clear: if one wished to preserve one's *castizo* (pure) identity, one generally shied clear of behavior associated with conversos, including the advocacy of reform. This is not to say that Old Christians were less blasphemous or anti-clerical than their converso neighbors. But this was an everyday querulousness that tended to stop short of attacking dogma or advocating a socio-religious system based on equality and merit, a concern that animated their New Christian co-religionists. In general, Spain's religious reform advocates were, for obvious reasons, conversos, not Old Christians.

In the 25 years that have elapsed since Ángel Alcalá published his edited volume on the conversos, cited above, the interest in Spain's converso phenomenon has continued to grow, inspiring innovative scholarship on New Christian identity, networks, resistance strategies, and reform. However, with the possible exception of Stephania Pastore's insightful *Una herejía Española* (2010), no recent study has attempted to explore in depth early modern converso heterodoxy or its trajectory. Building on the scholarship of Francisco Márquez Villanueva, Pastore's work examines the effect of Hernando de Talavera's evangelical message on early sixteenth-century converso activists, at the same time vividly illuminating the political and religious context in which this converso protest took place. However, while Pastore's work is an important contribution to converso studies and Spanish historiography, it tends, inadvertently, to reinforce the view that the converso involvement in religious reform was an early sixteenth-century phenomenon that had run its course before the last sessions of Trent announced a new, more oppressive, religious reality.

In writing the present work, I wish to chart converso non-conformism across the expanse of what Fernand Braudel called the long sixteenth century, opening up the cast of characters and their platform, and demonstrating how thoroughly the converso issue dominated Spanish society, humanism, and reform, both in a pre-Tridentine environment and subsequently. Indeed, much of the book focuses on Counter-Reformation Spain, where, I argue, a predominantly converso reform movement attempted to combat Tridentine dictates by emphasizing the importance of quietist practice, social toleration, and religious concord. This phenomenon continues to go unrecognized because, as I have noted above, the protagonists themselves were careful to disguise their identities and motives, and in this deception they have been aided and abetted by a modern scholarly community that has been slow to follow up on clues that contradict the established picture. Those of us who do spend time following such clues are fully aware that our endeavors will rarely allow us to state definitively that a Benito Arias Montano, a Pedro de Valencia, or indeed a Diego Velázquez de Silva were conversos. Nevertheless, one hopes that the evidence for such a proposition is compelling, and as such will lead to a more fruitful discussion on the nature of Spain's early modern reform movement and its advocates for change.

In the following pages I examine converso non-conformism and the socio-religious environment in which it emerged and developed. I do not focus on the first generation of converts to Catholicism, but their descendants, one, two, three, or even four generations removed from the conversion process, demonstrating how a minority of disaffected conversos promoted socio-religious change with the view to combating Old Christian prejudice. There is no doubt that many of these men and women were addressing deep psychological issues of self-worth and belonging. However, while the study offers some insights into what I refer to as converso disquiet, it does not pretend to be an exploration of the nuances of New Christian identity—an impossible task given my subjects' wariness of self-revelation. It is, rather, an investigation into Spain's distinctive reform environment, where the converso and the converso issue took center stage.

Acknowledgments

My thanks to William Childers, John Edwards, Mark Meyerson, and the late Francisco Márquez Villanueva for reading drafts of the book, or parts of the book, as it neared its completion, and for their trenchant comments. I would also like to express my gratitude to Mercedes Alcalá, Ruth Fine, Gregory Hutcheson, Steven Hutchinson, David Ringrose, Yosef Kaplan, and, especially, Ignacio Pulido for their encouragement and support.

I am extremely grateful for the financial support of the following institutions and foundations: the Spanish Foreign Ministry, grants for research into Spanish history; the Program of Cultural Cooperation between the Spanish Ministry of Culture and US Universities; the Maurice Amado Foundation for Research in Sephardic Studies; and the Saint Louis Center for Intercultural Studies. My special thanks to Saint Louis University, Madrid Campus, for its continuing support of my converso projects, in all their manifestations.

Finally, I am indebted to my wife Fabiola Martínez, for her love, good humor, smart advice (not always adhered to), and infinite patience.

Contents

1 Introduction   1

2 From Toledo to Alcala   11

3 From Alcala to Seville and Beyond   51

4 The Road Out of Trent   91

5 Four Humanists   117

6 Diego Velázquez and the Subtle Art of Protest   179

7 The Converso Returns   225

Notes   243

Select Bibliography   333

Index   357

List of Figures

Fig. 4.1	Lucas de Heere, *The Queen of Sheba before Solomon*, from Saint Bavo Cathedra, Ghent. Courtesy of the Flemish Art Imagebank, Ghent	105
Fig. 4.2	Dirck Crabeth, *Last Supper devotional portraits of Philip II of Spain and Mary Tudor* (central section), Janskirk, Gouda. Courtesy of Collection Rijksdienst voor het Cultureel Erfgoed, Amersfoort, NL	106
Fig. 5.1	Kings of Judah, Escorial Basilica. Courtesy of J.M. Monegro	132
Fig. 6.1	Diego Velázquez, *Kitchen Scene with Christ in the House of Martha and Mary*. Courtesy of the National Gallery, London. Bequeathed by Sir William H. Gregory, 1892	195
Fig. 6.2	Diego Velázquez, *Kitchen Maid with the Supper at Emmaus*. Courtesy of the National Gallery of Ireland, Dublin. Presented, Sir Alfred and Lady Beit, 1987 (Beit collection)	196
Fig. 6.3	Diego Velázquez, *Adoration of the Magi*. Alamy Images. © Heritage Image Partnership Ltd/Alamy Stock Photo	198
Fig. 6.4	Diego Velázquez, *An Old Woman Cooking Eggs*. © PAINTING/Alamy Stock Photo	199
Fig. 6.5	Diego Velázquez, *The Waterseller*. © Lebrecht Music and Arts Photo Library/Alamy Stock Photo	200
Fig. 6.6	Diego Velázquez, *Christ after the Flagellation Contemplated by the Christian Soul*. © Lebrecht Music and Arts Photo Library/Alamy Stock Photo	208

Fig. 6.7   Diego Velázquez, *Triumph of Bacchus* (*Los Borrachos*).
© FineArt/Alamy Stock Photo   212
Fig. 6.8   Diego Velázquez, *Las Meninas*. © classicpaintings/Alamy Stock
Photo   221
Fig. 6.9   Diego Velázquez, *Las Meninas* detail. © Paul Fearn/
Alamy Stock Photo   223

CHAPTER 1

Introduction

'[A]lthough they silenced tongues, they could not silence pens, which, with greater liberty than tongues, usually convey to those who one wishes to hear what is enclosed in the heart.'
Miguel Cervantes, Don Quijote I, XXIV

Velázquez's Cross

At some point between his entry into the Order of Santiago on 28 November 1659 and his death on 6 August 1660, Diego Velázquez stood before his painting *Las Meninas* and inscribed a red cross on his own doublet. This important detail had been absent from the painting during the first three years of its life; it had, however, been anticipated in the midget's breeches, the maid's sleeve decoration, the *infanta's* floral brooch, the small jug, and the dabs of paint on the painter's palette, all of which form a scarlet trail leading the viewer to a jet-black doublet that cries out for red paint. 'Knight me!' Velázquez demands from the confines of his own canvas, 'For I am a noble practitioner of the art of painting, and here is the proof, the *probanza*, *Las Meninas*.'

Ironically, in Velázquez's real *probanza*, the one he had recently undertaken to enter the noble Order of Santiago, his superior artistry was of no help. What interested the Council of the Orders was his family background, which was required to be untarnished by manual labor, trade, and, particularly, Jewish or Moorish blood. Unfortunately, Velázquez's family did not conform to these exacting standards, and thus in order to petition for his noble cross the painter had to lie about his ancestry. Of course, no one was deceived by this subterfuge, least of all the adjudicating committee for the Council, who pronounced him unfit for noble status.[1] And so finally Velázquez was forced to solicit, with the aid of Philip IV, a papal dispensation, permitting him to sport the Santiago insignia despite his common stock.

In all likelihood, Velázquez was aware that his cross would inevitably depend on papal goodwill and that the Santiago *probanza* was nothing more than a necessary and irksome process that he would have to submit himself to before he could place his case before a more sympathetic Holy See. The fact that Pope Alexander VII's vote of confidence would be made with regard to Velázquez's artistic fame, rather than his family's reputation, may even have given the painter some gratification; it would certainly have conformed to the image he entertained of himself and wished to convey to posterity through *Las Meninas*, that being of a man ennobled by his art.

Curiously, however, posterity has not always been receptive to *Las Meninas*' message. It is only recently that art historians have begun to examine the work against the background of the Renaissance painters' campaign for recognition as liberal arts practitioners—that is to say, as men engaged in a noble enterprise. But even this interpretation does not fully explain Velázquez's interest in proclaiming his noble artistic nature. In order to comprehend *Las Meninas*' message, we need to examine the painting with an eye toward Velázquez's immediate environment, in which two socio-cultural factions were in constant conflict. The more numerous of these two groups was Spain's Old Christian moral majority, which by the mid-seventeenth century had all but completed its task of constructing a national stereotype based on correct (Old-Christian) blood and orthodox Catholic practice. Its antagonist was a relatively small group of professional men, supported by a number of influential noble families, who favored a society based on a humanist socio-religious credo in which social worth was determined as much by merit as by genealogy, and religious observance was founded on evangelical (or Erasmian) precepts rather than Church tradition. It was to this second group, comprised predominantly of conversos, that Diego Velázquez gave his allegiance.[2]

It is my view that Diego Velázquez was from a converso background and that his humanist credo, so evident in his art, was influenced by his social caste. He was heir to a tradition of converso non-conformism in Seville, whose adherents confronted the prejudicial social and religious mores of Spanish society with humanistic arguments. These men were no social revolutionaries; they were, rather, private, low-key dissenters whose dissidence was contained in carefully nuanced literature directed toward their like-minded friends. Velázquez's early *bodegones* are themselves examples of non-conformist humanist texts, as are a number of canvases painted during his first years at the court of Philip IV. It was here that the young painter found himself enmeshed in a battle between the reforming faction of his patron, the Count-Duke of Olivares, and an opposing group of courtiers who attacked the *privado* for corrupting Spanish culture. At the center of this dispute was the capital's ever-growing community of Portuguese conversos, who had gravitated to Madrid to take advantage of the Count-Duke's favorable attitude toward Portugal's New Christian business community. This strained atmosphere is reflected by Velázquez in his painting *Los Borrachos*, which, I argue in Chap. 6, was a veiled attack on Spain's blood purity statutes and a prejudiced *vulgo* that supported them.

Diego Velázquez was a protagonist in an early modern social drama involving Spain's converso and Old Christian communities. This conflict had begun in the early fifteenth century, soon after the 1391 Jewish pogrom, which witnessed a wave of conversions to Christianity. These newcomers to the Christian religion were, quite logically, called converts, but so too were their children and grandchildren, who had been born, ostensibly, into Christian families. Obviously, as far as Spain's Old Christian population was concerned, the term 'converso' referred not only to neophytic religious status, but to a profound taint that neither time nor religious assimilation was capable of erasing.

The *limpieza de sangre* (pure blood) laws, starting with the 1449 *Sentencia-Estatuto* of Toledo, formalized what Old Christian society had long felt: the converts and their heirs were not authentic co-religionists and thus should not be allowed to become bona fide members of Christian society. These statutes forbade the conversos access to positions in religious, civic, and educational establishments, on the grounds that they were inherently untrustworthy. Under the terms of the statutes all candidates applying for entry into the above institutions were submitted to an official inquiry into their family backgrounds. If Jewish blood was detected in the candidate's ancestry, then he would be automatically disqualified from entry. In this way Old Christian society aimed to bridle the social ambitions of the converts and their heirs.

However, a number of wealthy conversos had already married into important noble families; under the conditions of the *limpieza* statutes, the descendants of these families would also be considered conversos, that is to say, second-class citizens. Thus it soon became apparent that the *limpieza* legislation affected not only the target group but potentially a large section of the Spanish nobility. In fact, by the sixteenth century few nobles, or even commoners, could be absolutely certain that they were not in some way 'contaminated.' Everyone could, however, make a demonstrative exhibition of their Old Christian mores, embracing, so to speak, pork and the saints while eschewing garlic, spices, eggplants, soap, and intellectual activity—Jewish perversities.

In this paranoid environment, the converso was the bogeyman whose bad blood surreptitiously corrupted the body and the body politic. Fomented by the Clergy, this prejudice was exploited by both Church and Crown in their campaign to homogenize, unify, and control a society that was anything but uniform. The key to this incipient state-building campaign was, naturally, blood: good Spaniards were those men and women with the correct Old Christian blood; bad Spaniards were the others, the conversos and the Moriscos (Christianized Muslims), who needed to be marginalized and contained through the *limpieza* laws.

Ironically, however, those statutes that had been designed to demoralize and oppress the conversos promoted a greater self-consciousness among them. This was particularly evident among a converso intellectual/ professional class, the group most affected by the *limpieza* legislation. Determined to contest the *Sentencia-Estatuto*, a number of influential conversos, including the highly respected Alonso de Cartagena, wrote long tracts defending themselves against accusations of inferiority, pointing out that their Jewish ancestors were God's chosen people, and thus were, if anything, superior rather than inferior to Old Christians. Other prominent conversos preferred, however, to avoid references to Jewish superiority, and instead turned to the Italian humanist movement for inspiration.

Humanism was attractive to converso professionals for obvious reasons. As members of Spain's socially dynamic middle sort, these men were drawn to a movement that challenged an old, static order in which the three estates were enjoined to maintain their social positions; as New Christians in search of an accessible religion and not an elaborate and alien doctrine, they were inspired by a Christian humanism that advocated a minimalist Christianity based on an evangelical message; and as members of a minority group victimized by an Old Christian society for its inferior blood, they were inspired by a credo that was predicated on the view that nobility was conveyed by *virtù* (or merit), and not by one's family tree. Through humanism the conversos were able to look upon themselves as a unique group; not the tainted and vilified *Alboraique* (hybrid animal) of Old Christian slander, but a body of virtuous, enlightened men, like those neophytes referred to by Saint Paul in his Epistles, who had chosen a new way forward.[3] Likewise, they could identify themselves with the *novus homo* of ancient Rome, high-minded public figures like Cicero and Horace, whose fame, prestige, and, ultimately, nobility rested not on their immaculate bloodline but on their talent, morality, and industry.

As adherents to a humanist credo, converso intellectuals could attack the unacceptable face of Catholic Spain discreetly as Christian and Social moralists and not vilified outsiders. Nevertheless, for many conversos who embraced a humanist credo this was not sufficient. For these men there still remained the need to defend the conversos against accusations of inferior blood, to attack Old Christian Spain's illiteracy and ignorance, and to celebrate a Sephardic cultural inheritance, which some did by promoting the view that the ancient Hebrew world was as culturally significant as classical Greece or Rome, and that the Hebrew Bible was central to the Christian tradition and not merely a prologue to it.[4]

Spain's converso non-conformists were, nevertheless, cautious activists, writing guardedly, or ambiguously, for both a general public and an intimate inner circle, or as Mateo Aleman puts it in *Guzmán de Alfarache*, for the 'vulgo' and the 'discreet reader.'[5] By 'vulgo' Aleman meant the uneducated, intolerant reader, for whom it was necessary to proclaim one's *limpieza de sangre* and Christian orthodoxy; the 'discreet reader' signified those people, a coterie of friends usually, who were aware of the deception.

The word *limpieza* itself held a special appeal for converso writers, allowing them to proclaim subtly that they were members of a hygienic, New Christian, culture, while feigning to be members of a soiled, Old Christian one that flaunted its clean blood. Thus the Córdoban humanist Ambrosio de Morales could state brazenly in his father's funeral oration: 'Here is written with much truth all that the deceased was: that is, of noble lineage and in all parts very clean [*muy limpio*].' Here the humanist plays with the word 'parts,' which could either connote branches of his family or body parts, and alludes to his subterfuge by emphasizing the statement's veracity.[6] Such puns were popular among converso writers, who wished to reveal their secret condition to a discreet reader while hiding it from all others. With the same dissimulative intention, Francisco Pacheco, in his *Retratos*, informs us that the Seville humanist Juan de Malara's parents were 'honorable and clean people' [*'gente onrada y limpia'*],[7] and that the painter Diego Velázquez (Pacheco's son-in-law) had 'cleanliness and good parts' [*'limpieza y buenas partes'*].[8]

The conversos' inclination to launder their family backgrounds is frequently lampooned by converso authors in Spanish picaresque fiction, a markedly New Christian literary genre. Often the novelists have their protagonists proclaim immaculate Old Christian ancestries, usually with roots in the far north of Spain, where it was believed few Jews had penetrated. However, this information is invariably contradicted by other biographical data that allude to their Jewish provenance. Thus in his *Crónica*, Francesillo de Zúñiga writes, 'in the mountains of the Asturias (which forms part of the Kingdom of Galicia) our Lord Jesus nurtured a poor boy called Pelayo of Visigothic lineage, from which I descended.' However, earlier he makes a clear reference to his Jewish lineage, when he writes that he is 'Duke of Jerusalem by direct succession, Count of Ruben and Tiberiades.'[9] In *La Pícara Justina*, another picaresque author, Francisco López de Úbeda, describes his heroine as 'la pícara montañesa,' a humorous oxymoron, combining *pícara* (invariably a conversa) with the adjective mountain-dwelling (an allusion to the Old Christian mountain dwellers of the Asturias). Later in the novel, Justina herself exposes the deceit, revealing that she is indeed a New Christian.

Coming from the mountains (the north of Spain) was recognized as a sign of Old Christian genealogy. Thus many conversos attempted to parry rumors of their Jewish roots with proclamations of northern ancestry. For example, the Córdoban poet Juan de Mena, accused by contemporaries of having Jewish roots, insisted that his ancestors came from the Valley of Mena 'in the land they call the Mountains' (Vizcaya).[10] Likewise, the Seville humanist Francisco Pacheco (the painter Pacheco's uncle), in his *limpieza de sangre* examination to become a canon, linked his family name with the village of Villasevil de los Pachecos in Cantabria, while Pacheco's friend, and fellow humanist, Benito Arias, actually added Montano to his family surname, intimating northern Spanish provenance. Benito Arias was indeed born in a mountain town, but this was Fregenal de la Sierra, in southern Extremadura, renowned for its large converso population. One assumes that he took the name Montano as a means of dissimulating his background, while, in a sense, proclaiming it, at least to a discreet circle of friends.[11]

The ingenious Miguel de Cervantes offers his own parody of ancestral cleansing in the opening lines of *Don Quijote*, informing us that, like the brave knight Amadis of Gaul, Quijote decided to add the name of his country to his own, calling himself Don Quijote de la Mancha, 'which in his opinion proclaimed his lineage and native land perfectly.'[12] But why would 'la Mancha' reference Quijote's lineage as well as homeland? The question was not one that Cervantes' general reader was likely to pose himself. However, the discreet reader would recognize that *mancha* (stain) was a term applied by Old Christians to conversos, whose blood was considered tainted, and that for this reason 'de la Mancha' (of the stain) 'perfectly' situated the ancestors of Cervantes' famous alter-ego both geographically and genealogically, as the author stated.[13]

As converso writers cloaked their backgrounds in double entendre, so too did they disguise their political and religious views in ostensibly orthodox discourses. Occasionally they even alluded to this subterfuge. This was the case of Aleman in the introduction to *Guzmán de Alfarache*, as I have already noted, and of Alonso Núñez de Reinoso in his novel *Clareo y Florisea*, in which the author writes, 'beneath its invention lie great secrets.'[14] The title of Juan Pérez de Moya's compendium of Greek myths, *Philosofía secreta*, is also an allusion to hidden messages—not merely the moral messages ensconced in the myths that he explicates, but also, I would argue, converso-humanist ones, which the author surreptitiously introduced into his glosses. In his exposition of the myth of Bacchus, Pérez de Moya notes that while the Greeks attributed the invention of wine to this god, the real inventor was Noah, at the beginning of the second age of man. It was during this same time, the author states, that men began to eat meat, God having told his people: 'I give you licence to eat all that you wish, that is to say freedom to eat herbs and fruit, with only this proviso: that you don't eat meat that isn't bled, because eating it with blood is cruel and bestial.'[15] While this comment has nothing to do with the myth of Bacchus, it is not, I would contend, a pointless aside; it is, rather, a surreptitious defense of Jewish dietary laws, from whose practice conversos were forced to desist.

Pérez de Moya's *Philosofía secreta* became an essential guide for many Spanish Baroque poets and painters interested in rendering a moralistic interpretation of Greek mythology. Diego Velázquez himself owned a copy of the work, and it is reasonable to assume that he referred to it, as well as to Ovid's *Metamorphoses*, to paint his *Triumph of Bacchus*, or *Los Borrachos* (*The Drunkards*). Indeed, like Pérez de Moya, Velázquez uses the Bacchus myth to make a surreptitious attack on Old Christian Spain—

not its bestial eating habits, but, I will argue, its spiritual and intellectual impoverishment, its ignorance and superstition, and most of all its prejudice against his converso friend, Juan de Jáuregui.[16]

BAD BLOOD AND FAITH

A veiled attack on *limpieza de sangre* legislation, Velázquez's *Los Borrachos* forms part of a larger conflict that began 150 years previous to the painter's birth, with the *Sentencia-Estatuto*. Up until this point Spain's converso elite had generally avoided a public examination of its religious identity, preferring to reserve its true religiosity for private discourse. However, the *Sentencia-Estatuto*, usually regarded as the first of the *limpieza de sangre* statutes, forced these high-placed bureaucrats and scholars to defend their socio-religious legitimacy, and in so doing address, in a civic arena, their own notions on what it meant to be a Christian and a Spaniard. It was thus in attempting to defend themselves against accusations of duplicity that conversos became leading proponents of religious and socio-political reform, advancing their views through the inchoate Spanish humanist and mystical movements, both of which they dominated. In support of this project, the conversos were able to count upon a number of noble families, in particular the Mendozas and Manriques, whose parvenu noble status, as well as their business and marital links to the New Christian community, often made them allies in reform.

Chapter 2 of this study examines the early converso-dominated reform movement, which developed in the royal court and certain noble households in the late fifteenth century before entering the new humanist university at Alcalá de Henares, where it took on the trappings of Erasmian Christian moralism. It was here that the converso humanists competed, or at times joined forces, with a predominantly converso illuminist movement, the *alumbrados,* who promoted the view that God's true temple lay within the hearts of the faithful, and that religious union was achieved not through the sacrament but through meditation on God's love. It was in this heady environment that Ignatius of Loyola was first introduced to a new, evangelical Christianity that later inspired his own reformist religious order, in its infancy also directed by converso scholars.

However, the growth of Lutheranism in Germany soon alerted the Crown and Church to the dangers of Spain's native reform movement; the result was a series of high-profile trials, in the late 1520s and 1530s, in which leading Erasmians and illuminists, almost all of whom converso, were prosecuted for heresy. These prosecutions effectively subdued the reform drive in Castile. However, by now an evangelical movement had also begun to emerge in Andalusia, promoted by the Archbishop of Seville, Alonso Manrique, who encouraged a group of young Erasmian scholars to transform religious practice in the south.

Chapter 3 focuses on the Andalusian reform movement in the first half of the sixteenth century, where the region's large New Christian population continued to struggle with its religious identity. As in Castile, members of the Andalusian converso community had formed intimate ties with members of the new nobility during the fifteenth century, among whom were the Portocarrero and Córdoba families. Significantly, both these noble clans supported the religious reform mission of the converso humanist Juan de Ávila, who spent his life disseminating a Pauline message of Christian equality and unity to the converso communities of Andalusia and Extremadura, through which he sought to create an advance guard of Christian reformers. In this enterprise Ávila was joined by a group of humanists, like himself educated at Alcalá de Henares, who entered the Seville Cathedral chapter in the 1530s, armed with an Erasmian and Valdesian reform message. These men broadcast their non-conformist views from the pulpit and, increasingly, within secret conventicles that examined proscribed Calvinist and Lutheran texts. In the late 1550s this dissident activity was exposed, leading to a spate of imprisonments and executions, once again stifling a largely New Christian movement for religious change.

Spain's mid-century Protestant trials took place against a background of increasing religious tension as each European principality attempted to impose respect for strict dogma—be it Catholic, Lutheran, or Calvinist—on its people. This situation invariably created frustrated groups of clandestine non-conformists, whose religious views were reserved for private discourse, or encrypted into works of superficial orthodoxy. It was with these Nicodemites in mind that a group of French humanists began to advocate the practice of *politique*, a practical political credo in which the state ruler was required to largely ignore his subjects' private heresies in the interests of social concord. In Chap. 4 I examine *politique* in post-Tridentine Spain, where certain converso humanists attempted to create a politically and religiously tolerant Philip II by promoting King Solomon as a royal role model. The object was to encourage a policy of peace and reconciliation, both within Philip's European dominions and in Spain, where the New Christians were still being stigmatized as an enemy within.

One of the more influential exponents of Spanish *politique* was the converso humanist Benito Arias Montano, who promoted Philip's El Escorial palace as a latter-day Solomon's Temple. In Chap. 5 I examine Montano and his close circle of friends, all of whom paid lip service to a Tridentine Catholic credo while advancing their own discreet message of religious transformation, toleration, and social peace within the realm. All were New Christians, I argue, whose humanist messages were relayed against a background of increasing anti-converso propaganda.

Post-Tridentine Spanish society was far from being a uniformly orthodox environment. The illuminist scandal in Seville during the 1620s, in which almost a thousand people approached the Inquisition to confess their religious misdeeds, gives some indication of the scale of heterodox activity in the Andalusian capital alone. It is my view that the young Seville painter Diego Velázquez alludes to this secret religious devotion in a number of his early canvases, including the famous *Waterseller*, which I discuss in Chap. 6. In Seville and later at court, in Madrid, Velázquez confronted the religious and social prejudices of his society in paintings that championed rationality, toleration, and quietist belief. They also proclaimed the nobility of his artistic endeavor, an obsession, in my view, related to the painter's converso roots.

Velázquez lived much of his adult life in an environment in which the conversos were constantly under attack, the main target being Madrid's large Portuguese community, who were considered bad subjects and worse Catholics. In the late 1650s, at the time of Velázquez's death, the Inquisition began to purge this wealthy group, leading many of its members to flee abroad, separating themselves and their capital from the Inquisitors' grasp. Subsequently, the converso issue gradually faded into the background, although it never really went away, as becomes clear from the modern historiographical debate on the conversos' significance to early modern Spanish culture. In Chap. 7 I examine this often tense academic discourse, which has developed against the backdrop of modern Spanish state building and the search for a unique national identity or volksgeist.

CHAPTER 2

From Toledo to Alcala

It has been estimated that as a result of the 1391 riots against the Jewish *aljamas* and the aggressive conversion campaign that followed, a third or more of Spain's Sephardic community converted to Christianity.[1] In this tense atmosphere few of the first-generation converts sincerely embraced the Catholic Church or Old Christian society; indeed, most congregated in converso neighborhoods, where the Jewish culture continued to exert a strong influence on their lives. For their part, Old Christians remained antagonistic toward the new converts, whom they regarded (with some justification) as lukewarm Catholics; and this antagonism grew throughout the fifteenth century, as a converso middle sort, free from the social and commercial restrictions applied to the Jews, assumed a prominent position in the business and professional life on the peninsula.

Those Jews who converted to Christianity in the wake of the 1391 pogrom found themselves in an advantageous position vis-à-vis both the Jewish and Old Christian communities. As New Christians they were no longer subject to the restrictions that had hampered Jewish merchants and professionals. As literate men (all Jewish males were required to gain a basic level of literacy in order to read the Torah), often with a sound knowledge of trade and finance, and with important contacts in Jewish financial and mercantile circles, they were able to compete with the Old Christian urban community at an advantage. A number of these new converts accumulated large fortunes, which they used to advance their social positions within their cities. One method of social advancement was through the purchase of administrative offices within the church and local

© The Author(s) 2018
K. Ingram, *Converso Non-Conformism in Early Modern Spain*,
https://doi.org/10.1007/978-3-319-93236-1_2

government; another method was to form marriage alliances with that other *arriviste* group, Castile's new nobility—families like the Ayalas, Mendozas, and Manriques, who through wise political maneuvering had risen rapidly to the top of Spain's fifteenth-century social hierarchy.[2]

The conversos' increasing commercial and social prominence in Castile's urban centers inevitably led to clashes with the Old Christian community. One of the most dramatic confrontations occurred in Toledo in 1449, where a converso agent of the Crown, Alonso Cota, was made responsible for collecting an extraordinary tax levied to aid Juan II's defense of Navarre against a French incursion. Predisposed to see this tax as an example of converso avarice and malice, the Old Christian community rose up against its New Christian neighbors, looting and burning their neighborhoods. Ordered to put a stop to the violence, the *alcalde mayor* (lord mayor), Pedro Sarmiento, merely used his power to inflame anti-converso feeling even further, and to introduce a statute, the *Sentencia-Estatuto*, prohibiting conversos from occupying public office— that is to say, from comporting themselves as nobles.[3]

The Toledo statute was soon rescinded and Sarmiento exiled from the city. However, it was clear to a number of influential conversos at court that the *Sentencia-Estatuto* needed to be condemned in writing before it induced other urban centers, where anti-converso sentiment also ran high, to pass similar legislation. The converso scholars Alonso Díaz de Montalvo, Fernán Díaz de Toledo, Alonso de Cartagena, and Diego de Valera all wrote lengthy replies to the statute.[4] All pointed out that the Jews had occupied a foundational role in Christianity, and all emphasized that through baptism all Christians were equal. Furthermore, Díaz de Toledo stated plainly that if followed to the letter of the law, *limpieza* statutes would effectively disenfranchise Spain's nobility, the majority of whom carried Jewish blood. And he noted, with some pride, that several of these noble families were genetically linked to his own. He also informed his readers that the conversos were the first among Christians, as it was they, and not the Gentiles, who were the descendants of God's chosen people. These combative sentiments were also echoed by Alonso de Cartagena in his *Defensorium unitatis christianae*. For Cartagena, Christianity was a redirection and a deepening of the Jewish faith: the Old Law had merely evolved into a more ideal form. Jews who embraced Christianity were embracing an evangelical spirit that had been present in their faith, in men like Moses and Aaron. The Gentiles did not have this foundation; none of their writings made reference to the coming of the Christ or to the Trinity.

They were sons who after a long absence returned home; the Jews (for which read conversos) were daughters who had never left the paternal house.

Nevertheless, it was clearly not enough to defend the conversos' Christian character; it was also necessary to attack the claim—implicit in Sarmiento's statute—that the New Christians, like their Jewish ancestors, were of an inferior caste, which militated against their suitability for public offices, traditionally regarded as the domain of Spain's Christian nobility. Alonso de Cartagena answered this attack by emphasizing the theological, moral, and civil nobility of the ancient Hebrew nation. This was not to infer that all Jews were nobles, Cartagena made clear, but to state that they had the capacity to form a noble class. While this argument may have served Cartagena, whose own ancestors had been members of a Sephardic elite, it was less effective for those conversos, the majority, who had acquired their status in fifteenth-century society through their own toil or that of a recent family member.[5] This was the case of Diego de Valera, the son of a court physician, who occupied a number of important administrative positions at the courts of Juan II and Enrique IV. In his *Espejo de verdadera nobleza*, written around 1451, Valera, like Cartagena, emphasized the noble character of the Jews: 'If we want authority for the nobility of the Jews, we can find many in the fourth chapter of Deuteronomy, which in speaking of the Jews states, "which other nation is as noble?" As if to say not one.' However, he rejected the proposition that nobility was based solely on genealogy. Men gained noble rank, according to Valera, when the civil authority recognized that they had qualities that separated them from the plebian estate. Genealogy might be a factor in gaining a noble title, but virtue (for which read merit) was no less important: 'and thus through virtue many men of low lineage were raised, ennobled and exalted, as others who lived vice-ridden lies lost the nobility and titles that their ancestor had gained through great works.'[6]

The view that character and not lineage was the decisive factor in attaining noble status was one that naturally appealed to Spain's converso professional class, beleaguered by accusations of inferior caste. Writing in the same period as Valera, the converso scholars Álvarez Gato, Pero Guillén, Juan Poeta, and Rodrigo Cota (the son of Alonso Cota, the man at the center of the 1449 Toledo riot) also championed character as the criterion for judging nobility, although these men wisely chose to present their views as Christian moralists and not New Christian professionals. 'I composed this couplet,' wrote Álvarez Gato, introducing a poem on social harmony, 'so that we can see clearly that we are all made from one mass, and that those who have more virtues than lineage should be regarded as the best.'[7]

In the 1460s and 1470s Gato, Cota, Guillén, and Poeta formed part of a literary circle established around the Archbishop of Toledo, Alonso de Carillo, a Renaissance-style patron in whose court scholars and cultivated knights rubbed shoulders. Taking advantage of his patron's interest in the martial arts, Pero Guillén used the knight errant as a symbol of nobility through merit, contrasting the nobleman who won his spurs in battle with his counterpart, the sedentary noble whose social status was merely a fluke of birth. 'And when a man is most clearly noble, then he must take greater care of his virtue, receiving wounds in just causes as signs of his great nobility; thus it follows that nobility is much greater when it is gained in dangerous circumstances and harsh places than that left through inheritance to successors.'[8] In using the active knight to illustrate true nobility, Guillén was linking his own cause to that of Spain's new nobility, men who had only recently gained their noble titles, and thus, like himself, were unable to boast impressive Old Christian pedigrees. Furthermore, these noble families had formed, in their rise to power, important marriage alliances with wealthy and influential conversos, and this made them as open to converso professional ideas as they were sensitive to *limpieza* attacks. Pero Guillén's patron, Archbishop Carrillo, was himself a member of one of these noble clans.[9]

The view that nobility should be acquired through merit is also prominent in the converso Fernando de Pulgar's *Claros varones de Castilla*, published in 1485. In this work Pulgar, also closely connected to the Carillo circle, takes 22 of his generation's most politically influential noblemen and clerics and demonstrates that their illustrious names were based on their 'virtues and abilities, both in learning and in arms [*'en las virtudes y en las abilidades que tovieron, asi en ciencia, como en armas'*]. Pulgar states directly that three of these figures, the prelates Alonso de Cartagena, Juan de Torquemada, and Francisco de Toledo, were conversos, making plain his view that Old Christian blood was not a *sine qua non* for religious office or noble status. Pulgar might also have stated that the majority of his subjects carried some Jewish blood, as his contemporary Díaz de Toledo had done in his *Instrucción del Relator*, but this would have made *Claros Varones* too obviously a converso apology, and may well have been detrimental to its author's purpose, that being to convince his readership of the importance of merit for noble status. Nevertheless, Pulgar does take the opportunity to attack, albeit subtly, the Old Christians' claim that they were spiritually and socially superior to their converso coreligionists. In his section on Alonso de Cartagena, Pulgar notes that the converso prelate was 'very clean in his person, his dress and his table, and whatever he touched he did so with great cleanliness, loathing those men who were not clean; because, he said, a man's outward cleanliness was a sign of his interior.'[10] Here Pulgar links spiritual purity and moral probity not to the Old Christian concept of clean blood but to physical cleanliness—a Jewish belief shared by many conversos. His account of Cartagena's domestic habits is in fact a veiled claim that it is this converso bishop, and not his noisome Old Christian antagonists, who is the more noble and spiritually upright. Later, in the sixteenth century, as anti-converso statutes proliferated in civil and clerical institutions, the emphasis on bodily cleanliness would became a converso literary topos, a barbed reference to unclean Old Christians, who languished in the conceit of their *limpieza de sangre* and *olor de santidad*.

While converso professionals increasingly exploited the view that nobility was determined by merit, the idea was not new; rather, it came via Italian humanist circles, where professional men with an even more highly developed group consciousness had been agitating for some considerable time for a social system that rewarded wisdom and ability. These Italian professionals—lawyers, professors, scribes, grammarians, civil administrators, court advisors, and, increasingly, clerics—found a model for their social pretensions in the statesmen-scholars of classical Rome (in particular Cicero), who had achieved fame, fortune, and noble status through their great talent and industry—what they called *virtù*. For the humanists, these classical figures became the gurus of correct thought and style, and they used their works to attack those elements in their own society that they found unpalatable—like, for example, the clerically oriented scholastic educational system. Thus, while classical authors were championed for their elegant Latin prose, their moral concerns, and their regard for the commonweal, the scholastics were berated for their rudimentary Latin, their penchant for recondite and otiose theological exegesis, and their mental, and often physical, isolation from their fellow man.

Of central importance to Italian humanism as a socio-political credo was moral philosophy, which humanists often used as a vehicle to attack church dogma and to promote a social ideal advantageous to themselves. They celebrated the marriage union (challenging the church's idealization of celibacy), they emphasized the dignity of man (confronting the concept of concupiscence), they championed both the active (secular) and contemplative (spiritual) life, and, above all, they advocated nobility through merit (*virtù*), citing classical authors as their authorities.[11]

As a credo, humanism took root not in the Italian universities, dominated by scholasticism, but in the noble houses of the fourteenth-century Florentine city republic, where a new breed of scholars was able to captivate the minds of patrician families like the Medici, themselves only recently advanced from middle-sort mercantile status. By the mid-fifteenth-century, humanist ideals had begun to penetrate Italian court society, the Italian nobility (often new nobility) having succumbed to the view that an interest in letters, even if feigned, would somehow reinforce their claim to classical noble ancestry.[12] At the same time, humanist ideas began to advance into the north of Europe, where they became increasingly associated with a secular middle-sort agitation toward church reform, or *devotio moderna*.

In Spain, however, the situation was somewhat different. Here there was a very clear division between Old Christian and converso professionals. For the conversos, increasingly under attack from the Church and the lay community, humanism represented an instrument for social and religious reforms, a means of combating the prejudices of their society. This attitude was not shared to the same degree by their Old Christian counterparts, who, like the rest of Old Christian Spain, were caught up in the euphoria of the late *Reconquista* and the conceit of their pure noble blood. For them the pressing religious problem was not a corrupt or intolerant Christianity but the Peninsula's two alien religions, Islam and Judaism. It is hardly surprising, therefore, that when a reform movement did emerge in late fifteenth-century Spain, it did so from among New Christians, conscious of the need to reshape their new religion and culture.

In Spain the humanist movement was from its inception dominated by New Christians, as often becomes apparent by the character of its offensive. First, as I have already noted, Spanish humanists advocated nobility through merit (*virtù* or *virtud*), not only as middle-sort professionals, curtailed by a Medieval social order, but also as New Christians chastised by Old Christian society for their Jewish (tainted) blood. True, the latter argument is not readily apparent in the works of men who, for practical reasons, were reluctant to reveal their Jewish roots. Nevertheless, a careful inspection of these humanists' works often reveals covert references to their own condition, particularly through double entendre references to cleanliness (*limpieza*), as exemplified by Fernando de Pulgar's description of Alonso de Cartagena, cited above.[13]

Second, while Spanish humanists proclaimed the philosophical, ethical, artistic, and literary excellence of the classical Roman world, they also often paid tribute to the Hebrew intellectual tradition, evoking the Old Testament Writings—the Psalms, Proverbs, Ecclesiastes, and the Book of Job—not only as spiritual guides but also as important works of moral philosophy and literature. While it is true that Italian and, particularly, Northern humanists were also increasingly attracted to the Hebrew Bible, their interest was largely philological, not cultural or literary.[14]

Third, Spanish humanists were often at pains to establish strong historical links between the ancient Hebrew culture and Spain. Thus Túbal, the son of Noah, was presented as either the first Spanish colonizer or, more significantly, the first civilized presence on the peninsula, a man who, according to the sixteenth-century Seville humanist Juan de Malara, introduced into Spain 'the practice of good customs and sacred laws.'[15] This link through Túbal to ancient Israel was established by Flavius Josephus in his *Antiquities of the Jews*, and subsequently repeated both by Saint Isidore in the seventh century and by Archbishop Jiménez de Rada in the twelfth. However, neither Saint Isidore nor Archbishop Jiménez de Rada focused on Túbal as a Hebrew or proto-Hebrew figure. Their interest, rather, was in demonstrating the longevity of the Iberian race and thus the preeminence of Spain as a national entity. In contrast, the anonymous author of the *Refundición de la crónica de 1344*, written at the time of the *Sentencia-Estatuto*, emphasized the Jewish character of Spain's post-diluvium colonists, whose numbers, he claimed, were considerably augmented by a later wave of Jewish immigration in the sixth century BC, at the time of the Babylonian captivity. These new Jewish immigrants, he informs us, subsequently dominated the culture of Toledo, making the city almost as prosperous and renowned as ancient Carthage or Rome.[16]

While other converso writers did not repeat the *Refundición* author's hyperbole, they did continue to stress the links between Spain and the early Jews. In his *Crónica de los Reyes Católicos* (1488), Diego de Valera stated that the Goths themselves were descended from an ancient tribe of Israel, evidently attempting to use Ferdinand and Isabel's obsession with their Visigothic ancestry to promote the converso cause. The same claim was also made by the Jewish scholar Salomon ibn Verga in his work *La vara de Juda*. Both ibn Verga and his fellow Jewish exile Isaac Abravanel also argued for a long history of Jewish settlement in Spain prior to the first century AD.[17] This Jewish settlement myth was repeated by a number of sixteenth-century converso writers, including Benito Arias Montano, whose *In Abdias* (1567) was written in defense of the claim that the Jews had arrived in Spain at the time of the destruction of the first Temple. Montano's argument was based on the Jewish prophet Abdias' statement that in the wake of the Judean defeat to Babylonia a community of Judean Jews had been exiled to Sefarad. Despite the fact that Saint Jerome had translated Sefarad as Bosphorus (Turkey), Montano associated the term with Iberia, following the reasoning of Jewish scholars, including Isaac Abravanel.[18]

The claim that Jews from Judea settled in Spain at the time of the Babylonian captivity was also repeated by the Jesuit scholar Jerónimo Román de la Higuera, who invented a series of false chronicles to give more substance to this and other of his historical prejudices. Significantly, Higuera's claims were made against the backdrop of the pure blood debate affecting the Jesuit Order, which led to the imposition of a *limpieza* statute in 1593 (see Chap. 5).[19]

Converso Humanists and the Noble Courts

In Spain, as in Italy, humanist ideas were at first propagated not in the universities but at court: either at the royal court, increasingly dominated by converso bureaucrats (*letrados*), or in the courts of a number of noble families who had formed professional relationships and, often, marriage unions with a wealthy urban converso patriciate, and in so doing had adopted the latter group's interest in intellectual pursuits.[20] A number of nobles were so inspired by this intellectual contact that they took up the pen themselves, despite the fact that among many of their noble peers scholarly activity was still considered a somewhat effete and undignified occupation, more appropriate for a Jewish scribe than for an Old Christian knight.[21] Fernán Pérez de Guzmán, Iñigo López de Mendoza (the Marquis of Santillana), and Gómez and Jorge Manrique, the four most cited examples of fifteenth-century noble litterateurs, were all formed in environments dominated by converso scholars.[22]

'That Seneca exhaled the Lucilius that is me,' wrote Fernán Pérez de Guzmán on the death of his friend Alonso de Cartagena, acknowledging his intellectual debt to the converso Bishop of Burgos.[23] This debt is clearly evident in *Generaciones y Semblanzas*, Pérez's book of noble prosopographies. Not only does the work reflect Cartagena's stylistic influences, it also mirrors the prelate's views on the importance of letters to a nobleman's formation. However, Cartagena's influence is most evident in Pérez's biographical sketch of the bishop's father, Pablo de Santa Maria, in which he praises the ex-rabbi's scholarship, and describes him as a man of great lineage, echoing Cartagena's views on his family's noble Jewish line. Furthermore, Pérez uses his prosopography of Santa Maria to defend the conversos against the recent Toledo attacks, insisting that their conversion under force impeded their adoption of Christian values. This reluctance to accept the Christian religion, writes Pérez, was especially prevalent among converts from humble backgrounds who, unaccustomed to self-reflection (a veiled attack on the conversos' Old Christian antagonists?), adhered to their religion for no other reason than that they were born into it. On the other hand, Pérez wrote, there were those New Christians whose devotion to Christianity had led them to reform corrupt religious establishments, while others, Alonso de Cartagena, for example, had written 'some works of great utility to our faith' [*'algunas escrituras de grande utilidad a nuestra fe'*]. One of these texts was, presumably, Cartagena's *Oracional de Fernán Pérez de Guzmán*, written for Pérez, in which the bishop anticipates Erasmus in his advocacy of a religion in which the evangelical message is guided by the rationality and eloquence found in the pagan writers.[24] Although Pérez de Guzmán considered himself a spokesman for a nobility assaulted by a growing bourgeois professional class, he had, through his close relationship with Cartagena, clearly imbibed the latter group's interest in socio-religious reform.

Like Pérez de Guzmán, the Marquis of Santillana (Pérez's nephew), also regarded Cartagena as his intellectual mentor, and often solicited the prelate's views on questions of scholarship and culture. It was in response to a question from Santillana that Cartagena wrote his *Doctrinal de caballeros*, a manual on correct noble comportment, executed by a converso for one of Spain's most powerful *grandees*. Naturally, the work emphasized the importance of study in a nobleman's formation: 'Gentleman need to be learned,' wrote Cartagena, 'because learning is the thing that most embellishes man and separates him from the other creatures.'[25]

Cartagena was only one of many converso professionals to have maintained close ties with the marquis. In fact, conversos administered the Mendoza estate at Guadalajara, from whence they were able to guide Santillana in his intellectual endeavors.[26] For although the marquis is often lauded as a man of great learning, he was in reality an enthusiastic amateur, whose poor knowledge of Latin required him to lean heavily on his converso friend Dr. Pedro Díaz de Toledo (the *relator* Fernán Díaz de Toledo's nephew) as translator and classical guide.[27] The relationship was not, however, all one sided. The marquis' interest in scholarship was used by Díaz in his *Diálogo e razonamiento en la muerte del Marqués de Santillana*, published on the noble's death, not only to extol Santillana's genius, but also to promote letters as a noble pursuit.[28] These views were echoed by the marquis' converso secretary, Diego de Burgos, in his *Triunfo del marqués*, another encomium published on Santillana's death. Before Santillana, wrote Burgos, no nobleman, neither layman nor cleric, had dared to dedicate himself to letters. Santillana had applied his talents to the emulation of the Greeks and Romans, and had restored Spain's past glory. Santillana, wrote his secretary, 'is the one that liberated Spain from blind ignorance, illuminating us in the light of real charity, and bringing to everyone's attention the knowledge that the best thing that men can strive for in this mortal life is learning.'[29]

For the converso professional Diego de Burgos, Santillana was an immensely important prize: he was a nobleman whose literary interests could be utilized—if enough care were taken—to make scholarship palatable to a semi-literate nobility, and in so doing raise the status of the intellectual, who was still perceived to be either an eccentric or a Jew. But to sell the image, it was necessary to pitch it in a way that would capture the target audience; hence, the use of martial imagery. Burgos' Santillana is not merely a scholar, he is an intellectual conquistador, a man who uses his literary skills, as a Spanish knight uses his sword, to free the country from barbarism. *Triunfo del Marqués* is at one and the same time an encomium, written by a retainer in praise of his noble master, and a subtle manifesto, written by a New Christian professional, advocating a society based on merit.

The Mendozas were at the vanguard of humanist studies and (as we will see) religious reform precisely because of their close relationship to a converso professional class that was intent on changing Spanish social and religious mores. Pedro González de Mendoza, Santillana's youngest son, an astute and ambitious man, who rose rapidly through the clerical ranks to become Archbishop of Seville (1473–1482), was, like his father, influenced by a close circle of converso advisors. In his chronicle of the Catholic Monarchs, Andrés Bernáldez intimates that Mendoza prevaricated in cleansing Seville of Judaizers, despite the many appeals of 'good Christian clerics,' because of his close links to the converso community.[30] This image of Mendoza as a man sympathetic toward the New Christians is also apparent in the letter written to the Cardinal by the converso scholar Fernando de Pulgar, attacking the Inquisition and its violence toward New Christians. It is quite obvious that Pulgar would not have shared his views with Mendoza had he not been certain that the prelate was of the same opinion. Indeed, it is probable that the letter was authorized by Mendoza, who promoted a campaign of evangelization within Seville's converso community in the hope that this would appease King Ferdinand and Queen Isabel sufficiently to obviate more radical measures. In charge of this evangelical program was the converso friar Hernando de Talavera, who created a basic catechism to aid the process. Unfortunately, no sooner had the campaign begun than an anonymous member of the converso community circulated a diatribe against the Church, lending support to the view, maintained by most of Seville's Old Christian community, that the conversos were unrepentant heretics.[31] Despite Mendoza's and Talavera's best efforts, the first tribunal of the Inquisition was established in Seville, in 1480, with horrific consequences.

Another Mendoza influenced by converso professionals and scholars was the Cardinal's nephew, Iñigo López de Mendoza, the second Count of Tendilla. Having distinguished himself as a diplomat in Italy, the count was, in 1492, presented with the governorship of the recently conquered Muslim kingdom of Granada. From the beginning of his office, and in opposition to a hardline faction at court, the count rejected enforced baptism of Granada's Muslim population; instead, he supported Hernando de Talavera, now Bishop of Granada, in his attempts to gradually educate the Muslims in the ways of the Christian faith. In his own campaign for a more equitable policy toward the city's Muslim population, Mendoza instructed his converso secretary and representative at court, Francisco de Ortiz, to cite the Roman occupation of Palestine, as recorded by the Jewish writer Flavius Josephus, as an example of how not to treat a subject nation. As Helen Nader points out in her work on the Mendozas, the count appears to have been oblivious to the fact that he was addressing a court intolerant of the Jews and indifferent to Jewish welfare, and that his use of Josephus to support his own views on religious clemency was, in the circumstances, singularly inappropriate.[32]

Iñigo López de Mendoza's son, Diego Hurtado de Mendoza, inherited his family's concern for scholarship and for a humanitarian approach to Spain's New Christians. In his three-volume account of the 1568 Morisco rebellion in the Alpujarra mountains, Mendoza showed himself sympathetic to the rebel leader Abén Humeya and the economic and social problems of Granada's Morisco population. Some scholars have attributed the picaresque novel *Lazarillo de Tormes* to Mendoza, based on the nobleman's Erasmian temperament. Although it is improbable that Mendoza was the author of this work, he certainly shared its anticlerical sentiments. It was Mendoza who, in 1530, wrote to his friend, the Bishop of Arras, that the best solution to the Protestant problem was to issue a general pardon to the heretics and accept them back into the Church. If, after publicly acknowledging their Catholicism, they wished to worship in private according to their conscience, or if they had opinions at variance with Catholic doctrine, they should be left unmolested.[33] This solution, later advocated by French humanists as an answer to the Huguenot problem, under the label *politique*, was one that Mendoza's circle of converso friends would have found particularly attractive.

Tied to the Mendozas through marriage, the Manrique family also maintained close contact with converso professionals.[34] Gómez and Jorge Manrique, members of the quartet of noble scholars mentioned above, were both associated with an otherwise largely converso intellectual group that formed around Archbishop Carrillo 1470s.[35] Gómez Manrique's sympathy toward the converso community was demonstrated when as *corregidor* (Crown representative) in Toledo he persuaded Queen Isabel to delay establishing an Inquisition tribunal in that city. When the tribunal was eventually established, he made every effort to ensure that its sentences for Judaizing were light ones, involving only the payment of fines.[36] This humane attitude toward the conversos was displayed by another family member, the Erasmian Alonso Manrique, who, while Archbishop of Seville (1524–1538), galvanized the converso Juan de Ávila into propagating evangelical Christianity throughout Andalusia. In his burlesque chronicle on the court of Charles V, Francisillo Zúñiga (another converso) associated the archbishop with a converso court society, and used the name Manrique as a synonym for New Christian, giving full reign to the rumor that the Manrique family ancestry was also in part Jewish.[37] It was the archbishop's son, Rodrigo Manrique, who wrote the following lines to Juan Luis Vives in 1534, lamenting the imprisonment of their mutual friend Juan de Vergara: 'You speak the pure truth: our land is envious and arrogant. I would also add barbarous. Thus they take it as a fact that anyone moderately well educated in letters is full of heresy, error and Judaizing ways, so much so that they have imposed silence upon learned men.'[38] Here, Manrique illustrates the major problem facing Spain's humanists: in the popular consciousness, intellectual inquiry was a Jewish trait; it was natural, therefore, that scholars like Vives and Vergara (both conversos) and Manrique himself (a noble closely linked to conversos) would be associated with Jewish perfidy.

The Conversos and Religious Reform

Jewish scholars often contrast the Spanish Jews' reaction to the pogrom of 1391 with that of their Northern coreligionists in similar circumstances during the First Crusade. Whereas the Northern Jewish communities resisted the Christian aggression, preferring martyrdom to the renunciation of faith, many of the Sephardim chose the path of least resistance, converting to Christianity. This capitulation is usually attributed to the lack of cohesion within the Jewish community itself, and in particular the rift that had developed between rank-and-file Jews and a wealthy and erudite Jewish courtier society, often indifferent to Judaic law. This courtier group had evolved in the rarefied intellectual atmosphere of Islamic Andalusia during the eleventh and twelfth centuries, where it had become influenced by Greek rationalist philosophy, very much in vogue in al-Andalus during that period. When these court Jews, or their intellectual heirs, later entered the Christian realm, they increasingly clashed not only with orthodox Jewish leaders but also with the Cabbalists, whose recondite, mystical interpretations of the Scriptures were, it seems, to some degree a reaction to the rationalism of the courtier society.[39] These conflicting intellectual and spiritual tendencies within the Jewish elite naturally created a certain insecurity in the Jewish *aljamas*, which was exploited by the new mendicant orders, the Franciscans and Dominicans, in their aggressive proselytizing campaigns during the fourteenth century, and by the same religious forces in the period immediately after the 1391 pogrom.

Of the Jews who converted to Christianity in 1391, or in the period directly thereafter, the majority undoubtedly did so out of fear and in the belief that they were not committing apostasy if after baptism they continued to observe the Jewish faith in private.[40] Others, especially among the courtier class, may have seen the pogrom as an opportunity to abandon traditional Jewish practice, which chafed their rationalist credo, and slough off the restrictions of their Sephardic caste. For these apostates, the Christian credo was no more compelling than the Jewish one, but conversion did bring with it important social and economic advantages. Skepticism and cynicism were not, however, peculiar to a converso intellectual elite. As the later Inquisition registers attest, these attitudes were found across the conversos' social ranks, expressed in the phrase: 'There is only birth and death and nothing else.'[41] While these views attest to the religious disillusion and despondency of many converts and their descendants, they may also reflect a specific antagonism toward Christian belief, which, much more than Judaism, emphasized salvation and the afterlife.

Not all of the post-1391 converts were secret Jews or cynics, however. There were also those who sincerely embraced Christianity—some from the outset, others later, as they began to process their conversion and its existentialist implications. Tainted in the eyes of both their erstwhile coreligionists and their new ones, these neophytes often saw themselves as latter-day Nazarenes, those early followers of Christ, who, in adhering to the precepts of Jesus, confronted the recondite law and pedantry of the pharisaic fundamentalists. Like the early Jewish Christians, they had not abandoned Judaism but had embraced a revolutionary version of it. Thus they were able to reconcile their Christianity with their Jewish background. This was certainly the attitude of the most famous convert of the period, Solomon Halevi or Pablo de Santa Maria, whose work *Scrutinium scriptorium*, written around 1430, some 40 years after his conversion, promotes the view that the conversos retained their status as God's chosen people, and thus were the first among Jews and Christians.

The father of Alonso de Cartagena, Pablo de Santa Maria is usually presented as a virulent antagonist of Judaism, his work *Scrutinium scriptorium* cited as proof of his anti-Jewish fervor. However, *Scrutinium* is more than an anti-Jewish diatribe; it is an attempt to situate the conversos within Christianity as distinguished protagonists. Jews were the original followers of Christ and leading figures in the early Church, Santa Maria noted, citing Saint Paul's Epistle to the Romans, and this status was now assumed by the modern Jewish converts. For as Paul had stated: 'If the first fruit is holy, then the whole batch is holy; and if the root is holy, then the branches are holy also.'[42] According to Santa Maria, the conversos were not only bona fide Christians, they were special ones, a new force that would revive Christianity, repairing the damage of the Medieval Church. This view was one that many other conversos would latch on to as they attempted to combat Old Christian prejudice and allay their own insecurities, creating a discrete role for themselves within Christianity.

In addressing the issue of converso religiosity, Pablo de Santa Maria was unusual among the early wave of converts. Most remained publicly mute about their religious views, feigning orthodoxy through observing Christian ceremony and ritual. However, this situation began to change with the 1449 *Sentencia-Estatuto*. Now it became clear to many conversos, especially among the professional elite, that they could no longer hide behind the mask of religious conformity; they had to confront their adopted religion head on and fashion a public Christian credo that they could genuinely uphold. Their ally in this venture was Saint Paul, the most erudite and cosmopolitan of the Evangelists, who had written of a Christianity founded not on ritual and ceremony but on an interior, mystical connection with the deity. Above all, Paul had emphasized that Christ's body was a metaphor for the Christian Church, in which all the members were of equal importance. It was this allusion that particularly appealed to the New Christians. Whether or not all those conversos who now cited Paul as an example of the true Christian message were themselves convinced Christians is, however, debatable. Some were undoubtedly believers; others may have seen Paul and Jesus as figureheads for a syncretic credo, based on the moral tenets found in pagan (in particular Senecan), Hebrew, and patristic texts. This syncretism is clearly visible in both Pedro Díaz de Toledo's *Introducción a los proverbios de Séneca* and Alonso de Cartagena's *Oracional de Fernan Pérez de Guzmán*. In the latter work, the author reveals his belief that the ways of God are unknowable and thus beyond speculation, a clear indication, it would seem, of the prelate's religious skepticism.[43]

In the mid-fifteenth century the interest in an interior, or Pauline, religious observance began to enter those religious orders in which the conversos maintained an important presence. Chief among these was the Jeronymite Order, a wealthy and privileged religious organization that appears to have been particularly attractive to New Christians. One of the order's early converso novices, later its general, was Alonso de Oropesa, the uncle of Fray Hernando de Talavera. In 1465, Oropesa published his *Lumen ad revelationem gentium* (*Light to Enlighten the Gentiles*), a work which anticipates Erasmus' *Enchiridion* in its allusions to the body of Christ as a symbol of religious harmony and unison.[44] However, Oropesa was interested in the Pauline allusion not only as a Christian humanist but also as a converso who was intent on defusing the tension between Old and New Christians in his own order. Unfortunately, the friar's attempt to create a harmonious religious environment was thwarted when, soon after his book was published, crypto-Jewish cells were discovered in the Jeronymite houses at Guadalupe and Toledo. Thereafter the Jeronymites took a reactionary turn, introducing a *limpieza de sangre* statute, in 1489, to discourage converso entry.[45]

The elite of what was still a fairly small and impoverished intellectual community, converso scholars were able to contest popular prejudice by circulating erudite treatises on an egalitarian and harmonious Christian body. However, this was not merely a defensive campaign against Old Christian calumnies. A number of converso intellectuals, both inside and outside the Church, clearly saw themselves as members of a vanguard for socio-religious reform. Like the early Jewish followers of Jesus, they were practitioners of a new, vital, and ethical faith, who had been vouchsafed the task of creating an age of peace and harmony. This millenarianism is very much in evidence during the early years of the Catholic Monarchs' reign, when court conversos praised the young rulers as a divine force for change. The belief, or hope, was that Ferdinand and Isabel would create a powerful, united Spain and, in the process, restore the conversos to the body politic.[46]

According to the great Spanish humanist Antonio Nebrija, Isabel's reign was like that of King Solomon, a period of pacification and growth which would lead, in its turn, to the great flourishing of the Castilian language and letters. The Queen had introduced 'laws that unite us and allow us to live together in this great company that we call the kingdom and republic of Castile,' and in so doing she had prepared the ground for a new society that, in Nebrija's words, would cultivate 'the arts of peace.'[47] Unfortunately, this was wishful thinking, especially as far as the New Christians were concerned, who, with the establishment of the Inquisition in 1478, became more than ever the alien within, the necessary 'Other,' upon whose back a homogeneous Spain would be constructed.

Living under the shadow of Old Christian malice and Holy Office persecution, it was inevitable that many conversos would pay lip service to organized Catholicism while seeking spiritual solace in a private, quietist world. In this endeavor they found support in the evangelical and mystical works of the Northern *devotio moderna* movement that, unsurprisingly, began to be published in Castilian at the turn of the century. Both Ludolph of Saxony's *Life of Christ* and Thomas à Kempis' *Imitation of Christ*, works that emphasized private prayer and moral self-renewal, became popular middle-sort devotional manuals in the period directly after the establishment of the Inquisition. However, the Northern writer who most animated the converso intellectual community, at least from the early sixteenth century onward, was *devotio moderna*'s enfant terrible, Erasmus of Rotterdam.

Although Spain was not one of the first nations to embrace Erasmus, it did eventually produce some of his most ardent supporters. Enthusiasm for the Dutch humanist was stimulated by the arrival, in 1517, of Charles V's Flemish court. Soon thereafter Erasmian ideas began to infiltrate certain noble households and the universities, in particular the University of Alcalá de Henares, recently founded by Cardinal Jiménez de Cisneros. In founding the university, Cisneros had envisaged an educational establishment of theological diversity, where both Thomist and nominalist theories would be available to the student body. Diversity was also visible in both the trilingual college of San Ildefonso, the ornament of the University, and the Complutense Polyglot Bible, a project directed by Cisneros in which, for the first time, Latin, Greek, Hebrew, and Aramaic versions of the Scriptures were incorporated into one work. This emphasis on linguistic study enticed converso scholars to Alcalá, many of whom now became Erasmus adherents. Among these men were Juan de Vergara, Bernadino de Tovar, Juan del Castillo, and the chancellor of the university, Pedro de Lerma, all of whom were later tried by the Inquisition for Protestant heresy.[48]

There is no mystery in Erasmus' appeal for the conversos. His interest in a faith in which pagan texts enriched the Christian message, his rejection of ceremonies and rituals, his focus on a Pauline message of equality within the Church, his belief that Christ had created a new man through His emphasis on interior religious reform, all were views that had been circulating in erudite New Christian circles since the mid-fifteenth century. For many converso scholars, Erasmus was clearly a fellow traveler in the war against Old Christian chauvinism and superstition. And they reveled in his attacks on an ignorant, corrupt Church, especially his comparison of ritualistic monks to Pharisaic Jews, which they used as a counter-punch against an Old Christian society that accused them of being impaired Christians.[49] Erasmus' greatest attraction for conversos, however, was his popularity. Indeed, it is likely that a number of converso nonconformists exaggerated their Erasmian philosophy before the Holy Office in a bid to disguise an illuminist orientation that was associated with crypto-Judaism.[50]

One of Erasmus' first Spanish disciples was the émigré scholar Juan Luis Vives, the eldest son of a family of converso cloth merchants from Valencia. Vives left Spain in 1509, at the age of 16, to study Arts at the University of Paris. However, in 1512 he cut short his university studies to move to Flanders, where, like many other converso émigré *letrados*, he hoped to enter the court of Charles, Duke of Burgundy, the future Charles V.⁵¹ Over the next five years the young scholar searched for a court patron, eventually gaining access to the household of Guillaume de Croy, Charles' Grand Chancellor. At the same time he entered a circle of Flemish humanists, developing his own humanist credo, predicated on the stoical principles of inner peace and equanimity.⁵² This stoical outlook was severely tested in 1522 when he learned that his father had been accused by the Valencia Inquisition tribunal of Judaizing, a crime for which he was subsequently burnt at the stake.⁵³ Vives alludes to the terrible event in a letter to his friend Francisco Cranvelt on 10 May 1523, on the eve of his departure, via England, for Spain, where he may have been considering visiting his father in prison:

> Tomorrow I leave Bruges for England, where I will say hello to [Thomas] More for you; from there I travel to Spain, but by sea, as by land one can barely survive in such calamitous times. I have left the visit until now in case some hope shines from Spain. Everything is darkness and night, no less in the events than in my spirit and resolve, which strips all the vehemence from my suffering. There is no shortage of people who say this has happened for the satisfaction of my soul. I hope that no such satisfaction occurs to them!⁵⁴

Although Vives made no further mention of his father's death in his correspondence, it is certain that the episode reinforced his personal campaign to transform a divided, violent Christian society into one based on rationality, peace, and harmony.

As Vives saw it, there were two major obstacles on the path to reform: a scholastic community that had abandoned Jesus' original message for worthless, arcane erudition, and an ignorant, unreflecting flock, or *vulgo*, mired in ceremonies and rituals.⁵⁵ This situation was not, however, peculiar to Christianity, as the humanist made clear in his posthumously published work *De veritate fidei christianae* (*The Truth of the Christian Faith*), in which a Christian (almost certainly Vives himself) confronts a Jew (or *marrano*) on his hidebound belief system, based on fear and hate, rather than on love, and on complex, meaningless rituals, many of which were absorbed into Judaism in a post-biblical age. When, in response to this attack, the Jew makes the same criticism of Christianity, the Christian agrees, but boldly states that in the case of his own religion the rituals could be ignored or annulled with no effect on the faith.⁵⁶

From *De veritate* it is evident that Vives had little interest in either his ancestors' original faith or the one they had been forced to adopt. He rejected both doctrines for an evangelical credo that Erasmus called the Philosophy of Christ. Vives devoted his life to spreading this philosophy abroad. However, the Spanish humanist was highly discriminative in his audience, believing that religious renewal would only come through an educated public that could appreciate the rationality of Christ's message. The ideal target was middle-class youth, who the author approached through his *Introductio ad sapientiam* (*Introduction to Wisdom*), published, significantly, in the year of his father's execution.

Above all, Vives told his young readers, virtue (i.e. service to God and love of man) should govern all of their actions. Through virtuous acts one gained honor and nobility, because 'true and firm nobility is born from virtue.' To be virtuous, one required knowledge, ingenuity, and fortitude, what the Romans called 'healthy understanding.' However, above all one needed to overcome one's passions and inner strife, especially rage, which brought with it such darkness that one could discern neither the truth nor how to achieve it.[57] This rage was cured by focusing on the message of Christ, which was peace, concord, and love. Those who continued to hate were not Christians, nor could they count on God's love. On the other hand, those who worked for a firm and perpetual peace among men, would, according to Christ, be called the sons of God.[58]

In order to achieve a peaceful and harmonious society, the members, especially its governors, should be at peace with themselves. Vives reinforced this stoical message in his later work *De concordia et discordia* (*On Concord and Discord*), published in 1529, a year after his deceased mother was declared a crypto-Jew, her remains disinterred and burnt at the stake. In *De concordia*, Vives contended that peace would not be achieved in Christendom until everyone concentrated on moral renewal. However, the onus was on the Christian rulers, whose misdeeds had the greatest effect on society. These men needed to be the role models for their subjects, containing their strong passions, especially anger and retribution, in order to create harmonious kingdoms. The rulers should be magnanimous, pardoning wrongs rather than seeking revenge, even against heretics; for anyone who wished a heretic burnt rather than redeemed had no interest in religious renewal, but only in retaliation. And in a clear reference to Spain's émigré conversos, Vives noted that some Christians were so disenchanted by their societies that they would rather live under the

Turks than those who acted like Turks (or tyrants) while professing to be Christians.[59]

Vives' *De concordia* was followed in the same year by a complementary work, *De pacificationes* (*On Peacemaking*), in which he outlined the qualities needed to become a peacemaker in civil society, the work being directed especially at magistrates and government officials, like the Archbishop of Seville and Inquisitor General Alonso Manrique, to whom it was dedicated. In his dedicatory note Vives, who knew Manrique personally, praised the prelate's pacific nature, urging him to employ this trait in his position as one of Charles V's inner circle of advisors. What was a royal counselor, Vives asked rhetorically, if not the moral conscience of the king, whose passions he needed to temper with calm advice. But Manrique was not only a royal advisor, he was also a bishop, or shepherd, like Christ, whose role was to pacify all his flock. This could only be achieved through love for all the parts of the Christian body. Finally, Vives turned to Manrique's role as Inquisitor General, the most important position in the Church, because the salvation, fortune, fame, and lives of so many were dependent upon the sound judgment and goodness of the incumbent. In a period of such confusion, it was essential to have someone at the ship's helm who could steer the vessel toward the correct port, that being toward peace and public tranquility.[60]

This view of Manrique as peacekeeper or pacifier was presented in the same year by another converso humanist, Charles V's secretary, Alfonso de Valdés. In his *Diálogo de Mercurio y Carón*, Valdés, through his mouthpiece Mercury (Mercurio), praises the Inquisitor General for combating the destructive impulse of Alastor, a spirit of blind retribution who continued to demand revenge for distant crimes, maintaining society in constant turmoil. Alastor worked especially through monks, who attacked the international harbinger of peace, Erasmus, as a heretic. Fortunately for the Spanish, the Inquisitor General, Manrique, was able to hinder the evil spirit in Spain, such that there was no longer 'dispute or debate' on this subject, a clear reference to the famous Valladolid debate of 1527, in which the Erasmians, led by Manrique, successfully defended the Dutch humanist against his Spanish detractors.[61]

Like Vives' *De concordia*, Valdés' *Diálogo de Mercurio y Caron* was a call for civic peace, to be achieved through following Christ's basic precepts.[62] The story takes place on the bank of the river Styx, where the messenger of the Gods, Mercury, and the Underworld boatman, Charon (Caron), discuss the political situation in Europe. Charon, who Valdés transforms into a transporter of Christian sinners to Hell, is worried that the peaceful intentions of Charles V, Erasmus, and Manrique will prove disastrous for his business. He thus plies Mercury with questions on the state of society, hoping for news of political strife and turmoil, which the god sadly furnishes. While the two talk, a series of sinners enter the boat, among whom are a bishop, a priest, and a theologian, prompting questions from the god and the boatman regarding their misspent lives. All have ignored the basic religious code of Christ, believing that their place in heaven was assured by their superficial religious observances and purchase of papal certificates of indulgence. Then Charon and Mercury spot a man walking in the opposite direction to the boat, on his way to heaven, and question him on his Christian existence.

He began to meditate on the ways of Christ when he was 20, he tells them, deciding that he had a choice: either he could believe in the veracity of the Christian message, in which case he needed to change his life, or he could reject it; either way there was no need to observe so many laws (*constituciones*) and ceremonies. And then, at the age of 25, God 'illuminated' him with understanding, at which point he left behind all superstitions and vices to follow true Christian belief, not as a priest or a monk, both of which he attacks, but as a married man.

The precise chronological details of the man's Christian 'conversion' process suggests that this account was based on Alfonso de Valdés' own situation, or perhaps that of his brother Juan, who while employed as a page in the household of Diego López Pacheco, the Marquis of Villena, had met and, it seems, been illuminated by the *alumbrado* Pedro Ruiz de Alcaraz, also from a converso background. Later, Juan incorporated mystical elements associated with the *alumbrados* into his own religious credo, a hybrid belief system influenced by Erasmian, Lutheran, and illuminist ideas.[63]

In his *Diálogo de doctrina cristiana*, published, like *Mercurio y Caron*, in 1529, Juan de Valdés gives voice to his reformist views in the form of a catechism, in which an Erasmian bishop replies to the earnest questioning of his two interlocutors, a monk and a priest. In reply to the monk's question 'What is the difference between a Christian and a non-Christian?' the bishop replies that besides baptism, Christianity is founded on faith and love, harming no one and, in short, following the example of Jesus. When the monk reminds him of ceremonies and Church tradition, he replies that these are only accessories, not the main elements ['*Mirad, padre, lo que yo dije que el Cristiano debe tener es lo principal, esto otro es accesorio*'].[64] And he goes on to list the fundamentals of faith, which, beside the Credo and Ten Commandments, are all contained in Mathew 5, 6, and 7 (the Sermon on the Mount).

Two years after its publication, Juan de Valdés' *Diálogo* was banned by the Inquisition, its author having already fled to Italy, where he would soon become an influential voice in an Italian religious reform movement. Meanwhile, in Spain the Erasmian honeymoon was coming to an end. In June 1529, Charles V left the peninsula for Rome, taking a number of influential Erasmians with him, including Alfonso de Valdés. In the political hiatus, Erasmus' enemies at court and within the Holy Office began to move against the Northern humanist's supporters. One of the first victims of the purge was the Inquisitor General, Alonso Manrique, banished to his Seville see by the regent, Queen Isabel, who was no friend of religious reform. The following year, at the Diet of Augsburg, Charles V was informed by a group of German princes and representatives of the free German cities that their territories were now Lutheran. Abruptly aware of the dangers Protestantism posed to his own kingdoms, Charles had little interest in checking the Inquisition activities against heretics in Spain. The result was a spate of attacks on humanists, almost all of whom were conversos, for adherence to illuminist (*alumbrado*) and Protestant beliefs. No one, it seemed, was safe. In 1535 Juan del Castillo, a member of Alonso Manrique's humanist circle, was burnt at the stake for Protestantism, with the archbishop unable, or unwilling, to help. At the same time one of Spain's most prominent Erasmus supporters, Juan de Vergara, languished in an Inquisition prison, despite the best efforts of his friend and employer Alonso de Fonseca, the Archbishop of Toledo, to free him.[65] The message for Spain's converso humanists was clear: if they wished to reform their society, they needed to do so with greater discretion, or *prudencia*.

The *Alumbrados* and Other Mystics

Increasingly separated from their Jewish roots, and yet alienated from Old Christian society, many conversos, especially intellectuals, sought an answer to their existentialist problems through a humanist, or Christian-humanist, credo. Others looked toward more radical solutions, following the messianic nostrums of popular religious visionaries, like those of the ten-year-old Inés Esteban of Herrera del Duque, whose prophesies excited converso communities across southern Extremadura and western Andalusia around the turn of the century. Inés claimed to have visited heaven, guided by her deceased mother, where in the highest reaches of paradise she had encountered the victims of the Inquisition bonfires. She also had visions of the prophet Elijah, who, she revealed, would soon appear on earth to announce the coming of the Messiah. On arrival, the Messiah would forgive the conversos for abandoning their true faith, before leading them to a promised land. Inés' notoriety soon brought her to the attention of the Toledo Inquisition tribunal, which burned her at the stake in July 1500.[66]

Inés' prophecies clearly appealed to those conversos who saw their recent suffering at the hands of the Inquisition as retribution for abandoning their ancestral religion. The young prophetess gave this confused and demoralized group a message of hope, contingent on their sincere return to the Jewish faith. Meanwhile, other converso prophets offered hope through the vision of a reformed and sanitized Christian Church in which the Holy Office ceased to exist. This was the case of Fray Melchor, who proclaimed that within 12 years, starting from 1512, the Roman Empire would be destroyed, the kings of Europe toppled, the clergy, except for a few reformers, beheaded, and the Church relocated to Jerusalem. Several years later another converso visionary, Pero López de Soria, like Inés Esteban, from a small town in Extremadura, prophesied that the Church would soon be illuminated by a new spiritual light, at which time the pope would establish his see in Toledo and create an egalitarian Catholic religion, uncorrupted by the evils of the Inquisition. This animosity toward a Church dominated by an evil Holy Office is also evident among Spain's *alumbrados*, a converso-dominated spiritual movement that rejected formal religious observance for private, mystical communion with the deity.

At the center of *alumbrado* practice was *dejamiento*, a mystical method based loosely on *recogimiento*, a Franciscan transcendental technique carried out under supervision in monasteries called *recolectorios*. Through *recogimiento* (gathering of the senses), Franciscan friars learnt how to distance themselves from all ideas, even the most saintly, silence the intellect, and obliterate all desire, so that they could fill themselves with the presence of God. *Dejamiento* (freeing of the senses) was similar to *recogimiento* in its goals. What most differentiated it from the orthodox practice was its adherents' belief that no particular method or ritual was required to achieve mystical union with God, only a sincere wish to open oneself to His love. It also appears that the practitioners of *dejamiento* believed that in abandoning themselves to God they achieved an immaculate state, during which time their acts were free from sin. Some may have seen this as a license to surrender themselves to general hysteria or sexual licentiousness;

most, it seems, viewed it merely as a challenge to the Catholic Church and its claim that only through the sacraments, indulgences, and dispensations could the individual gain God's grace. What drew people to *dejamiento* was, above all, its simplicity and informality. Unlike *recogimiento*, it did not demand special training or precise ritual; it was a mystical practice for a secular community that sought spiritual solace outside the parameters of an unloved Church.

Although it is impossible to determine exactly where and when the *alumbrado* phenomenon began, it is known that one of the first *alumbrado* conventicles was established around 1512 at the Mendoza court at Guadalajara, where a Franciscan tertiary, the conversa Isabel de la Cruz, preached her singular Christian ideology to the Duke of Infantado's household.[67] One of Isabel's disciples was the outspoken Pedro Ruiz de Alcaraz, a lay preacher who worked for the Duke of Infantado's son-in-law, Don Diego de Mendoza, the third Count of Priego, before taking up employment first with Don Benito Cisneros, the nephew of Cardinal Cisneros, and finally with Diego López de Pacheco, the second Marquis of Villena. It was while in the marquis' employment that Alcaraz came into contact with, and influenced, the young Juan de Valdés.[68]

At Alcaraz's Inquisition trial in 1519, the prosecution accused him of espousing the following errant views: Hell did not exist; Christ was not physically present in the Eucharist; fasts and other pious acts of contrition brought no benefits; the pope's indulgences and pardons were worthless; oral prayer was unnecessary—only mental prayer was required; confessions were pointless (he himself only confessed to appear to conform to the views of the ignorant masses); Saint Augustine's soliloquies were mere fantasies; married men and women engaged in the sexual act were closer to God than when they were praying; to save one's soul one had only to open oneself to God; and having gained God's love through this process of *dejamiento* one could not err either venially or mortally.[69]

A number of these views eventually led the Inquisition to suspect that Alcaraz, and other *alumbrados*, had been touched by the Lutheran heresy. However, in this the Holy Office was probably mistaken. The *alumbrados* may have entertained heretical ideas, but these ideas had their roots in *devotio moderna* (a common font for both Luther and the Spanish religious reformers) and New Christian iconoclasm. Alcaraz's own iconoclasm is evident in at least two ways. First, unlike the northern European devotees of *devotio moderna*, his theology is not Christocentric; at his trial it was stated that both he and his followers 'never mention the name of

Jesus Christ, nor the Virgin Mary, nor speak of the Passion of our Redeemer.'[70] Furthermore, he had often stated that God gave his love unconditionally to all peoples, not only Christians; Alcaraz's deity, it appears, was a generic concept, unburdened by the weight of Christian (or Jewish) dogma. Second, it is clear that Alcaraz was hostile not only toward the Catholic Church but also toward an Old Christian Spanish society. One witness at his trial observed that Alcaraz had actually rejoiced on hearing of the recent victory of the Barbary pirates against the Spanish forces.[71]

This antipathy toward Old Christian society emerges on a number of occasions in the *alumbrados'* trials. Alcaraz himself had noted that Fray Francisco de Ocaña, also influential at the Marquis of Villena's court, believed that all those who governed the Church were fallacious Christians and should be cast out 'like pigs,' a probable allusion to a pork-eating, or tainted, Old Christian presbytery. Another *alumbrado*, the wealthy Valladolid merchant Pedro de Cazalla, delivered the following harangue against the Spanish Crown and Inquisition, on being detained by the Holy Office officials:

> We didn't have a king [a reference to Charles V] but an idiot, and the devil had brought the Empress [Isabel of Portugal] to Castile, who was a viper like her grandmother [Isabela la Católica], who had brought the Inquisition to Castile and had supported it. Would to God that France declared war or that the Comunero revolt continued so that the Inquisition that ruined everything would be destroyed.[72]

The Comunero Revolt, referred to by Cazalla, was the uprising against Charles V between 1520 and 1521. At its height the rebels held much of central Spain, including the cities of Toledo, Segovia, and Valladolid. The revolt was fomented during Ferdinand of Aragon's Castilian regency, after the death of Philip I (the Handsome), in 1506. It was during this period that Ferdinand turned a blind eye to the Inquisition's indiscriminate attacks on a wealthy and politically powerful Castilian converso community. In fact, it now seems evident that the regent was deliberately targeting this group for its support of Philip I and his wife Juana (the Mad), who had inherited the Crown of Castile from Isabel. Ferdinand also did little to prevent noble violations of urban councils' territorial jurisdiction, something that also affected conversos, who often predominated in these institutions.[73] It was therefore not surprising that middle-sort conversos like Pedro de Cazalla were so active in the revolt.

However, Cazalla was no ordinary disillusioned converso, but the cousin of the *alumbrado* luminaries Maria and Juan de Cazalla. All three Cazallas had grown up in the Andalusian town of Palma del Rio, in merchant families closely associated with the Lord of Palma's court (see Chap. 3). In the 1480s the Córdoba Inquisition tried an older generation of the family for Judaizing. Some 40 years later Pedro and his cousins also fell afoul of the Holy Office, this time for illuminist heresy. Later still, in the famous Valladolid trials of 1559, six of Pedro's ten children were convicted of Protestantism, and four were burnt at the stake.

It was probably while growing up in Palma del Rio that Pedro and his cousins were first introduced to mystical practice, through the Franciscan monastery that dominated religious life in the town. Indeed, the monastery produced one of Spain's first important mystical theorists, Fray Bernabé de Palma, who outlined the *recogimiento* method in his *Via espiritus o de la perfección del alma*, banned by the Inquisition in its 1558 Index. Palma's preaching may also have inspired the young Francisco de Osuna (1492–1541), who took his religious name from his birthplace, the town of Osuna, some 60 kilometers south of Palma del Rio, where his family worked as retainers to the noble Girón family, later Dukes of Osuna.

Fray Francisco, who joined the Franciscan Order in 1513, became famous for his *Tercer abecedario* (1527), a mystical manual that influenced the later great Spanish mystics, Juan de Ávila, Teresa of Ávila, and John of the Cross, all of whom were conversos. While almost nothing is known of Osuna's own background, the friar's spiritual works, several of which were written while he resided at the Franciscan monastery at Salceda (near Guadalajara), also reveal very definite New Christian sensibilities.[74]

Francisco de Osuna entered the Franciscans in a period in which the order was undergoing rigorous internal reforms under the aegis of its general, Cardinal Jiménez de Cisneros. One aspect of these reforms was the establishment of eight *recolectorios*, where Franciscan friars devoted themselves to mystical communion with God. These establishments appear to have been a magnet for conversos, whose presence in the order increased dramatically during Cisneros' generalship. Some of these neophytes saw the order as a means of spiritual escape, others as a divine instrument toward social retribution and religious change. Among the latter group was Fray Melchor, mentioned above, who traveled from one Franciscan convent to another, prophesying a bloody revolution within the Catholic Church, followed by the institution's relocation to Jerusalem. At the same time, at Salceda the monastery's vicar revealed that a creature with stigmata would soon appear, introducing peace on earth among the Jews, Muslims, and Christians.

When Osuna entered the Salceda *recolectorio*, in 1517, he would have found the community of friars agitated by a volatile mix of millenarian fantasy and mystical visions—characteristics usually attributed to the *alumbrado* cell just down the road at Pastrana. In fact, there was very little difference between the religious ideas floating around in both communities, as Osuna would have discovered during his frequent visits to the local town in the company of his fellow friars. Several of these men soon became *alumbrado* devotees; one of them, Fray Pedro de Ortiz, even went as far as to denounce the Inquisition from the pulpit, when the Holy Office placed the *beata* and illuminist Francisca Hernández on trial for heresy. For this indiscretion the converso friar also found himself in the Holy Office prison.

It was in the *recolectorio* of Salceda that Osuna began writing his six *abecedarios espirituales*, the idea taken from the Old Testament spiritual guides of David, Solomon, and Jeremíah.[75] In his *Tercer abecedario*, published in 1527, Osuna is careful to draw a distinction between his own brand of mystical practice (*recogimiento*) and that of the radical *alumbrado* sect (*dejamiento*) that had recently been castigated in the 1525 Edict of Faith. Nevertheless, it is apparent in reading the *abecedarios* that the Franciscan friar carefully dissimulates his own non-conformist tendencies, as both Marcel Bataillon and Melquiades Andrés have pointed out.[76] He also demonstrates a converso self-consciousness, a characteristic which manifests itself, as Melquiades Andrés has noted, in his constant use of the Old Testament to explain his religious views, his attacks on race and blood prejudice, and in his defense of the conversos as both sincere Christians and true Hebrews.[77] Andrés particularly calls our attention to a passage in the *Cuarto abecadario*, in which Osuna writes:

> According to Saint Gregory, the carnal mother of Christ is the synagogue, and his brothers the Jews, whose lineage he took. But they did not wish to enter into the temple of the Scripture to look for him, but to remain outside on the edge and literal sense of the Sacred Scripture; and thus they did not see Christ nor will they see him until they enter from under the veil ... that Moses wore not to see Christ; and they are called dross because they are few and vile, nothing but the remnants of the good ones who have become incorporated in Christ; these [good Jews] are the head of the chosen ones, while the rest are the dregs which nobody takes notice of ... Thus the real

Israelites, those incorporated in Christ, enter through the word of the Scripture, which is the temple of God, to see Christ with the eyes of faith.[78]

Like Pablo de Santa Maria previously, Osuna attacks the Jews, but only to promote the conversos, the best of God's chosen people, who have abandoned a religion based on law for a new and better one, founded only on Scripture.

For obvious reasons Francisco de Osuna did not make overt references to his Jewish roots in his spiritual works; nevertheless, for those investigators interested in prying between the lines of his texts, there are a number of indications that the Franciscan friar was not merely a New Christian, but, on occasion, an indignant one. In reference to Osuna's converso character, Melquiades Andrés has already drawn our attention to the Franciscan's attacks on race and blood prejudice. However, there are in Osuna's works other, more subtle, indications of his New Christian provenance. In the *Tercer abecedario*, for example, Osuna attacks his society's morbid obsession with the agony of Christ during Easter Week, stating that these morose Christians are unable to enjoy mystical communion with God. On the other hand, joyful Christians, who are not obsessed with Christ's bodily suffering, are able to gain much from mystical practice.[79] Here Osuna discreetly distinguishes between true Christians, those who are genuinely disposed to embrace the transcendental aspects of their religion, and the impaired variety, obsessed with the image of an agonized Christ (the victim of Jewish and, by association, converso malice).

While Osuna directed this criticism at the Christian community in general, it is evident that his main target was his own order, who had made Jesus' physical agony during the Passion the center of its mystical process, helping to perpetuate the obsession with the Jewish crime of deicide.[80] In criticizing this morbid obsession, Osuna reflected the views of the *alumbrados*, who believed that the Passion should be approached with joy, not sadness, and that Maundy Thursday, like Resurrection Sunday, should be an occasion for rejoicing. This viewpoint was, incidentally, condemned by the Inquisition in its 1525 Edict of Faith, undoubtedly because it smacked of Jewish subversion.[81]

It seems that Osuna maintained somewhat of a tense relationship with his order. This was partly due to his obsession with mystical practice, which some of his fellow monks regarded as a sign of indolence. However, he tells us, in what appears to be an allusion to his converso background, that he was also attacked for his lineage, diet, and dress.[82] And while he does not elaborate on why his family background and eating habits should cause consternation within his religious community, he does indicate a possible reason for his fellow friars' criticism of his dress. It seems that Osuna was somewhat fastidious about personal cleanliness, writing that nice smells were much better than bad ones, which 'provoke indignation in the clean man [*el hombre limpio*].'[83] While this statement may appear innocuous, it is, I would argue, another carefully aimed barb against his own order, which venerated clean blood and a filthy body as a sign of Christian virtue.

Osuna's *Tercer abecedario* was published in 1527, in a period when the Inquisition was focusing its attention on the *alumbrado* mystical movement. This situation is reflected in the work, which attempts to distinguish between the good mysticism of his order and the bad kind practiced by the lay groups under attack. In practice, of course, the line separating the two groups was quite blurred, with a number of Franciscans eventually being prosecuted as devotees of the *alumbrado* sect. Osuna was not one of these, although it is significant that at the height of the prosecutions, in 1531, he left the Guadalajara area for Seville. Here, encouraged by the Erasmian Archbishop Alonso Manrique, Osuna continued to write his religious reform manuals.

Unfortunately, Osuna arrived in Seville at the moment in which his mystical devotee, Juan de Ávila, was being prosecuted by the local tribunal for *alumbrado* heresy (see Chap. 3). This event may have persuaded him to abandon the city, and the peninsula, for the more salubrious intellectual climate of France, moving first to Toulouse, ostensibly to attend the Franciscan General Congregation held in the city, and then to Paris, in search of publishers for his religious works. Finally, the Franciscan friar moved to Antwerp, where he published the *Trilogium evangelicum* (a study of Jesus' Passion, resurrection, and ascension), while proselytizing among a predominantly converso Spanish merchant community, attempting to temper their capitalist enthusiasm with his evangelical message. Finally, in 1536, after five years in exile, Osuna returned to Spain and obscurity. The only information we have on his last years appears in the editor's introduction to his *Quinto abecedario*, on poverty, published in 1541, which states simply that he had died.

While Osuna's sojourn north of the Pyrenees has elicited few comments from his biographers, it is noteworthy that his four-year absence from Spain occurred at a time when many reform-minded Spanish intellectuals took the road north to escape the Inquisition bonfires. In his

Quinto abecedario, the friar attacks a Church whose approach to its opponents was to set them physically rather than spiritually alight. And he commends his readers to Saint Paul, 'who did not threaten with fire, but inflamed with the spirit of Jesus, the best cure for [heresy].'

IGNATIUS OF LOYOLA AND THE FIRST JESUITS

Ignatius of Loyola had much in common with Francisco de Osuna. Like the Franciscan friar, he wrote a mystical manual, believed Christian ritual should be subordinate to private spirituality, and maintained close contact with a number of Erasmians and *alumbrados* who were later prosecuted for heresy. These commonalities were not, of course, coincidental. Like Osuna, Loyola's formative years were spent in environments where radical New Christian reform voices predominated. However, when, in 1553, the 60-year-old Loyola was persuaded to write his spiritual biography, he was careful to start the tale not in a religiously volatile New Castile, where he had passed his formative years in close proximity to converso nonconformism, but in his orthodox Old Christian homeland, Guipúzcoa, where he went, in 1521, to recuperate from a serious injury. It was here, in the innocent atmosphere of his childhood home, so the narrative goes, that Loyola's religious epiphany took place. It was here, he tells us, that he read Ludolph of Saxony's *La vite Christi*, had his first mystical vision (of the Virgin and Child), and resolved to make a pilgrimage to Jerusalem. Thus began a spiritual adventure that culminated in 1541 with the founding of the Society of Jesus.

As we might expect, the beginning of Loyola's spiritual autobiography follows a fairly conventional conversion narrative pattern, one modeled on that of Francis of Assisi: the prodigal son, corrupted by the values of court society, returns to the pious family home, where he sees the error of his ways, has an illuminating vision, and decides to devote his life to Christ. The work was clearly meant to serve as a salutary tale for Jesuit novices and a general public clamoring for religious monographs. But it was also a way to launder the Society's early history, emphasizing its orthodox mysticism, represented by the *Spiritual Exercises*, while downplaying its *alumbrado* and Erasmian tendencies. It was, at the same time, an attempt by the order to shed its image as a Jewish confraternity—for the Jesuits had already gained the reputation of being an organization dominated by New Christians.

Loyola's sympathetic attitude toward conversos should raise the question: was he himself from a Jewish background? The saint's biographers have, however, avoided this line of inquiry, preferring to focus on his paternal family's noble Basque roots for clues to his spiritual character. The Loyolas, it is true, were of an old Guipúzcoan family whose hidalgo lineage possibly stretched back to the thirteenth century. Ignatius' maternal family, on the other hand, were well-heeled parvenus, who had become wealthy through trade before turning their attention toward improving their social status. Ignatius' maternal grandfather, Doctor Martín García de Licona (his name was taken from the Basque port town), was both a trader and a *letrado* (bureaucrat), who had risen through the royal court's administrative ranks to become *auditor* for the Court of Appeal at Valladolid and advisor to the Catholic Monarchs.[84] In 1459 Licona bought himself a *mayorazgo* (title of mortmain) from an impecunious Guipúzcoan nobleman, Ladron de Balda, and with it noble status. Eight years later, in 1467, he married off his daughter, Marina Sánchez Licona (Loyola's mother) to Beltrán de Oñaz (Loyola's father), thus strengthening his family's noble status. For the Licona family the union was another step toward social respectability. For the Loyolas it was a profitable business transaction, bringing a considerable dowry of 1600 florins.

Were Ignatius of Loyola's maternal family conversos? The fact that Martín García de Licona was both a merchant and a *letrado* is certainly suggestive. However, even if the Liconas had Jewish roots, it is unlikely that Loyola would have been aware of this while growing up in the Basque country, where everyone maintained the conceit of an Old Christian hidalgo ancestry. It would thus have had no impact on his own attitude to New Christians. Did he, however, suspect something later as he established contact with a converso community in Castile, many of whose members had a similar profile to that of his maternal family? Loyola's early biographer, and fellow Jesuit, Pedro Ribadeneira, noted that on a number of occasions the Jesuit General had stated that he wished he were Jewish because Jesus Christ was a Jew. In the context of sixteenth-century Spain, where honor was predicated on *limpieza de sangre*, this was a most unusual comment for an Old Christian to make, especially one from the Basque country, where the denizens were inordinately proud of their pure blood. Was Loyola's statement an indication that he believed himself to be part Jewish? Or was it merely a fraternal gesture to a converso community who had accompanied him on his evangelical mission? Perhaps Loyola's strong bond with conversos is explained simply by the fact that after the age of 14 he spent much of his life in their company.

Loyola's relationship with conversos most likely began in 1506, when he moved south to Arévalo, becoming a page in the house of the court treasurer Juan Velázquez de Cuéllar, whose professional position brought him into constant contact with New Christian merchants.[85] As page to Velázquez it was inevitable that Loyola too would rub shoulders with these wealthy businessmen, some of whom would later finance the first Jesuit colleges in Spain. It was equally inevitable that he would witness at close quarters the Inquisition's attack on the converso merchant community, leading many to flee abroad and others to escape into private spiritual worlds, or millenarian fantasies in which they were delivered from Holy Office persecution.

When Loyola entered Arévalo, in 1506, there were four Inquisition tribunals in close proximity to the town—in Segovia, Valladolid, Ávila, and Medina del Campo—investigating the religious activities of the area's large and relatively prosperous New Christian communities, which had recently benefited from the expansion of Segovia's wool and textile industries. The tribunals kept close tabs on the smaller towns through a network of *familiares*, or honorary members, who often acted as informants. These individuals would have been a visible presence in Arévalo, monitoring the local population of conversos and Moriscos, many of whom were first-generation converts whose backgrounds were known to everyone in the town.

One of Arévalo's most famous New Christians is someone known to us today as the *Mancebo* (Young Man) of Arévalo. A contemporary of Loyola, the *Mancebo*, a Morisco, traveled around Spain in the first decades of the century, contacting clandestine Islamic cells with the aim of keeping the old religion alive. Significantly, the *Mancebo*'s own religious views, revealed in his *Sumario de la relación y ejercicio spiritual*, lean heavily on Thomas à Kempis' *Imitacio Christi*, indicating once again the appeal of the *devotio moderna* movement for New Christians forced to take stock of their spiritual lives.[86] The title of the *Mancebo*'s work also recalls that of Loyola's own religious guide, the *Ejercicios espirituales*, likewise inspired by the Kempis book.

Loyola told his fellow Jesuit Jerónimo Nadal that 'it was at Manresa that I saw the Gerçoncito [the *Imitacio Christi*] for the first time, and since then there is no book of devotion I like more.'[87] Loyola appears to have been unaware of the copy of Kempis' work in the Velázquez de

Cuéllar household. This was bought from the royal collection after the death of Queen Isabel in 1504, two years before Loyola entered the family's service. A number of other works in the Velázquez de Cuéllar library also call to mind Loyola's Spiritual Exercises, among which are *Reformación de las fuerzas de animo* and *Del regimiento de la conciencia*.[88]

While Loyola may not have been familiar with his employer's religious library, he would have been acquainted with his converso clients. Among this group was the family friend Pedro de Cazalla, who, along with his cousins Juan and Maria de Cazalla, was at the center of Castile's *alumbrado* movement, discussed above.[89] It was through Cazalla that Velázquez de Cuéllar's daughter Catalina de Velasco was introduced to the charismatic *beata* Francisca Hernández, later housing her in the family home at Valladolid for over a year prior to the *beata*'s arrest and prosecution for heresy. True, Catalina's relationship with the *beata* took place several years after Loyola had left the Velázquez de Cuéllar service. However, it does suggest that the founder of the Jesuits passed his formative years in an environment in which illuminist or heterodox ideas circulated freely. Moreover, we know from Loyola's fellow page, Alonso de Montalvo, that Loyola maintained a long-term correspondence with Catalina de Velasco after parting company with the family. It is likely, therefore, that he was well informed of the Velázquez de Cuéllar family's attachment to the *beata*.[90]

In 1517, when Juan Velázquez de Cuéllar died, Loyola moved north from Arévalo to Nájera, the seat of Antonio Manrique de Lara, Duke of Nájera, again entering a household closely associated with conversos and religious non-conformism.[91] The Duke of Nájera's uncle was the Erasmian prelate Antonio Manrique, who we have already met in connection with the converso humanists Juan Luis Vives and Alfonso and Juan de Valdés. The duke maintained a close relationship with his uncle, whose religious views he shared. More significantly, he was a friend and protector of the radical converso curate Francisco Medrano, a disciple, like Catalina de Velasco, of the *alumbrada* Francisca Hernández. During his four years in the service of the duke, Loyola would inevitably have become acquainted with Medrano and his illuminist ideas, once again suggesting that his own religious reflections had begun not in Guipúzcoa but in locations more often associated with mystical and non-conformist practice.

It was while fighting in the Manrique ranks against a French incursion into Navarre that Loyola sustained a serious leg wound, forcing him into a long convalescence at his family home. It was then, at the age of 31, that he decided to pursue a spiritual path, beginning with a pilgrimage to the Holy Land via another pilgrimage site, the monastery of Montserrat, near Manresa, where, he tells us, he wished to confess and prepare himself for his journey. But Montserrat was not only a place of pilgrimage, it was also an important center for mysticism, a practice introduced to the monastery in the late fifteenth century by García Jiménez de Cisneros, the cousin of the Franciscan general Cardinal Cisneros. These mystical ideas had gradually penetrated the lay community of Manresa, just as the mystical process practiced at the Franciscan monastery of Salceda permeated the nearby converso community at Pastrana.

Were Loyola's Manresa adherents, like the *alumbrados* of Pastrana, also from middle-sort converso backgrounds? While we have no information on their ancestries, we do know that the group was formed largely of artisans and merchants connected to the town's thriving textile trade. Among this group was the wealthy cotton merchant Inés Pascual, who became a lifelong patron of Loyola and his order. It was Inés who took the callow mystic under her wing, introducing him to her close circle of friends, who were soon captivated by his spiritual message and visions.[92] One of these visions, the most recurrent, Loyola tells us in his autobiography, was of Christ 'with no distinction in his bodily members.' The image evokes Saint Paul's metaphor of the Church as the body of Christ, equal in all its parts, a comparison that had long been used by converso reformers to emphasize the egalitarian nature of the Christian faith. Was it merely a coincidence that Loyola continued to have this vision throughout his sojourn in Manresa? Or was it a message to his Manresa followers that he was an emissary for a reformed, all-embracing Church in which conversos could find a place?

Not everyone in Manresa was impressed by Loyola's visions, however, as Inés Pascual's son noted much later:

> There were no lack of envious and malicious people who publicly attacked and muttered against these saintly exercises and against the person who practiced them and his followers, in particular Juana Serrano, in whose house he was a guest, and above all against my mother, Inés Pascual, saying that she was the inventor and instigator of these disturbances and novelties as she had brought their author to the town and had kept him and protected him there.[93]

This was the standard reaction to Loyola's early evangelical mission: for some, he was literally a Godsend; for others he was religiously suspect, his mystical reform movement regarded as detrimental to Old Christian social and religious values.

Loyola left Manresa for Barcelona in February 1523, remaining in the Catalan city for three weeks before continuing his journey to Jerusalem. On returning from his pilgrimage, in 1524, he renewed his ties with Inés Pascual, staying in the merchant's house in Barcelona for two years while he studied Latin under the Erasmian Jerónimo Ardévol. The classes were paid for by another wealthy patron, Isabel Roser, a member of the Ferrer family, who had also been among Loyola's followers in Manresa. During this period Loyola also formed a close relationship with Antonio Pujol, Inés Pascual's brother, a canon and scholar, who allowed him access to his library.[94]

It was while in Barcelona that Loyola also became acquainted with the court of the viceroy, Fadrique de Portugal, and in particular with two members of the viceroy's entourage, Lope de Cáceres and Calixto de Saa. These two young men later took up residence with Loyola at Alcalá de Henares, when he entered the Complutense University in 1526. Both men were from merchant backgrounds: Calixto de Saa was from a Portuguese merchant family; Lope de Cáceres was a member of the Caceres family of Segovia, a converso merchant clan that had been prominent in the Comunero revolt of 1520.[95]

In March 1526 Loyola moved from Barcelona to Alcalá, where he formed close ties with a Portuguese priest, Manuel Miona, who became his confessor, and the Alcalá printer Miguel de Eguía, who was in the process of producing a Castilian version of Erasmus' *Enchiridion*. Significantly, Miona and Eguía were members of a circle that had formed around the *alumbrada* Francisca Hernández, who by this time, as I have already noted, had developed a close friendship with Loyola's first patrons, the Velázquez de Cuéllar family. Both Miona and Eguia were tried for heresy in 1530.[96]

Writing in 1988, Loyola's latter-day biographer Ricardo García-Villoslada described the printer Eguia as a *hidalgo*. To be precise, the Eguias were wealthy wool merchants from Estella in Navarre who had used their own wool money to found entailed estates (*mayorazgos*) and fund chapels, thus giving themselves a noble veneer. Two members of the family later joined the Jesuit Order. As for Miguel Eguía, after serving a term in the Inquisition jail, he reentered Estella society, where he returned to his merchant roots while using his fortune to buy himself a position on the town council.[97]

Ignatius of Loyola was not long at Alcalá de Henares before his own evangelical mission came under the scrutiny of the Inquisition. In November 1526, Inquisition officials from the Toledo tribunal, acting on rumors that Loyola and his followers were engaged in clandestine illuminist activities, traveled to Alcalá to investigate the charges. However, after making some initial inquiries, the Holy Office agents turned the case over to the Archbishop of Toledo, Alonso de Fonseca, who in turn placed it in the hands of his vicar general, Juan Rodríguez de Figueroa. On 30 November 1526, Rodríguez interviewed Loyola at the archbishop's palace, at which time he informed him that he and his young followers should refrain from donning religious habits (Loyola and his friends were habitually clad in brown robes), which gave the erroneous impression that they were authentic, theologically trained friars. Three months later, Loyola was interviewed once again by Rodríguez, on this occasion in the archbishop's prison, where he had been interned following more reports of his illuminist activities. It was during this second interview that Rodríguez asked him if he observed the Sabbath—revealing that the vicar suspected he was dealing with a converso *alumbrado*.[98]

However, despite the fact that the depositions from a number of witnesses had presented Loyola as the leader of an illuminist conventicle, Rodríguez did not prosecute him; he merely banned him and his disciples from evangelizing in the town for three years. Why was the vicar so lenient? Why, indeed, was he even investigating a case that should have been directed by the Inquisition? Could it have been that pressure was placed upon the Holy Office by the archbishop, Alonso de Fonseca, perhaps at the request of Loyola's noble contacts, to hand the suspected *alumbrado* over to the archdiocese? It is significant that Fonseca, like the Archbishop of Seville, Alonso Manrique, was an Erasmus sympathizer, whose reformist views conflicted with those of the Holy Office. He was also a member of a converso clan, the Ulloas of Toro, who in the fifteenth century had formed marriage unions and political alliances with the heretofore modest *hidalgo* family, the Fonsecas.[99]

In little more than two generations the Ulloa-Fonseca clan not only established a number of important noble houses, it also produced three politically powerful clerics, all of whom were named Alonso de Fonseca. All three Alonsos were religious non-conformists; the first, who occupied both the Seville and the Santiago de Compostela sees, was often accused of dressing in a manner ill befitting an archbishop, for paying too much attention to astrological readings, and for publicly declaring himself to be in sympathy with Sadducean beliefs.[100] The second Alonso, nephew of the first, was a man of strong humanist convictions who, in 1475, as Archbishop of Seville, enticed the Spanish humanist Antonio Nebrija back to Spain from Italy to work in his court. The third Alonso, the product of the second Alonso's relationship with Maria de Ulloa (the Fonsecas and Ulloas formed endogamous alliances for several generations), was also closely attached to humanist reformers, promoting Erasmian views in his own see at Toledo. It was this Alonso who now came to Loyola's aid.

In his autobiography, Loyola states that after receiving the news that he would not be able to evangelize for three years, he traveled to Valladolid in order to place the matter in the hands of Fonseca. Here, he tells us, he talked on familiar terms with Spain's highest prelate, who 'offered him everything.' While Loyola does not elaborate on this cryptic remark, it seems evident that Fonseca had summoned him to the city to make him a very generous offer.

Although Loyola was careful to exclude background information on his meeting with Fonseca, it is clear that the event took place in Valladolid at the same time that Spain's clerical elite were gathered in the city to deliberate on the orthodoxy of Erasmus' religious works. Among the Dutch humanist's defenders in this tense debate was the Archbishop of Toledo, Alonso de Fonseca. Loyola would no doubt have followed the proceedings with some interest, although his attention may have been divided between the debate and another religious issue rocking the city: a growing illuminist movement, centered on the *beata* Francisca Hernández, who numbered among her followers several of Loyola's friends, including Catalina de Velasco, the daughter of Loyola's erstwhile patron, Juan Velázquez de Cuéllar. In fact, Hernández was now in permanent residence at Velasco's country home, just outside Valladolid. Loyola may even have met her during his visit to the city to talk with Fonseca. He would almost certainly have taken the occasion to meet with Catalina, with whom he corresponded for many years after leaving her father's service.

When Loyola met Fonseca in Valladolid in 1527, it was against a background of intense religious reflection and reform. Fonseca himself was part of this movement for change, lending his political support to Spain's Erasmian movement while financing the establishment of a *colegio mayor* at Salamanca University, with the aim of renovating the university's scholastic education.[101] When Fonseca spoke to Loyola at Valladolid, it is likely that he offered him the possibility of studying at this college, where he could gain his theological credentials before resuming his lay mission. Fonseca may even have considered guiding Loyola and his followers in their reform task, as his fellow Erasmian, Alonso Manrique, was soon to guide a group of reformers, including Juan de Ávila, in Andalusia. As it turned out, however, Loyola took advantage of Fonseca's hospitality for only six weeks. In September 1527, after having been questioned once again by religious authorities, he left Salamanca for the University of Paris, having decided, no doubt, that his increasing notoriety in Spain was detrimental to his plans for creating an evangelical organization.

It is in Paris, where Loyola studied from 1528 to 1535, that his close connections to a converso community become most evident. In fact, Loyola and a number of his student adherents were supported by converso merchant money for the duration of their studies. Some of this financial aid came from certain patrons in Barcelona, prominent among whom was Inés de Pascual; much of it came from the converso merchant communities of Bruges and Antwerp.[102] One of these wealthy merchants was Juan de Cuéllar, in whose home Loyola often stayed during his business trips to Antwerp. A merchant from Segovia, Cuéllar had for some reason left Spain in 1506, never to return. While it is unlikely that Loyola had known the merchant personally while he lived in Segovia, it is probable that through his early patron, Juan Velázquez de Cuéllar, he had become acquainted, in his youth, with other members of this merchant's extended family.

Another of Loyola's northern merchant patrons was Gonzalo de Aguilar, with whom he stayed while soliciting money in Bruges. Aguilar, a Burgos merchant, was married to Ana de Castro, a member of an enormously wealthy and politically influential converso merchant dynasty from Burgos. Loyola, it seems, was put in contact with Aguilar by Juan de Castro, a member of the Castro family whom he had befriended in Paris. While in Paris, Loyola also formed close attachments to Pedro de Garay, Pedro de Maluendo, and Alfonso, Bernadino and Jerónimo Salinas, all of whom were members of Burgos converso merchant families well situated in the business communities of Bruges and Antwerp. It is thus likely that Loyola also contacted these families while on his financing campaigns in Flanders. Later, a number of the merchants named above became benefactors of the infant Society of Jesus.

It was at the University of Paris that Loyola also gathered about him six men who, several years later, would become the first members of the Society of Jesus: Pedro Fabro, Francisco de Javier, Diego Láinez, Alfonso

Salmerón, Simón Rodríguez, and Nicolás Bobadilla. Of these men, it was an open secret that Diego Láinez and Nicolás Bobadilla were conversos, and there is also reason to suspect that Rodriguez, Salmerón, and Javier were from Jewish backgrounds. Indeed, most of the early Jesuit elite were New Christians. This group included Juan Alfonso Polanco, Loyola's personal secretary and framer of the Jesuit's *Constitutions*; Jerónimo Nadal, the order's roving trouble-shooter; and Pedro de Ribadeneira, Loyola's early biographer.[103]

A converso aura envelops both Loyola's biography and that of his order, especially during its infancy. This was not the organization that was later seen as a bulwark against Protestant heresy, but a non-conformist religious body that rejected monastic seclusion in favor of urban interaction, and scholastic exegesis in favor of mystical devotion and a humanist syllabus—characteristics that many churchmen associated with Erasmian heterodoxy. But what most conferred upon the Jesuits an air of radicalism, or even subversion, was their New Christian membership. It was this aspect that brought the order into conflict with the Archbishop of Toledo, Juan Martínez Silíceo, when, in 1551, they founded a college at Alcalá de Henares. Silíceo, whose animosity toward converso curates had led to the infamous Toledo *limpieza de sangre* statute of 1547, was adamantly against allowing a religious establishment into his diocese that was renowned for its New Christian composition.[104] The archbishop thus made it evident that his approbation for the college was contingent on the Jesuits adopting a *limpieza* requirement, similar to his own Toledo statute. This Loyola refused to countenance; however, to avoid an ugly and protracted conflict with the venomous primate, he gave Silíceo to understand that no conversos would be involved in the Alcalá college. There is no indication that Loyola took this assurance very seriously; in fact, without his investigating the backgrounds of the Jesuits involved in the college—something he refused to do—there was no possibility of his rigorously enforcing the ban.[105]

Pressure to prohibit New Christians from entering the Society did not only come from outside the order, however. There was also, in these early years, growing agitation among an Old Christian section of the Jesuits for a *limpieza* requirement. Despite this prejudice, Loyola remained firm in his conviction that the Society was to be free to all Christians.[106] Unfortunately, this situation began to change after Loyola's death, as the converso governing elite lost ground to its Old Christian rivals, and the Society evolved from a movement that advocated religious reform to one that defended conformity, tradition, and blood purity.[107]

CHAPTER 3

From Alcala to Seville and Beyond

According to the anonymous author of the fifteenth-century anti-Semitic text, *El Alboraique*, the conversos of northern Castile were natural converts and sincere in their new faith, while 'in the kingdom of Toledo, Murcia, Andalusia and Extremadura you will hardly find among them true Christians.'[1] Although it overestimates the northern conversos' sincerity, the statement does reflect a fundamental difference between the northern and southern communities: the southerners were more numerous and visible, thus representing a greater threat to their Old Christian antagonists.

Emanating from the once prosperous Jewish *aljamas* of Andalusia and La Mancha, the southern conversos formed larger communities, or support bases, than their northern counterparts, and this gave them a better opportunity of perpetuating their Jewish faith. It also encouraged them to form endogamous marriage unions, maintaining bonds of kinship and business alliances, through which they could better exploit the possibilities of the local economy. None of this went unnoticed by the Old Christian community, inclined for the most part to see conversos as a secret brotherhood of Jews bent on controlling or subverting Christian society. Always present, tensions between Old and New Christians could lead to violent outbreaks at the least provocation. These clashes were most likely to occur, however, in times of political instability, as during the final years of Enrique IV's ineffectual reign, when civil order often broke down completely, leaving the mob to vent its anger and frustrations against the traditional

© The Author(s) 2018
K. Ingram, *Converso Non-Conformism in Early Modern Spain*,
https://doi.org/10.1007/978-3-319-93236-1_3

scapegoat, the Jews; except that now the enemy was not the Jewish community, but a large and relatively prosperous converso one.

In 1473 anti-converso riots broke out in Córdoba, triggered, as assaults on the Jews and conversos often were, by a religious procession.[2] In this instance the violence was prompted, or so it was rumored, by a young converso woman who threw slop from a bedroom window onto a passing statue of the Virgin. In retaliation, the Old Christian processionists ransacked the city's converso neighborhoods, killing and pillaging for three days. The hostilities then spread to the nearby towns of Andjújar, Úbeda, Baeza, and Jaén, ravaging their converso districts. Without protection, the conversos fled south to Seville or to the town of Palma del Rio, where the Lord of Palma, Luis Fernández Portocarrero, offered them a safe haven. For this act of charity Portocarrero was no doubt remunerated handsomely. However, we should not discount the possibility that the nobleman acted out of genuine sympathy, or empathy, toward his New Christian refugees; after all, his own ancestors were also tainted: his mother's family, the Portocarreros, by Jewish blood[3]; his father's family, the Bocanegras, by trade.

Luis Fernández Portocarrero's great-great-grandfather was the Genoese merchant, Egidio Bocanegra, who in the fourteenth century placed his ships and his seamanship at the disposal of Alfonso XI in the defense of Spain's southern coast. For this service Bocanegra was presented with the small, depopulated town of Palma del Rio and its surrounding territory.[4] It was in a bid to bring prosperity to Palma that in 1350, or thereabouts, the Italian merchant introduced a large community of Mudéjar agriculturalists and artisans into the area. This community, one of the largest Mudéjar *aljamas* in Andalusia, maintained a stable population throughout the next century, numbering around 500 inhabitants, or 12 percent of the town's residents. In 1502, faced with a royal expulsion order, the majority of these Muslims converted to Christianity, although most continued to observe Islamic rites.

In contrast to Palma's fifteenth-century Mudéjar *aljama*, its Jewish one was quite small, having slumped after the 1391 pogrom and never really recovered. The town's converso population, on the other hand, was much healthier, expanding particularly in the last decades of the century, as Luis Fernández Portocarrero, the seventh Lord of Palma, gained a reputation as a nobleman friendly to the New Christians. Running parallel to the growth of Palma's New Christian community, and probably related to the phenomenon, was the growth of mystical practice, centered in the town's

Franciscan monasteries. One of Spain's great early modern mystics, Fray Bernabé de Palma, was born and brought up in the town, and served much of his adult life in the nearby Franciscan Monastery, Santa Maria de los Angeles.[5] The friar was much admired by the first Count of Palma, another Luis, and his wife Leonor de la Vega y Girón, and paid frequent visits to the Palma court to tend to the countess' spiritual needs. It is thus probable that he would have been acquainted with Juan and Maria Cazalla, whose parents formed part of the count's entourage. He may even have inspired the two young conversos to embark on a mystical religious path, although it is more likely that both the Cazallas and Bernabé imbibed from Palma del Rio's common mystical font.

It will be recalled that Juan and Maria Cazalla were investigated for illuminist heresy in the *alumbrado* trials of the 1520s and 1530s.[6] This was not the first time that members of the Cazalla family had been charged with heresy by the Holy Office. In 1488 Maria and Juan's father, Gonzalo Martínez, was convicted of Judaizing by the Inquisition tribunal of Córdoba, as was their wealthy and prominent uncle, Alfonso Cazalla, Luis Fernández Portocarrero's chief accountant. Remarkably, this indictment did not affect Alfonso Cazalla's status at the Palma court: he remained Portocarrero's financial advisor until the latter's death in 1503.[7]

The Portocarrero family was one of a number of noble Andalusian clans that developed close ties with a converso business and professional community in the fifteenth century. These relationships were at base marriages of convenience, sometimes literally, with the noble family offering protection and patronage in exchange for the conversos' business and administrative acumen. However, conversos were not only traders and bureaucrats; they were also scholars and educators, providing intellectual stimulus for the nobleman and tutelage for his children. It was inevitable in these circumstances that intimate bonds would often be established between noble families and their New Christian retainers. There was also a psychological complicity between the two social groups, as noted in the previous chapter. With few exceptions, the most important noble families in fifteenth-century Spain were recent arrivals, having ascended with the Trastámara dynasty. Like the conversos, they were *homines novi*, unable to boast flawless bloodlines, and thus they were also susceptible to attacks on their legitimacy, even more so in the case of those who had formed marriage unions with wealthy ex-Jews.

The strength of the relationship between certain Andalusian noble families and the middle-sort converso community becomes apparent when we examine the reaction of the nobles to the establishment of the first Inquisition tribunal in Seville in 1480. Noble families not only defended their converso accountants and advisors against the Inquisition officials, they also provided sanctuaries for converso merchants and artisans on the run from a rampant Holy Office. During the first months of Inquisition activity in Seville, 8000 persons are said to have fled to territory controlled by Rodrigo Ponce de León, Marquis of Cádiz, while many others made for Sanlucar de Barrameda, the *señorio*, or noble seat, of the Medina Sidonia family, a long-time ally of the New Christians. Other nobles who lent support to the conversos during this period were Fadrique Enríquez, the Marquis of Tarifa, and Alfonso Fernández de Córdoba, Lord of Priego and Aguilar, the head of a noble clan that was strongly influenced by converso religious reformers.

The Fernández de Córdoba family was characteristic of the new nobility; that is to say, they descended from a poor but ambitious northern hidalgo who came south in the late thirteenth century, looking to grab land in the *Reconquista*.[8] Later, in the fourteenth century, the family sided with Enrique Trastámara in his rebellion against his half-brother, King Pedro the Cruel, and as a result of this support was awarded large tracts of land in the province of Córdoba when the pretender became King Enrique II, in 1367. Having ascended several rungs of the noble ladder, the Fernández de Córdobas consolidated their position as a family of substance by forming lucrative ties to Córdoba's wealthy converso community. When this community found itself under threat in the violent anti-converso riots of 1473, it was Alfonso Fernández de Córdoba (or Aguilar) who came to its rescue.[9] Later, in 1506, it was Alfonso's son, Pedro, the first Marquis of Priego, who clashed with Córdoba's brutal Inquisition official, Diego Rodríguez de Lucero, storming the Inquisition gaol and releasing its inmates—almost all of whom were conversos convicted of Judaizing. In the same year, the marquis refused to allow Inquisition officials into his territories when they came to claim money from the converso community for a *composición*.[10] For these actions an enraged King Ferdinand stripped him of all his Crown offices, bonds, and grants.[11]

Pedro's daughter, Catalina, Marchioness of Priego, was also influenced by her close ties to the converso community, and in particular to the converso preacher Juan de Ávila, whom she supported in his missionary work, undertaken essentially among the New Christian community of Andalusia. It should be emphasized that in helping Ávila the marchioness was patronizing not the orthodox Catholic preacher of hagiographic fame but a controversial figure who had early in his preaching career been imprisoned by the Holy Office for his radical views. It was Ávila who introduced the marchioness' family to Ignatius of Loyola's recently founded Company of Jesus. Catalina herself was personally instrumental in founding Jesuit colleges in Córdoba and in the town of Montilla, where her family resided, while her son, Antonio de Córdoba, who had joined the Jesuits in 1554, was nominated the Córdoba institution's first rector. Again, it is important to stress that in supporting the Jesuits, the Fernández de Córdoba family were allying themselves with a religious group whose controversial character was intimately linked to its converso membership.

Unlike the Mendozas or the Manriques, the Fernández de Córdoba family did not produce men of letters. Their court at Montilla was, however, associated with scholarly activity. One member of this erudite enclave was the first marquis' physician, Dr. Antonio de Morales, a man renowned for his learning, who was the first occupant of the Chair of Philosophy and Metaphysics at the University of Alcalá. The marquis is said to have bought a building in Córdoba, reputed to have been built on the site of Seneca's birth, and presented it to Morales, stating that it was only fitting that another wise Córdoban live there. Dr. Morales' wife, Mencia de Oliva, was the daughter of another medical man and scholar, Fernán Pérez de Oliva, and the sister of the famous humanist of the same name. One of Mencia and Antonio's sons was the humanist Ambrosio de Morales, author of the *Crónica general*, a history of Spain up to the time of Charles V.[12] A second son, Agustín de Oliva, followed his father into medicine, although he too exhibited certain scholarly and literary pretensions, becoming known locally as both an antiquarian and a poet. Among Agustín's poetic output is a long dialogue between himself and a Córdoban schoolmaster named Diego López, in which both men accuse each other of belonging to New Christian families.[13]

The long poetic dialogue begins with López sending the physician Agustín de Oliva a pig, informing him snidely that if the meat makes him ill, he can use his own medicine to cure himself.[14] In reply to López's affront, Oliva writes back accusing his adversary of coming from a family of Judaizers; this in turn prompts López to charge Oliva with disguising his Muslim ancestry. There follows a long exchange of banter in which both men accuse each other of New Christian habits and foibles. Oliva states that members of the López family were silk merchants and tax farmers; López retorts that Oliva's family were pharmacists (*'Los Olivas de*

Montilla/y Olivos de aqui [Córdoba] especieros') and bankers ('*Pues Oliva se deriva/de Olivares cambiador/que diferencia ay Doctor/entre Oliva y Olivares*'). Both make allusions to *sambenitos* (the sackcloth worn by conversos convicted of heresy), although, understandably, neither man cites specific instances of Inquisition prosecutions. And both men accuse each other of having non-Christian eating habits—of consuming garlic, eggplants, only fish with scales, and of rejecting all pork products. In one passage of the document, López accuses Oliva of buying pork, but only to sell it later—a tantalizing remark, given the fact that at his death in 1591 Ambrosio de Morales, Oliva's famous brother, had stored in his house 16 pounds of ham, several pounds of which were moth-eaten.[15]

Oliva and López's final round of epistolary sniping takes place while the former is resident at the country estate of Luis Fernández Portocarrero—the second Count of Palma and grandson of the Luis Fernández Portocarrero we met earlier—where he is treating the nobleman for some illness. Oliva writes to López, telling him that the count has been inquiring about López's family, and that not wishing to lie, he had informed the nobleman about their Jewish roots. In reply to this attack, López states that he is not surprised the doctor associates with Portocarrero, as Palma del Rio was not so long ago another Mecca (a reference to the town's large Mudéjar population). He then writes to the count, via Oliva, denouncing the Oliva family as notorious New Christians. Portocarrero responds by relating what the doctor has informed him of López's family: 'that one of your grandfathers was converted into ash, sir.'[16] In his reply to this accusation López recommends that the count examine his own family's coat of arms, which, he states, has stains (*manchas*) on its Aragonese and Portuguese sides.[17] And at this point the work comes abruptly to an end.

The above exchange between Oliva and López was not an unusual one in early-modern Spain. Indeed, it would appear to have formed part of a literary subgenre already apparent in the fifteenth-century *cancioneros*, in which two converso poets entered into a literary joust, each party accusing the other of living a Sephardic way of life while pretending to be a good Christian. Like all *cancionero* poetry, these verses were written to entertain a court society, although in this case the entertainment could be vicious and vindictive, with the two antagonists verbally lacerating each other for the delectation of a royal or noble household. The Córdoban poet Anton Montoro (*El Ropero*), a friend of the second Count of Palma's grandfather, was himself involved in a number of these contests, although his own inclination was usually toward more ironic self-deprecation, an example of which is found in his reply to a 'gentleman' who sends him a pig:

> And you, Mister importunate
> so excessive in your gifts
> next time send me one
> that the rabbi has first cursed.
>
> [*Y vos, señor importune*
> *en las mandas muy prolixo*
> *mandad luego enviarme uno*
> *de los quell Rabí maldixo.*][18]

Sending ham to conversos appears to have been a popular practical joke of the day. In *Los judíos en la España moderna y contemporánea*, Caro Baroja includes a number of such exchanges. One of these concerns the Admiral of Castile, Fadrique Enríquez, and his retainer, the poet Gabriel de Mena. It is reported that one day Enríquez (whose grandmother was said to be Jewish) sent some pigs' trotters to the converso Mena with the following lines attached: *Estos pies de puerco tomo/El señor que no los come* (These pigs' trotters *are received by* the gentleman who does not eat them). In reply Mena merely added a 'd' to the first word in the second line so that it now read: *Estos pies de puerco tomo/Del señor que no los come* (These pigs' trotters *are received from* the gentleman who does not eat them).[19]

Agustín de Oliva's poem evidently forms part of a converso *cancionero* tradition. However, there is a notable anomaly here. One of the protagonists, Agustín himself, is from a Morisco background, or so his antagonist states. This is perplexing, not only because it does not conform to the literary genre, but also because Oliva's profile would suggest, if anything, that he was a converso: his profession, medicine, and the other activities which López attributes to his family—pharmacy and banking—were typically converso occupations. Moriscos could, of course, be physicians, and indeed many were; but the majority of these were members of Morisco elites found within the Kingdom of Granada and province of Valencia.[20] If López's claims were correct, the Olivas would seem to have been an exception to this rule—the remnant of a privileged and educated Castilian Mudéjar family that had converted to Christianity in the fifteenth century, and had integrated itself into what was a predominantly converso medical community, forming business and marital alliances possibly with the latter group. In attacking Agustín de Oliva, López may have chosen to concentrate on this Muslim side of the family, not the Jewish one, in order to make the contest more interesting and entertaining for the Portocarrero court, where conversos and Moriscos rubbed shoulders.

Whatever the nature of Agustín's New Christian ancestry, it was not something that he would have wished to air in public, and thus his poem would have circulated, if at all, within a reduced group of New Christian friends, probably associated with the Palma del Rio court. For the public, tailored version of the Oliva-Morales family's provenance, Agustín could rely on his brother Ambrosio, who was adept at using his own literary works to introduce references to his illustrious father, Dr. Antonio de Morales. In the prologue to his history of Spain, Ambrosio de Morales writes, '[M]y father was respected by almost all the noble families of Andalusia, for both his "good caste" as they say, and for his great knowledge of medicine, in which profession he was one of the most renowned men of his day.'[21] And in his *Antigüedades* the humanist notes that Morales senior was known 'as a man of singular intellect and excellent judgement ... celebrated in natural and moral philosophy [science and ethics], and in medicine, which was his principal profession, writing Latin with a felicitous style; and with very good taste in all manner of antiquarian pursuits. All of this in addition to his good caste and great kindness made him one of the most celebrated men of his day.'[22]

According to Ambrosio de Morales, his father was not only a renowned doctor and scholar, he was also of 'good caste,' an expression that had come to signify someone of Old Christian ancestry. But the term itself only meant of good background, or lineage. Morales never refers to his family as Old Christian, nor does he mention any of his ancestors, with the exception of his maternal grandfather, the physician Fernán Pérez de Oliva. One surmises that Morales wished to present his family in the best possible light without actually lying about its past—a typical case of converso dissimulation. This is most evident in his father's epitaph, in which the humanist wrote, with picaresque irony: 'Here it is said with much truth all that the deceased was: that is of noble lineage and in all his parts very clean (*por todas partes muy limpio*).'[23] The general reader would take this statement to mean that the humanist's father was untainted by Jewish or Muslim blood on all four branches of his family; however, literally speaking, Morales had only stated that his father was hygienic, a characteristic that often separated conversos from their Old Christian neighbors. The object, of course, was to deny one's past while surreptitiously affirming it. This, in effect, is what Morales' brother Agustín had done when he chose to enter into the poetic slandering match with the schoolteacher Diego López.

While we have little information on either the Oliva's or Morales' family histories, we can be certain that they were New Christians and that this taint continued to make life uncomfortable for them several generations after their ancestral conversions took place, even though there is no evidence, *pace* López's poem, that either family was drawn to Jewish or Islamic belief. In fact, both families appear to have placed their faith not in organized religion but in scientific inquiry and, increasingly, humanist reform. This is particularly evident in the works of Ambrosio de Morales' uncle, the humanist Fernán Pérez de Oliva, which demonstrate a peculiar New Christian sensitivity to the socio-religious tensions of his day.

Fernán Pérez de Oliva (1494?–1532)

Fernán Pérez de Oliva was born in Córdoba in or around the year 1494. We have no information on his mother, not even her name, although there are the usual perfunctory references to her coming from a distinguished family. His father, also named Fernán Pérez de Oliva, was a well-to-do physician and scholar who took a prominent role in the intellectual life of the city. Among Pérez de Oliva senior's friends was the physician Juan Díaz de Torreblanco, Miguel de Cervantes' great-grandfather, who formed part of a group of Córdoba scholars and businessmen that supported Christopher Columbus in his Atlantic enterprise. Pérez de Oliva senior's interest in science and, in particular, geography, something his son inherited, suggests that he too formed part of this group, and was personally acquainted with the great explorer. His son's work *Historia de la invención de las Indias*, written it seems at the behest of Ferdinand Columbus, the son of Christopher Columbus and the *Cordobesa* Beatriz Enríquez Arana, also suggests a certain familiarity between the Columbus and Pérez de Oliva families.[24]

An erudite man, Pérez de Oliva senior took personal charge of his son's early education, before dispatching him to the University of Salamanca, in 1508, to study philosophy and the humanities. From here the young scholar moved first to the recently established Complutense University, to perfect his Latin, and then, in 1512, to the University of Paris. Two years later he was in Rome, living with an uncle who was employed at the papal court and pursuing yet more studies in philosophy and the humanities. When this anonymous uncle died, Pope Leo X offered Oliva his office and benefices; however, the nephew turned down the offer, believing he would be unable to execute his duties and study at the same time. He then moved once more to Paris, where, he tells us, he studied a number of subjects, including Aristotle's *Ethics*. In 1524 he returned to Córdoba. Here he wrote the first of his two *razonamientos*, or critical studies, *El razonamiento sobre la navegación del Guadalquivir* (examined below). Two years later he moved once more to Salamanca (this time taking his nephew Ambrosio de Morales with him), where he temporarily substituted Doctor Juan Martínez Silíceo in the chair of Natural Philosophy.[25]

This teaching position at Salamanca was, it seems, Oliva's first taste of employment. His long duration as a student, over 16 years, is testimony not only to his love of letters but also to a not inconsiderable private income. We gain some indication of the extent of this income in a letter Oliva wrote to an archdeacon in Seville in 1525, in which he offers to exchange a number of the benefices he held in Córdoba for that of the archdeaconry. These benefices were in Montemayor, Belmonte, Cañaveral, Chillón, Santa Marina in Córdoba, and 'a very good one in Las Cabezas.' Clearly, the 33-year-old Oliva was not attracted to Salamanca University by its professorial salaries alone, which, in any case, were meager. Rather, he entered the university to help transform it from a conservative, scholastic institution to a progressive, humanist one, an objective indicated in his friend Cristóbal Villalón's *El Scholastico*, in which a loquacious Oliva expatiates on the dire state of university education at Salamanca.

El Scholastico describes a meeting held by a group of friends from Salamanca University in the summer of 1528 in a hamlet on the banks of the river Tormes, where the scholars have repaired to escape the city heat and to discuss the state of Spanish scholarship. Among this predominantly converso group are Villalón himself, Francisco de Bobadilla y Mendoza (subsequently the Bishop of Burgos and author of the famous *El tizón*), Francisco de Navarre, Alonso Osorio (son of Charles V's *mayordomo*, Álvaro Osorio), Antonio de Velasco (son of Juan Velázquez de Cuéllar, Loyola's first patron), and Fernán Pérez de Oliva, who generally leads the discussions.[26] The debates focus on a number of questions related to scholarly formation, all of which provide the author, mostly through the mouthpiece of Oliva, with an opportunity to attack a hidebound university system that continued to reward indolence and ignorance, while shunning classical scholarship, merely because it was written by pagans. In a passage that echoes both Antonio Nebrija in his *Gramática latina* and Desiderius Erasmus in his *Antibarbarorum liber*, Oliva inveighs against 'some foolish barbarians who interfere without knowledge or ability to teach, professing great literary ability, lauding their own nonsense, respecting barbarisms and solecisms through ignorance':

> These same people [Oliva continues] presumptuously criticize the doctrines and the works of the ancient men of wisdom, saying that these pagans corrupt good customs and damage judgement. And thus in my opinion these men of Arcady (complete intellectual asses) are a poison and pestilence for the good sense and inventiveness of the young, and the absolute reason for the ruin, loathing and exile of fine writing and knowledge.[27]

Moved by Oliva's words, Navarra, later Salamanca University's rector, urges those who have the ability to correct this situation, to do so. In fact, Oliva himself had already begun to move in this direction. In January 1528, some months before Villalón's informal colloquium took place, he had accepted the Archbishop of Toledo Alonso de Fonseca's invitation to be a founding member of his *colegio mayor*, the Colegio del Arzobispo, an institution created by the reform-minded prelate with the aim of offering students a humanist education based on Erasmian principles.[28] Shortly after the college's foundation, Oliva was made rector of the institution, a position he held up to his death in 1531. At the same time, and as a result of some elaborate behind-the-scenes machinations, he became university rector, a post that gave him an opportunity to initiate a number of reforms along humanist lines. Just five days into his tenure, he announced to the university senate that the university was in great need of Latin grammar courses.[29] The courses were duly organized and masters of Latin grammar appointed. One of the texts for study suggested by Oliva was Erasmus' *Copia verborum*.[30]

Oliva's entry into Salamanca University in 1526 had coincided with a period of tremendous optimism among Spain's humanist reformers. Humanism, led by its standard bearer Erasmus, was gaining adherents and prestige. Not only was Erasmus championed by the two most important clerics in the land—Alonso Manrique, the Inquisitor General, and Alonso de Fonseca, Archbishop of Toledo; he was also finding favor with Charles V himself, who had already invited him to share his views in person at the royal court. When Charles began to look toward Oliva as a possible instructor to his infant son Philip (probably on the recommendation of Archbishop Fonseca), both the candidate and his close circle of scholarly friends must have believed that the signs augured well for a future kingdom headed by a humanist monarch.[31] Unfortunately, Oliva died before he was able to take up the position, which passed to the scholastic Martínez Silíceo, who appears to have instilled in his royal charge a suspicion of both religious reform and conversos. It is tempting to speculate what would have happened if Oliva and not Silíceo had taken control of Philip's schooling, although it is unlikely that the Córdoban scholar would have lasted long at a court which after 1530 began to turn its back on humanist reformers. The fact that Silíceo substituted Oliva as the *infante's* educational guide was itself an indication that times had changed.[32]

Fernán Pérez de Oliva formed part of a wave of reform that had surfaced in the universities of Alcalá and, albeit to a lesser extent, Salamanca, in the second and third decades of the fifteenth century. The exponents of this reform were young intellectuals who had found in humanism a blueprint for a society directed by the classical *novus homo*—literate, ethical, industrious, and self-made. Pérez de Oliva's own works, *Razonamiento para la navegación del río Guadalquivir*, *Triumfo de Cristo en Jerusalen*, and his *Diálogo de la dignidad del hombre*, written between 1524 and 1531, reflect the reformist goals of this movement; they also allude, once again, to its New Christian character.

Oliva's *Razonamiento para la navegación del río Guadalquivir* is an essay recommending that the Guadalquivir river be made navigable from Seville to the author's home town of Córdoba.[33] The work was obviously written on behalf of a merchant lobby; nevertheless, it is also a very personal plea made by a man whose roots were in Córdoba's middle-sort community, and who had witnessed this community's steep decline in fortune. The author begins by reminding his readers of Córdoba's illustrious history, which he compares to that of Paris and Rome. However, he notes, contemporary Córdoba was a decadent backwater, abandoned by the one class—the merchants—whose money, work ethic, and civic vision could reverse its decline. Oliva then presents us with the two reasons for the merchants' absence. First, Córdoba had benefited throughout the Late Middle Ages from being a frontier town, where the Christian forces were armed, clothed, and provisioned for their confrontation with Islamic al-Andalus. But this source of income had come to an end with the defeat of the Kingdom of Granada in 1492. As a result, many of Córdoba's merchants had left for Seville to take advantage of the Indies trade, or for Granada, where the Crown was offering financial incentives to repopulate a city abandoned by Muslim artisans and traders. The second reason for the merchants' abandonment of Córdoba was, in Oliva's opinion, persecution. And while the author does not expand on this remark, it is clear that he was referring to the recent persecution of the city's converso elite by the Inquisition, and in particular by the Inquisition official, Diego Rodríguez de Lucero, who had established a reign of terror in the city from 1500 to 1507.[34] Córdoba now had the opportunity to heal the wounds caused by this vicious attack, Oliva writes, by supporting a project that would lead to the return of the merchants. These able and industrious men would help create a thriving city with a market, a mint, and prestigious public buildings; they would also help sweep the city clean of idleness and those vices it spawned: envy, gossip, discord, gambling, robbery, rape, and adultery, all of which he associates in particular with irresponsible members of the nobility.

The *Razonamiento para la navegación del rio Guadalquivir* is not only an apology for a middle-sort work ethic, it is also a veiled attack on Old Christian prejudice against the converso, a theme Oliva returns to in his *Triunfo de Cristo en Jerusalen*, written as an Easter address to the Fonseca College in Salamanca, probably in 1528.[35] As I have noted earlier, in Spain Easter was often an occasion for violent outbreaks against Jews and conversos, the hostility fomented by incendiary sermons delivered from the pulpit.[36] In his own Easter sermon, Oliva addresses this animosity toward the Other, contrasting it with Jesus' message of peace and accommodation.

Oliva begins his Easter sermon by juxtaposing Jesus' entry into Jerusalem on Palm Sunday with a Roman general's entry into Rome on his victorious return from 'cruel battles promoted by envy' [*'batallas crueles que la invidia les hazia'*]. For the Roman procession, writes Oliva, part of the city wall was pulled down to make the general's entry more spectacular. Through this gap came a long procession: first, those enslaved during the campaign; next the Roman citizens, waving palms and olive branches, signifying victory and peace; and finally, the triumphant military leader riding on a carriage, wearing a crown and a scarlet cloak embroidered with golden stars. Thus Oliva presents us with the realities of Pax Romana, a political slogan designed to mask the greed and envy of imperialist adventures, like the sack of Jerusalem and its temple in 70 C.E., celebrated on Titus' famous arch.

However, Oliva's description of the Roman victory procession had yet another function: it alluded to the triumphal Easter processions of his own day, in which the Roman Church also pronounced a message of peace while celebrating its own cruel and envious triumph over others, in this case the New Christians. As a contrast to this spectacle, Oliva offers a vision of the first Palm Sunday procession, which he takes as a model for peace and acceptance. In this procession Jesus had also broken down walls—not the walls of the city, however, but the walls that encased the Jews' hearts: 'See how those walls that enclosed the Jews' hearts crumble: see how the battlements fall to the ground through those words.' [*'¿Veis? Ya los muros se derruecan que tenían muy cerrados los pechos de los judíos; veislos ya dónde caen con aquellas vozes las almenas a donde están sus fundamentos.'*] And Oliva calls upon his Palm Sunday congregation to follow the Jews' example. They too must open up their hearts, he tells them, so they can receive Jesus' message. But first they must 'cast out ugly thoughts and make clean that which was tainted.'[37]

In Oliva's opinion there were three paths to perdition: ignorance, idleness, and negligence. But these could be combated by goodwill, as the angels had announced while Jesus made his way through the streets of Jerusalem: 'Glory to God in heaven and peace on earth to men of good will.'[38] And in this message, Oliva notes, the angels echoed King David, who wrote, 'I will listen to what the Lord tells me, because he will speak of peace for his people and for the saints *and those who convert to him.*'[39] Here, Oliva not only reminds his audience that the Jews were the first members of Christ's community, he also emphasizes the egalitarian nature of this early religion, in which old and new members were united in peace. However, in order to present this harmonious message, Oliva was forced to misquote Psalm number 85, which, in fact, makes no reference to converts at all, but reads rather, 'I will hear what God the Lord will speak: for he will speak peace unto his people, and to his saints: *but let them not turn again to folly.*'[40]

Jesus had come not in anger to punish them, but in peace to pardon them, Oliva tells his listeners; he had come not to condemn, but to save. And as proof of this, he cites the Old Testament prophet Zacharias, whose spirit, Oliva states, led the Palm Sunday procession: 'Do not fear, Jerusalem, for your king comes in peace to visit you.'[41] And if those people listening to his sermon really wanted to become part of this wonderful celebration, they could do so by following Jesus' carriage with palms and olive branches in their hands, while singing, '¡Hosana fili David! ¡Hosanna in excelcis! ¡Salvanos hijo de David! ¡Sálvanos en lo alto!' In other words, they could demonstrate their true Christianity through prayer, peace and victory.[42]

However, by victory, Oliva tells his listeners, he does not mean triumph over another culture or credo, but the triumph over base instincts and prejudice, or the opinion of the *vulgo*. Those who liberated themselves from this yoke also liberated themselves from the majority of sins. On the other hand, those who followed the *vulgo*, hoping to save themselves from the anger of the ignorant, would find that they too were condemned by God to Hell.

Oliva's Sermon for Palm Sunday is a subtle appeal for a harmonious Christian religion in which New Christians are equal participants. This religion is built not on public ceremonies and rituals, nor is it based on the subjugation of other cultures, but on toleration, rationality, and self-control. It is, in other words, the manifestation of a humanist ethical credo, in which wisdom and prudence define the true Christian, as Oliva makes clear in another work, his *Diálogo de la dignidad del hombre*, written in 1530, in which his protagonist Antonio describes rationality and restraint as defining the true Christian man.[43]

Based on Pico della Mirandola's *Oration on the Dignity of Man*, Oliva's *Diálogo de la dignidad del hombre* is a scholarly debate between two friends on the nature of man, with a third friend adjudicating the contest. Aurelio, the pessimist, believes that no more care has been taken in the creation of man than in the creation of the beasts. Indeed, in many respects man has fewer resources than the beasts, which need no tools, weapons, or clothes to survive. Nor is man ethically any better than the animals, as his lust for war and killing attests. He is capable of rational thought and of self-control, but his primitive urges almost always dominate his behavior. His lifespan is short, and if he happens to learn anything from life's experiences, he is left with little time to put these lessons into effect. He is vainglorious, constructing buildings and monuments to proclaim his immortality, choosing to ignore the fact that all such constructions crumble and fade. Even his written works will with time be forgotten. Thus nothing will remain of him except a few dry bones in a coffin, as inanimate as the stones that cover them.

In reply to Aurelio's grim analysis, Antonio concentrates on man's many perfections: his erect body, enabling him to look up to the stars, and not down at the ground like the beasts; his finely crafted hands; his well-sculpted face; his gift of language. But what most separates man from the beast is his rationality, which allows him to have control over himself instead of being prey to base instinct. This rationality, Antonio admits, may often be dominated by impulse, as Aurelio had claimed; nevertheless, this was not an inevitable condition of existence. For Antonio, free will is the key to the Christian man. It was his temple, created to honor God, to carry out His commandments and to merit His glory.[44]

Naturally, the judge, Dinarco, adjudicates in favor of Antonio's view of man, a wise decision given that the alternative would have been to vote in favor of a view that smacked of atheism. Nevertheless, far from condemning the loser Aurelio as a dangerous heretic, Dinarco praises his ingenuity of argument. A later editor of the text, Francisco Cervantes de Salazar, changed the tone of this judgment, believing that through some oversight, or carelessness, Oliva had not attacked Aurelio's views sufficiently for their lack of Christian dogma. But this was clearly no oversight. For Oliva non-conformist religious views were not acts of deviancy but manifestations of a God-given liberty of choice, as he makes clear through his mouthpiece Antonio:

> Thus this state of uncertainty in which God places man reflects the liberty of the soul: some want to wear wool, others linen, others leather; some love fish, others meat, others fruit. God wants everyone to use their free will, placing them in a state in which they can choose, and thus we should not see as something negative that which God has granted us as favored children.[45]

Both Aurelio and Antonio are religious non-conformists. For his part, Aurelio chooses to reject the idea of a divinity concerned with man's well-being or salvation—a view often expressed in Inquisition trials by the phrase, 'there is only life and death.' Antonio, on the other hand, embraces a concerned God, but in a Neoplatonic, Universalist sense, eschewing religious dogma for a credo based on moral transcendence. The two men, I would argue, represent contrasting responses to the converso's existentialist problem. Aurelio is driven by a sense of alienation and despair toward a crude Epicureanism or even atheism. Antonio, on the other hand, has found solace in a private, interior faith, based on *voluntad* or personal volition—a view evidently shared by his creator, Pérez de Oliva.[46]

Fernán Pérez de Oliva, it seems, confronted a bigoted, exclusionary Catholic Church by escaping into a personal, Neoplatonic religious credo. Other converso humanists met the same problem by attempting to transform the church into an accessible, egalitarian institution—one that would accommodate rather than alienate New Christians. This was the case of the preacher Juan de Ávila, who at the time of Oliva's death, in 1531, had recently embarked on what would become a lifelong evangelical mission in

Andalusia: an attempt to create a new church with converso evangelists at the forefront of change.

Juan De Ávila (1499?–1569)

Juan de Ávila was born around 1500 on the edge of Andalusia, in the southern La Mancha town of Almodóvar del Campo.[47] His father, Alonso de Ávila, was a wealthy merchant; his mother, Catalina Xixon, was, according to a number of sources, from the minor nobility. Although Ávila's converso background was an open secret during his lifetime, both of the *beato*'s early biographers were reluctant to make the information available to posterity. Luis de Granada, in a study published in 1588, avoids the subject altogether, stating only that the Ávilas were one of the richest and most honorable families of the town,[48] while Ávila's second biographer, Luis Muñoz, openly lies about his subject's background, presenting his family as 'pure and clean, without a drop of the blood that they say infects much that is good.'[49] In the introduction to the critical edition of Ávila's works, written in 1952, Ávila's latter-day biographer, Luis Sala Balust, states that Ávila's matriarchal family were *hidalgos*, citing information contained in the *beato*'s application for canonization. Balust determines that Ávila's father's family may have carried some Jewish blood, although, characteristically, this is presented as of remote origin, the unspoken conclusion being that Ávila's Jewish background had no significant effect on his religious character.

For an account of Ávila's childhood and formative years we still must rely heavily on Ávila's friend and disciple, Luis de Granada. There is no reason to suppose that in essentials this account is inaccurate, although it is undoubtedly tendentious, skirting material that would have provided Ávila's many enemies with further proof of his unorthodoxy. According to Granada, at the age of 14 Ávila was sent by his father to Salamanca to study Law. Four years into these studies and on the point of graduating, the future saint abandoned the university and returned to Almodóvar del Campo. Touched by a sudden religious epiphany, so Granada would have us believe, Ávila left university only weeks before obtaining his degree certificate. This may be true, although some modern scholars have speculated that a *limpieza de sangre* statute recently imposed by the university was the determinant factor in Ávila's decision not to graduate. In order to gain his degree, Ávila would have had to prove that none of the four branches of his family were sullied by Jewish blood. As this was an impossible task, he left empty-handed.[50] For the next three years, Granada tells us, Ávila meditated on religious themes in an alcove of the family home at Almodóvar del Campo, after which he moved to the Complutense University at Alcalá de Henares. Here he studied three years of liberal arts (*artes*), followed by three years of theology. It was probably at Alcalá that Ávila became acquainted with the works of Erasmus, which clearly influenced his own Christian humanist vision—although Granada, naturally, makes no mention of this.

In 1526, with 12 years of continuous study behind him, Ávila traveled to Seville, having made up his mind to sail to the Indies as a missionary. Once in the Andalusian capital, he formed a close friendship with two religious reformers, Fernando de Contreras and Domingo de Valtanás, who were instrumental in shaping his early evangelical career. Through Contreras, Ávila was introduced to the school for Christian doctrine, which became a model for his own schools, established throughout Andalusia in the following years. Contreras' school, founded in 1524, with the support of the Erasmian archbishop of Seville, Alonso Manrique, later became a clandestine center for Lutheran activity in Seville.

In his sixteenth-century biography of Contreras, the converso scholar Cristóbal Mosquera wrote that the priest was '*un amigo de limpieza.*' Given the debate taking place in the late sixteenth century on the justice of making *limpieza de sangre* a requirement for entry into the religious orders, a contemporary reader might, with good cause, have assumed that Mosquera was stating that the priest was an Old Christian supporter of pure blood laws. However, it seems that Contreras was a friend only of physical *limpieza*, and in particular, of clean saints: and thus for recreation, Mosquera tells us, he took the cathedral statues down to the river, with two or three companions, and gave them a good wash.[51] This story eventually found its way into the priest's *proceso* for beatification as evidence of the monk's religious devotion, even though it would seem to reveal an irreverent attitude toward mainstream religious observance on the part of Contreras and his biographer.[52]

It was Contreras who introduced Ávila to the Archbishop of Seville, Alonso Manrique, who, according to Luis de Granada, persuaded the *beato* to focus his missionary activity not on the New World but on Andalusia. At the same time, Ávila made the acquaintance of the Dominican friar Domingo de Valtanás, a vociferous opponent of *limpieza* statutes.[53] It was through Valtanás that he made contact with a number of wealthy and influential patrons, including the noble Priego family, with whom he maintained close ties throughout his life. It was also on the advice of Valtanás that Ávila moved, in 1527, to Écija, a prosperous town near Córdoba, which boasted a large converso merchant class. Here the young evangelist was supported by wealthy friends of Valtanás, don Tello de Aguilar and doña Leonor de Inestrosa.

Between 1527 and 1531 Ávila took his reform message to the towns around Écija, attracting, so Granada tells us, a large following. He also attracted some strong criticism. Soon rumors began to enter the Inquisition tribunal in Seville that the *beato*'s sermons contained heretical views, and that he was organizing clandestine meetings in which suspect mystical practices were encouraged. In 1531, Ávila was incarcerated in the Inquisition prison in Seville, where for the next nine months he was required to respond to his detractors' many accusations, among which were the following: Ávila had stated that those burnt by the Inquisition as heretics were martyrs; he had said that Christ was in the Eucharist like a man with his head covered (meaning, presumably, that it was impossible to identify his presence), and that the Virgin before conceiving Jesus had sinned venially, because nobody was exempt from original sin. Ávila was also accused of conducting a number of secret meetings in which those present were exhorted to forget their *Pater* and *Ave* in favor of quiet meditation, activities that smacked of *alumbrado* practice.

In July 1533, Ávila, who appears to have acquitted himself well in his defense, was released from prison with a warning to guard his tongue in the future, on pain of excommunication. There is no evidence to suggest that he was particularly chastened by his brush with the Holy Office; indeed, it appears to have strengthened his resolve to continue his evangelical mission, as is clear from a letter he wrote to his supporters in Écija while incarcerated: 'Oh my much loved brothers! God wants to open your eyes so that you understand how many favors he gives us that the world considers disfavors, and how honorable we are in being dishonored.'[54] Ávila goes on to tell his supporters that in the eyes of God they are honorable men and women, whose *limpieza* (purity) is a product of their suffering: 'And if you suffer somewhat from the tongues of bad people ... regard it as a reduction in your offenses and as a sign of reward from Christ, who wishes to clean you with the tongues of the filthy, and thus cleansed through suffering, your well-being is guaranteed in the next world.'[55] The pointed references to their unique *limpieza* suggest that his audience was very largely a converso one.

It was while Ávila was in the Inquisition prison that he began writing *Audi, filia*, a work in which he feigns a didactic exposition of Christian worship while setting forth his own vision for a new Church in which conversos and Old Christians enjoy equal status. The title *Audi, filia* is taken from a passage in the Hebrew Bible (Psalm 45: 11–12) in which, according to Ávila's interpretation, 'the prophet' David calls upon his people to embrace Jesus, the bearer of a reformed Jewish faith: 'Listen daughter, and see; bend your ear, and forget the house of your father. And the King will desire your beauty' [*'Oye hija, y ve, inclina tu oreja, y olvida la casa de tu padre. Y cobdiciará el rey tu hermosura'*]. While in the Hebrew Bible David delivers this message to the Jews, it is clear that Ávila sees it as applicable to Jew and Gentile alike or, more accurately, to conversos and Old Christians; both groups should abandon their old ways and follow the ways of Jesus, the religious catalyst:

> [Jesus] made peace between the rival nations, Jews and Gentiles, taking away the wall of enmity that had been between them, as Saint Paul said; placing together the ceremonies of the old law and the idolatry of the Gentiles so that both rejected the peculiarities and rites of their ancestors, coming to a new law under one faith.[56]

Although Ávila states that Jesus 'made peace' between the Jews and Gentiles, it is evident that the *beato* saw Jesus' mission—and by extension his own mission—as an ongoing one; the task was to unite the pagans (Old Christian society) and Jews (conversos resistant to Christianity) in a faith that shunned *ceremonias, ritos,* and *idolatria.*

While *Audi, filia* is a call for rapprochement between Old Christian and New Christian Spain, it is clear that the *beato*'s own sympathies lie with the beleaguered latter group, who are for him, as for many of his fellow con_verso humanists, the first among Christian equals. Jesus, he reminds his readers, preached only to the Jews. Later Christ's apostles took his message further afield, 'and now the name of Christ is preached in distant lands so that not only the Jews are enlightened, who believed Him, and for whom he was sent, but also the Gentiles, who were in the blindness of idolatry far from God.'[57] And several lines later Ávila returns to this theme: 'And Christ's preaching is light then and now for the Jews who wish to believe; because it is a great honor for them that the one known as the Savior of mankind, the true God and man, came from them, and principally to them.'[58] These two passages and many more were later changed by the Inquisition censors to conform to a more orthodox Christian view. The changes could not, however, totally disguise *Audi, filia*'s central arguments, these being that Christianity was based on simple moral tenets found in the Old Testament Scriptures, and that evangelical reformers like himself were members of a New Israel that was attacking latter-day paganism and prejudice. An example of this prejudice was his society's glorification of its noble lineage:

> Why do you boast the nobility of your lineage? [Ávila asks]. God made a man and a woman at the beginning of the world from whom everyone descends. Noble lineage does not conform to the equality of nature, but is the result of greed; and there can be no difference between the first and second born, thus the rich and poor, the free and the slave are of the same lineage, or they are not the children of God.[59]

Ávila's message is that genealogically all Christians are equal, and should be judged only on the strength of their faith. 'The true Christian faith is not any closer by saying, "I was born from Christians,"' Ávila tells his readers[60]; and the *beato* makes a number of pointed references to real or spiritual *limpieza* (as opposed to the false *limpieza de sangre*). It is through prayer that one gains God's '*preciosa limpieza*,' Ávila writes, for it is God who will cleanse us; and he quotes the Old Testament prophet Isaiah: 'The Lord washes clean the impurities of the daughters of Sion,' which the *beato* understands to mean that it is through faith in God that our stains are washed away.[61]

Soon after leaving the Inquisition prison in 1534, Ávila traveled to Palma del Rio on the invitation of the count, Luis Fernández Portocarrero, whom we met earlier as a protagonist in Agustín de Oliva's converso poem. It was while he was a guest of Portocarrero that Ávila revised his *Audi, filia*, which for many years circulated among a select group of adherents, in manuscript form, before being published by the Alcalá de Henares printer, Juan de Brocar, in 1556. The published work, much amplified to augment and, prudently, dilute Ávila's original message, was financed by Portocarrero himself. However, only three years after its publication, Ávila's work was placed on the Inquisition Index. In 1576 a new version was published, with some extensive amendments to rid the work of its Erasmian content and Jewish sympathies. In the censored version, the line, Christ was 'a light not only for the Jews who believed in him and to whom he was sent,' was changed to 'for the Jews who believed in him and who he preached to in person.'[62]

The line, 'because it is great honor for them [the Jews] that the Savior of the whole world came from them and specifically to them,' became 'And Christ's message thus preached is light, then and now, for the Gentiles who believe, and is light and honor to the Jews who also believe.'[63] In the 1556 version, Ávila had also stated that Pontius Pilate 'crucified' Jesus. In the censored version of 1574 this reads 'sentenced to death.' For Ávila, the villain is not the Jew but the Roman governor; for the Old Christian censors, Pilot was merely the conduit for Jewish malice.

Ávila remained a year in Palma del Rio before moving to Córdoba. Here he began to attract young disciples, among whom was Fray Luis de Granada, who, along with his friend Bartolomé de Carranza, had recently graduated from the Dominican college of San Gregorio in Valladolid. Fray Luis would later accompany Ávila on several of his proselytizing missions throughout Andalusia. A major focus of this program was the Kingdom of Granada, home to a large population of Moriscos and conversos, many of whom (in the case of the Moriscos, almost all of whom) continued to observe their old faith. Ávila not only targeted the New Christians himself, he recommended that others did likewise. In 1565 he wrote to the newly ordained Bishop of Granada, Don Pedro Guerrero, calling on him to direct his preachers specifically to the converso and Morisco communities of his diocese.[64]

Within a short space of time Ávila had acquired a number of illustrious supporters and patrons, through whom he was able to finance his many educational institutions. One of his most important benefactors was the Marchioness of Priego, Catalina Fernández de Córdoba, a fervent devotee who financed the *beato*'s evangelical school for poor children in the town of Montilla, her family seat. The marchioness also recommended Ávila's services to her son, Pedro Fernández de Córdoba, the fourth Count of Feria, a title he inherited from his paternal family, the Suárez de Figueroas of Zafra.

Like the Priegos, the Feria family maintained close ties with a middle-sort converso community, which they encouraged to settle in the town of Zafra and to establish what was to become one of the most important trade fairs in the peninsula. Here local converso merchants traded in spices, slaves, and textiles with their opposite numbers on the Portuguese side of the border, built splendid houses in the town square, and took control of the town's religious and cultural life.[65] Indeed, Zafra's conversos, or rather their taxes, had helped establish the Feria family as a wealthy noble house, whose expensive Renaissance-style fortress-palace became a center for humanist activity.

In July 1546 Ávila took his reform message to the conversos of Zafra and to other New Christian communities from Zafra south to Fregenal de la Sierra, a town whose population was reputed to be largely converso.[66] In the years to come this region would provide Ávila with many loyal disciples; it would also present him with some serious problems, as overly fervent supporters became too incautious in their mystical practices. In the 1570s the Dominican friar Alonso de la Fuente began to compile a dossier on mystical groups in Extremadura. According to the friar, these conventicles rejected the commandments of the Church and its fasts and sacraments for a life of mental prayer, meditation, and ecstatic trances, and were encouraged in their illuminist error by Ignatius of Loyola, Luis de Granada, and Juan de Ávila, whose works, *Ejercicios espirituales, Libro de la oración*, and *Audi, filia*, they read passionately and indiscriminately.[67]

During all the time that Ávila was proselytizing, he was also founding primary schools. Between 1535 and 1569 Ávila or his disciples founded a dozen of these establishments, whose name, *colegios de los niños de la doctrina cristiana*, accorded them a veneer of orthodoxy. In reality, of course, the schools were established to create a generation of literate Christian practitioners, and as nurseries for a new breed of prelate instructed in Ávila's Christian humanism. At the same time Ávila founded colleges for higher education in Granada, Córdoba, and Jerez de la Frontera; and in 1539, with the aid of a wealthy converso backer, Rodrigo López, employed at the papal court, he established the University of Baeza, an institution that became a placement center for converso scholars, many of whom were Ávila's close followers. The town of Baeza also became a center for the publication of religious texts—mostly mystical—supervised by Ávila himself.

In 1549 two prominent members of the University of Baeza's faculty, the Ávila disciples Bernadino Carleval and Gaspar Loarte, were arrested by the Inquisition and charged with possessing suspect religious works. Although both men were released some months later, the Inquisition continued to cast a suspicious eye over the university, attacking the establishment with increased vehemence in the 1570s, after Ávila's death. In these later attacks the university staff were berated for their opposition to the *limpieza de sangre* statutes and for claiming that conversos were purer Christians than their Old Christian neighbors. But what most concerned the Holy Office were the private prayer groups that a number of the professors had formed, which allegedly disrespected the holy orders and sidelined sound Catholic doctrine and vocal prayer in favor of mental prayer and meditation. To the Holy Office officials this was tantamount to illuminism, and they prosecuted Ávila's Baeza disciples as *alumbrados*.[68]

By the early 1550s, Ávila, in ill health, began to look to the recently established Society of Jesus to take over his educational establishments and accommodate his disciples. Loyola was enthusiastic. However, others, close to the General, advised caution. The Jesuits were already under attack for their heterodox views and converso composition. Did they really want to merge with another organization that was being tarred with the same brush? Ávila's organization was full of conversos, Padre Nadal informed Loyola in 1553. This in itself was problematical. But it was also apparent that a number of Ávila's disciples, less discreet than their master, were antagonizing the Inquisition. In the circumstances, too close contact with Ávila was not advisable.[69] Negotiations continued up until Loyola's death in 1555, with Ávila using himself as the bait: he too was prepared to join the Jesuits, but only on the condition that they took responsibility for a number of his colleges—in particular the University of Baeza—and his disciples. As far as the Jesuits were concerned, however, the impediments were too great. Ávila never entered the Company, and his organization began to stagnate and disintegrate even before his death in 1569.

In the years following Ávila's death, his apologists, their eyes set on the *maestro*'s future canonization, were at pains to present him as a man of essentially orthodox character, and they focused particularly on his interest in the Eucharist as evidence of his doctrinal correctness. But for Ávila the Eucharist and baptism (the only two sacraments he demonstrated any real interest in) were unifying agents in a new church based on the spirit of Jesus and the moral tenets of the Scriptures (that is to say, the Old Testament Scriptures and Saint Paul). Ávila's works barely disguise his indifference to Church tradition (the dogmatic pronouncements of the papacy), icon worship, and elaborate rituals.[70] And while he championed charitable work, he clearly did not believe that 'good works' were essential in order to gain God's grace, as is evident in his *Audi, filia*, in which he writes:

> Saint Paul states that righteousness (*justicia*) in the eyes of God is the righteousness of Jesus Christ, because it does not consist of our own works, but those of Christ, which are communicated to us through faith. And so our righteousness comes through Him, and God hears us not because of ourselves but because of Him.[71]

This was published eight years after the Council of Trent had ruled that Works were fundamental for attaining God's grace. Naturally, the highly censored version of *Audi, filia*, published in 1578, reworked this passage to stress the importance of Works.

In his lifetime Ávila was a controversial figure who was continuously linked to men of suspect religious practice, a number of whom were prosecuted in the famous Protestant trials of Seville and Valladolid in 1557 and 1558. One of these men was García Arias, to whom Ávila wrote in 1538, recommending that he read the works of Erasmus. In 1556, Arias, a member of the Jeronymite monastery of San Isidoro, Seville, was uncovered as the head of a group of heretical monks, almost all of whom were conversos, that flourished in the heart of the cloister. Although the Inquisition described this group as Protestant, the term is a singularly inappropriate one, implying that Arias and his fellow monks were led into heresy by reading Luther or Calvin. While it appears the monks had recently come into contact with some Calvinist texts, the truth is that their heretical views were those endemic to humanist and evangelical circles in Spain; there was no need for the Inquisition to look further afield for a source. Among Arias' sins, so we are told, was his denunciation of fasting, self-mortification and icon worship, and his substitution of canonical prayer, that is to say, vocal prayer, for the reading of the sacred Scriptures.[72] While the Inquisition chose to associate these views with those of Luther, they could just as easily have linked them to Erasmus or Juan de Ávila. Indeed, perhaps the only difference between Arias and the other two reformers was that he was less discreet. He did not heed the advice given to him by Ávila 18 years previously, in the same letter in which the *maestro* recommended that he read Erasmus. 'What happens in your heart in relation to God,' Ávila told him, 'be careful to keep to yourself, as a woman should keep to herself that which occurs in the marriage bed with her husband.'[73]

Converso Non-Conformism in Seville

It is no coincidence that Seville is closely associated with both the Jewish pogrom of 1391 and the first Inquisitorial activity almost a century later. The Jews had always been a highly visible component of society in the Andalusian capital, occupying important positions in trade, finance, and court administration both during Muslim and Christian control. It was this high profile that made them a target for popular malice and resentment and led to their downfall in 1391. In that year, Seville's large and flourishing *aljama* was decimated, its occupants—those who did not flee to safer zones—murdered or forcibly converted to Christianity. While Seville's Jewish population never recovered from the 1391 pogrom, the city's abruptly expanded New Christian community took advantage of the trading opportunities that the flourishing port had to offer. By 1480, the year the Inquisition tribunal was established in Seville, there may have been as many as 8000 conversos residing in the city, suggesting that possibly 20 percent of Seville's population was New Christian.[74] However, almost before the Holy Office had a chance to open its doors for business, the majority of these men and women had fled to the territories of sympathetic nobles: Rodrigo Ponce de León, Marquis of Cádiz, Enrique de Guzmán, Duke of Medina Sidonia, and Luis Fernández Portocarrero, lord of Palma.[75] Very soon the city was in financial straits, having lost not only a vital source of income, but also those agents—the converso tax farmers—who collected it.[76] Faced with an economic crisis, the Crown offered the conversos a deal: for a cash payment, a family could wipe the taint of a conviction from the Inquisition records. The conversos, at least the wealthier ones, accepted the offer and began to return to a city that was now caught up in the great Indies adventure.

In the first decades of the sixteenth century, Seville's converso community recuperated its losses. Wealthy converso merchants bought positions for their family members on the city council and in the cathedral, from which vantage points they once again took a prominent part in civic affairs. Many of these rich New Christian parvenus were interested in their secular or clerical offices only in as much as they guaranteed social respectability and financial security; others used their positions to create and promote civic reform. One of the more altruistic public figures was Rodrigo de Santaella (Maese Rodrigo), a wealthy canon who used his substantial fortune to found the Santa Maria de Jesus college, an institution of higher education (it eventually became the University of Seville), with academic professorships in theology, canon law, civil law, medicine, and the liberal arts. In the college's constitution, Santaella categorically prohibited his institution from discriminating against professors or students on the grounds of lineage. The college, wrote Santaella flippantly, was to admit all Christians, whether their ancestors were 'Canarians, Indians, Gentiles [Old Christians], pagans, Jews, Saracens, nobles, non-nobles, rich, poor, good, bad, urbanites, rustics, free men or slaves.'[77] And the prelate went on to justify this clause by citing Saint Paul's description of Christ as a unifying religious force that had eliminated differences between Jews and Gentiles. Unfortunately, Santaella died before the college was opened, in 1516, and was thus unable to impress his liberal attitudes upon its first rector Martín Navarro, who quickly wiped the non-discriminatory clause from the college's constitution and imposed a *limpieza de sangre* requirement.[78]

The College of Santa María de Jesus' *limpieza de sangre* statute (1519) was implemented at the same time as similar legislation was being passed in the cathedral chapter (1519) and in the Dominican college of Santo Tomás (1521). All three statutes reflected an atmosphere of open hostility toward a converso community that was once again prosperous and politically powerful. One Seville faction increasingly incensed by the conversos' presence in the city's public life was the noble Ponce de León clan, who viewed the close relationship between converso city councillors and its noble rivals, the Guzmán family, as prejudicial to its own interests. In 1520 the Ponce de León faction led a riot against the city's wealthy converso merchants, its aim being to break the conversos' economic power and oust them from local government. The rebels failed, however, to capture substantial public support, and were soon dispersed by the forces of Juan Alonso Pérez de Guzmán, the sixth Duke of Medina Sidonia, and those of Don Fadrique Enríquez de Ribera, a noble, like the duke, who maintained close ties to Seville's converso patriciate.

In fact, Don Fadrique Enríquez de Ribera was himself, so to speak, *manchado*, his great-great-grandmother being a Jewess from Guadalcanal, 80 kilometers to the north of Seville. However, it was not through the Enríquez but through the Riberas that this noble family's close contact with Seville's converso community was forged. Or, to be precise, it was through the illegitimate offspring of the Ribera family, who very often formed marriage alliances with wealthy conversos. Several of these alliances were with the Alcázar family, which may in itself account for Don Fadrique's defense of the beleaguered converso merchants in 1520—the merchant Francisco de Alcázar was on that occasion one of the rebels' primary targets. The Enríquez de Riberas' ties to the Alcázar family also explain Baltasar de Alcázar's long association with this noble house. This celebrated poet and humanist served Don Fernando's son Per Afan de Enríquez de Ribera, the first Duke of Alcalá, for over 20 years as his private secretary.[79]

The Enríquez de Riberas' close contact with Seville's converso merchants was also undoubtedly promoted through that noble family's commercial activities, for it gained the bulk of its income from the soap industry. A license to produce soap in Seville had been awarded to the Enríquez family by Juan II in 1423. Gradually, through further royal privileges and as a result of Don Fernando's mother Catalina de Ribera's canny business sense, the family gained a monopoly on soap production in the region. This lucrative business allowed Fadrique Enríquez de Ribera, the first Marquis of Tarifa, to convert one of the family residences into a splendid Renaissance palace, where he played host to the city's literary elite. The palace became known popularly as the *Casa de Pilatos* (the house of Pontius Pilot), a reference to Don Fadrique's trip to the Holy Land, via Italy, which apparently inspired him to expand and refurbish the family home. The name itself appears to have generated little curiosity on the part of local historians, and yet it is clearly derogatory. Branded, along with the Jews, as Christ's slayer, Pontius Pilot was one of the most hated men in Christendom. One is tempted to conclude, indeed, that the name is a snide reference to the Ribera family's unholy alliance with Seville's religiously suspect converso community, whose ancient ancestors, so it was believed, conspired with Pilot in deicide.[80]

As patrons of Renaissance art and literature, the Enríquez de Ribera family were at the vanguard of humanist reform in Seville during the sixteenth century. It was perhaps only natural, therefore, that certain members of the family would also become attracted to Seville's evangelical movement, which took root during the 1530s, and even to its radical offshoot, the so-called Protestant conventicle. The first Duke of Alcalá's illegitimate son Juan de Ribera, the product of his relationship with a member of the converso Caballería family, was closely drawn to the evangelical mission of Juan de Ávila and Luis de Granada.[81] He was also a champion of the young Jesuit Order, whose activities he encouraged while Bishop of Badajoz. Ribera was also suspected of encouraging illuminist activity in his Extemaduran diocese, although no case was ever brought against him. Ribera's aunt, Doña María Enríquez de Ribera, and her husband, Pedro Portocarrero, Marquis of Villanueva del Fresno, were adherents of the 'Protestant' prelate Constantino Ponce de la Fuente, and as such were investigated for heresy in 1557. Neither was placed on trial, although their converso secretary, Alonso de Baena, was convicted of Protestantism and sentenced to ten years' confinement. The Duke of Alcalá's secretary, Gaspar Zapata, another converso, was also convicted of Protestant heresy, albeit in absentia. Zapata, who had been arrested as early as 1550 for transporting Protestant literature, was burnt in effigy in Seville's 1562 *auto de fe*.

Protestant Cells

In the late-fifteenth and early sixteenth centuries Old Christian attacks on the converso communities—through Inquisition prosecutions and *limpieza* legislation—had done little to moderate the New Christians' tendencies toward religious non-conformism. It did, however, make them more circumspect in voicing their beliefs publicly, at least in the first four decades after the establishment of the Holy Office, in 1480. But by the 1520s this situation began to change, as Erasmian religious radicalism spread openly and, it seemed, with impunity, throughout the country. As far as Seville is concerned, the climacteric year would appear to be 1524, when the Erasmian cleric Alonso de Manrique was made archbishop of the see and soon set out to introduce a message of religious reform into his district. In this project he followed an earlier archbishop, Pedro González de Mendoza, who 45 years previously had promoted a new catechism with the purpose of integrating conversos into Christian culture, thus obviating the need for an Inquisition tribunal.[82]

More ambitious in his reform program than Mendoza, Manrique was particularly successful in attracting well-educated, religiously radical preachers and educators into the city, who were able to tap into a large reservoir of religious discontent. One of these men was Juan de Ávila; another was Juan de Castillo, a Toledan scholar, like Ávila a converso, who established a school in Seville under Manrique's guidance. When Manrique became Inquisitor General in 1526, Castillo and a number of his pupils accompanied the prelate to the Holy Office's headquarters in Toledo. Here, Juan, along with his brother and sister, Jerónimo and Petronila Lucena, became involved in Erasmian and illuminist conventicles. When Castillo's friend Juan de Vergara was charged with Lutheran heresy in 1531, Castillo, who had shared proscribed Lutheran literature with Vergara, fled the country. The Inquisition eventually tracked him down to Bologna, in 1535, and brought him back to Spain to stand trial. He was burnt at the stake in an *auto de fe* in Toledo on 18 March 1537.[83]

In disfavor at court since 1529, and confined to his archbishopric, Manrique was in no position to come to the aid of Castillo in his confrontation with the Inquisition. He was, nevertheless, still a powerful political presence in Seville, where, up until his death in 1538, he continued to attract men of reformist tendencies. Two of these figures were the preachers Juan Gil, always referred to as Doctor Egidio, and Constantino Ponce de la Fuente, who entered the city in the early 1530s, armed with a reform message they had acquired as young scholars at the Complutense University. Both men would soon become the nucleus of what appears to have been a predominantly converso religious reform movement in the city.

We have little information on Egidio's or Constantino's family histories, although the latter's converso background was common knowledge to his contemporaries. Constantino himself made a sardonic reference to the fact when he declined the position of *canonigo mayor* (principal preacher) in the Toledo Cathedral, stating he would rather that the ashes of his descendants rested in peace.[84] Some years after this, Constantino was nominated for the same position, but in the Seville Cathedral, which had been occupied by Constantino's friend Egidio until his death in 1554. This time Constantino accepted the offer, believing, no doubt, that the Seville canons (many of whom were of a similar background and religious inclination) would sidestep the *limpieza* examination, or at least would not be over-rigorous in their inquiry. However, the cathedral chapter was opposed by the new Archbishop of Seville and Inquisitor General, Fernando de Valdés, who reminded the canons, pointedly, of their obligation to comply with the institution's *limpieza* requirement: '[I]t is laid down that no one who is descended from parents or grandparents who are suspect in the holy Catholic faith can be admitted to the holy Church.'[85] The canons ignored the archbishop's interference, much to his fury. Contantino was elected the new *canonigo mayor*, although the appointment was short-lived. In 1558 he was accused of clandestinely proselytizing the Protestant faith and incarcerated in Seville's Inquisition prison, where he died while awaiting execution. His cadaver was burnt at the stake in the *auto de fe* of 1559 along with the remains of Egidio, who had died in 1555, sparing him the trauma of his second trial for heresy.

The debate continues as to whether Constantino was a Protestant, or whether he remained until his death an adherent, albeit a heretical one, of the Catholic Church. Certainly, as a young man studying at Alcalá de Henares he had become attached to an evangelical reform program that included certain propositions common to Lutheranism. This was understandable, given that both he and Luther were adherents of a Pauline credo. But Constantino's interest in Saint Paul was also intimately linked to his converso caste. For Constantino, as for Ávila, Saint Paul was not only a talisman for a simpler and more pious Christianity, he was also a figurehead for social and religious equality. This is evident in Constantino's catechism, the *Suma de doctrina Christiana*, in which he emphasizes that

Jesus took human form to free *all* men from their sins; although, like Ávila, he subtly notes that the first beneficiaries of this pardon were 'the same men whose lineage He had taken.'[86]

In dying as a man, God the Son had, with his blood, wiped clean the sins of mankind, Constantino tells us, and through baptism we continue to receive this cleansing: 'Because as baptism washes and cleanses the body with material water, so spiritually, by virtue of the blood of Jesus Christ our Redeemer, is the soul, and all of man, cleansed of the sins with which he was born, and all other sins that before baptism he committed: as occurs with those who convert and are baptized as men.'[87]

Constantino employs the term *limpieza* throughout his work to describe man's liberation from original sin. It is through Jesus' blood that we are cleansed—a *limpieza de sangre* that is not divisive, but all embracing. This *limpieza* is attained through baptism—which symbolically represents the original blood cleansing—and is maintained by keeping one's heart and soul *limpio* (that is to say, free from sin). Constantino also notes, again betraying his converso background, that the true Christian should maintain bodily cleanliness, because 'as the soul is the house and residence of God and the body is the house of the soul, He [God] wishes that all is sanctified for His service, and clean and pure, as befits a home where the Lord wishes to live.'[88]

Constantino recognizes, in the prologue to the *Suma*, that some readers will find the work 'base and gross Christianity and for people of little spirit or knowledge of God.' To these people he can only reply that he believes it 'sufficient to get us into heaven.'[89] The observation indicates that the author anticipated criticism for a work that focused on the Christian's moral duties, as outlined in the Decalogue, while remaining aloof to certain important aspects of the Credo, including four of the seven sacraments (he only mentions baptism, the Eucharist, and penitence), the veneration of the saints, and the importance of the pope as head of the Church. As José Nieto writes, 'The absence of the traditional Catholic clichés, seen as so crucial after the Lutheran attacks, speaks eloquently of Constantinian faith that in actions and in silence agrees with the basics of the Protestant Reformation.'[90]

While the *Suma* reveals Constantino as a man of clear non-conformist views, it obviously obfuscates the extent and character of his dissidence. It is probable, however, that in 1543, when the work was published, Constantino regarded himself as a Catholic reformer, stoically attempting to transform his faith gradually from within. If we were to liken his religious stance to that of a foreign evangelical group, then it would obviously be to the Italian *spirituali*, who were attempting a similar task, also based on an Erasmian and Valdesian reform program. In 1541 members of this group met with Lutheran representatives in Regensburg, Germany, with the goal of beating out a religious compromise. Much was expected from the meeting, but nothing was achieved. Indeed, in its aftermath the *spirituali* found themselves under attack for their dubious Catholicism.[91] A year later the Roman Inquisition was established and a number of leading reformers fled Italy for Germany or Switzerland. When, during the first Council of Trent, it became evident that there would be no changes in Catholic dogma, other reformers followed suit, or began to make contact with the Reformed Church through an expanding underground network, although this political move was not always accompanied by a corresponding radical change in their religious beliefs.[92]

A similar scenario is encountered in Spain among those clandestine evangelists prosecuted for Protestant heresy in the trials of Seville and Valladolid in the late 1550s.[93] While these men and women shared certain religious precepts with Calvinists and Lutherans—the lack of belief in purgatory, for example, or the rejection of saint worship—they remained largely ignorant of, or indifferent to, the niceties of the two Protestant Churches. This was not, of course, a problem while they gathered in their secret conventicles in Seville or Valladolid to attack Catholic dogma. It was a problem for those Spanish renegades who later found themselves on the run from the Inquisition, forced to carve out a religious niche in a Protestant environment north of the Pyrenees. This was the case of the radical monks Casiodoro de Reina and Antonio del Corro, who fled Seville for Geneva some months before the Protestant prosecutions began. Often regarded as dyed-in-the-wool Calvinists, Reina and Corro were in reality men of independent religious vision, who in exile moved in converso circles and clashed constantly with Calvinist authorities. Both men had embraced Calvinism as a means of confronting an aberrant Catholic Church, but increasingly found their generic reformism and irenic tendencies under attack in a Protestant Europe also sensitive to correct dogma.[94]

Reina and Corro were members of Seville's San Isidoro monastery, a Jeronymite institution renowned for its converso character.[95] Twelve of its members fled Seville in the mid-1550s, escaping what would almost certainly have been a death sentence for heresy. Their successful flight across Spain and France to Geneva suggests that they were aided by the same Calvinist organization that was responsible for bringing Protestant literature to the Andalusian port. One of the key figures in this secret enterprise was Marcos Pérez, a wealthy converso merchant stationed in Antwerp. Pérez used his wealth and extensive family organization, including the Núñez Pérez merchant family of Seville, to transport Lutheran and Calvinist texts from the book fairs at Frankfurt via Antwerp and Bordeaux to the Spanish ports, and thence, through his agent, Peter Tilman, to the fairs at Medina del Campo, from where the books infiltrated the towns of central Castile.

It is not clear what Marcos Pérez's motives were in financing a very costly clandestine book trade. Perhaps he merely wished to be a perpetual thorn in the side of a despised Catholic Church, or perhaps he believed that an underground reform movement, if extensive enough, could lead to open rebellion. This indeed occurred in his hometown of Antwerp in 1566 when religious riots developed into what would become known as the Dutch Revolt. Pérez himself was a leading figure in this revolt, using his wealth to finance rebel activity, and his many connections to unite, or at least attempt to unite, Lutheran and Calvinist groups behind a common anti-Catholic banner. Although a convert to Calvinism, Pérez was by no means zealous in his adopted faith, as he demonstrated by sheltering Casiodoro de Reina in 1564, when the querulous Spanish cleric found himself under attack by fellow Calvinists for his heterodox views. Pérez appears to have joined the Calvinist Church because it was the largest of the Protestant congregations in Antwerp and thus offered most scope as a political pressure group. Politics apart, the merchant followed a characteristically converso path of non-conformist non-conformism.[96]

In Seville, the first wave of attacks against Protestantism came in 1549, when the Inquisition prosecuted Doctor Egidio and a small group of Protestant book-smuggling accomplices based in Paris and Antwerp. Egidio's trial lasted over two years, during which time he was found guilty of and abjured the following beliefs: only faith was required to gain God's grace; acts of penitence were unnecessary, as Jesus had already absolved us of sin; only God merited worship, the worship of saintly images was idolatry and should be prohibited. For these so-called Protestant errors Egidio was sentenced to a year in the Inquisition prison of Triana and thereafter forbidden to leave Spain; also for a year after his release he was not to celebrate mass, and for ten years he was suspended from preaching. The sentence was not rigorously applied, however. In 1553 Egidio was restored to his position as preacher in the cathedral and was still practicing when he died two years later.

Egidio's 1549 prosecution appears not to have affected Seville's clandestine Protestant book trade. The canon's light sentence may even have led to overconfidence and carelessness on the part of the book traffickers. In 1557 one of the chief traffickers, Julián Hernández, delivered, by mistake, some Calvinist texts to a Seville clergyman who did not share the reformers' views. This literature was then handed to the Inquisition and an investigation was launched that would eventually lead to the prosecution of over a hundred people. Although the Inquisition records give us little indication of these heretics' caste, it is evident, at least, that most of the leading figures in the underground movement were conversos.[97]

The Inquisition prosecutions probably represented only a fraction of the people in Seville that were attracted toward the reform movement and who had read the prohibited texts. However, lack of space in the Inquisition prison and the snail's pace of the trials themselves prevented the Inquisitors from casting their net wider. Two of Seville's reforming faction who narrowly escaped prosecution during this period were the converso humanists Benito Arias Montano and Juan de Malara.[98] Another of the city's converso humanists, Sebastián Fox Morcillo, was not so lucky. Fox Morcillo, whose brother Francisco was one of six Jeronymite monks burnt at the stake in 1561 for Protestant heresy, had himself been accused of voicing heterodox beliefs while a student at the University of Louvain in the mid-1550s. In 1560 Sebastián, who had recently been appointed tutor to Philip II's son Don Carlos, was apparently lost at sea while fleeing an Inquisition inquiry.[99]

Valladolid

As the Protestant network was being prosecuted in Seville, yet another clandestine organization was unearthed in Valladolid, still the center of court life, although this privilege was soon to be usurped by Madrid. Like its Seville counterpart, the Valladolid cell was in fact a group of homegrown non-conformists who had recently begun to establish greater contact with Protestant agents. At the epicenter of this group was the converso Cazalla family, the sons and daughters of Pedro de Cazalla and Leonor de Vivero, who 30 years previously had played host to the *alumbrada* Francisca Hernández, and whose Valladolid home had been a center for illuminist and Erasmian debate.[100]

Pedro and Leonor's children had clearly inherited their parents' non-conformist views, but had been careful to keep them well hidden from the public gaze in the aftermath of the *alumbrado* trials. However, they had recently grown bolder, inspired no doubt by an expanding Protestant Church that was making tentative inroads into Spain. The family's contact with Protestantism, or so they claimed, had begun in 1554, as the result of a conversation between Pedro de Cazalla, a village priest, and the Italian Carlos de Seso, the *corregidor* (Crown representative) for the town of Toro. Seso had converted to Protestantism on a recent visit to his hometown of Turin, where he had made contact with a group of Nicodemists, and was now determined to spread the message abroad.

In his deposition before the Inquisition tribunal in 1558, Pedro de Cazalla claimed to have been initially shocked by Seso's religious views— the latter had stated, among other things, that there was no purgatory. He had thus brought the matter to the attention of his friend Bartolomé de Carranza, a Dominican friar and renowned theologian, who had seemed unconcerned by Seso's heretical opinions, and this, according to Cazalla, had caused him to reflect longer on them, eventually becoming convinced of their validity.[101]

Cazalla's explanation of his initiation into Protestant heresy should be approached with some skepticism, however. Coming from a nonconformist background, he would hardly have been surprised by Seso's denial of purgatory. He would also have known that his friend Carranza shared this opinion. Clearly, he contacted Carranza not to have him judge Seso's orthodoxy but to determine whether the Italian could safely be admitted into what was already a small, informal circle of discreet nonconformists, the majority of whom, like Pedro, were conversos. Among this group were Pedro's siblings, including his brother Agustín de Cazalla, and four of the Cazalla family's female cousins, whose parents, like the Cazallas, had been prosecuted as *alumbrados*.[102] Two of the cousins, Catalina and Maria Reinoso, members of the Baeza family, were nuns at the Cistercian convent of Bethlehem in Valladolid, where they spread the Protestant doctrine. Seven members of this community were later tried for heresy, four of them, including Catalina and Maria, being burnt at the stake.[103]

Also among the Cazalla heretical group was Pedro de Cazalla's childhood friend, Fray Domingo de Rojas, the son of the Marqués de Pozas, and a member of a noble clan with a pronounced converso character.[104] Like Cazalla, Domingo de Rojas had studied under Carranza at the San Pablo school in Valladolid, and maintained a close relationship with his *maestro* thereafter. The two had even traveled to the second Council of

Trent together, where Rojas, like Carranza, had made contact with the *spirituali*. On his return from Trent, a more militant Rojas began to share his views with members of his evangelical circle, including his own family.

Sometime in the early 1550s, probably around 1554, Cazalla, Rojas, and several other members of their non-conformist network, which extended west to Toro and Zamora, and north east to Palencia, moved from being passive religious malcontents to radical agents of Protestantism.[105] The catalyst may have been the Italian Protestant, or Valdesian, Carlos de Seso; although frustration at the conservative course taken by the Council of Trent (the second session ended in 1552) and greater contact with Calvinist propaganda, spread by Spanish (converso) agents based abroad, also undoubtedly contributed to the men's apostasy. At the same time, closer ties to Seville's non-conformists may also have inspired the Valladolid group to bolder action.[106] Animated by their new vision of themselves, Cazalla and his friends began to spread their message incautiously among their evangelical network, inviting condemnation and exposure. Word of their activities eventually reached the Inquisition in early 1558, several months after it had begun its investigations into the Seville conventicles.

The Inquisition began its prosecutions against the Valladolid group in May 1558. Unsurprisingly, many of those under investigation pleaded naivety. They did not fully understand the heretical nature of the views that they had been asked to support—in this they had been misled by their group leaders, Pedro de Cazalla, Carlos de Seso, and Domingo de Rojas. For their part, Cazalla, Seso, and Rojas implicated Bartolomé de Carranza, who had recently been made Archbishop of Toledo, the highest position in the Spanish church. They implied that the archbishop shared some of their views, including justification by faith alone, and that his own religious insouciance had encouraged them in their conceits. Unfortunately for Carranza these accusations surfaced at the same time that his *Catechismo christiano*, published in Antwerp in 1558, was being condemned as heretical by his fellow Dominican, Melchor Cano. Armed with this information, the Inquisitor General Valdés was able to convince Philip II that his new archbishop represented a threat to the country and should be relieved of his religious duties. On 22 August 1559 Carranza was arrested while visiting the town of Torrelaguna, north of Madrid, and transported to the Inquisition tribunal at Valladolid to stand trial for Protestant heresy.

Carranza was certainly not a clandestine Protestant, as Valdés undoubtedly knew; but neither was he an innocent victim of Inquisition aggression. He was rather an old-school evangelist, like Juan de Ávila, who managed for the most part to keep his radical views close to his chest. His goal, like Ávila's, was to transform Catholicism from within, introducing a humanist and spiritual program of renovation while skirting the more irksome elements of Church tradition.

Like Ávila, Carranza's interest in Erasmus began at the Complutense University, at which he studied from 1515 to 1520, and where his uncle Sancho, later an Erasmus supporter, taught theology.[107] Soon after leaving Alcalá, he entered the Dominican College of San Gregorio in Valladolid, an elite institution founded by the converso prelate Alfonso de Burgos with the aim of renovating his order.[108] It was while Carranza was still a student at this institution that the famous Valladolid conference was held on Erasmus' orthodoxy. One of those present was Bartolomé's uncle Sancho, whose interventions in support of the celebrated Dutch humanist clearly impressed another Erasmus champion, Alonso Manrique, Archbishop of Seville. Manrique subsequently offered Sancho the position of *canonigo magistral* in the Seville Cathedral, which he occupied until his death in 1531, at which time he was succeeded by Juan Gil (Doctor Igidio).[109]

Meanwhile, at the San Gregorio College, Sancho's nephew Bartolomé was also voicing reformist views: dismissing the power of the pope, while questioning the necessity of religious ceremonies or confession. These transgressions were reported to the Valladolid tribunal of the Inquisition in 1530 while it was engaged in a series of prosecutions related to the Francisca Hernández circle. Overwhelmed with weightier problems, the Inquisitors decided against prosecution.[110]

Carranza remained in Valladolid for much of his career, teaching first at the Dominican school of San Pablo and later at the College of San Gregorio, gaining a reputation, in the process, as an outstanding scholar and preacher. In 1545 and again in 1551 he formed part of the Spanish delegations to the Council of Trent, where he made contact with a group of like-minded Italian reformers (the *spirituali*), whose evangelical program, as I have noted, was inspired by the religious works of Carranza's friend Juan de Valdés.[111] The group was led by the controversial Cardinal Reginald Pole, who, like Carranza, was a secret supporter of justification by faith alone. In 1555 Carranza and Pole met once again, this time in England, where Mary Tudor and Philip II celebrated their recent marriage, while delegates from both royal households discussed the political and religious implications of the union.[112]

For Carranza, and many other humanists in the Spanish camp, Philip's marriage to Mary offered the possibility of a less rigidly dogmatic Catholicism, with Reginald Pole, now Archbishop of Canterbury, leading the way forward. If Pole could persuade Mary to introduce modest reforms to Catholic practice in England, perhaps the young and still malleable Philip could be induced to follow suit. Carranza's famous catechism, written at the behest of Pole, reflects the Spaniard's optimism about a moderately reformed Catholic faith. Unfortunately, this vision was soon blighted by the deaths of both Mary Tudor and Pole, in 1558, closely followed by the first Protestant convictions in Seville and Valladolid.[113]

Thoroughly shocked by the Protestant infiltration into Spain, Philip II was easily persuaded by Valdés to act forcefully against the malefactors, who the king was inclined to believe were all 'descendants of Jews.'[114] Valdés appears to have shared this view, carrying out routine *limpieza* investigations into the Valladolid group, including Bartolomé de Carranza.[115] The archbishop's investigation was conducted by the Inquisition tribunal of Calahorra, in Navarre, only 20 kilometers from his hometown of Miranda de Arga. The officials contacted the Carranza family notary in Miranda, asking him to select four men who, along with himself, would give evidence before the tribunal. All five witnesses appeared in Calahorra at the beginning of November 1559, and stated formulaically that the Carranzas were Old Christians and hidalgos, whose ancestors were from the Vizcayan Valley of Carranza. The Inquisitors sent the five testimonies to the *Suprema* with a letter explaining that as they believed there was nothing untoward to be discovered, they had suspended the proceedings.

Regarding this investigation, Carranza's latter-day biographer José Ignacio Tellechea has written, 'The results of the "limpieza" investigation into Carranza's background was so evident and obvious that the Inquisitors surrendered to the force of the testimonies and suspended the process.'[116] In fact the evidence was not evident at all, which suggests that there may have been some complicity between the Calahorra tribunal and the witnesses to make the investigation a swift and felicitous one for the accused.[117] Not that this made much difference to Carranza's fate. His trial dragged on for the next 17 years, first in Valladolid and then in Rome, with Philip II making sure that justice, as he saw it, was done. Finally, on 14 April 1576, Carranza was released from prison, having been condemned to abjure 16 of the Lutheran propositions of which he had been suspected.

He died three weeks later and was buried, appropriately for a Christian humanist, in the Basilica di Santa Maria sopra Minerva, in Rome.

With the Protestant trials and the arrest of Carranza, Spain now entered a period of increased social and religious repression, in which the Inquisition, confident of the king's support, struck out with greater determination than ever against the country's religious non-conformists. In this tense atmosphere it was inevitable that Old Christian Spain would be eager to flaunt its *limpieza de sangre* as proof of its religious and social legitimacy, and to penalize those other Spaniards, the New Christians, who lacked this stamp of approval. How Spain's converso humanists reacted to this affront is the subject of the next two chapters.

CHAPTER 4

The Road Out of Trent

On 4 December 1563, the fourth and final session of the Council of Trent officially came to an end. The Council had been convoked 18 years previously by Pope Paul III to discuss religious reform and to attempt to reconcile doctrinal differences between the Catholics and Protestants. When it became clear, however, that religious rapprochement was impossible, the Protestant delegates went home, leaving their Catholic counterparts, mostly Italians, to write a doctrinal and institutional reply to the new churches.

For the majority of Spanish humanists, Trent must have been a grave disappointment. True, the Council had made strides toward a more disciplined Church; the sale of indulgences had been banned, for example, and decrees had been passed requiring bishops to reside in their dioceses, give up their concubines, and make regular visits to the parish churches; furthermore, every diocese was ordered to establish a seminary for the education and training of the clergy, something that would have been welcomed by humanists, for whom clerical ignorance was a major stumbling block toward religious renovation. Nevertheless, on the subject of Church doctrine and ceremonial practice, the Council had voted in favor of tradition. Church authority was still to reside in both the Scriptures and papal decrees, all seven sacraments were to be observed, works (donations, fasts, acts of contrition) were to be considered as important as faith in acquiring God's grace, and the worship of the saints, through their icons, and the observance of ceremonies were to remain essential elements of Catholicism.

Faced with these well-broadcasted official rulings, Spanish humanists could no longer plead ignorance if attacked over their errant beliefs, as Juan de Ávila had done with regard to the first version of his *Audi, filia*. Their only recourse was to feign compliance with Trent, while subtly, surreptitiously, alluding to their true beliefs in works that circulated among like-minded friends. However, it was not always easy for men of strong humanist convictions to contain their contempt for an orthodox credo. In 1584 the celebrated humanist Francisco Sánchez de las Brozas (El Brocense) was summoned before the Inquisition's Valladolid tribunal, accused of making the following statements in front of his students in Salamanca: Church icons should be banned and would have been banned at Trent if it were not for the fact that the councillors were afraid of following Protestant dictates; the people who knelt down in front of the images displayed in the Easter processions were idiots; the Virgin had not given birth in a stable, this was merely an allegory; and theologians knew nothing; if he were a theologian he would burn them all himself.[1]

In the course of his trial, the Valladolid Inquisitors focused their attention not only on Brocense's religious views, but also on his background. What were the names of his paternal and maternal grandparents? The humanist stated that he did not know their names, nor did he know the names of his father's brothers and sisters or even of his own brothers. This reluctance to give the Inquisition information about his family has led a number of scholars to suspect that Brocense was a converso. Indeed, his family background conforms to a converso stereotype. He was born in Las Brozas, near the Portuguese border, an area that included substantial converso communities; his parents' names, Sánchez and Núñez, were favored by conversos in these borderland communities; his father, an upholsterer, was involved in textiles, an industry dominated by conversos; and three of his family members were medical men, a profession also dominated by conversos. Furthermore, Brocense married twice into a family, the Pesos, well known in Salamanca as converso merchants, moneylenders, and Judaizers.[2] Perhaps it was rumors concerning Brocense's wife's family that led the Inquisition tribunal to question the humanist on his own background; or perhaps the Holy Office had merely come to associate, with some justification, unorthodox views with converso roots.

The Tridentine Council's resistance to change was irksome to scholars like Brocense, brought up on Erasmian ideals; it was not, however, the only blow the Council dealt to Spain's humanists. It also warned against too great an interest in the Old Testament Scriptures, other than those narratives that foreshadowed the life of Christ and in particular the Passion. This ruling was a response to the Protestant Church's contention that the Scriptures were the sole religious authority. While Protestants began to pay greater attention to the Hebrew Bible and even to Jewish scriptural analysis, the Catholic Church, never totally comfortable with its Jewish ancestry, separated itself even further from the Old Law, at the same time underlining its adherence to its Medieval, Gentile traditions. The message was evident: Catholicism was the religion of the Gentiles; Protestantism was for heretics and traitors who had abandoned their faith and kind for an unholy alliance with those other willful deviants, the Jews. But the Council's ruling was not only an attack on Protestantism, it was also an affront, albeit unintentional, to those converso humanists for whom the Old Testament provided an indispensable antechamber into what was often an inimical Old Christian Church. The Old Testament was, indeed, fundamental to many converso humanists' Christian identity; it was a source of psychological comfort and intellectual and artistic inspiration, and was not easily abandoned.

In 1571 the Spanish Hebraist Fray Luis de León was imprisoned by the Inquisition tribunal at Valladolid, charged with: attacking the Septuagint, preferring rabbis and Jews to the saints as expositors of the Scriptures, circulating a Castilian translation of the *Song of Songs* and describing it as a love poem from Solomon to his wife, stating that in the Old Testament there was no promise of eternal life, and asserting that the Vulgate contained many falsities and that a better version could be made of it by a closer study of Hebrew sources. León's arguments are those of a Christian humanist who bases his biblical exegesis on philological criteria; they are also those of a converso for whom Christianity was an extension of Judaism, not a rejection of it; the two interpretations are inseparable.[3]

León's sense of his own unique, New Christian, identity (an identity influenced by his antecedents' culture) not only directed him toward Hebrew studies, it propelled him into the dangerous business of using the *Torah* and not the *Old Testament* as his biblical source; it also led him into many heated public disputations at the University of Salamanca, during which he was much too eager to demonstrate his superiority to Old Christian colleagues in Old Testament exegesis. Even before his brush with the Inquisition in 1571, León considered himself an outsider at Salamanca. This sense of isolation is evident in his poetry, in which he adopts the Horacian ode to express his own stoical views, his animosity toward the *vulgo* (specifically, ignorant scholastics), and his desire to retire to a quiet place—not a country villa, as in Horace's case, but 'an airy peak' ['*un cumbre airosa*']—where he can achieve spiritual tranquility, away from the malice of envious colleagues. However, as far as León was concerned, academic envy was only part of the problem; the real issue was Old Christian obscurantism and prejudice, as the friar made clear in both his poem 'On a failed hope' ['*En una esperanza que salió mala*'], in which he wrote 'In me the distant crime is castigated/and I become the criminal,' and the following defense of his Hebrew scholarship while in prison:

> I do not know whether I will find the appropriate words to explain what I feel. Yet, since the force and harm of my enemies thus compel me, your honest and religious ears will forgive me if my due and necessary defence requires that the veil be lifted with which Saint Jerome tried to cover the shame which he thought to have found in that place [the Hebrew Bible], and so I will speak about those things that nature made for an honest end with common words, words which, while turned awkward by their vicious usage, are made *clean* by a sane judgement that only deals with the knowledge of truth. For those who are *clean* and good, who do not pervert in any way the natural usage, all things natural are *clean* and only vice, which is a disorder of nature, offends them.[4]

León's statement is reminiscent of that made by Juan de Ávila to his supporters while incarcerated in the Inquisition prison in Seville. Both men subtly contrast true *limpieza*, which is the purity of those who seek the truth, with the false *limpieza* of their antagonists, which only serves to corrupt nature. In his *Los nombres de Cristo*, also written while he was in prison in Valladolid, León returns to the *limpieza* issue, contrasting the situation in Spain with the Christian society spoken about by Saint Paul, in which everyone was equal. According to León, his own government's desire to divide society into groups of honorable and tainted members was not only un-Christian, it was also clearly detrimental to the commonwealth:

> It not only damages its [the government's] honor when it uses fabrications to taint those who it governs, but also damages its interests and compromises the peace and conservation of its kingdoms. Thus in the same way that opposites may be brought together but cannot be mixed, so is it impossible to establish peace in a country in which the groups are held to be so different one from another, one group rejected and without honor. In the same way that a human body with damaged limbs and whose humors are in

disharmony is close to sickness and even death, we can see that a country in which many families are mistreated and wounded and because of customs and law cannot mix and harmonize with other groups and other families is a country about to sicken and on the edge of civil war. For each individual feels in his own self the wounds and insults with which society is rejecting him and will always be ready to rise, strike, and take vengeance.[5]

Far from reducing his fervor, León's long prison sentence appears to have steeled him in his humanist quest. At least, this is the impression one gets from reading *Los nombres de Cristo*, in which the friar blames barbarous theologians for creating a congregation too ignorant and confused to be given access to a vernacular Bible. As a corrective to the scholastics' 'harmful and vain books' [*'libros dañosos y de vanidad'*], León offers up his own work, a vernacular evangelical text, which makes constant, one might even conclude willful, reference to the Old Testament Scriptures.

It is also noteworthy that *Los nombres de Cristo* is dedicated to the royal councillor, later Inquisitor General, Don Pedro Portocarrero, a man whose family was closely linked to the converso community and to converso religious reform. Pedro's grandmother, Maria Osorio, was a member of a wealthy converso merchant clan from Toledo; his uncle, Pedro Portocarrero, and aunt, María Enríquez de Ribera, were associated with Seville's converso-dominated Protestant cell, only narrowly escaping prosecution themselves in the Seville trials of 1559.

As well as dedicating *Los nombres de Cristo* to Don Pedro, Fray Luis also dedicated a collection of poems to the nobleman, many of which, written in the Inquisition prison, attack the Holy Office. In one of these poems, León presents Portocarrero as an example of the right kind of nobility: not the nobility attained through an immaculate bloodline (something which, in any case, the Portocarrero family could not boast), but through personal merit: 'Yes, you are the generous young bud of illustrious parents, but this noble title is minor, surpassed by you yourself.'[6]

Luis de León's trial dragged on for five years until, overcome by inertia, the Valladolid tribunal was forced to present its findings and recommendations to the Supreme Council for adjudication. The Suprema, now headed by the moderate Gaspar de Quiroga, found in favor of the accused, recommending only that he be reprimanded in private. León was released from prison in December 1575 and immediately resumed his teaching duties. He is reported to have begun his first lecture to his students with the statement, 'As I was saying yesterday …'

Although Fray Luis' prison term was long, it was not, by Inquisition standards, particularly harsh. Certainly, the three converso scholars, Gaspar de Grajal, Martínez de Cantalapiedra, and Alonso Gudiel, all arrested around the same time as León for their 'Judaizing' tendencies, were subjected to much crueler treatment. Of these three men, Grajal and Gudiel died in prison. Martínez de Cantalapiedra survived his five-year confinement, but in broken health and with his reputation destroyed. Unlike León, he was not permitted to regain his teaching position at Salamanca. 'I have labored to interpret Scripture before the whole world,' Cantalapiedra told his prosecutors in 1577, 'but my only reward has been the destruction of my life, my honor, my health and my possessions.' And he concluded, as many humanists and conversos had done before him, that 'it is better to walk carefully and be prudent.'[7]

While post-Tridentine Spanish society could boast a number of important religious innovators, these men and women succeeded in changing the religious landscape despite Tridentine rulings rather than because of them. One of these figures, perhaps the most celebrated of Spain's post-Tridentine religious reformers, was Teresa of Ávila, a woman whose mystical practices ran counter to Trent's emphasis on a public, sacramental faith, and brought her into confrontation with both her own order, the Carmelites, and the Holy Office. That Teresa managed to avoid a serious clash with the latter institution, while establishing 15 Barefoot Carmelite houses in Spain and beyond, must be attributed to her impressive powers of dissimulation, for as an intelligent woman, a mystic, and above all a converso, her situation was, to say the least, a delicate one.

In 1485, Teresa of Ávila's paternal grandfather, Juan Sánchez de Cepeda, a wealthy Toledo silk merchant, confessed to the recently established Inquisition tribunal that he had committed 'many grave crimes and offenses' against the Catholic Church. This confession was made during the Inquisition's 40-day period of grace, in which conversos were encouraged to admit their apostasy in order to receive light sentences. During this period, 2400 conversos (15 percent of the city's total population of Old and New Christians) presented themselves to the Inquisitors for sentencing. It is unlikely that all these people were, in fact, Judaizers; they were, however, members of a minority group that often lived in the same neighborhoods, formed endogamous marriages and endogenous business unions, and maintained discrete cultural practices (bathing on the Sabbath, refraining from eating pork products), and this visible social nonconformity made them potential targets for Holy Office aggression.

Clearly, the majority of Toledo's conversos believed that it was wiser to genuflect before the Holy Office in this period of amnesty rather than await a later attack that would carry far greater consequences. What they did not realize, however, was that in volunteering information on their Jewish backgrounds they were presenting the Holy Office with important data that it would use against them and their families in the future. This, indeed, was the case of the Sánchez de Cepeda family.

As punishment for his grave crimes against the church, Juan Sánchez de Cepeda was ordered to walk, with his family, in penitential processions to Toledo's churches on seven consecutive Fridays. While the sentence was a light one, for Juan it undoubtedly represented an enormous blow to his civic dignity, and very probably led to his decision to move his business headquarters to Ávila, a small city 130 kilometers northwest of Toledo with a growing textile industry, and, significantly, no Inquisition tribunal. It was here, in 1519, that Juan's son Alonso Sánchez de Cepeda attempted to buy himself noble status.

A successful textile merchant like his father, Alonso Sánchez de Cepeda used his wealth to purchase the outward trappings of nobility. A city mansion adorned with coats of arms, a thoroughbred horse, and a number of expensive Toledo swords, all testify to Alonso's social ambitions.[8] All that was missing was an official certificate recognizing the merchant's *hidalgo* status. The opportunity to gain this came in 1519, when Charles I, in need of funds to press for the title of Holy Roman Emperor, introduced a new tax. Alonso and his three brothers refused to pay this tax, on the grounds that they were *hidalgos* and thus tax exempt. This refusal led to an investigation by the court of the Royal Chancery at Valladolid, which, in 1520, found in favor of the brothers. Contesting tax payment was, of course, a common stratagem used by conversos to acquire a certificate of nobility. It was expensive—witnesses and court officials had to be bribed—but generally effective. Unfortunately for the Sánchez de Cepedas, the Council of Finance appealed the Valladolid tribunal's decision, producing evidence from the Toledo Inquisition records that the family was of Jewish background. In light of this evidence, the tribunal was forced to amend its previous ruling. Alonso and his brothers could still flaunt their *hidalgo* status, but, according to the revised certificate, only in the district of Ávila.[9]

It is perhaps understandable, given the Sánchez de Cepeda family's background, that Alonso's daughter Teresa de Ahumada would herself become so obsessed with the question of social status and honor. Indeed,

Teresa entered the expensive and fashionable Carmelite convent la Encarnación precisely because it gave her the opportunity to act out the role of the noble, virtuous woman. Soon, however, the young nun became tormented by her spiritual vacuity, and this led to what appears to have been an intense neurotic illness. It was while convalescing from this infirmity, away from the convent, that Teresa read Francisco de Osuna's *Tercer abecedario* and took the first steps on a mystical path that would lead to the founding of her own religious order.

At the same time that Teresa was puzzling over her social and religious identity at la Encarnación, a group of humanist prelates—predominantly, if not exclusively, converso—began gathering together to discuss social and religious reform within the city. Influenced by the *devotio moderna* movement and, in particular, the evangelical program of Juan de Ávila, this coterie of reformers established a *colegio de niños* in 1556 and a seminary in 1572, both modeled on *el maestro* Ávila's own institutions. Members of the group also maintained a close relationship with the infant Jesuit Order, promoting the establishment of the *San Gil* Jesuit college in 1553.[10]

Teresa's mystical experiences and her critical attitude toward the religious life of la Encarnación convent eventually brought her into contact with Ávila's reformist faction. It was through her relationship with several members of this group that she became convinced of the need to found a reformed—Barefoot—branch of her own Carmelite Order. The first of these convents, named San José, was established in Ávila in 1562, and was soon followed by other religious houses in Medina del Campo, Malagón, Valladolid, and Toledo. Unlike the unreformed Carmelites, Teresa's order did not employ a *limpieza de sangre* statute, which may account for its high level of converso patronage, although converso middle-sort patrons may also have been attracted to religious establishments that emphasized quietist practice.[11]

One of Teresa's early Ávila patrons, and sponsor of the San José convent, was the wealthy widow Doña Guiomar de Ulloa. The Ulloas were a successful converso merchant clan that had used their affluence to establish their members in church and state offices and to forge a number of marriage alliances with Old Christian and New Christian *hidalgo* families.[12] Like the Fonseca family, with whom they were closely linked, the Ulloas were drawn toward Church reform; indeed one of their members, Juan de Ulloa Pereira, was an active participant in Valladolid's famous Protestant cell. It may have been through Ulloa Pereira that Doña

Guiomar and her religious circle were approached to join the cell. This meeting would almost certainly have occurred between 1556 and 1558, when Teresa of Ávila was Doña Guiomar's house guest. Neither Guiomar nor the members of her conventicle were tempted to enter the Valladolid group, so we are told; however, the very fact that they were approached by the clandestine Protestants suggests that they were considered fellow religious discontents.[13]

Closely associated with mystical (to many, *alumbrado*) practice, and tied to converso money, Teresa's reformed Carmelite convents attracted constant criticism during the first years of their existence. Aware of the precariousness of her organization, Teresa did all she could to allay her critics' fears. In both her autobiography and in *The Way of Perfection* Teresa is careful to emphasize the post-Tridentine, orthodox nature of her foundations. Her plan, she told her readers, was to create institutions in which groups of poor, secluded, unworldly nuns could pray for the Catholic Church in its struggle against the Lutherans. But it would be unwise to take all these statements at face value. Teresa may not have been well disposed toward Protestantism, but this had hardly propelled her toward founding a religious order. Her new organization was created in reaction to the moral laxity and intellectual poverty of the Spanish regular clergy, as becomes clear from her many criticisms of the religious in Spain in her works.[14] Her major influence was a pre-Tridentine evangelical reform movement, led by Juan de Ávila, a converso and mystic like herself driven by the need for personal and institutional purification. On the subject of Teresa's religious motivations, Rowan Williams writes perceptively:

> We do not begin to understand her as a religious, as a reformer, as a theologian, unless we see her as a 'displaced person' in the Spain of her day ... She cannot but do her religious reflection from the specific point of view she occupies: as a woman and a Jewess [*sic*], undergoing ecstatic experiences, and claiming certain kinds of authority, at a time when any one of these would guarantee her not being taken seriously in Church and society, except as a threat and a pollutant. Reading the *Life*, we become more and more aware of how she has to negotiate her way in an almost wholly suspicious environment. But, reading her work as a whole, we can see how the experience of impurity and dishonor itself becomes the keystone of a recovery of certain aspects of the primitive Christian story and proclamation no less radical than that of her reforming contemporaries in Northern Europe.[15]

In the tense atmosphere of post-Tridentine Spain, religious reformers like Teresa of Ávila were forced to move with extreme caution if they were to avoid a clash with the Holy Office. The Tridentine Council's call for a more pious and better educated clergy did, however, give them an opportunity to attack those bastions of religious conservatism, the regular orders, and in so doing take an important step toward creating a revitalized church. One of the religious orders' most powerful opponents during this period was Cristóbal de Rojas y Sandoval, a Teresa supporter, who from 1571 to 1580 was Archbishop of Seville.

Cristóbal de Rojas y Sandoval was born in Fuenterrabia, Guipúzcoa, in 1502, the illegitimate child of the Marquis of Denia, Bernardo de Rojas y Sandoval, and a certain Dominga de Alcega. In 1542, Don Cristóbal officially wiped clean the taint of illegitimacy by papal dispensation. However according to some, Rojas' 'natural' birth was not his only impediment; there was also the matter of his converso background. While Rojas himself remained mute on this subject, his nephew, Bernardo de Sandoval y Rojas, was less abashed. In defending Fray Agustín Salucio's tract against the *limpieza de sangre* statutes, in 1599, Bernardo, later Archbishop of Toledo, wrote: 'I certify to you father that I am the least pure-blooded man in the world.'[16]

While we have little information on Cristóbal de Rojas' early education, it is likely that his evangelical religious outlook was the product of the private, liberal tutelage he received on his father's estate at Lerma. Later, these religious tendencies were cemented at Alcalá de Henares, where he studied from 1524 to 1535, and at Charles V's humanist court, in which he passed his early career. Between 1542 and 1571 Rojas became, in succession, Bishop of Oviedo, Badajoz, Córdoba, and Seville. In each of these sees he undertook a progam of reform, attacking the regular orders, while favoring evangelical prelates. At Badajoz, Rojas encouraged preachers formed in Juan de Ávila's seminaries and members of the recently established Jesuits, and, according to the Dominican friar Alonso de la Fuente, turned a blind eye to the *alumbrado* sect that began to take root in the region during his office.

In 1565 Rojas, as the eldest bishop in Castile, was chosen to head the Council of Toledo, the most important of the five provincial councils established by Philip II to work out a program for enforcing the dictates of the Council of Trent. The choice did not meet with universal approval. Rojas had already gained a reputation for his bias against the unreformed religious houses, and some of the regular clergy felt that he would use his position as president of the Council to pursue his attacks with even greater vigor. The bishop's call to Juan de Ávila to present a guideline for reform only served to underline the clerics' fears. Soon anonymous letters were arriving at court, questioning the propriety of the Rojas' presidency: not only was the bishop's dogma dubious, so too was his Old Christian lineage. Disturbed by these letters, Philip II proposed an investigation to unearth and interrogate their authors. Rojas, however, demurred. As a man of Christian character, he explained, he would prefer to turn the other cheek rather than seek retribution. The matter was dropped.[17]

Meanwhile, as his opponents had feared, Rojas began to move against the relaxed religious houses of his sees: first Córdoba and later, from 1571, Seville. Rojas' occupancy of the latter see had coincided with a move among a group of Carmelite friars to make sweeping reforms within their own order, their initiative supported by two apostolic delegates with powers to found new, reformed convents and reform old ones. Rojas immediately lent his support to this movement and in 1573 helped establish a Barefoot, or reformed, Carmelite monastery within Seville.

Fearful that their own institution was about to be remodeled, the monks of the city's older, unreformed Carmelite monastery resisted the reformers, supported by the Carmelite General Giovanni Battista Rossi, who created a 19-man police force, 'Defenders of the Liberties of the Order,' to assist them and other unreformed Carmelite houses, physically preventing the apostolic delegates from entering and examining their institutions. The two opposing groups now entered into a long and bitter dispute which came to a head in 1576, when unreformed Carmelite convents throughout Andalusia openly clashed with the new apostolic delegate, Jerónimo Gracián (a Barefoot Carmelite friar and close friend of Teresa of Ávila), rejecting his authority over them.

In the summer of 1575, while the conflict continued to rage, Teresa of Ávila, in defiance of the Carmelite General's orders, arrived in Seville, where she founded yet another Barefoot convent. Inevitably, Teresa's institution soon found itself enmeshed in the local imbroglio. There were rumors that her Barefoot nuns were *alumbrados*, leading to an Inquisition investigation.[18] At the same time the royal court began to receive reports of corrupt practices, both religious and administrative, in the archbishop's palace. One of the authors of these reports was the Franciscan friar Bernardo de Fresneda, who in 1571 had succeeded Rojas as Bishop of Córdoba.

Confessor to the young King Philip II, Bernardo de Fresneda had for a number of years been one of the most politically powerful clerics in Spain. In 1559 Fresneda had conspired with Fernando de Valdés against the Archbishop of Toledo, Bartolomé de Carranza, whose rise to prominence, more meteoric even than his own, he envied, and whose position he coveted. It was even rumored during the first years of Carranza's imprisonment that, should the archbishop die, Fresneda would occupy his place. In the event, however, Fresneda did not receive the Toledo see but that of Cuenca, a bishopric close enough to Madrid to allow its incumbent to interfere in court politics, something Philip II found increasingly vexing. In 1571, the king transferred Fresneda to Córdoba, recently vacated by Rojas y Sandoval, with the instructions to behave like a model post-Tridentine bishop and occupy himself with the spiritual welfare of his flock.

In the spring of 1575, in conformity with the Tridentine dictate, Fresneda undertook a tour of his diocese, or at least the southern part of the diocese, an area associated with large converso communities. In the 1530s and 1540s Juan de Ávila had taken his evangelical mission to these same communities, offering crypto-Jews and lukewarm Catholics the opportunity to join a new church based on mystical communion and a moral code central to both Judaism and Christianity. Many of the conversos of the region had become Ávila adherents, although, as far as their critics were concerned, this had served only to underscore their tainted religious identity. In a letter to Philip II on returning from his 1575 tour, Fresneda wrote: '[O]f the ten thousand male and female conversos [in the region] no more than ten go to confession with Old Christians' [*'de los diez mill confessos y confessas no se confiessan diez con christianos viejos ...'*]. The bishop further noted that in several of the towns there were an enormous number of *beatas*, all of whom were conversos, who formed secret mystical conventicles in their homes. According to the prelate, these people were being encouraged by certain errant friars, mostly, but not exclusively, Jesuits, whom he referred to as 'teatinos.' But there was yet another, even bigger, culprit: the Archbishop of Seville himself, who had supported groups of *alumbrados* while Bishop of Badajoz and continued to lend his support to similar groups in Andalusia; indeed, many of the troublemakers in the region were clerics who had been formed in his Badajoz seminary and had followed him to his subsequent sees.[19]

One of the *agent provocateurs* singled out by Fresneda for attention was Fray Agustín Salucio, whom the bishop described as 'hijo de Genoves y no de buena madre,' that is to say, the offspring of an Italian trader and a converso mother. Salucio, of the Dominican Order of preachers, would later gain notoriety for his *discurso* attacking the *limpieza de sangre* statutes.[20] Written in 1599, Salucio's work was a reaction to an Old Christian society that continued to stigmatize and isolate New Christians through pure blood statutes. This legislation had proliferated in the post-Tridentine period as Old Christians, led by their king, had become increasingly inclined to regard conversos and Moriscos as the enemy within. The Morisco uprising of 1569 had added fuel to this prejudice, motivating Philip II to increase his vigilance of both minorities.[21]

In linking the Archbishop of Seville to converso non-conformism, Bernardo de Fresneda obviously hoped to appeal to Philip II's prejudices, in so doing blackening his rival's name and reform campaign. However, while Philip was suspicious of conversos, he was equally critical of the moral state of the monastic orders, and thus ready to support reformers like Cristóbal de Rojas and Teresa of Ávila in their mission to cleanse an Augean stable, sometimes clashing with members of the Spanish and Roman Curia in the process. This tension between King and Church was exploited by Spanish humanists at court to advance their own reform agenda, promoting the very orthodox Philip as a voice of common sense and flexibility, pitched against clerical intransigence. Thus Philip became the 'prudent' king, or the 'New Solomon,' an exemplum, according to the propaganda, of wisdom, discretion, and peace.

Modern historians invariably view the Solomon epithet as a reference to Philip's good sense and devotion to his state papers. In fact the term was never meant as a tribute to the king, whose plodding statesmanship drove secretaries and advisors to distraction; rather, it was seen as an image for Philip to live up to, an inducement to follow a more practical and humane policy toward his many subjects, both in Spain and abroad. The allusion began, naturally enough, in the Netherlands, where Philip's Dutch subjects hoped he would take the Solomon image to heart, treating them with tact and forbearance, even turning a blind eye to their private, unorthodox religious activities. The epithet was later promoted by humanists in Spain for similar purposes. However, for these Spanish propagandists, Solomon was not only a model for royal wisdom, or discretion, he was also a reminder of Christianity's links to Jewish religion and culture. In a Counter-Reformation environment in which the Old Testament was relegated to the status of a rarely perused prologue and conversos continued to be regarded as subversives, or an enemy within, Solomon was advanced surreptitiously as a figurehead, or ambassador, for peace, concordance, and assimilation.

A Spanish Solomon

The campaign to make Philip a new Solomon began in 1549, six years before he was crowned king, when, on his father's orders, he undertook a tour of the Habsburg's Dutch territories. The tour came at a time of social and religious unrest, with the Dutch cities protesting against increased taxes and loss of civil liberties. Particularly incensed by Charles V's recent clampdown on religious heresy, which had led to a spate of state executions, the Dutch wished to rehearse Prince Philip in his future duties to his northern subjects. They pointed out that as the warrior king, David, was succeeded by the prudent Solomon, so too the warrior Charles would be succeeded by his temperate son, Philip, who would then rule, as the welcoming committee of Tornay put it, 'in peace, honor and concord.'[22]

This reference to Philip as the prudent, pacific Solomon was repeated in Ypres, Lille, Brussels, Arras, and Ghent. It was also adopted five years later by the reform-minded Catholic bishop Reginald Pole in a speech before the English parliament, referring to the imminent marriage between Philip and Mary Tudor. Here Pole compared Charles V to King David, who 'was contaminate with Blood and War,' and thus 'could not build the Temple of Jerusalem, but left the finishing thereof to Solomon, who was *Rex pacificus*.' 'So may it be,' Pole continued, 'that the appeasing of Controversies of Religion in Christianity is not appointed to this Emperor but to his Son, who shall perform the building that the father had begun.' Like the Dutch burgers, Pole appears to have been urging Philip toward a peaceful reconciliation with Protestantism.

In 1559, four years after Pole made his impassioned speech for peace, the Dutch painter Lucas de Heere executed a canvas for Ghent Cathedral in which Solomon, modeled on Philip, is depicted receiving the Queen of Sheba—supposedly an allegorical representation of the Dutch territories (Fig. 4.1). The caption on the frame states: 'Philip, another Solomon, demonstrates his great wisdom.' This is a reference to Kings 10: 13–15, which relate that, on visiting Solomon's court, the foreign Queen of Sheba was impressed with the king's great learning. I would suggest, however, that Heere's canvas admits another reading: that of a pacific monarch establishing a harmonious relationship with a ruler of a different faith. Is it merely a coincidence that the Queen of Sheba is a tall, red-haired monarch, like the Protestant Queen Elizabeth, who had recently ascended the English throne on the death of her sister Mary, Philip's first wife? Is the painting not advocating a rapprochement between Catholic king and

Fig. 4.1 Lucas de Heere, *The Queen of Sheba before Solomon*, from Saint Bavo Cathedra, Ghent. Courtesy of the Flemish Art Imagebank, Ghent

Protestant queen, or even perhaps matrimony? It is noteworthy that the work was commissioned by Viglius van Aytta, a renowned jurist, Erasmian humanist, and advocate of religious peace. Viglius was a member of the Dutch regent Margaret of Palma's inner council, although Margaret herself suspected him of secret non-conformism. It is also significant that Lucas de Heere, the artist chosen by Viglius to execute the painting, fled the Netherlands for England after the Dutch Revolt of 1566, and there converted to Protestantism.

Philip seems to have been captivated by the comparison of himself to the wise King Solomon, although he had his own, very orthodox interpretation of its significance. This is evident in the stained glass window which he donated to Saint John's Church in Gouda, in 1557.[23] Here, in the upper panel, he is depicted in the Temple at Jerusalem, next to the Ark of the Covenant, making a very clear analogy between himself and Solomon. Philip, as Solomon, is in fact witnessing the consecration of the Temple, in

Fig. 4.2 Dirck Crabeth, *Last Supper devotional portraits of Philip II of Spain and Mary Tudor* (central section), Janskirk, Gouda. Courtesy of Collection Rijksdienst voor het Cultureel Erfgoed, Amersfoort, NL

which God was said to have been physically present. In a lower panel we see Philip and his wife Mary Tudor witnessing the Last Supper, showing their allegiance to the Catholic dogma of transubstantiation, in which God is once again said to be present (Fig. 4.2). As a good Counter-Reformation

Catholic monarch, Philip promotes the consecration of Solomon's Temple as a foreshadowing of the Last Supper and the said doctrine of transubstantiation, which, of course, is at the center of the Catholic struggle with Protestantism. Here the focus is not on peace and accommodation, but on a staunch defense of orthodox belief, the message reinforced by the king wearing knightly armor, showing his readiness to defend the faith. In 1566 Philip demonstrated this hardline approach to religious issues, when, in the wake of the Dutch revolt, he sent the Duke of Alba to subdue the rebels through savage martial law. As the duke terrorized the local population, prints began to appear of a blindfolded Solomon sitting back on his throne, passively witnessing a soldier cut a baby in two, unmoved by the mother's pleas. The cartoon was a scathing attack on the Spanish king, who had remained impervious to his subjects' subtle requests for prudent, Solomonic rule.

While the young Philip may not have been prepared to subordinate Catholic dogma to civic peace, there were those in his 1549 entourage who were more sympathetic to religious accommodation. Among this group were Bartolomé de Carranza, Constantino Ponce de la Fuente (both of whom were later tried and convicted of Protestant heresy), and Juan Cristóbal Calvete de Estrella, Prince Philip's tutor. It was Calvete who wrote an account of the prince's Netherland's visit, *El felicisisimo viaje del muy alto y muy poderoso principe Dom Phelippe*, in which the references to the new Solomon were carefully recorded.

Calvete did not return to Spain with the royal party in 1550, but remained in Antwerp, ostensibly to finish his chronicle, although it seems that he was also interested in making the acquaintance of other humanists in an intellectual environment that was rather more liberal than the one he was accustomed to in Spain.[24] One of Calvete's new friends was Cristophe Plantin, who was soon to become famous as the printer of the Antwerp Polyglot Bible (or King's Bible), edited by the Spanish humanist Benito Arias Montano. Plantin was also a member of the religious sect the Family of Love, a low-profile group that promoted private religious observance based on mystical or quietist practice. In contrast to Antwerp's other clandestine religious groups, the Calvinists and Anabaptists, the Familists did not advocate severance from the Catholic Church, which they regarded as an institution, like a strong monarchy, necessary for political cohesion. Rather, they feigned interest in church dogma and rituals in public, while following their own spiritual path, as outlined by their leader Hendrik Niclaes, in private conventicles.

The Family's mixture of Nicodemism—or secret religious practice—and public pacifism attracted many professionals and scholars, including the eminent Dutch humanist Justus Lipsius, whose influential Neostoical philosophy borrowed from the Familist credo. The sect also appears to have infiltrated humanist circles at the University of Louvain, which had become a haven for Spanish Erasmian scholars, who used the more relaxed environment to form religious debating societies in which non-conformist views circulated freely. One of these conventicles, formed by the converso humanist Pedro Jiménez, attracted a diverse group of Spanish scholars wishing to discuss, on a daily basis, points of doctrine expounded in the university classrooms.[25] From a report of the conventicle's activities, filed by the court informer, the friar Baltasar Pérez, it emerges that the meetings were attended by a very varied group of secular scholars and religious, among whom was Gaspar de Grajal, later prosecuted in Salamanca, along with Luis de León, for promoting Jewish Scripture. Most of the group were, like Grajal, converso intellectuals who had grown up in volatile, Erasmian environments in Spain, and whose attraction to certain elements of Protestantism was cemented during their travels abroad.[26] One or two may have been secret Calvinists, but most, it seems, were men who were looking to transform their Catholic faith, not necessarily abandon it.

Baltasar Pérez's secret report revealed that Jiménez' group maintained contact with both non-conformist circles in Antwerp and, more disconcertingly, members of the royal court in Brussels. Three members of the group, Sebastian Fox Morcillo, Felipe de la Torre, and Fadrique Furió Ceriol, were all promoted to positions at court just prior to, or immediately after, Philip's accession to the throne in 1554. Significantly, all three of these men wrote guides to good kingship for the young king, in which they advocated rational, prudent statecraft. One of these men, Fox Morcillo, the son of a Seville converso merchant, was the brother of Francisco Morcillo, who was among the monks from the Seville San Isidoro monastery burnt at the stake in 1560 for their Protestant sympathies. Sebastian, it is believed, died the previous year in a shipwreck while fleeing Spain to avoid a similar fate to that of his brother. However, it is not Fox Morcillo who interests us here, but his compatriots Fadrique Furió Ceriol and, particularly, Felipe de la Torre, whose *Institución de un Rey Cristiano* presents Solomon as a role model for Philip II.

All we know of Felipe de la Torre's family background and early life is that he was born in the Aragonese town of Tarazona and studied at Alcalá de Henares, graduating from the university in 1544. Soon after leaving

Alcalá he moved to Paris, joining a radical reform circle led by a Dr. Juan Morillo, himself a native of Aragon. Morillo had recently arrived in Paris from Trent, where, along with Bartolomé de Carranza, he had formed part of Cardinal Reginald Pole's *spirituali* (reformist) faction at the first Tridentine Council. However, he appears to have become disillusioned by the Council's conservatism, and set out to promote religious change through the creation of a clandestine network of activists, maintaining contact with radical groups in Castile and Aragon, including members of his native town of Biel, and the nearby community of Uncastillo. In his study 'A Hitherto Unknown Group of Protestants in Aragon,' Gordon Kinder examines this loosely knit collection of Aragonese dissidents.[27] He fails to note, however, that they came from an area renowned for its Jewish settlement. In Biel itself, almost half of the residents in the years prior to the 1492 expulsion were Jewish, and most of these subsequently converted to Catholicism. Morillo, I suggest, formed part of a disaffected Aragonese converso community, as did the other members of his network, including his Paris house guest, Felipe de la Torre.[28]

In 1554, as the French authorities were about to arrest Morillo and his Paris accomplices, the group fled to the Low Countries. Morillo himself moved to Antwerp, where he made contact with the converso merchant Marcos Pérez before crossing into Germany to become a Calvinist minister. At the same time, Felipe de la Torre entered the University of Louvain, forming part of Pedro Jiménez's reform circle, while writing his guide for the young Philip II, the *Institución de un Rey Cristiano*.[29]

In the introduction to the *Institución*, de la Torre tells his readers that he has written a moral guide for princes based on the Scriptures and the opinions of the Church Fathers. In fact, the Church Fathers' views on religious and ethical practice are all but absent from the work. Instead, de la Torre's guide focuses on the Old Testament, and presents the learned Jewish kings, especially the prudent Solomon, as role models for King Philip. Likewise, the author advocates Jewish Scripture as an important source of wisdom, recommending that Philip study the Sapienta, as did King Solomon, Israel's most prudent king. He suggests that Philip would also profit from studying the Hebrew histories, Joshua, Judges, and Kings, as well as the Chronicles, which should be supplemented by the classical pagan authors: Cicero, Seneca, Livy, and Plutarch. As to more modern works, the author recommends those by Constantino de la Fuente, Fray Luis de Granada, and Serafino da Fermo, revealing his own predilections toward a private, evangelical faith.

Having established the essential literary fonts for sound kingship, de la Torre now turns to the ruler's duties. As the representative of God, the king should reward good Christians and punish the bad ones, the latter group categorized as heretics and hypocrites. However, it is clear that for de la Torre, heresy is a perversion as prevalent among 'orthodox' Catholics as among dissident Protestants. 'One calls heretics by the following names,' he writes, 'false prophets, false Christs, false Apostles, false doctors, bad workers, dogs, profane men, arrogant men, incorrigible men, reprobates, lovers of themselves and their opinions, damned in faith, of corrupt understanding and tricksters, abominable, unbelievers, unfit for any good.'[30] As regards hypocrites, de la Torre turns to the Scriptures for inspiration:

> The Scriptures speak of hypocrites in the following terms, from which we can determine their ways: false brothers, sad hypocrites, whitewashed tombs, those who wish to be doctors of the law without understanding what they say or affirm, those who see themselves, in their own eyes, as wise and prudent but are only worthy of hate, being without kind wisdom, full of darkness and blindness, who resist the Holy Spirit and the truth, who close up the gates of heaven and do not enter themselves or allow others to do so.[31]

In fact, de la Torre's attack on hypocrites was based on Jesus' condemnation of the Pharisees, a detail that would be clear to many of his reform-minded readers, who would also relate it to Erasmus' *Antibarbarorum*, in which the humanist compared ignorant monks, mired in ceremonies, to Pharisaic Jews. As I have noted earlier, Spain's converso humanists were quick to repeat Erasmus' analogy in their war against Old Christian prejudice, linking their Old Christian antagonists with errant Jewry through pointless ritual, as the former had linked them to ignoble Jewry through common, tainted blood.[32]

Hypocrites, de la Torre informs us subtly, were those unrepentant churchmen who immersed themselves in ceremonies and tradition, like the Pharisees, while stubbornly ignoring the Scriptural source of Christianity. However, ignorance and arrogance were the least of these men's sins. They were also violent individuals who never grew tired of killing and spilling blood. They believed themselves to be saintly and clean (*limpia*), while, in fact, their own filth remained uncleansed. Here de la Torre draws a distinction between false and true cleanliness—that is to say, the clean blood which the Old Christian hypocrites believed they had and the moral or spiritual cleanliness, or purity, which they clearly lacked. These people should be prohibited from taking part in legal proceedings, writes de la Torre, and their false testimonies rigorously punished; for one of the things most despised by God, according to King Solomon, was false testimony. And de la Torre recommends that Philip take note of Solomon's words: 'The false witness shall not go unpunished. The liar shall not escape, and false testimony shall perish.'[33]

De la Torre's work is a call for toleration and respect within the Christian community. The figure of Christ unites everyone, he tells us: '[T]here is no difference between peoples or nations, Jews and Gentiles, Barbarians and Greeks; because their faith and religion took away all the differences and obstacles which distinguish the nations and united all in one Church and Gospel.'[34] To demonstrate the importance of this unity and brotherhood among Christians, from time to time God joins together realms, as he did recently in the case of King Philip [who had formed a marriage alliance with Queen Mary I of England in 1554]. In so doing, God obliges the ruler and his subjects to understand each other better and to treat each other with greater love and care.

Kings should be respected by their subjects, but in return they should rule wisely, with justice and generosity (*liberalidad*), creating a peaceful, united realm. And de la Torre once again turns to King Solomon as a model for change. Solomon succeeded his father, the warrior David, and established a realm of peace and unity, marked by the building of a temple in which the covenant—or true religion of the people—was kept. It was now incumbent on Philip, who, like Solomon, followed a warrior father, to construct his own temple (metaphorically speaking) to peace, in which a revitalized, evangelical Christianity would be practiced.

Like the Dutch city officials who received Prince Philip during his 1549 tour of the Netherlands, de la Torre makes use of the Solomon analogy to bolster his appeal for prudent and pacific rule, unswayed by Confessionalism. However, more than a call for religious concordance, de la Torre's *Institución* is a highly personal and emotional condemnation of Spanish society, its chauvinism, malice, and cruelty, all of which the author contrasts to an evangelical Christian message, itself linked to the prudence and wisdom of King Solomon and the Sapiential Books. Two decades later, de la Torre's fellow humanist Benito Arias Montano would attempt to convey a similar irenic message through associating Philip II's new palace at El Escorial with

Solomon's celebrated edifice in Jerusalem (see Chap. 5). Like de la Torre, Montano would employ Solomon as an emblem of peace and reconciliation, not only between Catholics and Protestants but also between Old and New Christians.

Peace and concordance were also at the heart of Fadrique Furió Ceriol's guide to good government, *El concejo y consejeros del príncipe*, published in 1559, three years after de la Torre's *Institución*, in which the author writes: '[T]here are only two lands in the whole world: that of good men and that of bad. All the good men, whether they be Jews, Moors, Gentiles, Christians, or of another religion, belong to the same land, the same household, and are of the same blood; and all the bad men likewise.'[35] This sentiment suggests that Furió, like his friend de la Torre, was attempting to create a tolerant regime in which New Christians could prosper without having to disguise their backgrounds, as he in fact had done, changing his name from Juan Miguel Ceriol to Fadrique Furió, and inventing noble military roots for his family.

Furió was not from a military background, as he claimed in the introduction to his work *Institutionum rhetoricarum*, but from an artisanal and trading one, as an examination of his two extant wills testify. In the first of these, recorded in his hometown of Valencia, in 1564, Furió states that his stepfather, Jerónimo Revert, and his brother-in-law, Bartolomé Revert, were *velluteres* (silk manufacturers), while his other brother-in-law, Joan Tarragó, was a *corredor d'orella* (an agent for merchant business transactions). In the same document, Furió nominated the merchant Nofre Adell as his executor, and Juan Baiarri, cloth dyer, and Julian de Moya, surgeon, as his witnesses. All of these professions were associated with a converso community in Valencia, suggesting that Furió himself was from that background. Later, in a revised will, recorded in Madrid, in 1592, Furió's witnesses were Miguel Barberán, silk manufacturer, and Martín Gelós, merchant, reinforcing the view that Ceriol, like his émigré compatriots Juan Luis Vives and Martín Cordero, was a New Christian.[36]

In a biographical report, written as part of his application for president of the Council of Aragon, in 1581, Furió tells us that he spent 18 years outside of Spain, in England, France, Italy, Germany, Switzerland, and the Netherlands. Although Furió does not elaborate on his life during this period, Luis de Requesens, governor of the Netherlands from 1573 to 1576, believed he spent his formative years at the court of the Erasmian bishop of Cologne, Herman Von Wied, who was excommunicated for his

Protestant sympathies in 1547. Later, in 1550 or thereabouts, Furió moved to the University of Paris, where, in company with his fellow Valencian humanist Juan Martín Cordero, he entered Dr. Juan Morillo's evangelical conventicle. In 1554, Furió, along with other members of the Morillo group, moved to Louvain. Here he published the *Bononia*—a dialogue between himself and the theologian Juan de Bononia, in which he enthusiastically advocated the translation of the Vulgate into native tongues, only five years after biblical texts in Spanish were placed on the Inquisition Index. The Bible was not a mysterious work, Furió wrote, but one written simply, in the everyday language of the apostles, for everyone's benefit, and should once again be made available to all Christians in their own languages.[37] For these radical views, Furió was imprisoned in 1559, although he was set free after three months' confinement, when the chancellor of the University of Louvain intervened on his behalf.[38] Soon after his release, Furió published *El concejo y consejeros del Príncipe*, in which he turned his attention toward good government and the need for council reform.

El concejo begins with Furió attacking the mirror for princes' genre for conflating the professional aspects of the office with the moral probity of the office holder. The latter was obviously important but it should not be confused with the former. A good prince was not just a good man (he may not even be a good man) but a good ruler, advancing his own and his subjects' interests and protecting himself and them from distress and ruin. Naturally, as far as the humanist Furió was concerned, sound kingship was based on a humanist education and outlook; thus a good prince was intelligent, widely read, and well traveled. He was also prudent and careful, attributes he would employ in choosing his counselors.

In Furió's view the existing system of government in Spain, in which the councils overlapped in their jurisdictions, should be reformed, creating seven new or revitalized bodies. The first of these was the Treasury, responsible for rationalizing the royal budget so that unnecessary expenses were avoided and taxes reduced. The second council was that of the State, referred to significantly as the Council of Peace, which vetted both civilian and military men for their public duties. The third council, the Council of War, determined the number of soldiers necessary in the interests of state defense alone; while the fourth council, named the Council of Maintenance, kept track of imported and exported goods, making sure the country was never short of staple products. The task of the fifth council, the Council of Law, was to calculate the number of officials necessary for governing the state, their mandate, and authority. It was also responsible for drafting new laws and scrapping old, obsolete ones that served only to keep an avaricious legal community in work. The sixth council, the Penal Council, would take charge of criminal proceedings and sentencing. Significantly, there was no Inquisition in Furió's state system, the determination and prosecution of heresy being left, presumably, to the dioceses. The seventh and final council was the Council of Merit, which rewarded people for their industry and virtue, recompensing both those who applied for such rewards and those who did not. This body would replace the Council of the Orders, whose criteria for awarding honors was based on blood rather than on ability.

Turning to the state councillors, Furió notes that these men should be intelligent, persuasive speakers, linguists, and historians, capable of applying their studies to the business of statecraft. They should also be world travelers, whose contact with other people would create an open-minded attitude. The very best and most intelligent of councillors were those who were not ill-disposed toward any nation. On the other hand, a sure sign of a weak intelligence was the tendency to speak badly of an opponent, or of the enemies of one's prince, or of those who followed other sects, whether Jews, Moors, Gentiles, or Christians.[39] But the worst of all possible councillors, according to Furió, were those men so devoted to the Church that to further its interests, right or wrong, they would turn a kingdom upside down. And he notes that the king should be aware of Churchmen's opinions, for 'behind the cross is the devil.'[40]

Commentators on *El Concejo* invariably compare it to Machiavelli's *The Prince*. This is understandable, given that both guides express a predilection for practical statecraft, untouched by religious dictates. Nevertheless, fundamentally they are quite different works. Machiavelli wrote *The Prince* as a survival guide for the ruler of a small Renaissance state, surrounded by potent and voracious neighbors. In contrast, Furió's work was written against a Reformation backdrop for a powerful ruler, who, at great cost to himself and his subjects, had assumed the role of Catholic standard bearer. Furió's objective was to direct his novice prince toward a new, practical, political credo, carried out by rational professionals, in which religious dogma played no part. In this respect *El Consejo* bears resemblance not to Machiavelli's *The Prince* but to Justus Lipsius' Neostoical treatise on statescraft, *Politicum civilis doctrine libri sex* (*Six Books on Politics or Civil Doctrine*), a practical guide for state governance, written in a period of increasing religious conflict.

Like Furió, Lipsius spent much of his life on the move, very often escaping religious strife. As a young man he studied first with the Jesuits in Cologne and later at the Catholic university in Louvain. After leaving university he was briefly the secretary of Cardinal Granvelle in Rome, before returning to Louvain in 1570. Two years later, while he was on a trip to Vienna, his house was sacked by Spanish troops. Lipsius reacted to this crisis by moving to the Protestant city of Jeno, where he converted to the reformed religion in order to teach at the city's university. However, a number of his fellow academics suspected that the conversion was motivated solely by practical necessity, and soon forced his dismissal. In 1574, Lipsius found himself back in Louvain, where his house was once again looted by Spanish troops. In search of greater security, he now moved to the new Calvinist university at Leiden, in whose relatively tolerant atmosphere he spent the next 13 years, composing his two major works, *De constantia libri duo* (*Two Books on Constancy*) and *Politicorum sive civilis doctrinae libri sex* (*Six Books on Politics or Civil Doctrine*), before returning once again to Louvain, where he was said to have died a good Catholic. However, according to his Calvinist friend Adrianus Saravia, Lipsius' religious views were more in keeping with those of the Family of Love than those of orthodox Catholicism. In a letter to the Archbishop of Canterbury, written in 1608, Saravia stated:

> He [Lipsius] never professed the evangelical doctrine; but, as far as I know, while he was living with us [the Calvinists of Leiden], he never openly opposed it. It seemed to us that in controversies he sided with the majority, that he liked peace and harmony and hated trouble-makers. But it is the custom of the H[enry] N[iclaes] family [the Family of Love] not openly to oppose the religion established by public authority; they wish to give the appearance of being adherents of that religion. He claimed to be disgusted by the crass idolatory of the Roman Church, which, however, he supported in his book on the idol of Halle. I was convinced by his words and actions that he was not averse to the religion that we profess. But I believed that the reason why, in these general, large-scale religious differences, he committed himself to no party was because he did not wish to offend any of his many friends who were of varying religious persuasions. He so adjusted all his writings that the subject of religion was not touched upon, and that the reader could not tell whether they were written by a Christian or a pagan.[41]

Published some 30 years after Furió's *El Concejo*, Lipsius' *Politicorum* found an appreciative audience among Spain's post-Tridentine humanists.

One of the work's most enthusiastic supporters was Benito Arias Montano, who wrote to Lipsius in 1593 informing him of his many adherents in Seville, among whom were the celebrated physicians Simón de Tovar and Francisco Sánchez de Oropesa, the canons Francisco Pacheco and Luciano de Negron, and the scholar Pedro de Valencia.[42] These men were not, of course, living in an environment assailed by civil war and religious upheaval, as was Lipsius; but they were members of a divided society, the divisions set by caste as well as by faith. As such, they were well able to empathize with the Dutch humanist's predicament and embrace his vision for socio-religious peace. In the next chapter, I examine four of Spain's prominent Counter-Reformation humanists and their call for a tolerant society; a plea, I will argue, closely related to their converso condition.

CHAPTER 5

Four Humanists

The late sixteenth century was a period of religious tension throughout Europe as Catholic and Protestant armies battled each other in defense of the true faith. But this tension was not only evident at an international level, between rival religious regimes, it was also present locally, where many men and women found themselves at variance with the official religion of their realm. John Calvin referred to those people who observed the Protestant faith clandestinely in Catholic lands as 'Nicodemites,' after Nicodemus the Pharisee, who visited Jesus in private; however, the term is equally applicable to Catholic adherents in Protestant realms, and to humanists everywhere who clashed with Confessionalism.[1] This was the case, for example, of the Dutch scholar Justus Lipsius, whose Neostoical philosophy—predicated on concealment—was an attempt to transform religious dissimulation from a vice to a virtue. Lipsius' philosophy, based on the stoical code of Seneca and the pragmatic politics of Tacitus, called for citizens to uphold the religion of their prince in public in order to avoid civil strife. However, in private they should be free to pursue their personal inclinations with the ruler's tacit consent. It was a type of practical statecraft that the French had begun to label *politique*.

Politique naturally appealed to Spain's converso humanists, who had operated under the shadow of the Inquisition for over a century, becoming adept at religious dissimulation. This deceit was now freely practiced across Counter-Reformation Europe, where it was often referred to euphemistically as 'prudence' or 'discretion.' The four protagonists of this

© The Author(s) 2018
K. Ingram, *Converso Non-Conformism in Early Modern Spain*,
https://doi.org/10.1007/978-3-319-93236-1_5

chapter were all 'discreet' men, who attempted to advance evangelical and humanist reform, while attracting as little hostility as possible from religiously orthodox antagonists. All four humanists were irenists, responsive to the messages of religious concordance from their European counterparts. But they were also, I argue, conversos, whose humanism and evangelism were shaped by their own unique situation as members of what Old Christian society labeled a tainted minority. All were born and brought up in Andalusia or southern Extremadura, in towns (Seville, Córdoba, Jerez de la Frontera, Zafra, and Fregenal de la Sierra) renowned for their large converso populations, and in which animosity toward the conversos continued unabated. Indeed, as I noted in the previous chapter, suspicion of the conversos grew after Trent, as the Church and the Crown became increasingly fearful of homegrown heretical groups, a problem both institutions associated with the converso and Morisco minorities. Old Christian suspicions were further aroused by the expansion of the Ottomon Turks into the western Mediterranean, where, it was feared, they were establishing contacts with the Morisco communities in the Spanish provinces of Granada and Valencia. This obsession with the enemy within led the Crown to examine the possibilities of a radical solution to the Morisco problem: the expulsion of the entire community, which finally occurred in 1609. It was in this atmosphere of suspicion and tension that four humanists and friends, Benito Arias Montano, Francisco Pacheco (the Licentiate), Pablo de Céspedes, and Pedro de Valencia, wrote their scholarly works, promoting concordance and synergism while simulating pure lineage and orthodox faith.

Benito Arias Montano (1527–1598)

Benito Arias Montano's religious non-conformism has already been mooted by Ben Rekers in his study of the Seville humanist published in 1970.[2] In this work Rekers presents the view that Montano converted to the religious sect the Family of Love while directing the Polyglot Bible project in Antwerp from 1568 to 1572. Rekers argued that Montano had arrived in Antwerp an advocate of Counter-Reformation Catholicism, but converted to an irenic, or religiously tolerant, outlook as a result of his relationship with the Antwerp printer Christophe Plantin and a number of the city's converso merchants who were Family adherents. Rekers further argued that on his return to Spain, in 1577, Montano spread Familist views among the the Jeronymite community of El Escorial palace-monastery, where he was employed as royal librarian, and among a small group of friends in Seville, including the cathedral canons Francisco Pacheco, Luciano de Negron, and Pedro Vélez de Guevara. Based on Montano's proximity to Family adherents and of his evident attraction to the mystical ideas of the Familist leader Hendrik Jansen van Barrefelt (Hiël), Rekers' view that Montano was attracted to the Flemish religious sect is clearly incontrovertible. However, his belief that this represented a radical change in the humanist's religious views is much less convincing. In fact, Montano's religious non-conformity began in his youth, within his extended converso-professional family, and these views were reinforced when, as a middle-aged man, he came into contact with the Flemish sect. Like the members of the Family of Love, Montano was an adherent of a minimalist Christianity that subordinated ceremonies, sacraments, and icons to an interior, mystical, religious practice, and like the Familists, he was used to disguising his true beliefs behind a cloak of religious conformity. Montano was attracted to the Flemish sect precisely because it reflected his own religious outlook, an outlook engendered in the converso environment of his youth.

Benito Arias Montano was born in 1527 in Fregenal de la Sierra, a small town in the province of Huelva, renowned for its large converso population.[3] We know nothing of Montano's parents, save for their names, Isabel Gómez and Benito Arias, and his father's occupation: he was a notary.[4] Montano tells us that his interest in Latin and Astrology began at his father's knee, which would indicate that Benito Arias took responsibility for his son's early education. Montano does not reveal how or where he became interested in the study of the Hebrew language and culture, but it may also have begun at the same time, under his father's guidance.

At the age of 12 or 13 Montano moved to Seville, where he was nurtured by friends of his father, Antonio de Alcocer and his wife Isabel Vélez. The Alcocers were an important converso merchant clan from Toledo who, like Saint Teresa's family, had gained their wealth through the silk trade.[5] Antonio de Alcocer was himself a successful *letrado* who maintained close contact with the Seville business community. One of his daughters, Isabel Vélez, married the wealthy converso merchant Diego Díaz Becerril; another daughter, Mencía de Alcocer, married another converso merchant, Gómez de León, who was imprisoned in 1559 for his involvement in Seville's clandestine 'Protestant' cell. During these 'Protestant' trials, Becerril acted as trustee for the property of Constantino Ponce de la Fuente, a man regarded by the Inquisition as the leader of the

'Protestant' group. Montano was very close to both Becerril and León, whom he referred to in his letters as his 'brothers.'[6] This term could be interpreted as merely an affectionate form of address; it could also have religious connotations—the fifteenth-century Flemish sect the Brethren of the Common Life addressed each other in this fashion, as did the *alumbrados* of Guadalajara and Valladolid in the early sixteenth century.

In Seville Montano was also closely associated with the Núñez Pérez family, whom he often described as his relatives (*deudos*). The Núñez Pérez were members of a powerful converso clan with family members in Lisbon, Bordeaux, and Antwerp. While Montano was in Antwerp directing the Polyglot Bible project, he formed a close relationship with a wealthy member of this clan, Luis Pérez, who was an adherent of the Family of Love. Luis Pérez's brother was the Calvinist Marcos Pérez, mentioned in Chap. 3, who was responsible for much of the clandestine Protestant literature shipments to Seville in the mid-sixteenth century.[7]

From 1548 to 1555, Montano studied Latin and Hebrew at the University of Alcalá de Henares. His knowledge of the latter language was such that his fellow students dubbed him a second Jerome, a reference to Saint Jerome's extensive knowledge of Hebrew, which he used to translate the Hebrew Scriptures into Latin. However, Montano's interest in Jewish culture was not confined to the scholarly examination of the Old Testament. Like Juan de Malara and Pablo de Céspedes (a close friend), he was also interested in establishing links between the ancient Jews and the Iberian Peninsula. Like Céspedes, Montano maintained that many of Spain's foremost towns were founded by early Jewish settlers and that the names of these towns were corruptions of Hebrew words.[8] In contrast to his interest in the Old Testament Scriptures, Montano demonstrated relatively little interest in the theology of the Church Fathers. He was, however, an avid reader of Erasmus, all of whose works were to be found in his student library.[9]

In 1553 Montano returned to Andalusia, where he now divided his time between Seville and his hermitage at Aracena, some 80 kilometers to the northwest, on the fringe of the Sierra Morena. The hermitage had been ceded to Montano by the Seville Cathedral, with the aid of his friend Pedro Vélez de Guevara (a relative of Montano's adoptive mother, Isabel Vélez), who was prior of the hermitages of the archdiocese. During the next six years Montano converted the rundown building into a comfortable country villa, where, accompanied by another scholar, named Ruano, and a servant named España, he devoted his time to the study of the

Scriptures. Montano also found time to study Medicine and Botany with his friend, the physician Francisco de Arce, also from Fregenal de la Sierra, and to graduate in Arts at the University of Seville, although it is unlikely that he did much studying at the university itself.[10]

In June 1559, three months before Seville's 'Protestants' were paraded through the city in the famous *auto de fe*, Montano was detained at his country villa by the mayor of Aracena and brought in chains to the Andalusian capital. The document describing Montano's arrest states that he had been accused by a certain Morales of Fregenal de la Sierra of 'el pecado etc.' Given the religious upheaval in Seville in 1559, given also Montano's own religious predilections, it is tempting to interpret this vague description as a reference to Protestant or even Jewish heresy, although other interpretations have also been mooted.[11] Whatever Montano's alleged offense, he was soon released from his prison cell, presumably for lack of evidence.

Soon after he left prison, Montano applied for and gained entry into the Order of Santiago. In May 1560 he was received into the order at the San Marcos priory of León, where he now donned a monk's habit, emblazoned with the red Saint James cross. A number of Montano scholars have pointed to the humanist's noble insignia as evidence for his Old Christian background. If he had been a converso, they argue, it would in all likelihood have been revealed in the rigorous *limpieza de sangre* investigations that preceded his entry into the order. In fact, while the order's investigations were often extensive, they were rarely rigorous. Candidates were usually able to direct the investigation toward friendly witnesses, some of whom were clearly bribed to present favorable information. Entering the military orders could be an expensive process; however, with careful preparation the results were usually favorable. Montano was himself very careful in planning his entry into the Order of Santiago. First he built a church dedicated to the saint in the village of El Castaño de Robledo, near his country retreat at Aracena. Then he founded a confraternity dedicated to the saint's cult. Only then did he make formal application for entry into the noble order. The entry procedure itself was rapid and, as often was the case, perfunctory. A dozen or so people were selected as character witnesses; all confirmed that the humanist's antecedents were *hidalgos*, unblemished by trade or Jewish blood. Once inside the order Montano demonstrated little interest in the saint, or indeed the cloistered life of the Santiago monastery; he did, however, wear his monk's robe, with its all-important noble insignia, everywhere he went.

For Montano, the Order of Santiago was a social carapace, protecting him from accusations of tainted origins or errant beliefs.[12] It was also a means of impressing influential clerics like the Bishop of Segovia, Martín Pérez de Ayala, who invited Montano to form part of a Spanish delegation to the third Council of Trent. Here the young humanist was able to show off his rhetorical skills in two well-received interventions: one on divorce, the other on communion. It is noteworthy that in support of his views the humanist cited the Scriptures but not Church tradition.[13]

It was while a delegate at Trent that Montano formed a close attachment to a number of Jews who were observing the proceedings. Montano was particularly impressed by a certain Simon de Mantua, whom he described as 'a man praiseworthy for his habits and integrity.' In a discussion on the Messiah, Mantua asked why it was that the world had not experienced the messianic peace that the Old Testament prophets had spoken of if, indeed, He had already arrived. In the face of this argument Montano admitted that he had no reply.[14] It was during the Trent conference that Montano also came into contact with a group of Jews from Milan (a city-state at that time under Spanish rule), who later solicited the humanist's help in renewing the Milan Jewish community's license for residency.

It may have been with this Italian Sephardic community in mind that Montano later wrote *In Abdías*, a defense of the claim that the Jews had arrived in Spain at the time of the destruction of the first Temple.[15] This claim was based on the Jewish prophet Abdias' statement that in the wake of the Judean defeat to the Babylonian king Nebuchadnezzar, a community of Judean Jews had been exiled to Sefarad. Despite the fact that Saint Jerome had translated Sefarad as Bosphorus, Montano followed the line of argument advanced by Jewish scholars, who associated the term with Iberia, offering some long and complex philological arguments in its defense. It is possible that he was introduced to this theory by the Milanese Jews he had met in Trent, who were trying to prove their ancient connection to Spain in a bid to remain resident in Philip II's Spanish Empire. But Montano's work would also have served Spanish conversos, who were attempting, once again, to contest their alien image by integrating their Jewish ancestors more fully into early Spanish history.

This cultural integrationism was again evident in Montano's *Instrucción Christiana*, also written in the period after his return from Trent, which formed the basis for his *Dictatum Christianum*, published by the Plantin Press in 1575. While the *Instruccción* is no longer extant, the *Dictatum* is available, providing us with an insight into Montano's religious frame of mind in the years directly after the last Tridentine council. Montano begins the *Dictatum* by reminding his readers of the calamitous situation of a Europe stricken by war. This is God's punishment, he opines, for the sins of a society in which Christians were either misguided followers of error-ridden Protestant sects or negligent members of a Catholic Church, so careless in their observance that they perverted the faith.[16] Almost everyone ignored the three fundamental obligations of the true Christian: fear of God, penitence, and charity. If Christians observed this simple 'dogma' (Montano evidently used the term as a pointed attack on a doctrine-ridden confessionalist Europe), then they would be filled with God's spirit, the first step toward social peace and harmony.

Christians only needed to be fearful of God, penitent, and charitable. Montano repeats these requirements like a mantra throughout his text. However, the humanist offers his own interpretation of what these divine requirements involved. By 'fear of God,' he meant the observance of the Ten Commandments; by 'penitence,' he referred not to the Christian sacrament but to the exercise of virtue; and by 'charity,' he emphasized the need for brotherly love. Evidently all three of these essential precepts could be followed by Christians in a Protestant as well as in a Catholic environment; there was thus no need to change faith to comply with the requirements of Montano's God. Moreover, all three prerequisites for being a good Christian also applied to being a good Jew; indeed, most of his models for correct Christian behavior were taken from the Hebrew Bible. In Montano's view there was no fundamental difference between the Jewish and Christian faith, as he makes clear through quoting Mathew 5, verse 17, in which Jesus states: 'Think not that I am come to destroy the law, or the prophets: I am not come to destroy but to fulfil.'[17] Montano's *Dictatum* is the work of a post-Tridentine Christian humanist who wished to remind all Christians—Protestants and Catholics alike—of the simple precepts of their religion. It is also the work of a converso Biblicist eager to encourage his fellow Christians to embrace rather than discard their Jewish religious heritage.

Montano's private meditations on faith were brought to a close in March 1566, when he was summoned to court and awarded the position of royal chaplain. He was thus conveniently on hand when, several months later, Philip II went in search of someone to oversee the Polyglot Bible project that was already underway in the Antwerp print shop of Christophe Plantin. Like its predecessor, the Complutense Polyglot Bible, the Antwerp

Bible was a humanist philological project, the aim of which was to reveal the earliest examples of the biblical message. However, since the Alcalá work, the philological studies of early biblical manuscripts had advanced apace, encouraging Plantin to float the idea for a new, improved, and expanded work. Unfortunately, a number of his collaborators in the enterprise were either Protestants or questionable Catholics. It was thus inevitable that Plantin's project would at some stage clash with Catholic officialdom, placing its patron, Philip II, in a very awkward position.

Philip should never have consented to patronize the Antwerp Polyglot Bible; that he did so reveals much about the nature of his rule. For although Philip was a diligent monarch who pored endlessly over his state papers, he was not as firmly in control of government policy as he liked to believe. In fact, he was often guided into decision-making by ambitious and skillful secretaries who selected the correspondence he read and the people with whom he met. One of these secretaries, the converso Antonio Pérez, was not only able to use his close proximity to the king to malign a political rival; he was also able to persuade Philip to have this man assassinated.[18] Pérez's contemporary, Gabriel de Zayas, does not figure as large in the history books as Pérez, yet it is clear that he too was a resourceful politician, with considerable influence on Philip II's decision-making. Indeed, it was in large measure through Zayas' maneuvering that the doctrinally dubious Antwerp Polyglot Bible gained Philip's support.

Although Gabriel de Zayas served as a royal secretary for over 20 years, our history books reveal almost nothing about this influential *letrado*. What we do know is that he was a member of a well-to-do family from Écija, near Córdoba, and that he studied classical languages at Alcalá de Henares.[19] It was at Alcalá that Zayas became friends with the humanist Ambrosio de Morales, through whom he may have first met Montano.[20] On leaving Alcalá, he entered the royal court bureaucracy under the protective wing of the converso Gonzalo Pérez, the father of the infamous Antonio Pérez and Philip II's most able secretary.[21]

Soon after he arrived at court, Zayas accompanied Prince Philip on a state visit to the Netherlands, where he became acquainted with Christophe Plantin, a French bookbinder and leatherworker who had moved to the flourishing city of Antwerp, in 1548, in search of work and a more liberal religious atmosphere. In 1555 Zayas commissioned Plantin to make a small leather box to hold a gemstone he wished to send to Spain as a gift for Charles V's queen, Margaret of Austria. It was while delivering the box to Zayas that Plantin was attacked and wounded in his right hand, as a result of which he was no longer able to continue bookbinding, and was forced to take up printing. This, at any rate, is the story told by Plantin's grandson, Baltasar Moretus, to the Jesuit chronicler Gilles Schoondonck in 1604.[22] It is likely, however, that Plantin's decision to enter the printing business was prompted not by an arm wound but by the offer of finance from a number of wealthy backers. Plantin's biographer, Colin Clair, believes that one of these men was Gabriel de Zayas; the others were prominent Calvinists or, like Plantin himself, devotees of the Family of Love prophet Hendrik Niclaes.[23]

When Plantin entered the printing business in 1555, Antwerp, along with Paris and Venice, was one of the three most important publishing cities in Europe; it was also a center for clandestine Protestant literature. Many of these Calvinist texts had already found their way into Spain through a secret supply network organized by the converso merchant Marcos Pérez. While the Protestant trials held at Valladolid and Seville at the end of the decade dealt a blow to this clandestine trade, they did not seriously affect the production of Protestant literature in the Netherlands itself, where dissenting religious sects, like the Family of Love, continued to attract new adherents. It is clear that Plantin's press was from its inception a source of non-conformist works, and that this clandestine production continued, off and on, throughout the next 30 years. In February 1562 it was reported to Margaret, Duchess of Parma, Philip II's half-sister and Regent of the Netherlands, that the printer Plantin, a man 'tainted by the heresies of the new religion,' had recently printed a heretical text in his Antwerp print shop. Margaret placed the matter in the hands of the Margrave, or Chief Constable, Jan van Immerzeele (unbeknownst to the regent, another secret Calvinist), who announced that Plantin had departed for Paris several weeks previously. Immerzeele also reported that he had searched the printer's workplace and interviewed his family, but had been unable to discover any evidence of heretical literature.[24] Thus Plantin was able to return to Antwerp, where he immediately entered into a business partnership with four wealthy merchants, Karel and Cornelis van Bomberghen, Joannes Goropius Becanus, and Jacopo Scotti, all of whom were Calvinists.[25]

While Plantin's business was expanding and flourishing, the political and religious situation in the Netherlands was rapidly deteriorating. In 1564, encouraged by the growing agitation against the Duchess of Parma's government, Calvinist ministers began holding open-air meetings to which large crowds were attracted. At the same time a faction of the Dutch nobility, led by William of Orange, began calling for the abolition of the Dutch Inquisition and for freedom of religious practice for Protestants and Calvinists. This religious agitation culminated in August 1566 with the so-called iconoclastic fury, during which time Catholic churches throughout the southern Netherlands were raided and burnt by militant Calvinists. It was during this period of religious strife that Plantin decided to approach Philip II with a proposal for a new Polyglot Bible.

The Polyglot Bible had occupied Plantin's thoughts for some considerable time before he offered the project to the Spanish king. The printer's initial plan was to publish the work under the patronage of the humanist Bishop of Arras, Cardinal Granvelle, an able and loyal statesman who, in 1556, had been appointed President of the Council of State for Flanders by Philip II. A hardline champion of Habsburg imperial interests, Granvelle was nevertheless a flexible Catholic who, unlike Philip, was prepared to sacrifice religious dogma for state stability. He was in fact a devotee of *politique*, an outlook he shared with his secretary Justus Lipsius and his printer friend Christophe Plantin, whom he supported in many of his publishing projects, and especially in the production of the Polyglot Bible.[26]

Unfortunately, Plantin's plan to publish the Polyglot with Granvelle as patron was dashed when, in the summer of 1566, the printer's business associates, the van Bomberghens, openly declared themselves Calvinists. It was now obvious that the Polyglot project would only succeed if it were financed and directed by someone of impeccable religious orthodoxy and enormous prestige. The obvious candidate was Philip II himself. The problem was how to steer the Spanish monarch around the thorny topic of Plantin's own heretical reputation. Luckily, in this task the printer was able to count on the persuasive skills of Gabriel de Zayas, who, in November 1566, became Philip II's Secretary for Flanders and as such was an important conduit between Philip and his Dutch subjects.

Plantin approached Philip II in 1566, already knowing that his friend Zayas would present him and his project in the best possible light. Indeed, it is likely that Plantin's formal application to the king via Zayas was preceded by an informal exchange between the secretary and the printer, to which Cardinal Granvelle may also have been party. The Polyglot Bible was, of course, presented to Philip as a monument to his Catholic piety, wisdom, and, above all, preeminence among Christian princes. In reality, however, the work was a 'pre-Tridentine' humanist project that attempted to undermine the authority of the sanctified Vulgate and in so doing challenge an orthodox vision of the Faith.[27]

The task confronting Zayas in 1566 was a delicate one. Not only did he have to whet Philip II's appetite for this dubiously orthodox religious fare (Plantin had already engaged the controversial biblical scholars Andreas Masius and Guillermo Postel as collaborators[28]), he also had to steer Plantin's proposal toward an adjudicating panel of scholars who would enthusiastically endorse the project. One of these adjudicators was Martínez de Cantalapiedra, who, along with Luis de León, was later imprisoned for attacking the Vulgate and promoting rabbinical scriptural exegesis; another adjudicator was Zayas' friend Benito Arias Montano, who was also chosen to head the project. All of this raises the question: was it merely a coincidence that Montano was called to court soon after Zayas became secretary for Flanders and shortly before Plantin offered the Polyglot to Philip II? Or did Montano himself form part of an elaborate plan to publish a work that challenged Tridentine orthodoxy? And was Montano's relative, the Antwerp merchant Luis Pérez, also involved in this plan? It is significant that the Familist Luis Pérez, a close friend of Plantin, advanced the printer money on several occasions during the Polyglot production process, enabling him to continue working on the Bible even when Philip II's promised aid was not forthcoming.

When Montano arrived in Antwerp in March 1568, he found that the Aramaic Old Testament and the Syriac version of the New Testament had already been edited and were ready for printing. Within two years of the Spanish humanist's arrival, the entire work was completed, a tribute to Montano's and Plantin's work effort.[29] Montano himself had written much of the *Apparatus*, which formed the eighth and final volume of the Polyglot, and included treatises on the culture and antiquities of the Jews. However, it is unlikely that the Bible would have been finished so rapidly had it not been for the fact that its censors, a team of theologians from the University of Louvain, had raised few objections to Montano's and Plantin's proposals, even though the two men had included, along with the Vulgate, a sixteenth-century translation of the Hebrew Bible by the Italian scholar Santes Pagnini.[30] When, however, Montano sent proofs of the Bible to a group of scholars at Alcalá de Henares, who had also been selected to examine the work in progress, the reaction was quite different. All three men (one of whom was Montano's friend Ambrosio de Morales) were worried that Montano may have taken his commission much too far, and all advised him to gain papal approval for the project before going to print, as security against later attacks from irate and indignant Catholic clerics. Montano ignored their advice, almost certainly because he too realized that the work was heading for trouble, and that its best chance of survival lay in it being presented to the pope as a printed and published *fait accompli*.

By the end of 1571 the Polyglot was printed and bound in eight volumes. As far as Philip II was concerned, however, the work remained unfinished while it lacked the pope's blessing. Thus in February 1572 Montano shipped a copy of the Bible to Rome for papal analysis. A month later Pope Pius V reported to King Philip's ambassador in Rome, Luis de Requesens, that the work would need to be subjected to a rigorous examination by a committee of theologians before he would be in a position to pass a definitive verdict (apparently, he set little store by the Louvain theologians' opinion). However, it was clear that His Holiness was already of the view that the work was tainted. He noted, for example, that one of the scholars involved in the project, Andreas Masius, was a man of evident heretical beliefs, and that the *Apparatus* (the eighth volume of the Polyglot, mostly composed by Montano) contained many references to the Talmud as well as to a treatise, *De Arcano Sermone*, that appeared to be Cabbalistic. In the circumstances, the pope felt unable to give Plantin's press the requested privilege to print the work.

On hearing the disturbing news, Philip II ordered Montano to travel to Rome in order to 'explain the matter in such a way as to put an end to any doubts.'[31] Fortunately for Montano, Pope Pius V died before his arrival and was succeeded by Gregory XIII, who, anxious to forge closer links with Philip II, proved to be much more malleable than his predecessor. Aided by Cardinal Granvelle, Montano was soon able to persuade the new pontiff to grant Plantin the all-important privilege to print the work.

As Montano explained it to Philip II, Rome had created problems for the Polyglot out of jealousy that such an important project had been instigated not by the papacy but by the Spanish monarch. However, it was not only the papacy that found fault with the work. One of the Polyglot's most virulent antagonists was the Spanish theologian León de Castro, the man responsible for the incarceration of Montano's friend, Luis de León. In 1574 Castro embarked on a rigorous campaign to prohibit the Polyglot, which eventually led to the establishment of a *Congregatio Concilio*, headed by Cardinal Bellarmine, to examine the work. In January 1576, after several months' deliberation, the council announced its verdict. In respect for Philip II, who financed the venture and with whose name it was associated, the council gave the Bible its lukewarm approval. At the same time it made clear that had the Polyglot been presented to it for adjudication in an unpublished form, it would have condemned it as a work unworthy of royal patronage. The Council noted that many of the authorities cited in the work were heretics, both Protestants and Jews, and it recommended that the pope make the *Apparatus* (containing Montano's treatises on Jewish culture and language) exempt from the privilege.

Pope Gregory XIII did not exempt the *Apparatus* from the privilege already awarded to the Polyglot; instead he diplomatically deferred final judgment on the whole eight-volume work to the Spanish Inquisition, now under the generalship of the moderate Gaspar de Quiroga. To assess the work, Quiroga chose the Jesuit scholar Juan de Mariana, who, like Montano, was a humanist, Hebraist, and converso. However, despite the fact that Mariano's sympathies probably lay with Montano, his analysis of the work concurred with that of the *Congregatio Concilio*. He criticized Montano for having quoted Sebastian Münster as an authority and for employing the scholars Lefèvre de la Boderie and Guillaume Postel, both of whom were of suspect doctrine, to prepare and comment on the biblical texts. He also criticized Andreas Masius' Chaldaic paraphrase, a work which relied almost entirely on rabbinical scholarship. Finally, he attacked Montano's treatises in the *Apparatus*, in which he quoted Jewish commentaries while ignoring the Church Fathers' views on the same subjects. Nevertheless, the Jesuit scholar approved the work, stating, generously, that he did not believe it was in conflict with doctrinal principle.[32]

When Mariano pronounced his verdict on the Antwerp Bible, Montano was once again in Spain, having been recalled by Philip II to occupy the position of royal librarian at the Escorial Palace. Montano had initially balked at the idea of returning to his homeland, pointing out to the king that his talents would be better employed in Antwerp, where his knowledge of the political situation made him a useful advisor to the newly appointed governor, Luis de Requesens. This was certainly true; however, it is also clear that he was motivated by other considerations. For one thing, he was anxious to avoid further confrontation with the dangerous León de Castro, who was still accusing him of Protestant and Jewish heresy. Above all, however, he had become accustomed to living in a heterodox environment among men who shared his non-conformist views.

One of these heterodox thinkers was Christophe Plantin; another was his relative, the wealthy converso merchant Luis Pérez. It was through the influence of these two friends that Montano had become increasingly opposed to Requesen's predecessor, the Duke of Alba, whose 'tenth penny' taxes and other draconian measures had caused much economic and social distress in Antwerp, besides debilitating its business community. In 1571 Montano had written to Zayas, in a letter he knew would be shared with the king: 'This land is now ill and people are dying of the plague. God help us. But above all it is afflicted by the publication of the ten percent edict. Because it is a fact that if this is not revised the merchandize of this land will be ruined, and this will occur very quickly ... it will ruin all the land and enrich its neighbors and enemies.'[33] Montano's views on the situation were supported by Cardinal Granvelle. They were also echoed by Fadrique Furió Ceriol in a tract outlining an alternative to Alba's aggressive tactics.[34] As a result of these criticisms of Alba's policy, Philip II recalled the duke to Spain in 1573, replacing him with the more conciliatory Luis de Requesens.

Furious with Montano for criticizing his policy, Alba wrote to Zayas shortly before his recall to Madrid, making his feelings known: 'As regards the continuance here of Dr. Arias Montano, I can tell you that the reason which prompted me to write that this was not desirable was the following: if a good shoemaker is commissioned to produce a painting he will make a botch of it, not even knowing where to begin.'[35] Alba was referring to the famous story of the great Classical Greek painter Apelles, who had accepted a shoemaker's criticism of his depiction of footwear in one of his works, but angrily rejected the man's other comments on his art, berating him with the cruel rebuke, 'Cobbler, do not judge higher than the sandals.' In alluding to this famous reprimand, Alba was making a snide reference to Montano's commoner status, which in the noble's view excluded him from pursuing the art of statecraft. However, it is also possible that the shoemaker jibe was a personal attack on the humanist's own background. A native of Fregenal de la Sierra, Montano was born into a community renowned for its converso shoemakers. Indeed, in the first Inquisition prosecutions against the town's converso community in 1491, three of the six Arias convicted of Judaizing practiced that trade.[36] Alba may well have been calling Zayas' attention to this fact. This was not the only time that one of Montano's contemporaries would make a cutting remark on his Jewish origins, as we will see.

Montano's period in Antwerp clearly had a profound effect on him, politically and religiously. It was here that the humanist became acquainted with the Family of Love—a relationship facilitated again by his friends Luis Pérez and Christophe Plantin, both of whom were Family adherents.[37] Whether Montano ever considered himself a member of the sect is debatable. Certainly he shared the Familists' disdain for the ceremonial and doctrinal trappings of organized religion, as well as their predilection for private, mystical practice. He was also taken with the biblical exegeses of the Family's leader Hendrik Jansen van Barrefelt (who had succeeded Hendrik Niclaes as head of the sect) and specifically with Barrefelt's interpretation of Saint John's Apocalypse, which he, Montano, plundered to write his own *Elucidationes in omnia Apostolorum Scripta*. However, while Montano believed Barrefelt to be a gifted interpreter of the more arcane Scriptures (his gift, according to the humanist, being that of the non-scholar unburdened by theological training), he did not consider him his mystical mentor. Montano's own mystical epiphany, as related to his friend Fray José de Sigüenza, had occurred at his country retreat at Aracena, in 1558, where God had revealed to him the meaning of the Scriptures in just one night.[38] This revelation did not, however, include the Apocalypse, which remained stubbornly intransigent until Barrefelt (who wrote under the pseudonym Hiël, 'the uniform life of God') had shed light on its mysteries, as Montano noted in the introduction to his *Elucidationes*:

> I confess that, although it is thirty years ago since, with divine help, I entered the way of the Lord and trained myself in the Holy Scriptures, yet I failed to understand almost everything in Saint John's Apocalypse, except for one or two, or at the most three, chapters, and those not consecutive, even after I had consulted many commentaries and interpretations. I often used to say that I, who admitted I did not understand it, understood the Apocalypse better than the commentators I had happened to read, since they went on expounding the text in their commentaries as if they had grasped the meaning and as if this were easy to express; but their various interpretations made the text still more obscure and more difficult for me to read than before. I continued in this opinion and this constant desire for understanding until by God's Providence it was brought about that, through the work and help of a certain living witness of Christian truth, to whom the very power and truth of Christ gave the name of Hiël [Barrefelt], another share of light was put before me, by which I could see all the mysteries of this book.[39]

The passage indicates once again that Montano had discovered in the Family of Love a sect that reinforced rather than changed his views on religious observance and Scriptural interpretation. What Montano had found in Antwerp were fellow travelers who had animated him in his own reform mission. It was this mission that the 48-year-old humanist now took to Philip II's palace-monastery at El Escorial.

A New Solomon's Temple

In constructing El Escorial, Philip II intended to create a magnificent monument to his religious piety and regal authority, without, as far as we know, including any overt allusion to King Solomon or his famous edifice. However, by the time the complex was finished in 1588, the palace-monastery had acquired a Solomonic veneer, its royal occupant widely compared to the wise biblical ruler. This transformation appears to have been initiated by Montano, who arrived at El Escorial in 1576, just in time to witness the termination of the royal basilica and to offer his recommendations on its religious iconography. Under Montano's influence, Philip now replaced the obelisks that adorned the basilica's façade with six statues of Jewish kings (Fig. 5.1). These were, from left to right, Jehoshaphat, Hezekiah, David, Solomon, Josiah, and Manasseh. David and Solomon were obvious allusions to Charles V and Philip II—the former a warrior king, whose bloodied hands precluded him from initiating

Fig. 5.1 Kings of Judah, Escorial Basilica. Courtesy of J.M. Monegro

the holy project; the latter, the prudent, pacific son chosen for the task. The other four rulers were all associated with promoting the Temple cult prior to the building's destruction in 580 BC. Obviously, the implication was that Philip II completed this genealogical line of pious Jews.[40]

Soon after the Jewish kings were added to the Basilica façade, Philip II and the prior of the Escorial's Jeronymite Order placed *Judgement of Solomon* canvases in their respective living quarters.[41] Whether these works, promoting peaceful settlement, were hung at the request of Montano is unknown; however, given the humanist's interest in the Escorial's iconography, as well as his influence over the Jeronymite monks (discussed below), this would appear to be the case. Certainly Montano was influential in designing the iconographic frescoes for the royal library, in which Old Testament figures symbolize four of the liberal arts, with the wise Solomon representing Arithmetic.[42]

Evidently Philip II was flattered by the comparison of himself to an Old Testament king renowned for his great wisdom, and thus readily consented to the Solomon references. He would also have seen the propaganda value of the comparison—a strident allusion to Spain as the New Israel, the nation designated by God to defend His divine, Catholic will. There is, however, another message contained within the Solomon allusion, one that undermines Catholic religious intransigence, supplanting it with a call for peaceful religious accord. This message was one close to the hearts of Spain's Dutch subjects, who had promoted the Solomon comparison during Philip's visit to the Netherlands 30 years previously. It was also one favored by the king's librarian, Benito Arias Montano, who had spent the last eight years in the Netherlands working in one way or another to promote this irenic vision. But Montano's Solomon had yet another function. It was a forceful riposte to orthodox churchmen like León de Castro, who, in labeling Old Testament scholars Judaizers, were further separating Catholic culture from its Hebrew progenitor and, in so doing, widening the rift between Old Christian and New Christian Spain. Like the Dutch citizens, Montano used Solomon and his temple as symbols of peace; however, his own irenic message was set against a peculiarly Spanish socio-religious backdrop.

Montano's tactic was the one used earlier by Felipe de la Torre in his *Institución de un Rey Cristiano*, in which the religiously non-conformist author presented ancient Jewish society as a model for correct Christian comportment, before calling upon Philip II to emulate Solomon and construct a temple to virtue. Montano had attempted a similar synergism in his *Dictatum Christianum*, discussed above, and in his controversial *Apparatus*, in which he included a long description of the Jewish Temple. It was thus natural that he would take advantage of Philip's interest in Solomon to further promote the message of Jewish-Christian concord at El Escorial.

Montano must have discussed his Escorial project with friends soon after entering the monastery, for in 1577 an excited Fray Luis de Estrada wrote to him from Alcalá de Henares, suggesting ways of amplifying the Temple imagery:

> And before I forget, I would like to tell you of a great temptation I have: and that is for you to ask his Majesty that he constructs in a chamber, among the other great things in San Lorenzo [El Escorial], an Old Testament tabernacle and a Temple of Solomon with the vestaments of the High Priest, because an image alone is not sufficient to understand the architecture, canopies and textiles; and if your grace orders models based on those printed in the King's Bible [the Antwerp Polyglot Bible], it would be the most wonderous thing to see since the time of Solomon; and if I were to order the tabernacle at least, I would make it in such a way that it could be assembled each year in the main chapel of the Basilica.[43]

However, Estrada was also aware that embarking on such a project had its dangers, wondering out loud if Montano's rival León de Castro would see this as another case of conversos promoting their ancestral religion: '[D]on't you worry that your competitor [Castro] will say that we are Judaizing?'[44] This possibility may indeed have occurred to Montano, preventing him from following up on his friend's suggestion. However, some years later the Jesuit Juan Bautista Villalpando did present Philip with a scale model of the Temple, contained within a replica of ancient Jerusalem. The gift was accompanied by the Jesuit's literary and graphic study of the Temple, *In Ezechielem Explanationes et Apparatus Urbis ac Templi Hierosolymitani*, published with the financial aid of the Spanish monarch.[45]

The model Temple presented to Philip by Villalpando was based on the vision of the prophet Ezekiel, in the Old Testament Book of Ezekiel, a work meticulously examined in a three-volume study written by Villalpando and his fellow Jesuit Jerónimo de Prado, and published between 1596 and 1605. Volume 1 of the work, authored for the most part by Prado, is a careful exegesis of the first 29 chapters of the Book of Ezekiel, in which the prophet communicates to his fellow Babylonian captives God's anger at their sinfulness. It is in retribution for these sins that the Almighty has placed them in captivity, and it is for this reason he will destroy their Temple at Jerusalem. The second volume, written by Villalpando after Prado's death in 1595, focuses on Ezekiel's vision of a future Temple that would serve as proof of God's forgiveness and his continuing love for his chosen people. Here Villalpando not only expatiates on the Ezekiel text, he also provides an elaborate series of graphics, visualizing a magnificent edifice which he claims was also a replica of Solomon's original construction. These views, he admitted, ran counter to those of most Catholic scholars, who saw Ezekiel's vision as a mystical representation of the Church of Christ. While he shared this opinion, he nevertheless also believed that God wished to make reference to a perfect place that had already existed in the Jewish culture, one that represented His timeless message of universal peace.[46] Having thus located Ezekiel's Temple firmly in Jewish antiquity, Villalpando devoted Volume 3 of the work, the *Apparatus*, to a background study of the ancient Jewish culture itself, as Benito Arias Montano had done previously in his Antwerp Bible.

Patronized by Philip II and closely linked to El Escorial, which Villalpando was careful to liken to the Temple, it is usually assumed that the *Explanationes* was yet another 'Counter-Reformation' exercise in glorifying Catholic Spain and its monarch. However, it is also clear that its focus on Old Testament culture was not at all in keeping with a Counter-Reformation Church, which preferred to emphasize the allegorical Christian message of the Old Testament, without celebrating Jewish achievements. Again I would suggest that Philip's Escorial project was being exploited by Hebraists to champion the ancient Jewish culture within a society that was bent on dismissing it as largely inimical and irrelevant.

Although we know little about the backgrounds of Juan Bautista de Villalpando (1552–1608) and Jerónimo de Prado (1547–1593), what we do know suggests that both were New Christians. Villalpando was the son of Gaspar Villalpando and Leonor de Cazalla Molina, both natives of Córdoba. Gaspar Villalpando's occupation—he was a physician—suggests Jewish ancestry, as does his surname, taken from the town of Villalpando near Zamora, and like Zamora (a surname also associated with conversos) the home of an important *Judería* up to the Jewish expulsion of 1492. Villalpando's mother's surnames, Cazalla and Molina, were also associated with conversos in and around Córdoba. More suggestive still of a converso background is the marriage union between Villalpando's sister Ana and

Miguel Jerónimo de Torreblanco, who was a converso on both sides of his family, and whose great-grandfather, Rodrigo de Chillón, a cloth dyer, was prosecuted for Judaizing at the end of the fifteenth century.[47]

Of Villalpando's education, an early biographical source states that his original intention was to study Arts at Alcalá de Henares, before a chance encounter with the architect Juan de Herrera in Madrid led to a change of focus.[48] It was while working as an assistant to Herrera, who from 1572 onward was the chief architect of El Escorial, that Villalpando became acquainted with Philip II's great architectural project. When Villalpando later joined the Jesuits he took his architectural skills with him, executing building projects for the order in Córdoba, Seville, and Baeza, while pursuing his studies in Hebrew and Theology.

It was at the Jesuit College in Córdoba that Villalpando met his later collaborator, Jerónimo de Prado. A gifted theologian, Prado was born and raised in Baeza, where he taught Scripture at the university founded by Juan de Ávila, an institution constantly under attack from the Córdoba Inquisition officials, suspicious of its converso faculty.[49] After Ávila's death in 1569, many of his disciples entered the Society of Jesus, attracted to the order by its emphasis on humanist education as well as by its refusal to implement *limpieza de sangre* examinations. Prado himself joined the newly founded Baeza Jesuit College in 1572, while continuing to teach Scripture at the university.

Villalpando and Prado were members of Jesuit colleges—Baeza and Córdoba—closely associated with conversos. It is noteworthy that in 1572, two years before Villalpando entered the Córdoban Jesuit College, the rector wrote to the Jesuit General Francisco de Borja, complaining that while his institution had an enrolment of 600 students, many of whom were from wealthy families, most entered for a humanist education alone, rather than to pursue a religious career. Those boys with a religious vocation, he wrote, tended to enter the Dominican college, which they stated was an institution for gentlemen, while the Jesuit college was only for Jews.[50] The characterization of the Jesuits as a Jewish order had been present almost since the Society's inception, leading Old Christian members to call for *limpieza* legislation. This was always firmly resisted by Loyola and his successor Diego de Láinez, himself a converso. However, the anti-converso lobby continued to grow during Francisco de Borja's office, effectively preventing Juan Alfonso de Polanco from becoming the order's fourth general after Borja's death. Instead, the General Congregation of 1576 elected the Flemish Everard Mercurian, who was then followed, in 1580, by the young Italian Claudio Acquaviva. It was during Acquaviva's tenure that pressure mounted for the order to impose a *limpieza de sangre* statute. This was enacted at the General Congregation of 1593, the year Villalpando and Prado's Ezekiel study received a papal license.[51]

Villalpando and Prado's *Explanationes* was written against a background of increasing tension within the Jesuits, a situation that reflected the antagonism in Spanish society itself between Old and New Christians. Reacting to this deepening anti-converso mood, a number of prominent converso Jesuits wrote in defense of the New Christians' contribution to their order and to Christian culture in general. In his *memoria* of 1593, the Italian Jesuit Antonio Possevino noted that the first converso Jesuits were renowned for their intellectual contribution to the order and their dedication to advancing the Jesuit message abroad. In this respect, he wrote, they were like the first Jewish Christians, who advanced Jesus' message. Indeed, Jewish converts to Christianity had made major contributions to the religion throughout the ages and up to the present time. The Spanish conversos, for example, had been instrumental in taking the Christian message to the New World as well as in 'repairing' the Faith in the Old one.[52]

While Possevino emphasized the Jews' contribution to Christian culture, his Spanish counterpart, Juan de Mariana, noted their influence on Spanish civilization. In his history of Spain, published in 1593, Mariana presented Túbal, the nephew of Noah, as the original colonizer of the peninsula. He also noted, vaguely citing 'Jewish books,' that many of Spain's early urban settlements, including Toledo, were founded by Jews who had fled Judah at the time of the Babylonian captivity.[53] Taking the Jewish contribution to Spanish culture many steps further, the Toledan Jesuit Jerónimo Román de la Higuera stated that the Jews were an important presence on the Iberian Peninsula as early as Solomon's reign, establishing communities in Toledo, Sagunto, and Numancia (all three of which were emblems of Spanish national pride). According to Higuera, these communities were augmented by other Jews entering the peninsula during the Babylonia captivity. Thus substantial numbers of Jews had entered Iberia before the death of Christ, a different type of Jew, Higuera noted, to the ones guilty of crucifying the Messiah. In fact, the Jewish communities of Toledo and Zamora had written a letter to their counterparts in Jerusalem at the time of the crucifixion, opposing the sentence. Finally, Higuera noted that after the death of Christ 500 of His early Jewish followers had left Jerusalem, eventually making their way to Iberia, where they took the Christian message to the Sephardic communities. And so it would seem that the first converts to Christianity on the peninsula were Sephardic Jews. Higuera's source for all this information on the Sephardim was the eleventh-century writer Julian Pérez, whose chronicle, fortuitously discovered by Higuera in Toledo, was based on ancient letters unearthed in the city's Santa Justa church. In fact the chronicle was a fake, invented by Higuera himself in order to advance his own singular vision of Spanish history.[54]

Like Mariano and Higuera, Villalpando also presented the Jews as early colonizers of Spain. In the second volume of the *Explanationes*, published in 1605, he noted that the tomb of one of Solomon's tax collectors had recently been discovered in Sagunto, testimony to a large and thriving Sephardic colony a thousand years before the birth of Christ.[55] According to Villalpando, the early Jewish diaspora community, inspired by God to disseminate his message, was much greater than modern society was aware; certainly as large as the Jewish population of the Holy Land, which he reckoned to be well over six million. Of this community Villalpando wrote praisingly:

> [T]he Promised Land [Israel] was in one sense an immense seedbed for the whole World; thousands and thousands of Hebrews dispersed throughout all the regions; and this occurred because of a divine plan. In those times the Hebrews were sincere in their belief in God, maintaining and teaching their religion: they were God's heirs, the chosen people; all the other nations walked far from the true Faith, walking dangerously along inaccessible paths, along the abrupt precipices of the Gentiles, following un-confessable superstitions, immersed in total ignorance of the divine and wrapped up in a dense fog of idolatry; falling down and losing their way. Thus divine providence willed that the Hebrews sowed their good seed and disseminated across three quarters of the globe, in each of the regions of these three parts, in each of their cities, their fortresses, villages and countryside; like a yeast that spoilt all the Gentile dough with the aim of creating a bread that could be presented at the divine table. For their part, the Gentiles brought forth no fruit, or a very small one; *this is precisely what the Gentiles will be reproached with at the solemn day of Judgement, and they will not be able to present excuses for their ignorance [Rom. 1,21]* (my italics).[56]

It was as a result of the size and scope of ancient Israel and its colonies—in Villalpando's view rivaling the modern Spanish Empire—that Solomon was able to build the grandiose edifice described by Ezekiel in his vision. Indeed the Jesuit tells us that the Temple was another wonder of the ancient world, a magnificent, perfect creation through which God introduced many important principles of architecture. These included the Corinthian order, erroneously attributed to the Greeks, who substituted their own symbol of peace, the olive leaf, for a Jewish palm frond on the capital.[57]

Villalpando's elaborate study of Solomon's Temple may have been a tribute to Philip II as a wise and prudent king and Spain as God's chosen realm, but it was also a celebration of the ancient Jewish culture and its continuing relevance to a modern Catholic one. Like Montano's Solomonic ornamentation of El Escorial, Villalpando's work championed religious synergism. In this respect, both Montano's and Villalpando's Temple projects bear comparison with the much more audacious Granada Lead Books fraud, carried out by, among others, the Morisco Miguel de Luna. Significantly, Luna spent time at the Escorial library in the 1580s as an Arabic translator, where he was able to observe at close quarters Philip II's susceptibility for Solomon imagery, something he was careful to incorporate into his own integrationist project.

The Lead Books Fraud

The Granada Lead Books fraud began in 1588, when a lead box was discovered by workmen as they were dismantling the old minaret of what had been the city's central mosque. Inside the box was a bone, a piece of cloth, an image of the Virgin, and a parchment, purportedly written by the first Bishop of Granada, a certain Cecilius, who, along with his brother Tesiphon, was presented as an early Arab convert to Christianity. The parchment text, written in Latin, Greek, and Arabic, revealed Cecilius' own history besides recording and interpreting a millenarian prophesy by Saint John. It also disclosed the origins of the relics: the bone belonged to Saint Stephen and the cloth to the Virgin, who had used it to wipe away her tears at Christ's crucifixion. All of this was revealed to the Bishop of Granada by Miguel de Luna, who, in his capacity as professional translator, was called in to render the document into Castilian and verify its authenticity.

Several years later, after a series of bound lead discs (or 'Lead Books'), inscribed with Arabic script, were found on the city's Valparaiso hill, Luna's services were once more called upon. The translation was, however, made difficult, Luna noted, by the Arabic letters, which he called

'Solomonic,' a neologism that was clearly meant to convey the writings' antiquity as well as their recondite or hermetic qualities—the ancient Jewish King Solomon being associated with the hermetic arts. The discs' magical properties were also conveyed by the material on which they were written—a base metal which, presumably, given alchemical treatment, would turn into a noble one. Evidently, the authors of the discs wished to ensure the success of their synergistic venture by appealing to both historical narrative (albeit falsified) and the occult. They were also clearly mindful of Philip II's attraction to the historic Solomon, as well as his weakness for the Solomonic, or hermetic, arts.[58]

Pieced together, the Lead Books of Granada reveal the following story: in the first century, soon after the death of Christ, the Virgin Mary sent Saint James and six companions, including the Arabs Cecilius and Tesiphon, on an evangelizing mission in Iberia (Hispania). As part of this venture they took with them a prophesy revealed to the Virgin by the Angel Gabriel, known as 'The Certainty of the Gospel,' which declared, among other things, that God had chosen the Arabic language 'to exalt his holy law and his sacred gospel and his holy church at the end of Time.'[59] The group was ordered to bury Mary's gospel in a holy place, revealed to them by an apparition of a dead man (as it transpired, the Valparaiso hill in Granada). They were then to continue on their evangelical mission, remaining on the peninsula until they had converted at least one person to Christianity. Unfortunately, the pagan Celto-Iberians of Hispania were unmoved by the Good News. It was not until the group reached Córdoba, on their return from Galicia, that they gained their first convert, an Arab named Aben Almogueira, who then accompanied them back to Granada.[60] It was here that Cecilius, now recognized as the city's bishop, was martyred in Nero's anti-Christian pogrom.

A shamefully patent advertisement for Arab preeminence within early Christianity, it seems inconceivable that the Lead Books could have gained support among Granada's Old Christian community. However, the authors of the Books were not only promoting the Arab (Morisco) community, they were also celebrating Granada as the site of Spain's first Christian Church, something that had an enormous appeal to all sections of the city's Old Christian population. The Books also contained other revelations that were likely to appeal to Spanish Catholics, among which was the Virgin's affirmation that she was indeed immaculately conceived, thus supporting Spain's Marianists in their campaign to have the belief dogmatized. There were also concessions to the Catholic Church's obsession with reliquary, the fraudsters having placed pieces of bone and ashes in the area where the Books were located, which the Books themselves revealed to be the remains of Spain's first Christian martyrs. Significantly, the authors avoided mention of the Trinity, and were careful to describe Jesus not as the son of God, but as the spirit of God; nevertheless, there was a lot here guaranteed to appeal to Granada's Old Christian community, and to encourage it to accept some less palatable philo-Morisco elements.

Not everyone in Granada was convinced of the Books' authenticity, however. The chronicler Luis del Mármol Carvajal even suggested that the bishop, Pedro de Castro, investigate the translator Miguel de Luna himself.[61] Castro did not heed the suggestion, even though Luna had recently published a philo-Muslim work based on a document he claimed to have discovered in the Escorial library. The work, *La verdadera historia del rey Don Rodrigo*, was, according to Luna, his translation of an eighth-century manuscript written by an Arab eye-witness to the Islamic conquest of Spain, which presented the Muslim conquerors as wise and able rulers who encouraged cultural and ethnic mixing, a policy that led to socio-religious integration and peace throughout al-Andalus.[62]

Although Luna's *La verdadera historia* should have given Bishop Castro pause for thought, he was already too captivated by the Lead Books' magic to reflect on the credibility of their translator. Others in the cathedral were more circumspect, however, recommending that the Turpiana parchment and the Books be scrutinized by outside experts. Ironically, the first of these learned adjudicators was Benito Arias Montano, who in 1593 was invited to Granada to examine the parchment. Aware of Castro's own bias toward the find, Montano politely refused to make the trip, pleading ill-health. Undeterred, Castro arranged for him to inspect the work in Seville, a short distance from his Aracena retreat, where he quickly determined that its Latin was a modern variety, not an ancient one. Two years later, Montano was once more contacted for his expert opinion, this time on the Lead Books. Again his view was that they were forgeries: the Arabic script was not one he had ever contemplated in either an ancient or a modern document, and the works contained important terminological anachronisms and errors of historical fact.

Montano did not offer an opinion on the real authors of the Books or their motives; however, there can be little doubt that he saw the works for what they were: an attempt by the now much reduced Morisco community of Granada to ingratiate itself with the Old Christian authorities. He may even have been somewhat sympathetic to their goals; he was, after all, engaged in a similar fight against Old Christian prejudice. The difference, of course, was that he did not forge documents to advance his cause. As a humanist attempting to separate myth and superstition from Christian practice, he would have found this abhorrent. He would also have noted that in advancing their own cause, the Moriscos had prejudiced that of the *judeoconversos*, whose Jewish ancestors were eclipsed by the Arab converts in the Lead Books' evangelical narrative. Montano expressed none of these concerns publicly, although he undoubtedly discussed them with his friend and amanuensis Pedro de Valencia, who, as we will see, later penned a more hostile attack on the Books, in which he emphasized the forgeries' detrimental effect on the Judeo-Christian tradition.

Unsurprisingly, Bishop Castro did not request Montano's expert advice further, preferring to count on scholars who could be relied upon to deliver a positive verdict on the Lead Books' authenticity. By carefully choosing his collaborators, while vigorously resisting the call for the documents to be sent to Rome, Castro was able to protect the finds and promote their legitimacy up until his death in 1624. Thereafter the Lead Books were dispatched to the Holy See, where, after decades of deliberation, they were ruled anathema by the papacy in 1682; not that this verdict diminished their stature in Granada itself, or that of their supposed author Cecilius, who became and has remained the patron saint of the city.

Benito Arias Montano's Private Faith

Ironically, Benito Arias Montano, the man called upon by Bishop Castro to assess the Lead Books' find in 1593, was himself a clandestine dissident who had been working for much of his professional life on transforming Spain's socio-religious mores. Latterly this secret campaign had taken place at Philip II's showcase palace at El Escorial, which Montano identified as an important center for reform. We have already seen how the humanist changed the Palace iconography to present a message of religious peace and concordance. However, Montano did not stop there. He also focused his attention on the Escorial's community of Jeronymite monks, sowing a reform message within the community, based on his own religious views and those of his Familist friends in the Netherlands. The objective, it seems, was to influence a religious group close to the king, who would in turn promote evangelical reform within the palace. A curious letter, written by the Antwerp printer Christophe Plantin in 1580, in reply to one of Montano's Jeronymite pupils, gives some indication of Montano's proselytizing activities:

> I was overjoyed by your letter, Reverend Father of Christ, for various reasons, of which the chief is that it tended to the greater glory of God, and the other that you can now be a comfort to our Montano, since you tell me that you have entered the true path, following Him who by the grace of God preceded you in it...But what use is all this to you since, as your letter states, you now have before you someone whose example you can rightly follow? For, to tell you the truth, I cannot accept any of the praise you heap on me in your letter. And so take care, Reverend Father, if, as you write, you love me and wish to be loved by me in return, which through the grace of God I am bound to do, lest you ascribe to me, a bodily, visible and thus corruptible person, what belongs to another, to the invisible and incorruptible God.[63]

It is clear from Plantin's caveat that he was perturbed by his correspondent's unconstrained euphoria and, it seems, imprudent remarks. Unfortunately, the monk's letter has not survived, and thus we can only guess at the nature of its contents. We do, however, have a much more informative account of Montano's religious instruction at El Escorial, this provided by another Jeronymite pupil, his friend and disciple Fray José de Sigüenza.

In 1592 José de Sigüenza was denounced to the Inquisition by a number of fellow monks for certain heretical beliefs which, as it became clear in the trial that followed, he had imbibed from his mentor Montano. In the trial Sigüenza was reported as proclaiming, 'If I have Arias Montano and the Bible, I don't need any other [religious] books.'[64] Sigüenza did not deny the comment, although he tried to dismiss it by stating that he did not read much (clearly untrue), and that Montano provided an accessible summary of a broad theological corpus. In the course of the trial Sigüenza was also said to have made the following disrespectful remarks: 'the saints say fanciful things at times and not the sense of the Holy Scripture'; 'one wastes a lot of time in studying Scholastic Theology, which is of little use'; 'in order to understand Holy Scripture one should not follow the Saints but the Hebrew [texts], ignoring the views of the Saints and Scholastic Theology'; 'many barbarians and Gentiles, Turks and Moors, although they have no knowledge of our faith, can be saved just by believing in only one God and abiding by natural law'; 'my advice is to stop reading devotional books, just read the Gospels and entrust yourself to God, who will illuminate you.'[65]

Despite the fact that Sigüenza's prosecutors had called for a death sentence, the friar managed to escape this ordeal, with nothing more serious than a short term of imprisonment. This sentence must certainly have come as a surprise to Montano, who had left El Escorial for Seville at the beginning of the trial, undoubtedly fleeing what he believed to be his own imminent incarceration. In Seville, at least, he was surrounded by his family and intimate friends. He was also next to a port, which would offer him the chance of rapid escape if the Inquisition turned its attention toward his own 'heretical' activities.

Montano would, of course, have had little difficulty in escaping Spain, given his close relationship with the Núñez Pérez family, who had contacts throughout Europe. This merchant family had maintained a close relationship with Montano during his career, helping to transform his bureaucratic emoluments into a small fortune.[66] For his part, Montano had been of service to the Núñez Pérez clan on at least two occasions: once in Antwerp during his Polyglot Bible period, when he had acted as a channel for Luis Pérez's and his merchant friends' grievances against Alba to Philip II; and later, in 1577, on his return from Antwerp, when he had become involved in a dispute between a group of Spanish converso merchants operating out of Lisbon and the Portuguese king.

The Portuguese affair began in 1576, when King Sebastian demanded that the Spanish merchant community residing in Lisbon pay a fee, similar to that paid by Portuguese converso merchants, which would indemnify them in the event that they were prosecuted by the Portuguese Inquisition for Judaizing. This royal requirement obviously posed a major problem for the Spanish merchants: if they paid up, they would be admitting to having converso roots, something they had always been very careful to deny, at least officially. If they did not pay, then they undoubtedly risked the ire of the Portuguese king. Their response was to wax appalled and offended, and to write to King Philip, through their spokesmen Alonso Núñez Contador, Gonzalo Pérez Martínez, and Diego López, asking that the royal chaplain, Benito Arias Montano ('who has had contact with us before and knows us and our families'), be allowed to investigate the case. In 1578 Montano traveled to Lisbon, where he spoke with the merchants, many of whom were members of the converso merchant families he was acquainted with in Seville and Antwerp. As a result of Montano's report, in which he assured Philip II that the merchants were men of proven *limpieza de sangre*, a clear lie, the Spanish king intervened on their behalf and the Portuguese monarch withdrew his demand. It is inconceivable, of course, that the Lisbon merchants would have written to the king, soliciting Montano's services, without first contacting the humanist himself, who, as they pointed out, was well known to them. It is thus likely that the Lisbon trip was stage-managed by Montano and the merchants, with Montano using his position at court to deliver some converso friends from a potentially ruinous situation.[67]

In March 1578, having concluded his Portuguese business, Montano returned to Spain via his Aracena retreat, laden with a cartload of seashells that later decorated his roof. This was not merely gratuitous adornment. For Montano the shell was a manifestation of the perfect symmetry of God's universe; it was also a symbol of his own stoical philosophy, protecting him, wherever he went, from the barbs of his many detractors.[68] No sooner had he arrived in Aracena than these attacks began once again, this time emanating from a Seville Dominican monastery, whose friars were walking around the city 'mocking my writings and my name.'[69] While Montano does not elaborate on the nature of the Domincians' attack, it is likely that they were making allusions to his Jewish sympathies, as the Dominican León de Castro had done in previous years. Judging by Lope de Vega's snide allusion in the following verse, it would seem evident that rumors of Montano's own Jewish background were now widespread. Lope wrote:

> Cured ham of the Spanish pig
> Of the famous Aracena mountains
> Where Arias Montano fled from the world
>
> [*Jamón presunto de español marrano,*
> *de sierra famosa de Aracena,*
> *adonde huyó del mundo Arias Montano*][70]

However, the first line of the verse, as Lope was aware, could also be read as 'suspicious ham from the Spanish Judaizer [*marrano*].' Thus Lopé's satirical verse plays on the fact that the area in which Montano was born and which he chose for his country retreat was renowned for both the quality of its pigs and the size of its converso or, as was commonly believed, crypto-Jewish population.

Living in an area in which pigs were so prominent, it was a difficult task for conversos like Montano to avoid eating ham without inciting rumors of Jewish practice. Montano himself seems to have solved this problem by stating that he did not eat any type of meat, and if he did so on occasion, it was without enjoyment. This did not, however, prevent his good friend Gabriel de Zayas from dispatching two legs of ham to him in May 1577, in the wake of León de Castro's accusations of Judaizing. The gift would seem to allude to a ribald type of Spanish genre poetry (see Chap. 3), in which conversos sent each other pieces of ham, provoking mutual accusations of Jewish practice. Unfortunately, we do not know what Zayas wrote in the letter that accompanied the gift. We do have Montano's reply, however: 'I beg your honor not to send hams, not even one. I would prefer that you served them to yourself and ate them, for this would give me most pleasure.'[71] It would seem that Montano was turning the tables on his friend, inviting him to eat the ham and prove his own Old Christian legitimacy, a common ploy in this converso game.

Given the rumors that were circulating on Montano's philo-Semitisim, it was inevitable that his frequent escapes to his Aracena retreat would be associated with clandestine religious practice. This was indeed a reasonable assumption, although the secret religious activity was not Judaism, as many claimed, but an evangelical and mystical Christianity, in which the Hebrew Bible was considered an important spiritual guide. This credo, I would suggest, was shared by a small circle of Andalusian friends who were frequent visitors to Aracena. From Montano's letters to Zayas and Plantin, as well as from a number of other sources, we are able to create a composite picture of the humanist's close circle during this time, whose character was clearly converso: the merchant Diego Núñez Pérez, to whom Montano was related; the cathedral prior Pedro Vélez de Guevara, who was a relative of Montano's adoptive mother, Isabel Vélez; the physicians and scholars Francisco Sánchez de Oropesa, Simón de Tovar, and Francisco de Arce (who Montano referred to as 'my instructor in surgery'); the Hebrew scholars Juan de Cano and Pedro de Valencia (Montano's secretary and disciple); and the cathedral clerics Luciano de Negron (scion of a wealthy banking family) and Francisco Pacheco (second cousin to the painter Francisco Pacheco, Diego Velázquez's mentor). It is from Pacheco's *Second Sermon on Liberty* (examined in this chapter) that we gain an intimate picture of this group of friends, brought together by Montano in his isolated country house to discuss their private religious beliefs without fear of reproof.

It is tempting, of course, to compare this Seville group of non-conformists described by Pacheco in his *Sermon on Liberty* with Montano's circle of Familist friends in Antwerp; and in many respects the comparison is an apposite one, the members of both groups being attracted to stoical and quietist practice. However, once again it is important to emphasize that the Seville group's views were formed independently of the Family of Love, in a peculiarly Spanish, New Christian setting. Thus while Montano undoubtedly relayed Familist secrets to his Seville friends (it would be naïve to believe otherwise), there is little to suggest that he created a Familist cell on Andalusian soil.

After his 1578 trip to Portugal Montano spent 18 months at Aracena, writing scriptural commentaries while instructing his young secretary Pedro de Valencia in Hebrew and Aramaic. He left reluctantly for El Escorial in September 1579, but returned south often during the next decade, finally retiring to Andalusia in 1592 to escape the possible consequences of José de Sigüenza's trial for heresy. During the last six years of his life, Montano divided his time between his country house at Aracena and a villa on the outskirts of Seville, devoting himself to his scientific and scriptural studies. These included his *Commentaries on Thirty-One Psalms of David*, an intimate valediction to his friends, whose humanist character he explored through reference to the Old Testament poems.[72]

Just before his death, in June 1598, Montano took up residency in the Santiago monastery in Seville. Once again, however, his association with the order appears to have been superficial. In fact, Montano all but ignored the monastery's cloisters during his final days, preferring to spend his last moments in the house of his converso merchant friend Diego Núñez Pérez, whose daughter, Ana Núñez, prepared his corpse for burial.[73]

Did Montano move to the Núñez Pérez house so that his body could be washed and prepared for burial following the Jewish custom? It is certainly tempting to think so. Not that Montano was ever a Judaizer in the strictest sense of the term; he was, however, a religious non-conformist who fashioned a private credo for himself in which the Jewish religion and cultural heritage figured prominently. Despite all the pressures on him to abandon this interest, he never did so. Rather, I would suggest, he carried his Jewish interests as a badge of honor, a mark of solidarity with his Sephardic ancestors. Montano was above all a man of independent religious views. It is not unlikely that he took this attitude to his deathbed, where he died, as he had lived, steadfastly following his own religious course—one designed for his salvation as a humanist and New Christian.

Francisco Pacheco (1540?–1599)

There is much about canon Francisco Pacheco's biography that is a mystery. First, the canon's date of birth. On his tombstone Pacheco is presented as dying at the age of 64, which would mean he was born in 1535. However, in a document signed by the canon shortly before his death, his birth date is presented as 1532, and in two much earlier documents, as 1540. Equally mysterious is Pacheco's university career. In 1570 he stood before an academic committee, claiming that he had graduated from Seville University in 1555 with a diploma in arts and letters, and had then gone on to study for his bachelor's degree (for three years from 1560 to 1563, and one other year subsequently) in theology. He was now asking for official recognition of these studies, and to support his case he presented four students who testified that they had studied with him during his time at the university. As a result of these testimonies, and without any official record of his attendance at the Seville institution, or any evidence that he had taken an exam, he was awarded a degree in theology on 20 March 1570. It is perhaps noteworthy that one of the members of Pacheco's adjudication committee was Pedro Vélez de Guevara, a good friend of both Pacheco and Benito Arias Montano, and a powerful presence in Seville's cathedral, whose support could quite easily have influenced a university committee in its task of reaching the right decision.

The third mysterious aspect of Pacheco's biography is his lineage. In a *limpieza de sangre* examination undertaken from 1 to 24 September 1592 to gain his canonry, Pacheco stated that his father was Hernando Aguilar Pacheco, from the town of Villasevil de los Pachecos in Cantabria, and that his mother was Elvira López de Miranda, whose family came from Miranda de Ebro.[74] The apostolic notary in charge of the investigation, Juan Santillana, was thus dispatched to the village of Villasevil, where he interviewed seven people, four of whom were, unlikely though it may seem, nonagenarians. All stated that Hernando Aguilar Pacheco (Pacheco's father), who had left the village some 80 years previously, was the son of Juan Vallejo Pacheco of Villasevil and Mencia Villegas de Castaneda from Santa Maria de Cayon, half a league away from Villasevil. No one knew Francisco Pacheco, but all said that they understood he was the son of Hernando Aguilar Pacheco and a certain Elvira López de Miranda, whom Hernando had met and married in Jerez de la Frontera. All the witnesses described both paternal grandparents as *hidalgos* and Old Christians, without any Jewish or Moorish stain; indeed, all noted that the area was famous for its Old Christian character.

Having concluded his investigation in Villasevil, Santillana traveled to Miranda de Ebro, a prosperous commercial center in the province of Burgos, in which, prior to the 1492 Expulsion, when the López Miranda family abandoned the town, the Jews represented a quarter of the population.[75] Unsurprisingly, given the length of time that had elapsed since the family's departure, the investigator was unable to find anyone who was able to provide him with information on them. Thus the next step was to return south and conclude his investigations in Jerez de la Frontera, where Francisco Pacheco was born, where his parents were married, and where three generations of his mother's family, the López Mirandas, had resided. If the object of the exercise was to determine whether or not Pacheco was from an Old Christian background, then a visit to Jerez de Frontera was essential. However, inexplicably, Santillana concluded his inquiries in Miranda de Ebro. On 30 September 1592, Francisco Pacheco was awarded his canonry, although no information was provided to the adjudicating committee on the background of his mother's family.

Why had the *limpieza de sangre* investigation not included Jerez de la Frontera, only a day's journey from Seville? The most likely explanation is that an investigation in Jerez would have revealed a different family background to the one Pacheco wished to promote officially within the cathedral. Indeed, Pacheco's claim that his surname was taken from a Cantabrian village had become something of a cliché in sixteenth-century Spain, employed particular by conversos who wished to add substance to their protests of Old Christian hidalgo roots. The surname Pacheco was, in fact, quite common in Jerez de la Frontera, as an examination of the city's notarial archives attests. The name may have been assumed by members of a merchant community in the mid-fifteenth century when Juan Pacheco, the Marqués of Villena, was Jerez's *Corregidor*, and created a large client network within the city.[76] This, I would suggest, is a more feasible source of the canon's family surname than a Cantabrian village.

A better clue to Francisco Pacheco's background is provided by his mother's family, the López, a name popular among Jerez's converso community.[77] Pacheco's mother Elvira López de Miranda was the sister of María López, the painter Francisco Pacheco's grandmother. María's son, Juan Pérez, and two of her grandsons, Juan Pérez and Pedro López, were tailors, while a third grandson, Mateo Pérez, was a linen worker, trades traditionally associated with Jewish and converso artisans.[78]

Francisco Pacheco's converso origins are not only suggested by a family background he was careful to hide, however; they are also apparent in his coterie of friends and in two of his works, *Sátira apologética en defensa del divino Dueñas* (1569?) and *Dos sermones sobre la instauración de la libertad del espíritu para vivir recta y felizmente* (1575), both of which were modeled on Horace's critical satires and epistles. The first of these works, the *Sátira*, is an attempt to draw a distinction between a small group of intellectual poets and the mass of versifiers who plied their rhymes in the streets of Seville. Pacheco refers to the second group as a *musaica pestilencia*, corrupting an anti-semitic term used by Old Christian society (*mosaica pestilencia* or Jewish plague) in order to express his own prejudice for ignorant bards and their false muses:

> What beast will have the patience
> To pick up a pen and go to war
> Against that musaic pestilence
>
> [*Qué bestia habrá que tenga ya paciencia
> Que tome la pluma y haga guerra
> Contra aquesta musaica pestilencia*][79]

The satire, Pacheco tells us, in a short, tongue-in-cheek introduction to the work, came about in the following way. One day, in 1569, he and his friend, Licentiate Dueñas, were in conversation in the cathedral when a certain scandalous youth and 'poet' by the name of Cuevas, the son of a physician, had walked by without doffing his cap. Insulted, Dueñas had cited some verse which made an allusion to bad manners. This angered the young man to such an extent that he got together with some of his poet friends and wrote a satire against Dueñas. This, in turn, inspired a whole spate of satires, in which the two rival poetic groups attacked each other's artistic credentials and family lineage. Some had even fled the city, Pacheco tells us, waggishly one assumes, after being accused of being 'submissives' (*'someticos,'* for which read sodomites and Jews, *semiticos*).[80] In the middle of this melee, Pacheco himself had written a satire in defense of Dueñas, which he had read out on *las gradas* (the cathedral steps, a public meeting place), in the Plaza de San Francisco, and in other public places. Shortly thereafter, two 'poets' from the rival groups had loudly discussed the merits of the poem outside the house of the *corregidor*, who immediately arrested them and many others besides, so that very soon the city jail was full of poets. At which point Pacheco, according to his satirical account, wrote yet another satire, this time in defense of the jailed poets. Placated by these verses, the *corregidor*, who considered himself something of a bard (Pacheco quotes some of his inane doggerel), immediately released all the poet prisoners.

Pacheco's short introduction sets the tone for the satire itself—a trenchant and ribald attack on bad poetry, full of sexual and scatological innuendo, with numerous sly references to the New Christian character of the city's literateurs. Many of these references are unfathomable to a modern reader; others are much more evident: the poet Fernando de Herrera's Jewish background, for example, is indicated in his verbal joust with his poetic rival, 'el gorrero' (the scrounger): 'They call each other Jewish sons-of-bitches/the poets' songs don't lie'[81]; or the humanist Juan de Malara's semitic features, an allusion to which is subtly inserted into a passage in which Pacheco notes how few financial rewards his friend had gained from his epic poem *Hercules animado*: 'And if he [Malara] hadn't already been defeated enough, Hercules, in revenge, struck his big nose with his club'[82]; or even a subtle hint, perhaps, at his own New Christian origins: 'I once passed a time in this self deceit [writing bad poetry], producing more verses in an hour than [the physician] Bernal kills patients in a year. That was certainly a Moor's life [wretched period].'[83]

While Pacheco's poem is clearly styled on the satires of Horace (a poet favored by Spain's post-Tridentine humanists), it would also appear to borrow heavily from a homegrown tradition of poetical satire, visible in the fifteenth-century *cancioneros*, in which conversos make humorous and very often vicious allusions to each other's Sephardic backgrounds. Pacheco's satire was not meant as an attack on converso poets, however, but rather as a commentary, in Horation mode, on the prejudices and pretentions endemic to his own society, in which the *limpieza* issue was at the forefront. In his *Dos sermones sobre la instauración de la libertad*, written several years after the satire, Pacheco once again turns to Horace as a model for social criticism. He also adopts the Roman's Epicurean ideals (*autarkeia*, or inner self-sufficiency) as a means of combating the vicissitudes of his society.

Pacheco's *Dos sermones sobre la instauración de la libertad*, both of which are directed to his friend Pedro Vélez de Guevara, chart the decline of society from a mythical Golden Age to its present state of corruption.[84] The first satire begins with an image of an Arcadian idyll, where there were no laws, no money, no kings, titles, or clerics greedy for the bishop's miter, and in which man's life 'passed by in a golden happiness while he was his own master.'[85] Then impicty and greed entered this utopia in tandem, impairing man's sense of freedom, his virtuous conduct, and his wisdom. Soon ambition triumphs over liberty and virtue; men thirst for private property, and laws appear to defend it. Forgetting the true faith, men begin to worship stone idols; they convert God into a magus who exists only to satisfy their own private caprice. Monarchies arise, accompanied by wars. People are enslaved. A nobility emerges, obsessed with its titles and coats of arms. It promotes the idea that 'a man's value rests in his blood,'[86] ignoring the fact that all men have been created equal 'with the same clay and breath from the same flame.'[87] And yet the stupid *vulgo* holds these men and their ill-attained wealth and titles in high esteem, while it regards men who gain their living in peaceful pursuits as lesser mortals.[88]

Pacheco now focuses his attention on court society, where the king and nobles strut like peacocks in their fine apparel, a colorful veil hiding a putrid and corrupt core: '[W]hat ambitions, what spirits, worse than the excrement of slaves, what rage and what brutal voices, what atrocious thirst for blood and money! ... with what miserable ambition and greed do they, when consumed with envy, squash everyone else, not allowing anyone to be equal with themselves.'[89] This same greed for power and riches also affects clerical society, where men like Apicio (a pseudonym), like an astute politician, uses his wealth, influence, and charm to buy himself a bishop's miter, whereupon he fills his bishop's court with family, courtesans, and social parasites.

As a contrast to this noble and clerical corruption, Pacheco presents us with two *letrado* friends, Juan de Ovando and Juan López de Velasco, men who devote their lives to the state, an onerous task for which they gain little praise:

> What man in his right mind would envy you, Velasco, for having received the heavy tasks and affairs of such a large realm, for executing those decisions made by the great Philip after consulting you, and to place on your shoulders the worries that such an enormous universe creates? ... how many times have we seen that a preeminent post like this one and the favor it conveys have enveloped the unprepared man in envy, and that fortune, like a great storm, has torn him from on high, leaving him speechless![90]

Faced with social violence, deceit, corruption, and hypocrisy, Pacheco turns to the Stoics and Epicureans as guides to inner serenity, albeit without mentioning the two philosophies by name. Instead he refers to his *autarkeia*, in general terms:

> As far as I'm concerned, my only pleasure is the precious wellbeing that costs me little. I only have to wish for it and calm my mind, dispersing the

clouds that cover it. This is the liberty of the spirit that has a guilt-free conscience and is free from mean ambitions and fear, despises riches and vain honors, and does not countenance any servile act. This virtue is the only one I pursue with all my heart.[91]

In his second sermon, Pacheco elaborates on this philosophical code, likening the spiritually tranquil man to a person safe on a headland, observing a stormy sea beyond. Separated from those people who traverse the treacherous waters in search of power and wealth, he has protected himself from the volatile world they inhabit. This man resides in a private fortress, insulated from 'society's whirlwind' and the 'ignoble *vulgo* ... motivated by a persistent desire for vengeance or by a fit or rage.'[92] And the humanist contrasts this inner spiritual sanctum with a turbulent Christendom, dominated by laws and edicts that do nothing to put troubled minds at ease. The ideal spiritual environment, Pacheco opines, is a pastoral haven, like Benito Arias Montano's country house at Aracena; and he calls upon Vélez de Guevara, the recipient of the sermon, to escape with him to Montano's retreat, where, with luck, Montano himself will turn up, playing a song that makes the river Jordan sing, the peaks of Mount Hermón shimmer, and Nazarite nymphs, on the Jordan's banks, applaud.[93]

Here, in Aracena, among their friends Montano, Juan de Caño, a certain prelate named Parma (all of whom are Hebraists), and Francisco Yáñez (the grandson of Nebrija), they will celebrate the daily mass 'with pure tongues and minds' [*'con las lenguas y las mentes limpias'*].[94] Here they will immerse themselves in their pastoral setting, preparing simple food from the produce found in Montano's garden. And after they have eaten their modest fare they will engage in urbane conversation, enlivened by jokes and laughter. Caño will talk of the enigmas of the Scriptures; Montano will regale them with his great knowledge of astrology and botany, 'and many other things contained in divine books but unknown to all'[95]; and Parma will lecture them on the mysteries of the sacred word, 'which the translator of the Chaldean Bible has written correctly and in concordance with our muses.'[96] Here, Pacheco makes a discreet reference to Andreas Masius' controversial Chaldean, or Aramaic, Old Testament, which formed part of Montano's Polyglot Bible. However, while Pacheco voices his support for Masius' text, labeled rabbinical by a papal council, he is careful to point out that his own interest in Hebrew and Aramaic Scriptures is that of an orthodox Catholic who wishes only to unmask 'the circumcised trickster, refuting him with his own tongue and with all the incredible and grandiose things stated by the Church Fathers in order to shape our conduct and secure our beliefs.'[97]

But Pacheco's protest rings false. Montano's reclusive group may not have been Jewish apologists, but neither were they orthodox Christians. They were, I would argue, disaffected converso humanists who, in promoting the Hebrew Bible's importance to Christianity, were asserting their own authenticity as Catholics and Spaniards. The abiding image is of a secret support group who have gathered together to pursue their mutual interests—scientific and religious—in private. They are in essence an Epicurean 'Garden' community, searching for freedom and happiness away from the constraints, conventions, and prejudices of their society; except that their spiritual home is not a sleepy suburb of ancient Athens, but an antique Jewish Arcady, on the banks of the river Jordan.

Pablo De Cespedes (1548?–1608)

When Pablo de Céspedes appears in scholarly works on Golden Age Spain, it is usually in his capacity as an artist or art theorist. However, a number of letters and papers housed in the Granada Cathedral archive present the humanist as a keen Hebraist, eager to promote the ancient Hebrew language and culture, and forge a link between classical Semitic civilization and Spain. In his study based on these Granada documents, Jesús Rubio Lapaz argues that Céspedes, like his friend Benito Arias Montano, linked Spain to the ancient Hebrews as a Counter-Reformation propagandist who wished to strengthen Philip II's image as a great Catholic prince.[98] However, this view is not borne out by Céspedes' biography or his works, neither of which suggest that the Córdoban humanist was a partisan of Philip II's imperialist vision or his orthodox Catholic ideology.

As a prebendary in the Córdoba Cathedral, a position he held from 1577 to his death, Céspedes never gave mass, rarely attended the ceremony, and insisted on passing through the cathedral when this and other ceremonies were taking place. For this demonstration of disrespect toward Tridentine practice he was admonished on a number of occasions by the bishop, finally being issued an official reprimand (*expedente canonico*) in 1589. He was also known to make sarcastic remarks on the value of the Sacrament and the existence of purgatory, and to praise the English Queen Elizabeth and the Great Sultan, whom he referred to waggishly as 'The Lady Queen' and 'The Gentleman Great Turk.' At a dinner held at the Jesuit College in Córdoba to mark the anniversary of

Loyola's beatification, he stood up and calmly stated that his century had produced three great people: Loyola, the Turkish pirate Barbarrosa, and Elizabeth I of England.[99] Significantly, Céspedes' heroes came from three different religious environments, with the Jesuit General Loyola, not Philip II, representing Catholic Spain.

Céspedes was not a Counter-Reformation Catholic apologist, but an old-style Erasmian humanist, attracted to evangelical practice and a rational, or what he considered rational, pursuit of knowledge. He had little or no interest in theological texts or doctrinal manuals, both of which were conspicuously absent from his extensive library.[100] His passion, as the Granada documents testify, was for philological and historical study, with a predilection for promoting the ancient oriental, Semitic cultures as a direct font for an early civilized Iberia. This interest in an ancient Hebraic Spain, I will suggest, was not that of a post-Tridentine Catholic propagandist, but rather of a converso humanist who wished to challenge Rome's religious hegemony and his own society's pure blood prejudice.

The problem with Céspedes' converso identity, however, is that it rests on circumstantial evidence. What little we do know about his antecedents is provided mostly by a *limpieza de sangre* report to which Céspedes was subjected in 1577 in order to occupy the position of prebendary (*racionero*) in the Córdoba Cathedral. Like the majority of *limpieza de sangre* examinations for church office, this was a carefully orchestrated affair, paid for by the candidate and organized by his own nominees, all three of whom, it seems, were related to Céspedes himself.[101] These men were able to choose and rehearse the witnesses who were to give depositions to the cathedral canon, Dr. Diego Muñoz, the man chosen to oversee the investigation.

In their genealogical investigations, the Church was interested in only two issues: the candidate's legitimacy and his Old Christian ancestry. Céspedes had stated that he was the legitimate son of Old Christian parents, Alonso de Céspedes of Ocaña, near Toledo, and Aulalia de Arroyo from the village of Alcolea de Torote, a few kilometers east of Alcalá de Henares. His paternal grandparents were given as Alonso de Céspedes and Francisca de Mora, and his maternal grandparents as Cebrián Arroyo and Pascuala Martín. To corroborate this information, Dr. Muñoz traveled to Ocaña and Alcolea in the late summer of 1577, where he took depositions from witnesses presented to him by Céspedes' legal appointees (*procuradores*). In Alcolea, six witnesses were brought forth, none of whom appeared to have known Céspedes' father Alonso, although several knew Pablo. All stated that his mother's family was free of Jewish or Moorish taint. One of the witnesses, Licentiate Andrés de Muñoz, a priest, added, apparently without irony, that Céspedes' uncle (and *procurador*), Pedro Martínez de Arroyo, was a *familiar* of the Toldedo Inquisition tribunal, and that the witness knew this for a fact because he had been called upon to give evidence in that *limpieza de sangre* investigation also.

In Ocaña, Céspedes' representatives Alonso de Céspedes and Francisco Álvarez were able to provide only two people to testify to the Céspedes' Old Christian roots, one of whom was a family member. Even after being given another day to drum up more witnesses, the representatives returned empty handed. Thus the investigation moved several kilometers away to the villages of Noblejas and Dos Barrios, the respective birth places of Céspedes' grandfather, Alonso de Céspedes, and grandmother, Francisca de Mora. Here Céspedes' representatives were able to present Muñoz with nine witnesses ready to testify to the Céspedes and Mora families' clean blood, two of whom were related to Pablo. None of the witnesses offered details on the family's background or circumstances, but this was normal practice; the object of the majority of *limpieza de sangre* investigations was to conceal information, not reveal it.[102] It is, however, significant that in the fifteenth century Ocaña had one of the largest Jewish *aljamas* in Castille, numerically smaller than that of Toledo, but proportionately much larger. In the expulsion year of 1492 this community numbered some 1500 people, or 25 percent of the town's total population. Ocaña's late fifteenth-century converso population is less easy to estimate, although judging by the early prosecutions for Judaizing in the town, it is also likely have been large. It is possible indeed that in the period directly prior to 1492 the combined population of Jews and conversos in Ocaña would have represented around 40 percent of the town's inhabitants.

Ocaña became a major target for the Toledo Inquisition tribunal soon after it was established in 1485. While the records for most of these trials have been lost, we do have a list of some of the town's conversos, compiled by the Bishop of Calahorra, in 1537, from Toledo tribunal documents, and among the names on the list are Céspedes and Mora: Francisco de Céspedes (prior), and Juan de Mora, Pedro de Mora, and Diego de Mora (apothecary). The surname Mora was indeed one favored by Jewish converts in the region, becoming notorious in the late sixteenth century when the Mora clan of Quintanar de la Orden, a town to the southeast of Ocaña, was the central protagonist in a famous trial for Judaizing.[103] There is no evidence that Pablo de Céspedes' paternal grandmother was related to this Mora family; nevertheless, her surname suggests a New Christian background.

As for the Céspedes side of the family, it seems that they were members of a small middle-sort clan that emerged in the mid-fifteenth century when a Juan de Céspedes married a Maria de la Torre in Ocaña and had four sons: Gutiérrez, Diego, Pedro, and Alonso. Gutierrez moved to Noblejas at the end of the century, where his son Alonso, Pablo's great grandfather, was born.[104] Meanwhile, Gutierrez's brother, another Alonso, married a Maria Hervás (the surname indicates a Jewish background[105]), producing a son, Francisco Hervás, who entered the Church, as did many of the Céspedes. One member of the family, a Pedro de Céspedes (the names Pedro and Alonso recur across several generations) became an important member of Toledo Cathedral in the first decades of the sixteenth century, occupying the position of chaplain in the New Kings' Chapel before gaining a prestigious canonry, which he shared with a Francisco de Mora—very obviously a relative.[106] This Pedro de Céspedes is known to us as one of a small group of cathedral officials, among whom was the great Spanish humanist Juan de Vergara, who opposed Archbishop Silíceo's famous 1547 *limpieza de sangre* statute. He was also one of six chaplains who had voted against the New Kings' Chapel *limpieza* legislation when it was proposed 17 years previously, in 1530.[107]

From information volunteered by one of the witnesses in Pablo de Céspedes' *probanza*, it appears that his grandparents Alonso de Céspedes and Francisca de Mora married in the village of Noblejas around 1517, before moving to Ocaña. When Alonso died some ten years later, his widow left the town with her three children, Alonso, Pedro, and a girl whose name is not recorded, for the home of her cousin Francisco López Aponte (or Aponte Morales) in Córdoba. This López was the original occupant of the cathedral prebendary that was inherited by Francisca's son Pedro in 1547. Later, in 1577, Pedro shared the title with Pablo, in what scholars have so far accepted as an act of avuncular devotion, although we should not rule out the possibility that Pablo's generous uncle Pedro was in fact his father.[108]

Pablo de Céspedes' ancestry remains somewhat unclear to us, as does his childhood and formative years. We are not even sure when he was born. In his *Retratos*, the painter Franciso Pacheco states that when Céspedes died in 1608 he was 60 years of age, establishing a date of birth of 1548. As Pacheco was not only Céspedes' first biographer, but also a close friend, one would expect him to be reasonably accurate on this point. Nevertheless, Pacheco's biographical data is not always reliable. For example, he tells us that when Pablo entered the University of Alcalá de Henares, he lodged with his relative, the Toledo canon Pedro de Céspedes. We know, however, that the Canon died in 1554, when Pablo was presumably still a child. He also tells us that Céspedes returned to Spain, after a seven-year sojourn in Italy, in the year of the Portuguese King Sebastian's death in Algeria (1578). From other sources, however, we know Pablo returned to Spain in 1577, the same year he took possession, or part possession, of the Córdoba prebendary.[109] It is thus tempting to question other information provided in Pacheco's biographical essay. Is it feasible that a graduate of classical languages would spend seven (or possibly nine) years copying art works in Rome, as Pacheco states? Céspedes was not from a background that permitted dilettante pursuits, so we must discount the fact that he was in Rome to pursue an expensive hobby. But neither is it likely that a young man who had trained to become a *letrado* would later opt to become a painter, or artisan. And even if this were the case, why would he approach the task in such an autodidactic fashion? Did Céspedes really travel to Rome to become a painter, or was there some other motive behind his long visit?

Pacheco provides a clue to an alternative motive when he casually states that while in Rome Céspedes lodged in the household of the Bishop of Zamora. This bishop was none other than Diego de Simancas, the Inquisition legal official given the task of leading the prosecution against Archbishop Carranza.[110] Pacheco does not allude to Carranza's trial; he does, however, note that Simancas was a native of Córdoba and that Céspedes knew some of his family who still resided in the city. In fact, Diego de Simancas' brother, Juan de Simancas, received a *juro* or bond from Pablo's uncle Pedro in May 1577, to the value of 400 ducados, at the time that Pablo was applying for entry into the cathedral chapter, suggesting that the transaction was connected to Céspedes' application.[111]

It is significant that Céspedes' dates in Italy almost exactly coincide with those of Diego Simancas, suggesting that he formed part of Simancas' household for the duration of the official's assignment, leaving the city soon after the Carranza trial was concluded in April 1576. This is not to infer that Céspedes formed part of an anti-Carranza faction. Indeed, everything we know about him suggests the opposite. In all probability he attached himself to the Simancas household in an attempt to secure a lucrative sinecure in the Córdoba Cathedral, where the Simancas family were the ruling faction, and where Diego Simancas expected to be given a bishopric as a reward for heading Philip II's legal team in the prosecution of Carranza.[112] I would suggest that Céspedes, as one of the less significant members of the Simancas entourage, had little to do in the eternal city but distract himself with his humanist activities, including the study of Renaissance art.

There is, however, the possibility—slight, but worth mentioning—that Céspedes was acting as a spy, infiltrating Diego de Simancas' Roman delegation on behalf of a pro-Carranza faction in Spain. In this respect, it is noteworthy that another Céspedes, a certain licentiate, represented Carranza's interests in Rome during the first years of the archbishop's imprisonment, when the Spanish primate was still held in Valladolid. This Céspedes, described by Philip II's ambassador Francisco de Vargas as 'insolent and disrespectful,' was one of Carranza's most fervent devotees. He was also mistakenly identified by the nineteenth-century biographer of the Inquisition Juan Antonio Llorente as Pablo de Céspedes, an error later repeated by Marcelino Menéndez Pelayo in his *Historia de los heterodoxos españoles*. We now know that the licentiate was around 50 years of age in 1559, ruling out the possibility that he and Pablo de Céspedes were one and the same person.[113] But could the two have been related and in league together in Rome? Certainly what we know of Pablo de Céspedes' character and humanist network would seem to place him in a pro-Carranza camp. Indeed, directly before moving to Italy he spent several years at Alcalá de Henares, studying under Ambrosio de Morales, a discreet defender of Carranza.[114] Could he then have gone to Italy to spy for a pro-Carranza group? Or did he go there merely with the intention of ingratiating himself with the Simancas family? With little information available to us on Céspedes' Roman circle and movements, his motivation remains hidden. It does, however, appear likely that his trip to Rome was inspired by considerations other than artistic ones.[115]

Céspedes returned to Córdoba in the summer of 1577, gaining entry into the cathedral chapter almost immediately, probably with the help of the Simancas family. Thereafter, he turned his back on clerical office, dedicating himself to his real interests: humanist study, painting, and a close circle of friends in Seville and Córdoba, among whom were Licentiate Francisco Pacheco, the poets Fernando de Herrera and Luis de Góngora, and the Dominican friar and author of the famous anti-*limpieza* tract Agustín Salucio.[116] Unfortunately, most of Céspedes' own artistic and literary output has not survived the centuries. We do, however, still have access to a number of letters and essays written toward the end of his life, which testify to his passion for philological and antiquarian study. They also reveal, as I have already noted, a keen interest in a post-diluvian Hebraic culture and its connection to Spain.

In one of the documents Céspedes argues that the site occupied by Córdoba's cathedral was not only that of the great mosque—a building he praises for its fine workmanship—but also of Roman and Hebrew temples.[117] The opinion that a Roman temple, dedicated to the God Janus, had once stood on the cathedral site had already been mooted by Céspedes' friend Ambrosio de Morales, among others; the view that a Hebrew temple had preceded the Roman structure was, however, original to Céspedes, who argued, in a long, quasi-scientific discourse, that the original building was erected by Noah's heirs, who had entered Spain after the death of the biblical figure.

According to Céspedes' account, these early colonists had entered the peninsula through the mouth of the Guadalquivir River and had followed its course until it came to the point where it was no longer easily navigated. Here they had constructed their colony—Córdoba—and a temple to Noah, which they named, in their Hebrew dialect, Ian Noah or Noah's Altar. Over time this temple had grown in size, finally imitating King Solomon's magnificent temple in Jerusalem, with the same classical features, the so-called Corinthian columns, later attributed to the Greeks. The conduit for this cultural exchange between pre-Roman Córdoba and Jerusalem was, in the humanist's opinion, the Carthaginians, who had established important cities in Spain in this period. And he singles out the city of Sagunto as an entrepôt for the Semitic civilization, a city described by Céspedes' friend and fellow *Cordobés* Juan Bautista Villalpando as a Jewish colony in the time of Solomon. Céspedes himself does not make such a bold statement; nevertheless, he clearly infers that areas of pre-Romanic Spain maintained close cultural ties with ancient Israel, including Córdoba. Over time, however, Córdoba's Hebraic culture had declined and with it the belief in a monotheistic religion. At this point the city's Solomonesque temple became the center of a pagan cult, its name Ian Noah corrupted to Ianus, or Janus, the god subsequently worshipped in its precincts. This two-faced pagan deity was, according to Céspedes, an imitation of Noah, who was also depicted in antiquity as bicipital in view of the fact that he had contemplated a pre- and post-diluvian world. Céspedes' intention was obviously to demonstrate that a Hebrew culture was established in Córdoba prior to the Roman presence, and that this culture had not only left its mark on classical Iberian society, but had also provided the foundations, quite literally, for Catholic worship.

In another of the Granada documents, Céspedes builds on his thesis that the city was founded by Noah's ancestors, arguing that an etymological analysis of the names of a number of the area's settlements, including Córdoba, reveals their Hebrew origins.[118] According to Céspedes, Córdoba itself was derived from a Hebrew phrase meaning 'fortified plain' in which virtue, diligence, and industry were cultivated. This city, established on a bedrock of humanist principles linked to a Hebraic culture, was, Céspedes informs his readers, the home to many enlightened men, first during the Roman occupation (Céspedes notes that the Stoic Seneca was a Córdoba native) and later during the Moslem caliphates. In the latter period, Céspedes writes, the city's schools produced 'such excellent men in philosophy and medicine that even kings came from distant lands and other provinces to find a cure for their incurable illnesses, as was the case of King Sancho, known as the Fatman, who was restored to health by Córdoba's physicians.'[119] Cespedes also notes that in the period after the *Reconquista* Córdoba continued to produce important scholars, presenting as an example the poet Juan de Mena, who was considered the prince of Spanish poets ['*estimado y tenido príncipe de los poetas españoles*']. Finally, the humanist pays tribute to the noble Fernández de Córdoba family and their efforts to rid the city of '*tiranía Barbara*' and '*maldita superstición,*' under Moorish rule, and return it to its ancient liberty and rightful lord, the king of Spain.[120]

Although Céspedes ends his essay with a brief attack on Islamic Spain, this appears perfunctory, out of keeping with the rest of the piece, which celebrates cultural pluralism, not nationalist or religious sectarianism. For Céspedes, Córdoba's greatness is based not on its Catholic dogma, but on virtue, diligence, and industry, characteristics found in four different cultural settings: Hebrew, Roman, Muslim, and Catholic. Even when Céspedes celebrates the Fernández de Córdoba family for their part in expelling the Muslims from the city, he praises them not as defenders of the faith but, significantly, as warriors against 'superstition' and 'barbarous tyranny.' As Céspedes' informed readers would know, the Fernández de Córdobas were well-known antagonists of the Inquisition, ridding the city of the tyrannical Inquisitor Diego Rodríguez de Lucero in 1506, for which the family was severely punished by King Ferdinand of Aragon, at that time regent of Spain.[121] These same readers would also be aware that the Fernández de Córdobas were closely associated with Spain's evangelical reform movement, first as supporters of Juan de Ávila, and later as patrons of the *Colegio de Santa Catalina*, the converso-dominated Jesuit college established in Córdoba in 1559, and to which Céspedes himself was closely attached. The unwritten message, I would suggest, is that the mission to liberate Spain of tyranny and superstition, of which the Fernández de Córdoba family formed a part, had not ended in 1492, but was an ongoing one.

Céspedes' essays celebrating Córdoba's Hebrew heritage were not written as Counter-Reformation propaganda, but rather as a challenge to it, promoting the city's glorious humanist past, in which the Hebrew and Islamic cultures were prominent participants. This was at root an exercise in cultural syncretism, similar to that being undertaken by Montano and Villalpando at El Escorial and, more radically, by the Morisco translator Miguel de Luna in Granada. Indeed, Céspedes may well have been inspired to write his study on Córdoba's Hebrew past from following the events taking place in Granada, where the Sacromonte lead discs, translated by Luna, a man he clearly admired, revealed an early Christian Spain dominated by Jewish and Arab evangelists.[122]

Céspedes appears to have been on close terms with Luna, as he was with Montano and Villalpando, with whom he shared an interest in Hebraic study and Solomonic architecture. In another essay found within the Granada collection, Céspedes supports Villalpando's view, outlined in his *Ezechielem explanationes*, that the so-called Corinthian column was found in ancient Jewish architecture before being incorporated into Greek monuments. However, he disagrees with the Jesuit's claim that the column originated in a God-inspired First Temple, preferring a rationalistic approach to its creation. According to Céspedes, the column first appeared in ancient Babylonia, where a civilized society, without access to trees or stone, created the ceiling supports for its ceremonial buildings out of palm fronds, closely bound together to form pillars. Later this palm aesthetic was incorporated into stone and marble columns, spreading throughout the region to Israel, where they were used in early Jewish architecture, including Solomon's Temple. Two of these 'Solomonic' columns were now to be found in Saint Peter's Basilica in Rome, Cespedes notes, having been brought to the city in the time of the Emperor Titus, where they were reputed to have the power 'to expel evil spirits.'

For Céspedes' latter-day biographer, Jesús Rubio Lapaz, his subject's interest in proving the Oriental provenance of the Corinthian column is further proof that he was a spokesman for Counter-Reformation orthodoxy. By locating the column within ancient Jewish society, according to Lapaz, Céspedes was attempting to legitimize Church architecture, as a good Catholic.[123] But the Counter-Reformation Church had few scruples about the pagan origins of its architectural motifs; nor was it prone to seek legitimacy through contact with the Jewish culture, ancient or modern. Céspedes' interest in the Solomonic column was not a reflection of a trend within Rome, but rather within post-Tridentine Spanish humanism, where Hebraic scholars were attempting to champion the Hebrew Bible and culture in the face of opposition from an Old Christian Church and society. His motives, like those of his friend Benito Arias Montano, were personal, not institutional.

Pedro De Valencia (1555–1620)

Pedro de Valencia was born to Ana Vazquez and Melchor de Valencia in the southern Extremaduran town of Zafra on 19 August 1555, and baptized in the church of Santa Maria de la Candelaria on the 25th of the same month.[124] His father was a *letrado* from Córdoba who was employed by the Duke of Feria in his Zafra court. The surname Valencia suggests that the paternal family stemmed from Valencia de las Torres, or perhaps Valencia de Mombuey, both of which were located close to Zafra. Pedro's mother was the daughter of the wealthy merchant Juan Ramírez (the elder), originally from Segura de León, a small town some 30 kilometers to the south, who took up residence in Zafra earlier in the century.[125] The Ramírez family resided in one of the large houses in the main square, a favorite dwelling place for Zafra's merchant elite, who benefited from the trade fairs encouraged by the noble Feria family. The majority of these merchants were conversos, who established complex trading networks with family members across the border in Portugal. The Ramírez family were themselves renowned conversos, according to an Inquisition report in 1625, as were the González family, with whom they were linked through marriage.[126] Pedro de Valencia's godfather Luis González was the grandson of a Jew who had left Zafra in the expulsion year of 1492, only to return as a Christian three years later to reclaim his property.[127]

If we pry further into Pedro de Valencia's family background, we find evidence of frequent endogamous unions, a phenomenon common to converso families, especially those who were fairly recent converts, and thus had certain family secrets to hide. Pedro's maternal aunt, Isabel González, married a Juan Ramírez from Segura de León, while his godfather's son, also named Juan Ramírez, married an Isabel Ramírez, almost certainly a cousin. Pedro himself married his first cousin (the daughter of another maternal aunt), applying through his friend and mentor Benito Arias Montano for a papal license to do so.

It seems evident that Pedro de Valencia was not only from a converso family, but also from one that had recently converted to Christianity, and for which its Jewish ancestry continued to pose a challenge. Valencia's interest in justifying the Jewish proscription on mixing meat and dairy products provides us with a glimpse of these private tensions.[128] Other allusions, albeit more subtle ones, are present in certain of his social and religious discourses, as the humanist attempts to create a more caring society, tolerant of its marginal groups. Valencia's reformist character may have been forged as a pupil at Juan de Ávila's school in Zafra. Like all of Ávila's institutions, the Zafra school was established to create a new evangelical Christian who would help disseminate humanist values, including the message of equality among co-religionists. The young Valencia would have attended Ávila's school prior to transferring to the Jesuit College in Córdoba, which had also been a Juan de Ávila institution before the *maestro* ceded it to the Society of Jesus several years prior to his death in 1569.

After four years in the Córdoba Jesuit College, studying Arts and Theology, Valencia enrolled in the University of Salamanca to read Law. The choice of degree was probably made by his father, who envisaged a bureaucratic career for his son similar to his own. Valencia's own interests were located elsewhere, however, in biblical studies, or more particularly the philological study of the Latin, Greek, and Hebrew Bibles. He even took Greek classes with the great Salamanca humanist Sánchez de las Brozas (El Brocense) in order to advance his humanist studies in private. There is no evidence that he studied Hebrew while at the university, but then the Salamanca climate was not congenial to the close scrutiny of Jewish texts. The Hebrew scholars Luis de León, Gaspar de Grajal, and Martín Martínez de Cantalapiedra, all languished in prison during Valencia's time at the university, accused of promoting a Jewish interpretation of the Old Testament, which was considered tantamount to Judaizing.

Valencia completed his degree in 1576 and returned to Zafra to become a lawyer, although he continued to demonstrate more interest in humanist and biblical studies than in the Law. One of the texts that occupied much of his time was Montano's Polyglot Bible, which he commissioned a family friend, Sebastian Pérez, to buy from a Lisbon bookseller immediately after its publication in 1577. A friend of Montano, Pérez later introduced Valencia to the famous humanist at the latter's Aracena retreat, some 30 kilometers south of Zafra. Soon after the meeting, which took place in the spring of 1578, Valencia took up residence with Montano, agreeing to act as his amanuensis in exchange for private tuition in Hebrew and Aramaic. Here he was introduced to a circle of humanists that included Francisco Pacheco and Pablo de Céspedes.[129]

In entering Montano's employment, Valencia was not only attaching himself to a renowned philologist; he was also allying himself with a controversial biblical scholar who subordinated Catholic doctrine to personal mystical practice and a Christian humanist credo, the latter rooted firmly in the Old Testament Scriptures. Valencia clearly shared these reformist views, as he demonstrated in a series of social and religious critiques, beginning with the irenic *Academica*, an account of the conflict between the ancient stoics and skeptics on the problems of determining truth. Like Lipsius' *Politica*, published in 1589, the work was an attempt to reach a peaceful solution to Europe's religious impasse. However, while Lipsius looked at a stoical credo for a solution, Valencia turned to the ancient skeptics and their view that true knowledge was impossible.

Pedro de Valencia's *Academica* is a call for religious toleration in Europe, carefully disguised as an objective account of a famous philosophical debate between the ancient stoics and their rivals, the academic skeptics, concerning the nature of truth. According to the stoics, Valencia tells us, the wise man would know when a perception was true by *phantasia kataleptike*, or the overwhelming conviction that it was so. In contrast, their opponents, the academic skeptics, believed that intellectual conviction, however strong, was not a valid criterion for establishing the truth, and that the wise man would, of necessity, be an agnostic, practicing *epoche* or the suspension of judgment. This would not, however, lead to his intellectual or moral stasis, as he would temper his skepticism through the doctrine of probability, allowing him to decide on the best course of action without being fully convinced that his decision was based on true perceptions.

Valencia's work charts the long discourse between the stoics and skeptics, from the early dispute between Zeno and Arcesilaus through to the neo-skeptical works of the Roman writers Cicero and Sextus Empiricus. It was from Cicero's *Academica (De Natura Deorum)* that Valencia took the title of his work, and from which he gleaned much of his knowledge on the issue. Valencia's own approach to the debate, or so he tells us, was merely that of a disinterested scribe 'devoting our strength to the appropriate task of the grammarian, as Galen says, that being to record and bring to light all the words of the ancients.'[130] There is, however, nothing disinterested about the *Academica*. It is, rather, a guarded attack on dogmatism, both ancient and modern, with Cicero and, more importantly, Saint Augustine being cited by the humanist as supporters of a more prudent skeptical viewpoint:

> And in this way those who follow what is probable and act ethically will achieve happiness. All these ideas are very much those of the academic skeptics. Thus, as can be deduced from Saint Augustine, the skeptics considered wise and good—and happy to the degree men can be so—those that looked for truth, even though they did not achieve it, but strived for what was possible ... And in my opinion Saint Augustine is a great authority even in a matter of this nature.[131]

In writing the *Academica*, Valencia clearly wished to promote a skeptical approach to truth, one that was in keeping with his own views, revealed in later essays, on the need for prudent action in civil and religious matters. However, he was careful to present the work as little more than an exercise in illuminating a pagan debate. While of interest, it was only of secondary concern to a Christian, he stated, who knew that only God was in possession of real wisdom. It was God, not the philosophers, that one needed to approach in order to be enlightened, Valencia tells his readers in the work's closing paragraph. Yet he also notes that divine enlightenment would not be forthcoming to the 'lovers of false wisdom,' but only to those people who 'make themselves stupid to become wise.'[132] In other words, although not expressly stated, the good Christian is not the dogmatist, but the skeptic, who lives by the Socratic axiom 'all I know is that I know nothing.'

According to Valencia, the *Academica* was written in just 20 days at the request of a friend, García de Silva y Figueroa (the illegitimate son of the First Duke of Feria), who apparently wished to gain a better understanding of the debate between the skeptics and the stoics. We should not pay too much attention to Valencia's claim, or disclaimer, however. The *Academica* was not a casual exercise in explaining an ancient debate, but a piece of subtle propaganda, produced by an irenist for a like-minded readership, including the dedicatee García de Silva, a career politician and diplomat who later established links with Lipsius and his disciple Johannes Woverius while stationed in the Netherlands.[133] Among the work's other readers was the converso physician Simón de Tovar, a member of Montano's circle, who persuaded Valencia to publish it with the Plantin Press in Antwerp. The book was released in 1597, as pressure increased on Philip II to recognize the independence of the Calvinist northern provinces and restore peace to the region.

Valencia's *Academica* is the work of a Christian humanist who wished to resolve the religious conflicts in Europe through an appeal for sensible, prudent behavior. It is also the work of a converso who was sensitive to intolerance and religious division in his own society, widespread evils officially endorsed by *limpieza de sangre* legislation. Valencia later confronted this socio-religious discrimination in his *Commentary on the Epistle to the Galatians*, written in 1607, a decade after the *Academica* was published, in a period in which Spain's converso community, recently augmented by religiously suspect Portuguese New Christians, again found itself under attack. Reacting to this situation, Valencia turned to Saint Paul, as converso apologists had done previously, evoking the saint's message of a Christian Church united through the body of Christ.

Valencia's commentary on Galatians was one of a number of works written by converso scholars around the turn of the sixteenth century addressing the issue of converso marginalization. If anything, this problem had worsened in the post-Tridentine period as the clergy and the Crown obsessed on the need to create a homogeneous Catholic society as a bulwark against a rampant Protestant Church in Europe and an expansionist Ottoman Empire in the Mediterranean. In this tense atmosphere, it was inevitable that the socio-religious minorities would be targeted as the enemy within, to be constrained and subdued by Holy Office surveillance and *limpieza de sangre* legislation. It was also inevitable that religious institutions, like the Barefoot Carmelites or the Jesuits, who had initially rejected *limpieza* statutes, would be placed under increasing pressure by their Old Christian membership to implement them. In 1593 the Italian General of the Jesuit Order, Claudio Acquaviva, bowed to pressure and introduced a statute. This was contested in the same year by one of the Jesuit's most celebrated scholars, Pedro de Ribadeneira, himself a converso, in a letter listing 13 reasons against the introduction of blood purity legislation. Above all, Ribadeneira reminded the pro-*limpieza* group that the statute went against the original Jesuit constitution that judged would-be members by the strength of their faith, not by the purity of their lineage. He also noted that it was personal prejudices and not blood or lineage that created tensions within institutions, a pointed attack on the Old Christian *limpieza* lobbyists; and he forecast that the statute would cause only tension and schism within the order. None of this was of any avail; the statute remained in force for the next 350 years, although it was moderated somewhat in the Sixth General Congregation of 1608.[134]

Worried that the proliferation of *limpieza de sangre* statutes might itself represent a threat to social harmony, the aging Philip II convened a council in 1595 to examine the issue. Headed by the Inquisitor General Pedro de Portocarrero, a close friend of Fray Luis de León, the council discussed the possibility of limiting *limpieza* investigations to a period of 100 years, thus restricting inquiries to the recent generations of a person's family, where there was usually less official evidence of Jewish taint. Unfortunately, Philip II died while the council was still in deliberation, leaving the *limpieza* issue unresolved. However, in 1599, the Dominican scholar Agustín Salucio, evidently urged on by Portocarrero, wrote a discourse emphasizing the grave social and political consequences of maintaining *limpieza* legislation in its current form. The work was presented as that of a disinterested party who had dismissed the emotive arguments of the pro- and anti-*limpieza* camps, addressing himself only to the practical implications of *limpieza* legislation. The Dominican friar was not, however, the dispassionate observer he claimed to be. The descendant of a family of money lenders, officially Genoese, in reality Genoese and Spanish converso, Salucio was highly sensitive to the problems posed by the pure blood statutes, an attitude he shared with many members of his intellectual circle, which included Pablo de Céspedes, and the Licentiate Francisco Pacheco.[135]

Salucio had three major criticisms of the statutes. First, they were illogical, focusing on genealogical rather than religious violation. Second, the blood taint was often regarded as perpetual, giving the New Christians no incentive to integrate into Old Christian society. And third, those most damaged by the legislation were a productive middle sort and lower nobility, the two groups that most often carried Jewish blood. Their antagonists were the deprived masses, who regarded their own blood purity, erroneously, as an emblem of virtue and social status, and the idle high nobility, who used *limpieza* statutes as a means of impeding the social advancement of their more dynamic middle-sort rivals. All of this created tension that would lead inevitably to civil strife, as Luis de León had warned in *Los nombres de cristo*, when he wrote:

> There is no possibility of peace in a kingdom in which the parts are directed against each other, and are so distinct, some highly honored, others clearly humiliated. And as a body whose humors are not in harmony is very much inclined towards illness and death, so too the kingdom, where many orders, strong men and private houses are upset and wounded, [...] and where the

laws do not allow the groups to mix, will be subject to illness and will take up arms [against each other] at any moment.[136]

This violent outcome, according to Salucio, was unavoidable, particularly given the situation of the Moriscos, a large and growing minority whose alienation from Spanish society was driving it toward a clandestine alliance with the Ottoman Turks. However, the problem had a simple solution: the limitation of the *limpieza de sangre* statutes and the encouragement of mixed marriages, whose progeny would be regarded not as New but Old Christians. In this way, 'Old Christians and Moriscos and Conversos would form a united body, all Old Christians and secure, something quite easily achieved, and would forget the infidelity of their ancestors.'[137]

Despite gaining support for the discourse from a number of highly placed dignitaries, including the Inquisitor General Pedro Portocarrero and the Archbishop of Toledo, Bernardo de Sandoval y Rojas, both of whom were members of mixed-blood noble clans, Salucio was unable to convince the *Suprema* or the Royal Council of the efficacy of his argument. The work was soon vilified by both institutions and banned from publication. Manuscripts did, however, continue to circulate among interested parties at court, keeping the *limpieza* debate alive during the reigns of Philip III and IV, but without ever seriously threatening the statutes themselves. Clearly, most Spaniards did not believe, as Salucio did, in the desirability of socio-ethnic unity, especially if it came at the cost of miscegenation. Indeed, it was probably this suggestion, above all others, that condemned his discourse to failure.

Characteristically, Pedro de Valencia did not attack *limpieza de sangre* head on, as Salucio had done, but rather through the exposition of an ancient debate, a tactic he had previously employed in the *Academica*.[138] This time Valencia chose Saint Paul's 'Epistle to the Galatians,' in which the apostle emphasized the need to follow Jesus' precepts and not those of the early Jewish converts, who insisted on the preeminence of Jewish Christians and Jewish Law within the new sect, contradicting Jesus' spiritual and egalitarian message.

Jesus had come to make peace between Jews and Gentiles, Valencia tells his readers: 'reconciling both in one body ... you that were far from God [the Gentiles] and those who were close [the Jews].'[139] Yet despite their propinquity to God, the majority of the Jews resisted the new evangelical message. Even those Jews who followed Jesus often continued to observe the Old Law, ignoring the fact that it was now obsolete. These Christian Jews refused to accept that they and the Christian Gentiles had been cleansed and sanctified through the blood of Christ, and that circumcision or any other purification was unnecessary to enter the nation of God. This error was attacked by Saint Paul in his letter to the early Christians of Antioch, the 'Galatians,' whom he had converted from paganism to Christianity only to discover that they had since been influenced by a group of Christians from Jerusalem who propagated antiquated Jewish Laws. It was these Jewish proselytizers, Valencia notes, who were the real *flajos* (weak ones) and not the recent converts among the Galatians.[140] Unfortunately, however, these errant Christian Jews were able to intimidate not only Gentiles but also other Jews, including Saint Peter himself, into readopting the Old Law, abandoning the true Christian path through fear of social ostracism. As a result, the Jerusalem Church remained a Judaizing establishment up until the Jewish expulsion from the city, in 135 AD, a disaster incurred, according to Valencia, through divine dissatisfaction with both the Jewish and Jewish-Christian communities.[141]

While Valencia cleverly chose to emphasize the spiritual and egalitarian aspects of Christianity by attacking an errant group of early Jewish Christians, his discourse had clear implications for a contemporary Spanish Church that had forgotten or ignored the central precepts of Christ's message: that all were made equal through Christ's death. Like the early Christianized Jews, this modern Catholic community had behaved with hubris and chauvinism, and as a result was also in danger of incurring God's wrath. This at least would appear to be Valencia's covert warning to his fellow countrymen.

Valencia's discourse on Saint Paul's epistle was written in the first decade after Benito Arias Montano's death, when he found himself liberated from his secretarial duties and able to concentrate on his own humanist works. Like Montano, Valencia was at heart a Christian moralist, although his lack of formal theological training undoubtedly dissuaded him from concentrating on biblical commentaries as his *maestro* had done. His focus, rather, was on Spain's social and economic ills, which he examined in discourses directed toward powerful members of the court, like the royal confessors Gaspar de Córdoba and Diego de Mardones, who were in a position to influence royal policy. One might describe Valencia as an *arbitrista* if it were not for the fact that even in his own day the term was often used as a pejorative for pseudo-scholars who peddled trite or fantastic formulas for Spain's salvation.[142] Valencia's studies, on the contrary, addressed themselves to practical problems and ethical, sensible solutions. His views were, in many respects, similar to those of Martín González de Cellorigo, whose *Memorial de la política necesaria* is usually cited as one of the more trenchant contemporaneous examinations of Spain's seventeenth-century crisis.[143] Both González de Cellorigo and Valencia pinpointed the same obstacles in the path of social and economic harmony: the easy wealth of the Indies, which, instead of enriching the country, was impoverishing it; the widespread belief that honor and virtue resided in idleness; the lack of domestic industry; and the neglect of agriculture, which both men saw as particularly detrimental to the country's wellbeing.

According to Valencia, Spain had forgotten that a country's prosperity depended on its close relationship to the land. The major culprit was the Spanish nobility, who preferred to sit on vast stretches of *dehesa* (pasture) instead of turning some of the terrain into productive wheat fields. These nobles should be encouraged to hand over unproductive land to peasant farmers at a modest rate of interest, thus creating a thriving rural labor force, an essential component of a dynamic and successful society.[144] Furthermore, the king should reduce tariffs on staple food items, like bread and wine, the high price of which was creating hardship throughout the countryside. And Valencia reminded the monarch that his role was that of a father or good shepherd whose job was to produce a healthy flock for his own benefit and the benefit of his realm.[145]

While Valencia's views made little impact on government policy, they did gain him some attention at court and led to his being awarded, in 1607, the position of Chronicler of the Realm, which required him to take up residence in Madrid. One of Valencia's early commissions as a royal servant was to design the emblems for a series of frescoes in the Pardo Palace on the virtues of good kingship as practiced by Philip III. As was customary, Valencia represented the four cardinal virtues, Prudence, Justice, Fortitude and Temperance, with classical goddesses. However, in the case of Justice, the humanist yielded to his own bucolic bias, substituting the scale-carrying Astrea for a representation of the Roman agricultural goddess Ceres, who was also regarded as the protector of plebeian rights. Thus Valencia's Justice carries in her right hand 'an olive branch and in her left an ear of corn, which means that from the good administration of Justice there follows peace, security and plenty, so that the fields are cultivated and Man's labors are blessed with rain from Heaven.'[146] Some 20 years later, the court painter Diego Velázquez incorporated Valencia's goddess into a painting on the Morisco expulsion, placing her next to Philip III, who is looking out at a group of forlorn men and women boarding the boats that will take them away from Spain. However, Velázquez's corn-carrying deity has traded her olive branch for spears and her white robe for Roman armor. She thus serves as a reminder not of Philip III's regal virtue and justice, but of his infamy and deceit, which has resulted in the expulsion of an industrious section of the population.[147]

Having been an advocate of toleration toward the Morisco community, Valencia would undoubtedly have approved of Velázquez's use of his emblem to subtly criticize the 1609 expulsion. In his *Tratado acerca de los moriscos de España*, written in 1606 for Philip III's confessor Fray Diego de Mardones, Valencia urged the king to deal leniently with his Morisco subjects, encouraging them to integrate through a gradual, peaceful program of evangelization. In contrast to Jaime Bleda and other apologists for the expulsion, who presented the Moriscos as congenitally bad Christians, Valencia was dismissive of biological essentialism. He preferred, rather, to examine the issue in its socio-cultural context, concluding that while the Moriscos had made little attempt to embrace Christianity, Old Christian Spain had done virtually nothing to encourage their integration.

Valencia was under no illusion as to the dimensions of the problem. It was clear to him that most of those Moriscos residing in the Spanish Levant considered themselves Muslim, and that many of these harbored a grudge toward the Christian community. However, he also attempted to see their continuing isolation from their perspective: despite being denizens of Spain, despite looking like their Old Christian neighbors, they were not accepted as bona fide Spaniards. They were like the Heliots, whom the Spartans constantly complained about without attempting to integrate into Spartan society.

There were, Valencia opined, good practical reasons for taking a hard line against the Morisco community, but a nation's leader should not be moved solely by expediency. Indeed, God condemned and destroyed kings and kingdoms that did not follow the ways of justice. This was the case of Jeroboam—Valencia noted in a pointed warning to Philip III— who veered from the prudent path of his father, Solomon, with fatal results. The Spanish king needed to choose a practical solution to the Morisco problem that was also an ethical one. This ruled out expulsion, as there was nothing ethical or practical in uprooting thousands of productive citizens and handing them to the Turkish enemy. There was, however, an alternative: national dispersion. This strategy had already been employed after the second Alpujarras rebellion; however, the dispersion was a limited one, and the Morisco groups were quite large, discouraging assimilation. The Moriscos should now be relocated in smaller groups. At the same time, the Church should be obliged to lead the Old Christian community in fasts, donations, and prayers, through which they would demonstrate concern for the Moriscos' spiritual welfare. This would certainly be an improvement on the present policy of doing nothing, save calling them Moorish dogs.[148] Finally, the civil and religious authorities should encourage Old and New Christians to form mixed marriages (an idea advanced several years previously by Agustín Salucio), thus 'doing away with Gentiles as well as Jews and Muslims, joining them all in a new body and republic.'[149] This ethno-cultural mixing, Valencia notes, was already practiced by other nations, who managed to blend together their diverse groups rather than making an issue about their differences, as Spain did. And as an example of royal open-mindedness, Valencia called attention to Alexander the Great, who refused to divide the world into Greek friends and barbarian enemies, as counseled by his advisors (an allusion to Philip III's pro-expulsion court), but judged all by the criterion of virtue, making friends with the good and rebuking the bad, irrespective of nation. This policy was adopted by all prudent princes of well-governed, non-barbarous, states. Those rulers who failed to apply it should heed God's warning to the Babylonians and all other empires: 'Woe to you, destroyer, you who has not been destroyed! Woe to you, betrayer, you who has not been betrayed! When you stop destroying, you will be destroyed; when you stop betraying, you will be betrayed.'[150]

Valencia's impassioned appeal for clemency had no impact on the king and his all- powerful first minister, the Duke of Lerma. In fact, it is likely that the decision to expel the Moriscos had already been taken by the time Valencia dispatched his discourse to the king's confessor Mardones, at the beginning of 1606; the only pending issue was when the process would begin. This came on 4 April 1609, on the same day that Philip III signed a 12-year truce with the Dutch secessionist provinces. In concluding the two pieces of political business at the same time, Philip III and Lerma could demonstrate that they had secured peace for Spain on two fronts. They had also guaranteed that troops would be available at home if the Moriscos attempted a rebellion. As it turned out they went reasonably quietly, as their Muslim ancestors had done in 1502.

Valencia would obviously have had mixed feelings about the April 4th announcements: on the one hand delight over the truce, on the other despondency over the expulsion, which augured badly for conversos, who were also regarded by many as an enemy within. Over the next 20 years these anti-converso sentiments grew as a Portuguese New Christian (*marrano*) community entered Spain's commercial centers, especially Madrid, escaping the Lusitanian Inquisition only to attract the suspicion of its new hosts. It was in this tense atmosphere that Valencia found himself defending Montano's Polyglot Bible, a work once again attacked for its pro-Jewish sentiments.

The author of the new attack was Fray Andrés de León, a member of the Friars Minor, who in 1615 sent a report to the Royal Council stating that he had made a new Latin translation of the *Parafrasis chaldaica*. This version, he stated, had been approved by a commission of cardinals in Rome, who had also discredited the earlier translation made by Andreas Masius in Montano's Polyglot Bible. Given the importance of this new translation and its usefulness to the university community, León continued, he was requesting a license to publish the work. In response to the request, the Royal Council asked the rector of the University of Alcalá to establish a committee of adjudication. A year later, in May 1616, León met with the committee to distribute copies of his manuscript, one of which soon fell into the hands of Pedro de Valencia, who proceeded to prepare his own detailed examination of the work.

In preparing his report Valencia was aided by his cousin, and brother-in-law, Juan Ramírez Moreno, who had also studied under Benito Arias Montano and was thus well prepared to assess León's linguistic expertise and root out the flaws in his translation. The pair's *Advertencia* was submitted to the Alcalá group in September 1616, accompanied by an official note from the Royal Council asking the committee members to take the critique into consideration when preparing their own assessment of León's work. Clearly, Valencia was pulling strings at court in order to force the committee's hand: anyone who was disposed to approve León's translation would first have to answer his and his cousin's careful linguistic criticisms.

According to Valencia and Ramírez, León's translation was impaired throughout by the friar's dogmatic bias. In examining and translating an ancient work, they noted, it was the scholar's duty only to verify the original's authenticity, not to determine whether it was in accordance or discordance with the Vulgate, or whether it was favorable to Christians or to the Jews. León transgressed this rule, frequently changing the original Aramaic meaning when it conflicted with a Catholic message. In so doing he had not only created a hybrid, useless text, he had also seriously compromised the credibility of the Catholic Church. At the University of Alcalá, five members of the nine-man assessment committee coincided with Valencia and Ramírez in their condemnation of the new *Paraphrasis*, and thus León was denied his royal license to publish. The friar was not yet ready to give up on his work, however, which he believed was a necessary orthodox riposte to Montano's earlier 'rabbinical' translation. His mission was something akin to that of the Archbishop of Seville, Pedro de Castro, who in championing the authenticity of the Lead Books of Granada was also defending truth against heresy; this at least was the message León conveyed to Castro in a series of letters soliciting the archbishop's help while pledging his own support for the prelate's Lead Books' campaign. León was also careful to point out to the archbishop that they were both being assailed by a common enemy: Pedro de Valencia, who besides defaming the friar's translation was also bent on exposing the Granada texts as fakes.[151]

León was right, Valencia was a forthright critic of the Lead Books, sharing Montano's view, presented to Castro in 1596, that they were forgeries. It was not until 1607, however, that he became officially involved in the affair, when the new pope, Paul V, wrote to Philip III requesting information on the finds, which the Holy See had still not been allowed to scrutinize. Responding to the request, the king established a committee of investigation, headed by the Archbishop of Toledo, Bernardo de Sandoval y Rojas, who then asked Valencia for a preliminary study. He also appears to have given him license to express his criticism as candidly as possible, a freedom Montano clearly did not enjoy in writing his earlier assessment of the books for the Archbishop of Granada.

He had been asked on several previous occasions to comment on the Granada discoveries, Valencia tells Sandoval in his discourse, but he had declined because he did not feel at liberty to state his true opinions. The Archbishop of Granada had clearly made up his mind about the works before requesting scholarly analysis, and was only interested in assessments that confirmed his own views. In this conceit he was supported by many powerful men who regarded the Lead Books as a great treasure, and a *vulgo* who were always animated by such stories. In the face of this passionate approbation, few scholars were prepared to offer an objective opinion. However, trusting in the Archbishop of Toledo's support, he would set forth his views simply, 'without covering up anything out of fear or respect, respecting above all God, whose cause was at stake.'[152]

Valencia divided his 1607 discourse into two parts. In the first he presented a long series of previous criticisms against the Turpiana parchment and the Lead Books, including those made by Montano; in the second part he offered some personal reflections on the documents, concluding that they were contemporary forgeries made by Muslims or Moriscos who wished to subvert the Judeo-Christian message, promoting the Arabs, not the Jews, as God's chosen people.[153] The Lead Books were not only meant to challenge the early Christian tradition, of course, as Valencia was well aware. They were also intended to promote religious syncretism and social integration, something close to the humanist's own heart. However, while Valencia actively advanced the message of Christian unity in his works, like his mentor Benito Arias Montano, he was not prepared to invent stories to suit his purpose. The authors of the Lead Books, on the other hand, had spun fantastic tales that would make Spain a laughing stock when they were eventually examined by experts in Rome, as Valencia made plain in his discourse: 'The risk to Spain´s reputation is very great, because on reading these books in Rome, they're going to realize what they are [forgeries], and wonder why they have made such an impression on us.'[154] There was yet another possible negative consequence. Once exposed as cheap forgeries, the Lead Books would surely confirm the Old Christian authorities in their belief that the New Christians were denigrators of the faith, thus harming the campaign for integration. While Valencia did not express this view in his official report, it must surely have been one that he entertained in private.

There is no evidence that Valencia's 1607 report was transmitted to Pope Paul V. However, the pontiff did read another critical study of the Lead Books, written by the Jesuit, and Morisco, Ignacio de las Casas, and this reinforced his own skeptical opinion of the works. Nevertheless, the pope's demands that the books be sent to Rome for examination continued to be resisted by Pedro de Castro, who argued that they were Spanish relics, not Italian ones. In the meantime Castro actively promoted the Books' authenticity, using his personal fortune to construct a collegiate church on the Valparaiso hill, where they had been discovered, dedicated to their veneration. Even after Castro abandoned his Granada see for that of Seville, in 1611, he continued to control the expanding cult, taking the Parchment and Books with him to his new diocese to prevent them from being sent to Rome by his successor.

While Castro was able to control access to the Granada finds, he was not able to prevent scholarly examination of a transcription of two of the works made for Philip II in 1596. In 1616 an Arabic scholar, Francisco de Gurmendi, translated these works into Latin, and sent them to the Royal Council, which in turn passed them on to the Holy See. This prompted another call for an inquiry, supported by Philip III's latest confessor, the Dominican friar Luis de Aliaga, who appears to have been responsible for creating an anti-Lead-Book lobby in Madrid, organized around Pedro de Valencia. This group, which met regularly at Valencia's house, and included Francisco de Gurminda and Valencia's nephew Juan Moreno Ramírez, was given the task of preparing a *memoria*, or government report, on the works. However, Castro soon learned of the group's activities and intervened to prevent their study being completed, citing an earlier papal brief, issued by Clement VIII in 1596, forbidding discussion of the subject.[155] This prohibition was reinforced by Castro with a threat of excommunication for incompliance, and backed up by an Inquisition order for the submission of the group's papers to the Holy Office, effectively putting an end to the report.[156]

The *Paraphrasis* and Lead Books episodes appear to have left Valencia in a state of deep depression from which he did not recover. The humanist died in Madrid on 10 April 1620, at the age of 64. A year later Philip III succumbed to a sudden illness, leaving his realm in the hands of his 17-year-old son, also named Philip, and the young man's *privado*, Gaspar de Guzmán, the Count of Olivares, who came to power armed with a radical program for reform. If Pedro de Valencia had lived he would almost certainly have formed part of Olivares' reform group, which comprised a number of men from the count's native Andalusia. Among this coterie was Valencia's fellow *Zafrense*, the humanist Juan de Fonseca y Figueroa, and a young painter from Seville named Diego Velázquez, who, I will argue in the next chapter, also viewed the world through a converso-humanist lens.

CHAPTER 6

Diego Velázquez and the Subtle Art of Protest

Given the fact that the great Renaissance and Baroque painters were very often men of intellectual curiosity who moved in humanist circles, it would seem likely that their art would demonstrate, on occasion, the same heterodox attitudes that we have come to associate with the works of their humanist literary colleagues. Over 40 years ago, Anthony Blunt wrote that the French painter Nicolas Poussin was clearly not in sympathy with the Roman Catholicism of his own day, a fact that became apparent when one examined his circle of friends, his comments on religious matters, and above all his paintings.[1] A similar assessment has been made of Titian, based on his close contact with a coterie of heterodox writers (several of whom, including Titian's tenant Andrea di Ugoni, were tried for heresy), and upon the worldly, at times almost profane, quality of his art.[2] In his essay, 'Tiziano e la religione,' Augusto Gentili argues that Titian's non-conformism is expressed covertly in a number of his works, including his *Entombment*, in which he makes a direct allusion to his own religious dissimulation by using himself as the model for Nicodemus.[3] Like Poussin and Titian, the Flemish painter Peter Paul Rubens also found his own humanist ideas in conflict with the confessionalism of the post-Tridentine church. In fact, Rubens' personal religious credo was strongly influenced by Justus Lipsius' Neostoicism, a philosophy based on the pagan scholars Seneca and Tacitus which advocated prudence and dissimulation in the interests of religious peace.

It is clear that in the Counter-Reformation environment humanist writers and artists alike looked for ways to articulate their dissident religious

© The Author(s) 2018
K. Ingram, *Converso Non-Conformism in Early Modern Spain*,
https://doi.org/10.1007/978-3-319-93236-1_6

views while observing the necessary formalities of an orthodox faith. The trick, of course, was to pay lip service to orthodox themes, while subtly inserting a personal, dissident message for the delectation of a close circle of friends. For humanist painters, one way to contest orthodoxy was through novel renditions of standard themes. According to David Davies, this is the case of El Greco, who was attached to a predominantly converso coterie of humanist clerics in Toledo, and whose idiosyncratic forms and colors were attempts to reflect the mystical ideals of this group. While El Greco did not actually reject Tridentine orthodox artistic themes, he presented them in such a way as to subordinate external demonstrations of faith to a private mystical, or illuminist, religious experience.[4] This is also the case of Diego Velázquez who, like El Greco, was closely connected to a group of humanists, again predominantly converso. Like El Greco, Velázquez, who I will argue was himself from a New Christian background, feigned compliance with the religious dictates of Trent while stealthily inserting a personal, non-conformist message into his art, first in Seville and later at the court of Philip IV, where he became a propagandist for the Count-Duke of Olivares' reform program.

Velázquez's Family Canvas

As Velázquez's first biographer Antonio Palomino tells the story, it was at El Escorial during Easter week 1658 that Philip IV offered Diego Velázquez a noble title, inviting him to choose the military order he would most like to enter. Velázquez, who entertained few doubts as to his noble artistry, chose the highly prestigious Order of Santiago.[5]

Before the painter could claim his knighthood, however, he had first to demonstrate that his was a noble background, unblemished by Jewish or Moorish blood, unsullied by artisanal or mercantile endeavors, and free from Inquisitorial prosecution. On 15 July 1658, Velázquez presented his genealogy to the Council of the Orders. His father, he informed the Council, was Juan Rodríguez de Silva, his mother Gerónima de Velázquez. Both parents were natives of Seville, as were his maternal grandparents, Juan Velázquez and Catalina de Zayas. The painter's paternal grandparents were, he stated, Diego Rodríguez de Silva and Maria Rodríguez, and were from the city of Porto in the north of Portugal.[6]

As Spain had been at war with Portugal since 1640, the Council of the Orders decided, after some deliberation, to conduct its Portuguese investigations in and around the Spanish town of Tui, which lay some 100 kilometers north of Porto, in the region of Galicia. The other investigations were to take place in Madrid and Seville.

On 1 November 1658, the two investigators, Don Fernando de Salcedo and Don Diego Lozano Villasandino, both members of the Order of Santiago, arrived in Galicia to conduct their inquiries. During the next month the two men interviewed 75 people. The majority of the interviewees, as was to be expected, had no knowledge at all of Velázquez's paternal grandparents, although a number of them pointed out that the name de Silva was considered a noble one, without hint of Jewish or Moorish blood. One witness, Juan Feixo de Noboa,[7] a second lieutenant in the Spanish infantry, stated that he had heard mention of Velázquez's grandparents while he was stationed in Porto in 1640, and that they had the reputation of being nobles whose blood was clear [of racial impurity]. Another military man, Captain Diego de Vegas Hoyos,[8] told the investigators that he had met an Alonso Rodríguez de Silva in Porto in 1627, who had claimed to be a relative of Diego Velázquez. Alonso had heard it said that Diego Rodríguez de Silva and his wife were Old Christians, and that they had not been involved in any mechanical or otherwise low or vile work. Two or three of the other witnesses also made specific reference to the Rodríguez de Silva family, albeit without offering any more concrete evidence as to its noble or Old Christian status.

From 20 December 1658 to 11 January 1659, Salcedo and Lozano were in Madrid, taking depositions from another 23 witnesses, a number of whom were knights of the Orders of Santiago or Calatrava. The painters Francisco de Zurbarán and Alonso Cano were also interviewed.[9] Zurbarán stated that he had known Velázquez for 40 years. Although he did not know either the paternal or maternal grandparents personally, he did know that the Velázquez were people of high standing and that the Silvas came from an area of Portugal (the northwest, between the rivers Douro and Minho) where their surname was famed for its noble and illustrious character (an observation made by a number of witnesses). Alonso Cano, who had known Velázquez for 44 years, could offer no information on the painter's background, save that he understood his parents were nobles, legitimately married, and untainted by Jewish or Moorish blood, or at least he had heard nothing to the contrary. The other Madrid depositions were of a similarly monotonous and inconclusive character: the Silva surname was a noble one; the Silva grandparents were said to be from noble and Old Christian backgrounds, as were the Velázquez; no one in the painter's family had been engaged in an artisanal, mercantile, or otherwise base profession, as far as anyone knew.

The Seville depositions, taken between 31 January and 16 February 1659, were somewhat more informative as to Velázquez's noble background. Most of the witnesses stated that the acid test of a man's noble status in Seville was provided by his exemption from the meat tax; and that Velázquez's father, Juan Rodríguez de Silva, his grandfathers, Juan Velázquez and Diego Rodríguez de Silva, and his maternal great-grandfather, a certain Andrés de Buenrostro, all enjoyed this privilege. The investigators also produced information from the meat tax registers, located in the city council offices, corroborating these statements. Juan Velázquez and Andrés de Buenrostro were exempted on 7 July 1600, and 13 February 1609, respectively, while Diego Rodríguez de Silva's and Juan Rodríguez de Silva's successful petitions (for which no dates were given) were recorded on pages 33 and 168 of the 1613–1642 register. To conclude their report, the investigators also submitted information from the church of San Pedro's records, confirming that Diego Velázquez was baptized on 6 June 1599, and that he was the legitimate child of Juan Rodríguez de Silva and Gerónima Velázquez.[10] Curiously, no information was supplied on Velázquez's parents' marriage, despite the fact that this event was also recorded in the San Pedro church registers.[11]

Don Fernando Antonio de Salcedo and Don Diego Lozano Villasandino submitted their report to the Council of the Orders on 26 February 1659. Five weeks later, on 2 April 1659, the Council published its findings. The good news was that no evidence had been submitted to suggest that Diego Velázquez's family was converso; unfortunately, neither was there any firm indication that his antecedents were nobles—the exemption from the meat tax having been rejected, unsurprisingly, as proof of blue blood.[12] Velázquez could, therefore, only enter the noble Order of Santiago, the Council informed the king, with papal dispensation. On 1 October the pope issued the necessary brief, and on Friday, 28 November 1659, in a formal ceremony held in the *Convento de Religiosos de Corpus Christi*, Diego Velázquez became a knight of the Order of Santiago.[13]

Antonio Palomino tells us that the Council of the Orders obstructed Velázquez's petition out of envy of the painter's position of privilege at court.[14] This may have been so; nevertheless, Palomino's statement is misleading, intimating that the Council had victimized a man of noble lineage. While it is possible that the Council was not well disposed toward

Velázquez's candidacy,[15] this does not alter the fact that the evidence presented to it in support of the painter's noble ancestry was scant. It was also, as the Council may well have surmised, false.

In fact, the painter was flagrantly transforming his family tree. Velázquez was not from a noble background, and even if exemption from the meat tax were proof of noble provenance, the Velázquez family would still fail the test, for the Juan Velázquez who appeared in the meat tax registers of 1600 was not Diego Velázquez's grandfather. The painter's grandfather was the *calcetero* (hosier) and merchant Juan Velázquez Moreno, who died of the plague in 1599.[16] Furthermore, Velázquez's maternal grandmother was not Catalina de Zayas, but Juana (or Ana) Mexía Aguilar.[17] Thus, while the man who gained exemption from the meat tax in 1609, Andrés de Buenrostro, may have been the legitimate father of a Catalina de Zayas, he was certainly not Diego Velázquez's great-grandfather.

Velázquez had lied about the paternal side of his family too. It was his paternal grandmother that was the Rodríguez de Silva; his paternal grandfather was merely a Rodríguez. Doubtless, the painter had presented his grandfather as a Silva to give the impression of an even stronger link to the noble clan he claimed to be part of. These discrepancies would, naturally, have come to light had the Council of the Orders been allowed to view Velázquez's parents' wedding record; that indeed, one suspects, is why the investigators never submitted it.

The two investigators had clearly ignored material that was detrimental to Velázquez's petition; they had also selected witnesses who, through friendship or, perhaps, venality, were disposed to corroborate the false genealogy. These deceptions were, of course, not unique to the Velázquez case. Antonio Domínguez Ortiz notes that such were the irregularities in the military orders' genealogical investigations that in 1654 (four years before Velázquez's petition) the Council of the Orders opened a full-scale inquiry into the situation.[18] Ruth Pike's investigation into the converso origins of the Sevillian dramatist Diego Jimenez Enciso presents us with a specific example of the intrigue and corruption that often accompanied the military orders' inquiries into candidates' backgrounds.[19] In the 1620s Enciso, a converso with enemies on the Seville city council, had tried to gain greater social status by securing Santiago knighthoods for his two nephews. While the investigations conducted by the Santiago officials supported the Enciso version of the family ancestry, certain letters sent to the Council of the Orders indicated that the Encisos were a converso merchant family, one of whose members, the silk merchant Juan de Jerez, appeared in the Seville *composición* of 1510.[20] By bribing witnesses, the letters claimed, the Encisos had succeeded in disguising their true origins. Accusations of misconduct were also made against Juan de Jáuregui's investigating committee when the Seville poet (a friend of Velázquez's mentor, Francisco Pacheco) applied for entry into the Military Order of Calatrava in 1627.[21] Those witnesses who had presented information on Jáuregui's converso background had been filtered out of the report, it was claimed, while others had been bribed to testify to his Old Christian origins. In a subsequent inquiry into the allegations, it was revealed that the poet was a member of the Sal family, a successful converso merchant clan which had used its wealth to buy prestigious government offices, thereby dissimulating its converso background.[22]

Had Diego Velázquez, like Juan de Jáuregui and Diego Jimenez Enciso, coached or bribed his witnesses into lying about his Old Christian background? The Council of the Orders had stated, it is true, that Velázquez's blood was clear of blemish; however, this conclusion was based solely on the testimony of witnesses who, as we have seen, had lied about the painter's noble ancestry. Had these people also lied to hide the candidate's Jewish lineage?

The possibility that the Velázquez family, or at least the paternal line, were conversos has already been broached by the Spanish art historian Julián Gállego in his study *Velázquez en Sevilla*.[23] Velázquez's paternal grandparents must have entered Spain, Gállego determines, in the last quarter of the sixteenth century. It was during this period that Portuguese conversos began crossing the border, fleeing an Inquisition that was proving to be even more rigorous in its prosecution of Judaizers than its Spanish counterpart.[24] What Gállego does not mention is that two of the more popular surnames adopted by Portuguese conversos were Silva and Rodríguez, as a glance at the seventeenth-century Inquisition trials of suspected Judaizers will testify. Indeed, it appears that the name Silva suffered a loss of prestige in the seventeenth century, due to its association with Portuguese conversos.[25]

There is yet a further indication that Velázquez's Portuguese roots may have been Jewish ones. This concerns the painter's reaction to the news that the investigation into his Portuguese family was to be conducted on the stretch of the Portuguese border closest to the city of Seville. On 29 June 1658, Velázquez wrote to the king, beseeching him to have these inquiries take place not on the border but in the Spanish capital, as had previously been the policy when men of Portuguese backgrounds had petitioned for knighthood.

Velázquez was right: in the past, military order investigations into Portuguese candidates had taken place not in Portugal but in Madrid. However, it had become clear that this practice was aiding many Portuguese conversos to gain noble titles, and for this reason had been abandoned. As the Council of Orders pointed out to the king in a letter of 5 July 1658, the practice of conducting the Portuguese inquiries in Madrid had given rise to a number of problems. The Council had thus changed its investigation policy, and it was not recommendable that Velázquez be made an exception to this ruling. However, given the close relationship that existed between the king and the candidate, the Council was disposed to conduct the Portuguese investigations on the northern Portuguese border closest to the city of Porto, where the candidate had stated his family was from. (As Spain had been at war with Portugal since 1640, investigations could not take place inside Portuguese territory.)

Velázquez had claimed his Portuguese ancestors were from Porto, it would seem, with the intention of directing the genealogical investigation away from their true domicile. Unfortunately for the painter, the Council had ignored the bait, opting to conduct its inquiries on the Portuguese border closest to Seville. It was this decision that prompted Velázquez's anxious appeal to the king. The Council then responded by informing the candidate that it would follow his instructions and conduct the investigation in a safe place—in other words, not in the south, which was clearly making him uneasy, but on the border closest to Porto, where the painter had wanted the inquiries held all along (*'que es donde da el pretendiente sus origines por la genealogia que a presentado en el Consejo'*).[26]

In all probability Velázquez's paternal family did not issue from the northwest of Portugal, as the painter claimed, but from Portugal's southeastern borderland. It was along this thin strip of rugged terrain, Caro Baroja informs us, that the vast majority of Portugal's converso population resided[27]; and it was from here that the majority of *émigrés* issued in the late sixteenth century, bearing names like Núñez, Castro, Silva, and Rodríguez. Most of the men and women who crossed the border were involved in activities related to the textile industry (weavers, tailors, cloth and clothes merchants), time-honored practices of a Jewish community resident in the Spanish-Portuguese border area.[28] Once in Spain these new arrivals gravitated toward converso communities (usually in Extremadura and Andalusia), where they formed business and marriage alliances with Spanish socio-cultural counterparts, often involved in like activities. This, I would suggest, is the profile of Diego Velázquez's paternal grandfather, Diego Rodríguez, who, in 1597, married his son Juan to Gerónima Velázquez, daughter of the clothes merchant Juan Velázquez Moreno.[29]

While Velázquez's paternal family remains hidden from view, his maternal family has recently begun to reveal itself through Seville's notarial archive, which presents us with some interesting details on his grandfather Juan Velázquez Moreno's business activities. In his notarial contracts, Velázquez Moreno refers to himself as a maker of velvet breeches, a craft, like silk weaving (to which it was linked), or tailoring, associated with converso artisans.[30] Making expensive breeches was, however, only one of Velázquez Moreno's activities; he was also a merchant, a renter of property, and, on occasion, a moneylender. His associates were men in the clothes trade and silversmiths; his friends were Seville notaries.[31] He was clearly literate, as testified by his signature, executed in bold, confident strokes, which dominates all his notarial contracts. He was, in short, an exemplum of the Seville converso merchant.

Of Velázquez Moreno's wife Juana, or Ana Mexía, we know nothing save that she was illiterate and that her surname was one associated with conversos.[32] We have no idea when the couple married, which may suggest that the wedding took place before the Tridentine ruling on marriage records was enforced. It is also possible that the two opted to form a marriage union outside the church, using a notary to record a civil process. If this is so, the evidence remains buried in the un-indexed tomes of Seville's notarial archive. The Seville archive does reveal, however, that the couple had at least three surviving children: Ana, Fernando (a notary), and Gerónima, Diego Velázquez's mother, who was at least ten years younger than her brother and sister. [33]

Gerónima was probably no more than 17 or 18 when she married Juan Rodríguez de Silva, on 31 December 1597. The ceremony was not held in the local church of San Pedro, but in the family home close by, Velázquez Moreno having applied for a special license to have the ceremony performed in a secular setting.[34] It was in this house that Diego Velázquez was born in late May or early June of 1599, in the same year that both his maternal grandparents, whom he later tried to erase from his family tree, died of the plague.

Private Subtexts

Soon after Juan Velázquez Moreno's death, Juan Rodríguez, his wife, and infant son Diego moved to the district of San Lorenzo, where, in short succession, four more children were born. It was perhaps this growing family that persuaded Rodríguez to apprentice his eldest son, at the age of 11, to the painter Francisco Pacheco. However, it is also likely that he had noted some artistic promise in the boy, and believed that he, Diego, might make good use of this in a city in which wealthy religious institutions and well-heeled merchants were vying for professional painters' services. The fact that Rodríguez chose Francisco Pacheco as Diego's master also indicates that he had put some serious thought into his son's career; for while Pacheco may not have been the most talented painter in Seville, he was certainly one of the better connected ones.

The painter to whom Diego Velázquez was apprenticed in 1610 was, like his young charge, from a tailoring background. According to a *limpieza de sangre* examination undertaken by Pacheco between 1593 and 1595, his father and two of his four brothers were tailors.[35] His father, Juan Pérez, had practiced this trade not in Seville but in Sanlucar de Barrameda, the seat of the powerful Medina Sidonia family, where Pacheco was born in 1564. It was in Sanlucar that Pacheco's grandfather, also named Juan Pérez, gained his living as a seaman, working on the Indies fleet. The Pacheco family's professional activities and residence both suggest that Francisco Pacheco, like his young apprentice, was from a converso background.

From the *limpieza* document we learn that Pacheco's paternal grandmother was named Maria López, which strongly suggests that it was through her that the painter and his namesake, the celebrated Seville humanist, Licentiate Francisco Pacheco, were linked. It is probable that Maria López and Elvira López Miranda, Licentiate Pacheco's mother, were sisters; thus, the Licentiate was the painter's second cousin and not his uncle, as the latter was wont to state. On her birth certificate Francisco's daughter Juana, later Diego Velázquez's wife, was registered as Juana Miranda, again suggesting that the Licentiate and the painter were linked through the Miranda López family, which, according to the Licentiate's *limpieza de sangre* report, had left Miranda del Ebro at the time of the Jewish expulsion to set up home in Jerez de la Frontera.[36]

It is, of course, quite natural that the ambitious young painter Francisco Pacheco would wish to create the impression of a strong familial relationship with the Licentiate, who, as a canon in Seville Cathedral, was both a potential source of clients and, equally important, a link to Seville's intellectual elite. It was through his association with this elite group that Pacheco looked to convert his image as base artisan to that of noble (humanist) artist.

Pacheco was obsessed by the image of the artist ennobled through his talent, as is evident from an examination of his two major prose works, *Retratos de varones insignes* and *El arte de la pintura*. The first of these works is a series of pen-and-ink portraits and short prosopographies of Seville's humanist or humanistic community, which attempts to polish the scholars' literary, moral, and genealogical reputations. It is also a vehicle for Pacheco to showcase his own artistic virtues and to have them praised by friends in exaggerated poetic encomiums proclaiming his noble artistry. Following the same lines, the second work is both a guidebook for noble artistic practice and a declaration of the author's own elevated position within the painting community, a position attained, so he would have us believe, through his clear understanding of the technique and theory of pictorial expression. In contrast to this vaunted image, however, Pacheco's canvases, often rigid and aseptic, indicate a man of only modest talent. The abiding impression is of a pedant, whose inflated view of himself stands in marked contrast to his artistic ability.

Self-promotion apart, however, Pacheco was a man of some learning, who clearly saw himself as spiritual heir to those humanists I have examined in the previous chapter. Indeed, he seems to have been animated by the idea, first expressed by Juan de Malara in his *Philosophia vulgar*, of creating an informal academy of men who would work together to promote the humanist enterprise within the city.[37] Among Pacheco's own scholarly network were the painter Pablo de Céspedes and the Jesuits Juan de Pineda and Luis de Alcázar.[38] Younger friends and collaborators included Juan de Jáuregui, Juan de Fonseca y Figueroa, and Francisco de Rioja, all of whom, along with Velázquez, would become members of the Count-Duke of Olivares' inner circle at court.[39] Pacheco also maintained a close relationship with Don Fadrique Enríquez de Ribera, the third Duke of Alcalá, who, like his father, the second Duke, promoted humanist discourse in the city, some of which took place under the roof of his famous palace, the *Casa de Pilatos*. It was here, in 1605, that Pacheco painted the *Apotheosis of Hercules*, a ceiling fresco celebrating individual accomplishment, in this instance rewarded by a place among the gods.

It was in the humanistic atmosphere of Pacheco's household that Diego Velázquez was educated between 1611 and 1623, and it was here that his art soon took on a realist quality that was its enduring trait. However, Velázquez's early works allude not only to a humanist formation but also to an intensely spiritual, or mystical, one. It would seem that Pacheco's apprentice grew up in an environment in which classical learning and private spiritual communion went hand in hand, an impression reinforced by an examination of Pacheco's *Arte de historia* or his library, both of which reveal a man of quietist inclination. Indeed, recent studies suggest that Pacheco's religiosity may have been rather more radical than his literary works or library suggest. There is even some indication that Velázquez's master and father-in-law was connected to the Congregation of the Pomegranate (*Congregación de la Granada*), a secret sect investigated by the Seville Inquisition a year before Velázquez left Seville for the royal court in Madrid.

The Inquisition inquiry, which began in 1622, was directed initially toward the *beata* Catalina de Jesus, a native of Baeza and adherent of Juan de Ávila's disciple Pedro de Hojeda, himself prosecuted for heresy in 1590.[40] Catalina's own non-conformism was an amalgam of the mystical-iconoclastic views of Juan de Ávila (advocacy of mental prayer, rejection of church rituals and saint worship, contempt for the Inquisition) and the more eccentric characteristics (claims to prophetic abilities, for example) common to *alumbrado* leaders. These beliefs appear to have struck a chord with a large section of Seville's population. In their early letters to the Supreme Council, the Seville Inquisition officials described the *beata*'s following as massive, a view confirmed by the number of people—almost a thousand—who came forward during a period of grace to confess their religious errors. It was while this investigation was taking place that the Inquisition also began to hear reports of a strange, hermetic group known as the Congregation of the Pomegranate which, they were informed, had been operating in the city for over 50 years.

According to the Dominican father and inquisitor Domingo Farfan, in his 1626 report on the sect, the Congregation was formed in 1541, or thereabouts, in Lebrija, by a locksmith, Gómez Camacho, who saw himself as the voice of Jesus, sent to change the Church in preparation for the Second Coming.[41] The first time we catch sight of Camacho, he is being interviewed by the Seville Inquisition tribunal, accused of defaming the Church through a series of anti-clerical visions, one of which was of an abused Christ sold for 30 pieces of silver, not by the treacherous Jew,

Judas, but by the religious orders and the secular clergy.[42] Responding to these accusations, Camacho stated that he had heard a voice telling him: 'Go, go and deliver my people from Captivity,' and in this he understood that he was to become the intermediary for other servants of God who were 'hidden, shackled, and mistreated and who did not dare come forward for fear of being treated badly like others before them.'[43] It seems that Camacho saw himself as a representative of a beleaguered converso community, a man chosen by God to announce His imminent arrival, at which point His people, the conversos, would be delivered from their enemy, an oppressive Catholic Church. If this event occurred after his death, Camacho believed that he would be resurrected, along with a select group of adherents, who would then be martyred in a struggle against the anti-Christ.

Camacho's millenarian fantasy of cleansing a corrupt Church was not unusual in a Spanish illuminist movement directed for the most part by conversos with an axe to grind against a prejudicial Church and a vindictive Holy Office. More original is his devotion to the Virgin Mary, who, along with other saints, was usually ignored by early converso illuminists. In contrast, Camacho and his followers saw the Virgin as a figure of liberty, leading her people against their enemies at the end of time. This vision exactly reversed that of Old Christian Spain, which in the late Middle Ages had co-opted the Virgin, in her guise as John the Evangelist's 'woman clothed with the sun' (Revelation 12: 1–3), as a standard bearer for its fight against the anti-Christ, Islamic Granada.[44] In their appropriation of the image, Camacho's sect had made the Virgin the representative of good New Christians against a dragon that was the Catholic Church.

After his release from Inquisition confinement, in 1543, Camacho settled in Lebrija, where he soon attracted a group of adherents, appropriately associated with the town's Immaculist convent. In fact the Immaculist order, founded by the Portuguese Beatriz de Silva in 1484, appears to have been regarded as a safe haven by wealthy conversos, who were often involved in founding the order's first convents.[45] Whether the prioress of the Lebrija convent, Francisca de Vera, was a converso is not known. It is, however, likely that Camacho's disciple and successor Rodrigo Álvarez, the son of a Portuguese physician, was from a New Christian background.[46] In the 1550s Álvarez continued Camacho's mission in and around Lebrija, before moving to Seville, where, in 1566, he joined the Jesuits. Here he gained a reputation as an expert on orthodox mysticism, while continuing to peddle, in private, his own prophesies. Ironically, it was Rodrigo Álvarez who was given the task of appraising Teresa of Ávila's mysticism when, in 1577, her Seville convent was denounced as a center of *alumbrado* practice.[47]

After Álvarez's death, in 1587, the sculptor Juan Bautista Vázquez had two visions of him as a new Jesus, both of which were circulated among his followers. In the first of these the sculptor saw Álvarez, dressed in his Jesuit robe, descend from heaven holding aloft a burning axe, one half of which was old, the other half new. He was followed by a multitude of cardinals, bishops, priests, and people of all estates. He was also accompanied by a heavenly voice, declaring: 'This is not a new light, but that old light of the early Church.' This image of Álvarez as a latter-day Jesus was reinforced by Bautista's second vision, in which God poured crystalline water over the Jesuit, who caught it in a glass held next to his chest; and from this glass of pure water many people came to drink.[48]

On continuing Gómez Camacho's prophetic mission, Rodrigo Álvarez had been vouchsafed a secret by his master. While the Inquisition inquiry of 1623 was unable to discover what this was, it did learn that Álvarez passed it on to six other people, a group of disciples known as 'the six of the special spirit' (*los seis del particular espíritu*). Among these men were two silversmiths, Juan del Salto and Alonso Pérez de Vargas, a Portuguese painter, Vasco Pereira, and a priest, Hernando de Mata, who, in 1587, became the new head of the sect. During his time as leader, Mata created yet another inner group of six, among whom were the priest Bernardo de Toro (the next and final head of the sect) and Juan de Pacheco's friend and collaborator, the sculptor Juan Martínez Montañes. Beyond the inner circle was an ever-growing group of followers, known as the *comunes*.

It was during Hernando de Mata's leadership that the sect became known as the Congregation of the Pomegranate, the name taken from the cathedral chapel dedicated to Our Lady of the Pomegranate, to which Mata was assigned to give Sunday sermons. Mata's private group of adherents met in the Courtyard of the Oranges, directly outside the chapel, where they were introduced to the sect's peculiar credo, at the center of which lay the immaculately conceived Virgin.

By the time of Mata's death, in 1612, the Immaculist cult had grown considerably in Seville, promoted by the Franciscans and Jesuits, but also by the Congregationalists (among whom were moonlighting members of the Society), motivated by their own particular agenda. This growing support for the *Inmaculada* created tensions with the city's Dominicans, led by the prior of the Dominican monastery of *Regina Angelorum*, Domingo de Molina, a vociferous opponent of the cult. At the 1613 feast of the Immaculate Conception, Molina was particularly combative, declaring from the pulpit that the Virgin 'was conceived like you and I and Martin Luther.'[49] This assault was met with processions throughout Seville, celebrating the *Inmaculada*, many of which were orchestrated by the Congregation, whose new leader, Hernando de Toro, put music to a poem by a city versifier, Miguel Cid, championing the Virgin's pure conception. Four thousand copies of these poems were then printed, financed by another Congregation member, Mateo Vazquez de Leca, and distributed throughout the city.

In reply to this propaganda, an anonymous author, presumably a Dominican close to Domingo de Molina, wrote the following verse:

>Most holy rag dealers and scriveners
>Virtuous lackeys and squires
>Wise mulattos, learned shoemakers
>*Religiosos*, arresting officers [*corchetes*]
>Divine pages, sovereign tailors
>Watercarriers, shepherds, barber-surgeons
>To arms, to arms victorious people
>Pillars and teachers of the church
>Pay no attention to any saint
>Define, blaspheme ... now
>And persecute the Order that has so
>Persecuted your lineage
>Well, then, sagacious soldiers
>The pastor, to clear the way for us,
>Has tied up the black and white dog.[50]

This anonymous author's attack is directed against a laity that sets itself up as a religious authority without proper training. However, the target is not lay society in general, but those members of it that hold a grudge against the Dominicans, an order inextricably linked to the Inquisition, for persecuting their ancestors. In other words, according to the writer, the *Inmaculada* protest in Seville was at root a New Christian one, supported by rag dealers, scriveners, shoemakers, tailors, and barber-surgeons (traditional converso professions), and directed against an order associated with their persecution. The writer also notes that the pastor (the Archbishop of Seville) was aiding and abetting the New Christians by tying up the black-and-white dog (the Dominicans) so that it could not protect the flock.

The archbishop referred to is none other than Pedro de Castro, who, as Bishop of Granada (1589–1610), championed the Lead Book discoveries on Valparaiso Hill. Castro was particularly enthused to learn from these forgeries that Saint Peter himself had stated that the Virgin's conception was immaculate. Evidently, this revelation was used as bait by the Morisco forgers to gain the Old Christian authorities' approbation for what were some fairly implausible claims concerning Arab involvement in the early Spanish Church. However, Mary was not used cynically. Like the Congregation of the Pomegranate, the Lead Books falsifiers clearly saw the *Inmaculada* as a talisman for a reformed Christianity, with themselves as an important component of this new Church.[51]

Pedro de Castro's personal interest in the Immaculate Conception, animated first by the Granada finds and now by the Congregation's obsession, propelled him, in 1615, to finance a two-man delegation to Rome (formed by the Congregation members Bernardo de Toro and Mateo Vazquez de Leca) to call for the belief's dogmatization. The papacy remained unconvinced, however, and continued so for the next two hundred years. It was not until 1854 that the *Inmaculada* was legitimized in dogma; although, in 1617, Pope Paul V did issue a papal brief stating that the cult should not be criticized in public, a declaration greeted in Seville with jubilation and an increased demand for images of the Virgin.

In the period directly following the papal announcement, Francisco Pacheco painted three *Inmaculadas*, with the Virgin each time in the company of a Congregation member. The first of these paintings was of Miguel Cid, who wrote the celebrated poem in support of the Virgin; the second was of Mateo Vazquez de Leca; and the third, according to a recent study, was of the head of the Congregation, Bernardo de Toro.[52] The fact that Pacheco was chosen by members of the sect to execute their devotional portraits may have been purely casual; nevertheless, it is noteworthy that in his *Retratos*, the painter not only includes studies of two of the sect's leaders, Álvarez and Mata, he also writes about them in a way that suggests he was a follower.[53] Álvarez, he tells his readers, entered the Jesuits after meeting the 'saintly' Gómez Camacho, and among other things he had the gift of prophecy, even divining the date of his own death. He also reveals that he had been personally present at Álvarez's funeral, where he witnessed a number of people taking pieces of his clothes, 'with which God has made great miracles.'[54] Of Mata, Pacheco states that, like Álvarez, he was given the gift of prophecy. He also notes that those present at Mata's funeral snatched flowers and pieces of his habit as if they were relics. Furthermore, he discloses that in 1608 Mata requested a portrait from him in which he, Mata, was to be depicted next to his predecessor Álvarez, and that in executing the canvas Pacheco should be inspired by the story of the Old Testament prophet Elisha, who, led by God, appointed Elijah as his successor.[55] The anecdote suggests that Pacheco was not only on familiar terms with Mata, he was also privy to the Congregation's secret mission.

It is also noteworthy that three of Pacheco's collaborators in his artistic and literary works were men closely associated with the sect. These were the painter Vasco Pereira, the sculptor Juan Martínez Montañes, and the Jesuit father Juan de Pineda, who was later accused by the inquisitor Domingo Farfan of having many Congregation papers in his possession.[56] Finally, there is Pacheco's *Last Judgement*, executed in 1613, in which he places a portrait of himself among the saved, for, as he notes in his *Arte de la pintura*, 'it is certain that I will find myself present on that day.' How do we interpret what would seem on the surface to be a piece of gratuitous impudence? Could it be that Pacheco was oblivious to his own arrogance, concerned only with the wish to announce surreptitiously his membership of a sect whose raison d'être was the final combat against the anti-Christ?[57]

Although it is impossible to gauge the extent of Pacheco's involvement in the Congregation, it is evident that it ran deeper than a mutual concern for the Virgin Mary. Whether this attraction was shared by his apprentice and future son-in-law is a moot point. Nevertheless, even if Velázquez was not a devotee of the sect, the setting and tone of his early religious canvases strongly suggest that he too was attracted to clandestine illuminist practice. There is something perplexing, even disconcerting, about Velázquez's early religious *bodegones*. It is as if he is offering us a tantalizing glimpse of a secret, and while we are not exactly sure what this is, we know, instinctively, that it is not orthodox. In this respect Velázquez has much in common with Caravaggio, a painter he clearly admired. Both are non-conformists, robbing the Church of its institutional iconography and transforming it into a personal, subversive one. However, while Caravaggio's non-conformism is that of the populist, taking the Scriptures to the streets, Velázquez's is that of the domesticator, taking them home with him, to an interior space.

Velázquez appears to choose his religious subjects precisely because they allow him access to a domestic environment in which he can stealthily convey a private, quietist religious outlook for his own benefit and that of a close circle of likeminded clients.[58] In both his bodegones *Christ in the House of Martha* and *Mary and Kitchen Maid with Supper at Emmaus*, the

Fig. 6.1 Diego Velázquez, *Kitchen Scene with Christ in the House of Martha and Mary*. Courtesy of the National Gallery, London. Bequeathed by Sir William H. Gregory, 1892

young painter adopts a Flemish artistic practice of juxtaposing contemporary domestic scenes with scriptural events, the scriptural story rendered in the background of the canvas. These religious paintings were favored by the Catholic Church for their didacticism, emphasizing both the biblical roots of Catholic dogma and its continuing relevance in the everyday lives of the faithful. However, Velázquez's bodegones subtly subordinate Catholic dogma to a private, interior religiosity.

In *Christ in the House of Martha and Mary* (Fig. 6.1) Velázquez makes reference to Jesus' visit to the home of the two sisters Mary and Martha, who then invite him to dinner (Luke 10: 38–42). However, while Martha prepares the food, Mary chooses to engage Jesus in a conversation on spiritual matters. Irritated, Martha asks Jesus if He approves of her sister's conduct, to which He replies: 'Martha, Martha, thou art careful and troubled about many things: But one thing is needful; and Mary has chosen that good part, which shall not be taken away from her.' While the Catholic Church attempted to put a brave face on this passage, claiming it underlined the importance of both faith and good works for gaining salvation, it is clear that good works are presented, at best, as an optional extra. Perhaps it was this doctrinal ambiguity that underlay the story's appeal to Velázquez, whose own rendition of the scriptural passage appears to focus on the insignificance of Martha's religious role.

In the foreground of Velázquez's canvas, an old woman (a mentor figure) draws our attention to a young, unprepossessing servant (an allusion to Martha) who is gloomily preparing food in a kitchen, clearly unimpressed with her task, while, in an interior space, a comely girl, with blonde tresses, is in conversation with a seated man. We assume that this background scene is an allusion to Luke's story. However, in Velázquez's rendition Martha has no contact with Jesus, her place taken by the old woman mentor figure, who, with pointed finger, draws the viewer's attention toward the spiritual Mary. It would thus appear that the painter is paying lip service to Tridentine orthodoxy while alluding to a domestic religious practice based on faith alone.

Like his *Christ in the House of Martha and Mary*, Velázquez's *Kitchen Maid with Supper at Emmaus* (Fig. 6.2) also appears to emphasize Catholic orthodox practice through a reference to Scripture. According to the biblical story (Luke 24: 13–35), after His resurrection, Jesus meets two of his followers on the road to Emmaus. At first the two men fail to recognize the Savior; it is only when Jesus breaks the bread in two at supper that His identity becomes suddenly apparent. This scene was taken by the Counter-Reformation Church as an allegorical reference to transubstantiation, or the insistence that at the mass Christ is physically present in the Host. However, Velázquez chooses to present us with a kitchen scene free of sacramental symbolism. There is no bread (invariably a staple in renditions of the story); only a table unencumbered by food (save for a fist of garlic), behind which stands a young

Fig. 6.2 Diego Velázquez, *Kitchen Maid with the Supper at Emmaus*. Courtesy of the National Gallery of Ireland, Dublin. Presented, Sir Alfred and Lady Beit, 1987 (Beit collection)

black servant or slave, whose posture, body placed against the wall to avoid detection, suggests that her interest in the dining-room conversation is something other than spiritual. Indeed, she appears to be eavesdropping on a private religious gathering taking place in the adjacent room, a practice common to servants, who were very often the Inquisition's source of information. Once again, I would suggest, Velázquez's subject is not Tridentine orthodoxy but private, or secret, religious practice, undertaken in interior rooms away from the servants' gaze.

Velázquez invariably takes institutional religious subjects and transforms them into private ones. Even the Virgin Mary is transformed from a stylized icon into a comely young girl (*Immaculate Conception*), or a young bride and mother (*Adoration of the Magi*, Fig. 6.3). In the latter painting, executed in 1619, Velázquez evidently employs the biblical story to celebrate the birth of his first child Francisca, held by her mother, Juana Pacheco (Mary), and observed by Velázquez's father-in-law, Francisco Pacheco (as Joseph). However, in order to present his domestic drama, the artist was forced to take liberties with standard iconography. As Pacheco notes in his *Arte de la pintura*, the first of the three magi to pay his respects to the Savior is the eldest, represented with white hair and beard, who offers the infant gold (a symbol of kinghood).[59] In his own rendition of the scene, Velázquez changes the order so that the younger man is the protagonist, offering his gift of myrrh (symbolizing mortality) to the painter's infant daughter.[60]

Significantly, the most spiritually evocative of all Velázquez's early works, *An Old Woman Cooking Eggs* (Fig. 6.4) and *The Waterseller* (Fig. 6.5) do not depict religious scenes at all, but private, everyday ones. In *An Old Woman Cooking Eggs*, two people are caught in a moment of intense spiritual contemplation while involved in the act of preparing a meal. The simplicity of the food, three eggs, alludes to the simple religious message of the Bible, based on Christ's birth, resurrection, and second coming (thus the third egg remains in the woman's hand). At the same time the carafe of oil, held by the boy, is a symbol of purity and anointment, as is the goblet of water which the same boy holds in *The Waterseller*. The woman, who bears a strong resemblance to the figure in *Christ in the House of Martha and Mary*, once again appears to be a mentor, instructing her young charge in practical and spiritual matters. Here, spirituality is once again a private affair, passed from the old to the young in a household setting. Indeed, I would suggest that Velázquez's scene presents a

Fig. 6.3 Diego Velázquez, *Adoration of the Magi*. Alamy Images. © Heritage Image Partnership Ltd/Alamy Stock Photo

Fig. 6.4 Diego Velázquez, *An Old Woman Cooking Eggs*. © PAINTING/ Alamy Stock Photo

domestic mysticism reminiscent of that which the Holy Office had come to associate with *alumbrado* heresy.

Like *An Old Woman Cooking Eggs*, *The Waterseller* captures an intense, mystical moment between an old man (the mentor) and a young boy (the pupil). Here, the two figures are united spiritually through a finely cut glass goblet (or chalice) which they both delicately clasp. Clearly, this very dignified waterseller is no ordinary vender plying his trade among the general public; he is, rather, a private individual, catering to a select clientele in a rarefied atmosphere beyond the public's gaze. This impression of covert practice is reinforced by a third figure, a shadowy presence who appears to drink in secret. Indeed, the scene evokes Juan Bautista Vasquez's vision of Rodrigo Álvarez (mentioned above), in which the Congregation leader is baptized by God, the water caught in a crystal goblet next to his chest, from which his followers drink.

Fig. 6.5 Diego Velázquez, *The Waterseller*. © Lebrecht Music and Arts Photo Library/Alamy Stock Photo

It has been suggested that the fig at the bottom of the glass of water held by the old man and the boy is a visual pun on the name Juan de Fonseca y Figueroa, for whom the painting was executed.[61] This does not, however, explain why the glass is full of water; surely, if this were merely a pun on the owner's name, the fig would be in an empty goblet, more accurately reflecting the name Fonseca (dry font). I would suggest that Velázquez was not merely interested in including a reference to Fonseca y Figueroa, his friend and patron, but in linking him with the private, mystical religiosity depicted in the canvas. In placing the fig in a glass of crystalline water, Velázquez is, I believe, associating Fonseca with a pure, reformed Christianity. Whether or not he is linking him to the Congregation is a matter of conjecture.

Juan de Fonseca y Figueroa, the recipient of Velázquez's tribute, was a member of an illustrious family closely associated with religious reform. Fonseca's ancestor, Juan Rodriguez de Fonseca, was the famous Erasmian Archbishop of Toledo, examined in Chap. 2 of this work. Another family member, Juan de Ulloa Pereira, was convicted of Protestantism in the 1559 Valladolid trials and punished with life imprisonment. The family's origins, at least on the paternal, Fonseca, side, were converso. This appears to have created an impediment for Juan's father, who wished to join the Order of Santiago in 1561, and his elder brother, Pedro, who applied for entry to the lesser Order of Alcántara in 1598. In Juan's *limpieza* examination to become a canon of Seville Cathedral in 1606, the problem was not mentioned. The investigators may have been unaware of it, or may simply have been instructed, as was often the case, to let sleeping dogs lie.[62]

Juan de Fonseca was a man with important connections, among which was his cousin Gaspar de Guzmán, later Count-Duke of Olivares.[63] Of Fonseca, Olivares wrote: '[W]e were close friends from early youth, the foundations of our friendship being ties of kinship and his great natural talents.'[64] In fact, the two coincided at Salamanca University as adolescents, and these student ties were renewed on Olivares' return to Seville, in 1607, to take charge of his family estate. When, eight years later, Olivares was called to court, Fonseca left his cathedral sinecure and followed suit. Later, on Olivares' accession to power, Fonseca was awarded the important position of *sumiller de cortina* in the royal chapel.

Soon after Fonseca arrived at court, other members of Olivares' Seville circle found their way to Madrid. These were Franciso de Rioja and Francisco de Calatayud, who were made court secretaries, and the poet and painter Juan de Jáuregui, who eventually became groom to the queen. Then, in 1623, Olivares was persuaded by Fonseca to summon Pacheco's young prodigy Diego Velázquez to the capital to paint a portrait of Philip IV. Velázquez' portrait was approved by both king and *privado*, and on 6 October the 24-year-old painter entered a royal court now dominated by Olivares and his program for socio-political change.

At the Court of the Count-Duke

With the death of Philip III, in May 1621, the Duke of Lerma's political faction fell from power at court, replaced by that of Don Gaspar de Guzmán, the Count of Olivares, who, as Philip IV's favorite, now became the most powerful man in Spain. For the ambitious Olivares this was a dream come true. Not only did it provide him with the means to gain further titles and enter Spain's elite group of grandees (something his predecessor, the Duke of Lerma, had exploited to the full), it also afforded him the opportunity of achieving lasting fame as a great, and virtuous, public figure.

To realize this goal Olivares turned to a reform program that had been mooted many times in humanist circles over the previous half century, including the circle he himself had belonged to during his recent sojourn in Seville: the reduction of emoluments for an idle nobility parked permanently and ineffectually at court; the rational distribution of taxes, taking the burden off the shoulders of the Castilian peasantry; the encouragement of domestic industry and the erection of import barriers to stimulate the national economy; the introduction of sumptuary laws to discourage profligate spending among the aristocracy; and the abolition, or at least curtailment, of *limpieza de sangre* legislation, thus giving conversos the opportunity to enter civic and ecclesiastical positions without running the *linajudo*'s (informer's) gauntlet. Olivares himself was a vehement opponent of the *limpieza de Sangre* statutes. In a Council of State meeting, convened in 1625 to discuss this issue, the *privado* stated: 'The law prohibiting honors is unjust and impious, against divine law, natural law, and the law of nations ... Without crime, without sin or offence against God, they [the conversos] find themselves—even when they excel all others in virtue, sanctity and scholarship—condemned not only without being heard, but without even the possibility of being heard ... In no other government or state in the world do such laws exist.'[65]

Olivares' interest in repealing the *limpieza* laws was not, however, impartial. The *privado*'s paternal grandmother, Francisca de Ribera Niño, was the daughter of Charles V's wealthy converso secretary, Lope Conchillos. Olivares was thus as sensitive to the *limpieza* issue as were his converso advisors, who were forced to lie about their backgrounds to gain public office. In his application for entry into the Military Order of Alcántara, in 1623, Olivares stated that all four branches of his family were Old Christian, free from Jewish stain. No one, of course, contradicted him, even though his converso background was an open secret at court.[66]

Olivares clearly had ulterior motives for supporting the abolition of the *limpieza de sangre* statutes. Nevertheless, it would be a mistake to view his anti-*limpieza* stand as being motivated entirely by self-interest. It is clear that Olivares' family maintained close ties with Seville's converso community long before Pedro de Guzmán y Zuñiga, the first Count of Olivares, married his converso bride in 1560. Indeed, it is to be supposed that the marriage took place precisely because Pedro's father, Juan Alonso Pérez de Guzmán, the third Duke of Medina Sidonia, was singularly, or cavalierly, unimpressed by the *limpieza* neurosis that was affecting sixteenth-century Spain. Olivares had inherited this attitude. Not only was he vociferous in his condemnation of the *limpieza* statutes, he was also unabashed about his interest in the Jewish culture, applying to the Inquisition for a license to own censored Hebrew literature. He even formed a close relationship with the Moroccan Jewish scholar Jacob Cansino, who acted as his emissary between the Madrid court and the converso (*marrano*) merchant community of Lisbon. In 1627, Olivares enticed a number of these Portuguese converso merchants to Madrid to act as the Crown's bankers, ignoring demands from the papacy and Holy Office to desist from such a dangerous enterprise.[67] Once at court these wealthy merchants were shielded from the Inquisition by the *privado*, who also aided their entry into the noble orders, through a measure known as the *patria común* (common nation), allowing Portuguese candidates to sidestep detrimental *limpieza de sangre* investigations. It was this same measure that Diego Velázquez would later try to take advantage of in his *limpieza* examination for entry into the Order of Santiago, in 1558.

Closely attached to a converso-humanist reform program, it was inevitable that Olivares would often clash with a court anxious to guard its noble privileges and the pretense of its honorable, Visigothic ancestry. One of the more vehement confrontations occurred in 1628, when Olivares lent his support to a campaign to make the recently canonized Teresa of Ávila co-patron of Spain (alongside Santiago, or Saint James the Greater). Whereas Saint James, known by all as the Moor Slayer, was associated with a pure, *castizo*, orthodox society and its drive against alien and heretical cultures, Saint Teresa's image was much more ambiguous. She herself had been attacked on many occasions by the Holy Office for her rejection of orthodox practice in favor of dangerous, mystical meditation. Furthermore, she had, in her own religious organization, manifested a preference for merit over clean blood. Olivares undoubtedly saw Teresa as a symbol of the new, revitalized Spain that he was in the process, or so he believed, of creating. However, the Count-Duke may also have had more personal reasons for supporting Teresa as co-patron of Spain. He was, in fact, related to the saint through his converso grandmother, Francisca de Ribera.[68]

It was over the Teresa of Ávila co-patronage issue that Olivares first clashed with the splenetic Francisco Quevedo, who, backed by an anti-Teresa lobby, published in 1628 two tracts: *Memorial en defensa de Santiago* and *Su espada por Santiago*.[69] Quevedo's impassioned essays elicited equally emotional responses from members of Olivares' close circle, including the poet Juan de Jáuregui, who soon entered into a protracted dispute with the Manchegan poet, whom he dismissed as a typical member of Spain's ignorant *vulgo*. There was nothing typical about Quevedo, however; he was, rather, a complex, tortured soul, whose aggressive *castecismo* may well have been a reaction to his own family background, with its hint, on his mother's side, of converso ancestry.[70]

An intense, almost pathological anti-Semite, Quevedo increasingly blamed Spain's decline on a Machiavellian Jewish (converso) financial community, symbiotically linked to the Olivares government.[71] These attacks culminated in Quevedo's work, *La isla de los monopantos*, in which Olivares, transformed into Pragas Chincollas (an anagram of his own name, Gaspar, and his great-grandfather's surname, Conchillas), is linked to an international conspiracy of Jews, whose intention is to subvert Christian society. It was very probably as a result of this defamatory text that Quevedo was arrested by Olivares in January 1639, and incarcerated in the San Marcos prison in León, where he lingered until the *privado*'s fall from power, four years later.[72]

While Olivares' early reform program did little to relieve the Crown of its financial problems, it did serve to associate him and his regime with unorthodox views. This negative image was reinforced in 1628, when he became implicated in an investigation into the *alumbrado* activities of Madrid's San Plácido Convent, a Benedictine institution founded by his close friend, the converso Jerónimo de Villanueva, *protonotario* for the Crown of Aragon.

It is apparent that Villanueva founded the Benedictine convent, which, through a special license, he controlled totally, as a reformed religious institution in which Catholic dogma and ceremony were subordinated to intense mystical practice. Unfortunately for the *protonotario*, the unconventional mystical methods of the convent's religious advisor, Francisco García Calderón, soon created a community of confused and hysterical nuns. Inaugurated in 1624, the San Plácido Convent had only been functioning for a year before the majority of its religious inmates, including the abbess (the institution's co-founder, Doña Teresa de Silva), began experiencing prophetic visions. Believing that the nuns were demonically possessed, or so he later claimed, García Calderón attempted to exorcise their demons, while taking scrupulous notes of their prophecies, all of which were of a similar millenarian character: the San Plácido Convent would soon be the source of a reformation, not only of the Benedictine Order, but of the entire Church. The head of this reform movement would be García Calderón, who, accompanied by 11 nuns from the convent, would set out to redeem the world. On the death of the incumbent pope, Urban VIII, Cardinal Borgia would occupy the Holy See; Borgia would then be succeeded by García Calderón, who would rule for 33 years. During this period Jerónimo de Villanueva would be made a cardinal and would aid the new pope in his religious revolution.

Rumors of the San Plácido nuns' visions soon reached the Inquisition, which mounted an inquiry into the convent's religious activities. In the course of this investigation, the Holy Office discovered that García Calderón had introduced a type of *dejamiento* mysticism into the convent, convincing the nuns that in their mystical, transcendental state they were free from sin. It appears that the monk had maintained close physical, or even sexual, contact with a number of the nuns; likewise, Jerónimo de Villanueva, who lived next door to the convent and was a constant visitor, was reported to have been on intimate terms with the abbess, Doña Teresa de Silva.

The Inquisition was in no doubt that García Calderon and the nuns of the San Plácido Convent were engaged in *alumbrado* heresy. García was sentenced to permanent incarceration, and the nuns, including Teresa de Silva, were dispersed to other Benedictine convents. Jerónimo de Villanueva escaped prosecution, undoubtedly due to his close relationship with Olivares. The San Plácido affair was not yet over, however. In 1643, after Olivares fell from power, the Inquisition reopened its files on the convent's activities, this time charging Villanueva with heresy. In its renewed attack, the Holy Office also made much of the fact that Villanueva, a converso, was a distant relative of the physician Pedro de Cabra, who had participated in the assassination of the first Inquisition official in Aragon, in 1485. The goal was clearly to link the Olivares regime once again to Jewish subversion. On 7 February 1647, the Supreme Council pronounced sentence on Villanueva: a three-year banishment from Madrid. Although the sentence was light, the trial affectively destroyed his career.[73]

An enormous scandal, the San Plácido affair generated all kinds of scurrilous rumors concerning the religious and sexual behavior of the royal court. Several of these focused on Philip IV, who was believed to have been romantically attached to one of the convent's nuns. It was even stated that Velázquez's *Christ on the Cross*, painted for the convent around the time of the first trial, was executed by the painter on the orders of a troubled and repentant Philip. In all probability, however, the painting, whose quietism is reminiscent of Velázquez's earlier bodegones, *The Waterseller* and *An Old Woman Cooking Eggs*, was commissioned by Villanueva himself to emphasize the essentially spiritual objectives of a convent closely associated with the Olivares regime; it was also, I believe, painted to contest an incipient protest movement, the Degradation of the Cross cult, that was using the image of an agonized, crucified Christ to attack the Olivares court faction and its intimate ties to Madrid's Portuguese converso community.

The Degradation of the Cross affair began in the summer of 1630, when a group of Portuguese conversos, recent arrivals to Madrid and living on Calle Infantas, were reported to the Madrid inquisitors as secret Judaizers.[74] After some initial inquiries, the accused were transferred to Toledo, where they were further interrogated by tribunal officials eager to gain information on the nature of their crimes and the extent of the capital's Jewish network. In the meantime, however, the six-year-old son of one of the prisoners, who had been left in Madrid, was questioned by the Madrid inquisitors and revealed that his parents and their neighbors had ritually strangled and tortured a wooden image of Christ on the Cross. Furthermore, the child told the inquisitors that the image had spoken to all present, asking them why they were harming Him. This information was now conveyed to the Toledo officials who, during the following months, interrogated and tortured the six detainees until all admitted the ritual deicide and confirmed the miracle of the talking Christ statue. All were now condemned to be burnt at the stake, after being paraded in an *auto de fe*. This was originally scheduled to take place in Toledo on 16 June 1632. However, the Inquisitor General, Cardinal Antonio de Zapata, a sworn enemy of the Olivares regime, soon changed the venue to Madrid, where it was calculated to have greater political impact.

As was to be expected, the *auto de fe*, staged in the Plaza Mayor on 29 July 1632, unleashed a wave of resentment against the capital's Portuguese conversos and against Olivares himself. The Count-Duke's enemies at court took full advantage of this situation, organizing, in the weeks and months following the *auto*, a series of palace devotional displays, emphasizing the 'Jewish heresy.' It was also at this time that Francisco Quevedo published his pamphlet, *Execración contra los judios*, in which he called for the banishment of the conversos from the Iberian Peninsula.[75]

Meanwhile the Confraternity of Saint Peter Martyr, supported by Cardinal Zapata, applied to Philip IV for a license to create a religious foundation devoted to building a church on the spot where the heretics' houses had been razed. In reply, the king, undoubtedly coached by Olivares, stated that the queen, Isabel de Bourbon, had already suggested such a project, the details of which were to be worked out by a government committee dedicated to this end. This committee was indeed established, but was soon packed with Olivares nominees, who spent the next ten years delaying all plans for the temple's construction.

While the Count-Duke was able to resist the construction of a shrine dedicated to the Degradation of the Cross, he was not able to quell the popular support for this project. In the decade following the Portuguese conversos' execution, at least five of the capital's religious confraternities devoted themselves fully to the Degradation cult, organizing festivals and processions, and publishing innumerable tracts to ensure that the infamy remained alive in the city's collective memory. Finally, in 1644, a year after Olivares' fall from power, and only days after Queen Isabel's death, Philip IV signed a decree for the construction of a church and convent dedicated to the Degradation. In giving the royal assent to the project, Philip was following the wishes of his deceased wife, a young woman whose interest in the foundation appears to have run parallel with her enmity toward the Count-Duke.[76]

The church and convent (named the *Convento de la Paciencia*) dedicated to the Degradation of the Cross were completed in 1651 and decorated with five enormous canvases, graphically depicting episodes in the Degradation legend.[77] I would suggest however, that Diego Velázquez had already alluded to the event around the time of the *auto de fe* itself, in 1632. The painting, now titled *Christ after the Flagellation Contemplated by the Christian Soul* (Fig. 6.6), depicts a reclining Christ tied to a column

Fig. 6.6 Diego Velázquez, *Christ after the Flagellation Contemplated by the Christian Soul*. © Lebrecht Music and Arts Photo Library/Alamy Stock Photo

after his flailing, observed by a small child and an angel. The sorrowful child meets Christ's gaze and seems to beg forgiveness, we assume for the sins of mankind, although we might also read into his supplication the personal plea of a small boy whose fantasizing has led to a human tragedy. Velázquez's painting is not about guilt, however, but compassion. Like *Christ on the Cross*, also painted against the background of the Degradation of the Cross affair, it transports the viewer onto a spiritual plain, exalting the Christian message of exculpation and peace.[78]

While Velázquez's depiction of the flagellation is unusual, it is not unique. Juan de Roelas presented a similar scene in a canvas executed in 1616 for the Encarnación Convent in Madrid, only a few minutes' walk from the royal palace. In the convent's inventory the painting is recorded as '[a] naked Christ flogged and wounded, with his hands tied, thrown to the floor, with an angel and a small child at the side of the column and above this a sign which states: "Child suffer for me—as you have placed me here."'[79] It was this inscription, I would suggest, that inspired Velázquez to use the Roelas canvas as a model for his own work on the flagellation. However, unlike Roelas, Velázquez places his child not in the background but up front, where he is transformed from an apparition into a flesh-and-blood protagonist of an awful drama.

A member of the Olivares group—or clan, as it was soon to become known—it was inevitable that Velázquez would become personally caught up in the group's battles against conservative (orthodox) political and religious forces; it was equally inevitable that he would be attacked, like Olivares himself, for his non-conformist attitudes. In particular, the young painter was targeted by a group of older colleagues, who saw him not only as a troublesome innovator but also as a serious rival for court emoluments. In his work, *Discursos practicables del nobilisimo arte de la pintura*, the painter Jusepe Martínez speaks of a rivalry between the newcomer and two of his elder colleagues, Eugenio Cajés and Vicente Carducho, who dismissed him as nothing more than a painter of heads.[80] Carducho's negative assessment of Caravaggio, in his *Diálogos de la pintura* (published in 1633), also appears to have been an attack on Velázquez, who was clearly influenced by the Italian's innovative works. In Carducho's opinion, Caravaggio was an anti-Christ, 'without precepts, without doctrine, without study ... with nothing but nature before him, which he copied in his amazing way.'[81] In other words, Caravaggio and, by implication, Velázquez were mere imitators of nature, ingenious craftsmen who lacked the intellectual expertise and the moral (or religious) principles that defined the noble artist. The true painter, in Carducho's opinion, was someone like himself, who concentrated on historical themes, dominating perspective and narrative to reveal important philosophical truths, rather than merely mirroring his environment.

Irritated, it seems, by these attacks on his protégé, in 1627 the Count-Duke ordered a contest in which Velázquez would compete against the court history painters, Vicente Carducho, Eugenio Cajés, and Angelo Nardi, for the best rendition of the 1609 expulsion of the Moriscos; the winner's work was to be hung in the *Salon Nuevo* of the Alcázar palace. On the surface this was a strange assignment, the 1609 expulsion having taken place under the administration of the Duke of Lerma, a man vilified by Olivares as an inept and venal public official. The episode was also a clear demonstration of Spanish society's rejection of its industrious New Christian subjects, an attitude the Count-Duke had vociferously attacked during his first months in office. In choosing the theme, Olivares appears to have been bowing to pressure from his antagonists at court for an official celebration of an event that symbolized Spain's purity of blood and faith.

In fact, the competition was a carefully stage-managed event, in which biased adjudicators voted for a politically acceptable canvas painted by Olivares' favorite, Velázquez.[82] The Count-Duke thus used the competition to subtly criticize the policy of the previous regime and to chastise two court painters, Carducho and Cajés, closely associated with the Lerma faction, or its remnants, at court.

Unfortunately, Velázquez's winning canvas was destroyed in the palace fire of 1734. There is, however, a brief description of the work in Antonio Palomino's biography of the painter. Palomino writes:

> In the middle of the painting is King Philip III in armor and with a baton in hand pointing at a group of sobbing men, women and children who are being directed by some soldiers; and in the background some carts and a large ship with some boats to transport the group ... At the right of the king is Spain, represented as a majestic matron, in Roman armor, sitting at the foot of a building. In her right hand she holds a shield and spears, and in her left hand some ears of corn. At her feet on a plinth is the inscription: Philippo III HiSaint. Regi Cathol.[83]

While the description is slight, the general impression is of a work that emphasizes the great pathos of the expulsion. Indeed, in placing the king and the iconic Spain (or is the armed maiden an allusion to the Church militant?) in armor, Velázquez evokes an aggressive act perpetrated by a militarist state against a passive and defenseless group. It is also significant that Velázquez's 'majestic maiden' is a corruption of Ceres, goddess of agriculture. The real Ceres was worshipped for giving humans the gift of the harvest and for this reason was depicted with a wheat sheaf in one hand and a farming tool in the other. Significantly, it was this image that the humanist Pedro Valencia took as a representation of Justice in his series of emblems for Philip III (see Chap. 5). However, Velázquez's aberrant Ceres has abandoned tools for weapons. The implication would seem to be that she has gained the fruits of the land not by her own labor but by force. Given the fact that the exiled Moriscos were above all a rural community, renowned for their agricultural skills, it would seem that Velázquez's armed maiden was a subtle allusion to Philip III's (and Lerma's) rapacious attack on a productive minority.[84]

As a member of the Olivares group, the young Velázquez found himself in a volatile situation during his early years at court, as his protector attempted to dispel the inertia of the previous regime and introduce basic reforms, including the abolition of the *limpieza* statutes, so entrenched in Spanish society. Olivares himself was an aggressive opponent of pure blood legislation, forcing the Council of the Orders to adopt the *patria común* measure, allowing Portuguese candidates for knighthood the right to forego background investigations in their native land. This measure was, however, of no use to Olivares' friend, the Spanish poet and scholar Juan de Jáuregui, when he applied for entry into the noble Order of Calatrava in 1628, only to be denied access on account of his Jewish background.[85] In a society in which honor was linked to clean blood, or the pretense of clean blood, this was undoubtedly a huge blow to the poet. It would also have been a cause for concern for other members of the Olivares circle, including Velázquez, who may have been counting on the Count-Duke to oil their paths to knighthoods. It was in the wake of Jáuregui's failed bid for a noble title, and, I would argue, as a reaction to it, that Velázquez painted *Los Borrachos* (*Triumph of Bacchus*, Fig. 6.7).

Interpreters of Velázquez's *Los Borrachos*, and there have been many, tend to fall into two categories: those that present it as a court burlesque, and those who depict it as a pictorial morality that alludes to the dangers and/or virtues of wine drinking.[86] The painting is neither. It is, rather, an intensely personal comment on a Spanish society in which two opposite and inimical doctrines were in conflict: the humanist's and the *vulgo*'s. The traditional Bacchus is the god or demi-god of excess and abandonment; however, there is also another Bacchus, the god described by Pérez de Moya in his *Philosofía secreta* as a civilizer and pacifier.[87] It is this rational, patrician judge that Velázquez depicts in his canvas. Thus his true adherents are not the drunken group of peasants in the top left of the canvas, but the two garlanded figures (the garland being a reference to their artistic status) and the cloaked man, all of whom turn their attention toward the god.[88] In contrast, the four peasants remain oblivious to Bacchus' presence. One man begs money unsuccessfully from another (in this society religious ritual is not accompanied by charity), while in front of him two somewhat

Fig. 6.7 Diego Velázquez, *Triumph of Bacchus* (*Los Borrachos*). © FineArt/Alamy Stock Photo

inebriated companions gaze out at the viewer. One of these men holds out a bowl of wine in a ritualistic gesture, seemingly inviting the viewer to partake of its contents. This wine is not, however, the amber-colored liquid contained in Bacchus' followers' glasses, with which they toast the god, but a blood-red libation. Clearly, Velázquez is drawing a distinction between the two types of drinker. In one representation, the wine—a nectar—is associated with elevated consciousness and veracity (that is to say, with Bacchus' image as the purveyor of truth and civilization); in the other, it is associated with the *vulgo*, who view it as a means of inebriation, a magical ingredient in the Eucharistic rite, and a symbol of their socio-religious purity. The god Bacchus, with his face averted from the peasants and his legs crossed—a classical pose signifying judgment—is judging against their credo.[89] The three figures who look toward him are doing likewise.

Los Borrachos is a pictorial juxtaposition of the two ideological camps that were at loggerheads in the Madrid court and capital during Velázquez's first years in the city. But there is much more to the painting than this. Like *Christ and the Christian Soul*, the Bacchus canvas is a very personal reaction to a specific incident, in this case the poet Juan de Jáuregui's rejected application for a noble title, the theme being suggested by Jáuregui's famous poem *Orfeo* (*Orpheus*, the follower of Bacchus), published four years earlier, and dedicated to the Count-Duke of Olivares.[90] In the poem, closely based on Ovid's tale in *Metamorphoses*, Orpheus is attacked and killed by a group of wild Bacchus followers, the Thracian women, who are unable to appreciate the beauty of his musical gifts. In punishment for this crime, Bacchus transforms the assassins into trees and shrubs, rooting them into the earth. It is this moment of judgment that Velázquez alludes to in *Los Borrachos*, making reference to the Thracians' punishment through the god's cross-legged pose and the tiny, leafy bird that flutters next to his feet, an allusion to the bird in Ovid's poem:

> And as a bird, its foot held in a snare
> Hidden by a clever fowler, feels it's caught
> And flaps its wings and by its flutterings
> Tightens the trap, so each of them was stuck
> Fast in the soil and struggled, terrified,
> In vain, to escape and as she jerked away,
> The lithe root held her shackled.[91]

And thus in punishment for their insensibilities the Thracian women are relegated down the chain of being from humans to plants. Velázquez's composed Bacchus does not wreak such horrible vengeance on his peasants, representatives of a hide-bound society that has denied the poet Jauregui noble status. He does, however, reverse their decision, crowning the poet with an ivy wreath in recognition of his noble enterprise. Thus Velázquez predicates noble status on merit and not on correct (Old Christian) blood, as indeed he does in a later work celebrating his own noble enterprise, *Las Meninas*.

In *Los Borrachos*, Velázquez places Jáuregui with his back toward us in order to disguise his features; he does, however, make subtle allusions to the figure's poetic character, through the emblematic garland of ivy with which Bacchus ennobles him, and to his ambitions to enter a military order, through the prominent sword strapped to his back. He also offers clues to the identity of the garlanded man crouching in shadow at the bottom-left-hand corner of the canvas. This, I would suggest, is Juan de Fonseca y Figueroa, who introduced Velázquez to the court in 1623. Fonseca died in March 1627, a year or so before the canvas was executed, and for this reason is placed in silhouette, or as a 'shade,' outside the central group, on the side of the canvas otherwise occupied by the netherworld figures of Bacchus and the satyr.[92] Significantly, the silhouetted figure embraces a large earthenware jar, reminiscent of the one in *The Waterseller*, painted by Velázquez for Fonseca several years earlier.[93] Like Jáuregui, Fonseca was a poet and sometime painter, hence the garland; he was also a member of Pacheco's humanist circle in Seville, Olivares' clan at court, and the scion of a family that had also been denied access to the military orders for its tainted ancestry.

The other member of Bacchus' mortal group of adherents is the old man, who kneels in front of the inebriate peasants. Unlike the other members of the Bacchus group, he wears no garland, indicating that he is neither poet nor painter. However, neither is he a member of the peasant group. In appearance and demeanor he is reminiscent of Velázquez's Waterseller, a solemn, dignified man who stands out from the crowd. There are no clues to his identity, although the fact that his features are plainly visible suggests that he was not a prominent personality at court who might be readily identified. He may even have been an archetype, fashioned by the painter to represent an honorable member of the general populace, someone who questioned his society's mores—including its prejudice for pure blood.

THE PORTRAIT OF THE ARTIST AS A NOBLEMAN

By 1628, the year he painted *Los Borrachos*, Velázquez stood incontestably at the pinnacle of the court's painter hierarchy, both as a portraitist and as a historical narrator. However, he was still, as Carducho had pointed out, a talented novice with much to learn about artistic representation. These limitations were made apparent in September 1628, when the great Flemish painter Peter Paul Rubens paid a visit to the Madrid court and executed a series of paintings which gained the plaudits of all who viewed them. One of these highly praised works was an equestrian portrait of Philip IV, which the king now hung in the *salon nuevo*, opposite the equestrian portrait Titian had executed of Charles V. The portrait took the place of an earlier, similar work by Velázquez, which was now relegated to one of the lesser state rooms.[94]

It would be reasonable to assume that Velázquez viewed Peter Paul Rubens' visit to Madrid with some trepidation. Rubens was not only regarded internationally as a great and innovative painter, he was also considered to be a gentleman scholar and an experienced and savvy politician; it was in the latter capacity that he now visited Madrid, carrying a diplomatic brief from Brussels, where he was employed at the court of Philip IV's aunt, Isabella. It was thus inevitable that the Flemish painter would steal the Spaniard's thunder. However, despite Rubens' superior social position at court, he appears to have been on quite close terms with his young colleague; the two painters even visited El Escorial together to examine the palace-monastery's collection of art. It is, of course, not surprising that Rubens took an interest in the Spanish painter. Velázquez was one of the Count-Duke's court favorites; he was also clearly a very talented painter, head and shoulders above most of his court contemporaries, and, like Rubens, an adherent of a modern, naturalistic approach to painting. But the two men were not only united by their artistic skills and predilections; they were also both products of post-Tridentine humanist environments, heavily influenced by Neostoicism, or the philosophy of political restraint and religious dissimulation.[95]

Peter Paul Rubens is regarded as the exemplum of the Baroque Catholic artist, an exciting, dynamic stylist who proclaimed a new, exultant, and self-confident Catholic Church, the bold defender of Roman orthodoxy. However, there was nothing conventional about Rubens' religious background; he was, rather, the product of a non-conformist, or Nicodemist, upbringing, in which religious affiliation was determined by practical considerations. One suspects that Rubens, like the Flemish scholar Justus Lipsius, with whom he was closely linked, adhered publicly to an orthodox Catholic faith because it made life easier for him.

In 1566, at the time of the Dutch iconoclasm, Rubens' father, Jan, a wealthy lawyer and alderman, joined a group of Antwerp citizens (including the converso merchant Marcus Pérez), who openly declared themselves in favor of a Calvinist Flanders.[96] On the arrival of the Duke of Alba's troops, the following year, Jan Rubens was forced, like Pérez, to flee the city. Unlike Pérez, however, he did not move to Calvinist Leiden but to Catholic Cologne, where his Protestant faith continued to cause him problems. Finally, in the interests of a peaceful existence, or so it would seem, Jan Rubens reconverted to Catholicism.

In 1587, on the death of Jan Rubens, his wife, Maria Pypelinckx, and her four surviving children, including the ten-year-old Peter Paul, moved back to Antwerp, waving the flag of Catholic orthodoxy. Whether or not Maria was sincere in her religious display is, however, debatable. The fact that her eldest son Philip soon became a disciple of Justus Lipsius, a man renowned for his religious flexibility, should perhaps alert us to the family's continuing non-conformism.[97] In Peter Paul Ruben's *Four Philosophers* (1611), the painter depicts his brother Philip and Joannes Woverius sitting with their mentor Lipsius under a bust of the great Roman stoic Seneca. Notably, the painter includes himself in this work, albeit to one side of the three humanist intellectuals, showing his affinity with Lipsius' philosophical views.

As the Rubens scholar Frances Huemer points out, Rubens' artistic vision was guided by Lipsius' views on constancy and moderation.[98] It was also clearly influenced by an irenic ideology in which citizens were urged to contain their religious fervor in the interests of political and social harmony. The painter's pacifist sentiments are clearly present in his canvas *The Adoration of the Magi*, painted in 1609 to commemorate the 12-year treaty between the Protestant United Provinces and Spain. Here the artist presents a Christian world united in its reverence for the Christ Child and prosperous in the peace engendered by His birth. Although originally executed for the Antwerp Town Hall, the painting eventually found its way into the Madrid Alcázar collection, where Rubens re-encountered it during his 1628 visit. With a peace treaty again on his mind, this time between Spain and England, for which he was about to set sail on an ambassadorial mission, Rubens now began to revise the work, adding new sections to the canvas, and including himself among the worshippers, in the guise of a noble knight on horseback, chivalrously setting forth to restore the peace between Protestant and Catholic foes. Once installed in the English court, the painter-ambassador returned to the peace theme, executing the *Allegory of Peace*, in which Minerva repels the warrior Mars, Peace offers her breast to the young child, and harmony and prosperity abound. A relatively small canvas, executed for private rather than official display, *Allegory of Peace* clearly displays Rubens' personal commitment to the reconciliation of Protestant and Catholic foes.[99] These irenic sentiments are also evident in Velázquez's 1634 canvas, the *Surrender of Breda* (*The Lancers*). Although painted to celebrate the Spanish forces' defeat of the Dutch in 1624, the painting rejects triumphalism for a message of goodwill and reconciliation between two opposing forces.

Did Rubens ever discuss his Neostoical credo or irenic views with Velázquez? It is tempting to imagine such a conversation taking place during the painters' visit to the Escorial monastery—perhaps next to the frescoes of the royal library, designed by Lipsius' friend Benito Arias Montano.[100] It is not inconceivable that the two men would have used these days together to talk more openly about themselves and their opinions on the role of the humanist artist. Rubens may even have taken the occasion to talk to Velázquez about the benefits of a trip to Italy to study the great Renaissance artists. More than anyone else at court, the great Flemish painter would have been aware of Velázquez's technical deficiencies, in particular his limitations in anatomical draftsmanship and composition. He would also have been in a position, as someone who knew the Italian art world very well, to suggest practical ways in which the talented young painter might benefit from study in Italy. Certainly, the suggestion would have appealed to Olivares, who had for some time been grooming Velázquez for the role of court Apelles.

Velázquez left for Italy in July 1629, where he spent almost 15 months revolutionizing his artistic technique. Unfortunately, our major source for the visit, Francisco Pacheco, tells us almost nothing about how this transformation occurred; instead he concentrates on how splendidly his son-in-law was treated by his noble hosts. This highly idealized view of Velázquez's time in Italy was, in all likelihood, written some years after the visit took place, when the painter was preparing his assault on a noble title. In the circumstances, Pacheco's major concern was not historical accuracy but effective propaganda. The truth, however, is that the young painter's Italian hosts considered him a lowly and somewhat embarrassing house guest, as a letter written by Averardo de Medici, the Florentine ambassador to Madrid, to his employer, the Duke of Tuscany, reveals. In response to a letter from the duke, asking how his court should receive Velázquez, Averardo suggested polite condescension: 'I recommend that you commission him to do your portrait and then give him a chain with your medal. Treat him with kingly gravity and treat him well within the compass of his profession, because with these low-class Spaniards [spagnoli bassi] you lose the same by esteeming them too little as you do by esteeming them too much.'[101] In another letter of introduction, this time written to the Duchess of Palma by her ambassador in Madrid, the Italian official described Velázquez as 'an usher to the king,' which was 'a bit better than a doorman and less than a chamber assistant.'[102] The fact that Velázquez was also the king's favorite painter was clearly of little importance; even in

Italy the office of painter was normally considered a manual art, some rungs below an usher on the palace hierarchical ladder.

Obviously Velázquez was under no illusion as to his position in court society, despite his father-in-law's panegyric. However, he was clearly aware that the social limitations imposed upon him by his profession were not insuperable; both Titian and Rubens, for example, had transcended their artisan status to claim noble honors. This was something that was well within his grasp also, but first he needed to broaden his artistic education in Italy, studying the techniques of the great Renaissance colorists and draftsmen: Michelangelo, Leonardo, Rafael, Giorgione, Tintoretto, and, of course, Titian.

Titian is without doubt the single most important influence on Velázquez's mature style, and yet the Venetian master is totally absent from the early works. There are two reasons for this peculiarity. First, Velázquez's early mentor, Francisco Pacheco, was much more inclined toward the Florentine school of draftsmanship than toward the Venetian colorists; he was also of the opinion that Titian's later works were too casually executed to be considered great works of art. Second, the young Velázquez may have found the subject matter of Titian's works, or rather the very irregular copies that reached Seville, too fanciful or perhaps just old-fashioned, far removed from his own artistic vision, dictated by the naturalism, or street realism, of Caravaggio. This prejudice seems to have survived into his early years at court, despite the rich collection of Titian canvasses that called out for his attention.

It took Peter Paul Rubens, a Titian devotee, to open Velázquez's eyes to the Venetian's artistry. While at court, Rubens painted the entire royal collection of Titian's works and almost certainly commented on them as he did so. It is to be supposed that Velázquez was often present during these master workshops, where Rubens not only demonstrated Titian's brilliant technique and creative genius, but also his rebellious, even non-conformist spirit—something that Velázquez may previously have been oblivious to. But Velázquez was also drawn to Titian for reasons other than artistic merit. As he prepared to consolidate his position as the court's foremost painter, he must surely have been aware of the Venetian's pre-eminent position within the court of Charles V, where he was regarded as a new Apelles and decorated with a noble title. Velázquez obviously realized that in his own bid for noble recognition, a positive comparison with the Venetian master would go a long way.

However, while Velázquez was eager to demonstrate that he was an aristocrat among artists, he was also aware that his artistic abilities would only take him so far along the path to his title; they would not in themselves secure him a noble insignia. Indeed, to gain recognition by one of the noble military orders, he would need to officially disguise his profession, presenting himself as the son of *hidalgos*, uncorrupted by trade and, more importantly, Jewish and Moorish blood. In the 1630s, when he probably began to consider the possibility of buying himself a knighthood, the *limpieza* statute may not have appeared such a daunting impediment. He was, after all, required only to present information about his paternal family line (investigations into candidates' maternal family were not introduced until 1553), and here his Portuguese ancestry would allow him to take advantage of Olivares' *patria común* measure.[103] There was, nevertheless, a small problem. Up until now the painter had made little of his Portuguese surnames, no doubt wishing to avoid association with Madrid's vilified Portuguese converso community. Nevertheless, if he wished to claim Portuguese *hidalgo* status, it was evident that he needed to boast about his Portuguese background rather than disguise it. And thus from the early 1630s onward he began incorporating the name Silva into his signature on a regular basis.

Unfortunately, however, in 1643, while Velázquez was still in the process of preparing the ground for his assault on a noble title, Olivares fell from power. With the *privado*'s exit, Velázquez's stock at court also declined, with the result that he was in no position to advance his claim to noble entitlement. It was not until the end of the decade, after Olivares' nephew, the Count of Haro, took effective control over court politics, that Velázquez's situation improved sufficiently for him to contemplate entry into a military order once again. The first major step toward this goal was taken during the painter's second trip to Italy (1649–1651), when, after painting his highly celebrated portrait of Pope Innocent X, he solicited a letter from the pontiff supporting his application for a noble title.

Back at court, Velázquez continued his preparations, selecting and rehearsing friendly witnesses, carefully mapping out a genealogical route that would guide the later investigators around troublesome obstacles. This was an enormously costly and time-consuming business, made infinitely more difficult after 1653, when he discovered he would also have to submit his maternal family to public scrutiny. It was thus not until the mid 1650s that he was ready to receive royal nomination for entitlement. Philip IV was duly nudged, and the title process began in earnest.

How confident was Velázquez that he would dupe the Council of the Orders into awarding him his title? The fact that he began his title preparations by soliciting a letter of support from Innocent X suggests that he was expecting the application to run into difficulties, and that these would only be resolved by papal intervention.[104] Even so, he may have been surprised by the tenacity with which the Council of the Orders resisted his petition, first discounting the noble pretensions of his maternal family and then, once this impediment had been resolved through papal dispensation, dismissing those of his paternal line also. Finally, the humbled candidate had to trouble the Holy See not once but twice for exemptions.

While the Council of the Orders was correct to suspect Velázquez was of common stock, its reaction, one suspects, was not that of an entirely dispassionate committee. Indeed, it seems likely that Velázquez's major problem was not so much his humble origins as his high profile at court, in particular his close association with the Olivares regime and its relaxed policy toward awarding knighthoods. His application for entry into the Order of Santiago was, in fact, reminiscent of that of earlier Portuguese candidates, who fraudulently gained their titles through the Count-Duke's connivance. Naturally, the Council drew the logical conclusion: this latest Portuguese candidate, like the previous ones, was using his money and influence to undermine their authority and circumvent their rules. Resistance to his application was thus a matter of honor.

Vehemently opposed to Velázquez gaining the Santiago crest, but unable to block his entry into the order, the Council finally resorted to humiliating the painter, asking that he gain dispensation not once but twice for his lowly forebears. All of this must have been extremely distressing, and worse was to follow. Soon rumors began to circulate at court that Velázquez was an unfaithful servant, and this malicious gossip continued after his death in August 1660. Finally, Velázquez's friend and executor Don Gaspar de Fuensalida, a court official, was called before Philip IV to reply to these accusations. According to Antonio Palomino, Fuensalida explained that the painter was the victim of envy, assuring the king of his 'fidelity,' 'legality,' and moral rectitude.[105]

What was the nature of these rumors alluded to by Palomino? The biographer is reluctant to tell us, although it seems likely that they were, at least in part, related to irregularities in his conduct as *aposentador mayor*, a position he held from 1652 to his death. It appears that during this time, in which he was in charge of a large budget for certain salaries and other palace payments, he had managed to retain a considerable sum of money for his own use.[106] This was certainly fraudulent behavior, but it was not particularly unusual at court. Nevertheless, Velázquez's enemies wished to present the misconduct in terms of *lèse majesté*, a term now being applied

Fig. 6.8   Diego Velázquez, *Las Meninas*. © classicpaintings/Alamy Stock Photo

to a Portuguese financial community that was accused of using its privileged situation to ruin the kingdom. The inference could hardly have been lost on Velázquez's contemporaries: the painter was yet another malevolent Portuguese converso, enriching and ennobling himself at others' expense.

How different all this was, or seemingly so, from the world of *Las Meninas* (Fig. 6.8) painted just four years earlier, in which Velázquez invites us to contemplate a genteel court environment on a tranquil spring afternoon. The sun filters in through an open doorway and high windows, bathing the protagonists in a golden glow; attendants stand by, idly chatting; the *infanta* plays with her maids; a dog sleeps, indifferent to the midget's teasing; and the noble painter conveys the best of all possible worlds onto canvas. But as is often the case in a Velázquez painting, appearances are deceptive. What seems to be an inconsequential *entremés*, or interlude, concerning the *infanta* and her maids, is in fact an Ovidian drama in which the painter confronts his court detractors head on with what he considers incontrovertible evidence of his noblility.

Painted in 1656, as Velázquez prepared himself for the Council of the Orders' investigations, *Las Meninas* is above all a disclaimer. It states: I am not a fraud whose claim to noble entitlement rests on lies and deceit—on the fabrication of a noble Old Christian ancestry—but a great painter whose nobility is based squarely on his artistic genius. And to prove this is no idle boast, I submit as evidence this technically brilliant and intellectually complex work of art.[107]

Conceptually, *Las Meninas* has much in common with *Los Borrachos*, painted 30 years previously, in which Velázquez overturned the Council of the Orders' decision concerning Juan de Jáurequi, awarding him a noble wreath for artistic merit. The difference is that *Las Meninas* was conceived and executed before Velázquez underwent the investigation for knighthood, not after it; thus the painter and his painting were left in limbo for three years, awaiting the outcome of the *probanza*. This situation is reflected in the painting itself, which depicts Velázquez standing in front of a canvas of similar dimensions to those of *Las Meninas*, with brush poised to add some detail. Of course the only detail missing from *Las Meninas* in 1656 was the red cross of Santiago, the emblem that would vindicate Velázquez's claim to noble status, which the painter later included (Fig. 6.9).

Painted two years before Velázquez' *probanza*, *Las Meninas* reveals a painter quietly confident of his possibilities of knighthood. This confidence was not in any way inspired by the Council of Orders (which he no doubt suspected would reject his petition), but by the king, who had obviously informed Velázquez of his commitment to the venture's success. And so Velázquez painted himself onto the canvas with his brazen black chest extended for an award he believed would soon be forthcoming through papal dispensation.

Fig. 6.9 Diego Velázquez, *Las Meninas* detail. © Paul Fearn/Alamy Stock Photo

Nevertheless, the painter was also aware, as a reader of Ovid, that artistic temerity often led to disaster, and that his own challenge to the gods, or fate, might yet end badly. For this reason he chose as the backcloth to his personal drama two images from Ovid of talented artists bested by resentful deities. The first of these is an allusion to Peter Paul Ruben's *Palas and Arachne*, which depicts the young weaver physically assaulted by the goddess Athena for her presumptuous claim to greater talent. The second image is taken from Jacob Jordaens' *Apollo as Victor over Pan*, in which a furious and unprepossessing Apollo berates Midas for favoring the musical accomplishments of the pipe-playing satyr (here presented with human legs), while receiving the winner's garland from a cowed and chastised judge, Timolus. Both works demonstrate the dangers of pitting one's talents against those of the Parnassus gods. Significantly, however, neither alludes to the challenger's artistic inferiority; on the contrary, they infer that Arachne and Pan are the victims of rancorous bullies, ill-disposed to accept lesser beings as creditable opponents, let alone worthy victors. In other words, the artist's challenge ultimately fails not through an insufficiency of talent but through lack of social status.[108]

There was, of course, an important difference between Velázquez and the mythological figures Arachne and Pan. His temerity had ended in triumph, not tragedy. It was, however, as Velázquez knew, a pyrrhic victory. Few at court were disposed to regard the painter as a bona fide nobleman; most saw him as a fraud who had gained his title through false pretenses. Despite the noble emblem of the Order of Santiago he boasted on his chest, he was still considered of common stock. Worse, his Portuguese provenance clearly singled him out in the eyes of many of the courtiers as a man of tainted caste: another of the Count-Duke's illicit *marranos*.

It was perhaps unfortunate for Velázquez that at the time of his *probanza*, the Inquisition was making a concerted attack on the capital's Portuguese financiers, focusing on their dubious Christianity to strip them of their lucrative positions in the Treasury. After a massive *auto de fe* in Cuenca, in 1654, it was said that 200 converso families fled Madrid for foreign parts.[109] This exodus continued during the next decades as wealthy members of the converso community were continuously targeted by the Inquisition. By the end of the century, most of the wealthier Portuguese businessmen had left the city, with the result that accusations of converso financial and religious corruption within the court declined. This did not mean, however, that Spain's long obsession with the conversos came to an end. For this obsession was not so much with heresy as with genealogy: the conversos' Jewish essence. If this Jewish malady were allowed to reign unchecked, it was believed, it would infect the entire kingdom, impairing everyone's virtue and honor.[110] Even after the Inquisition ledgers ceased to record accusations against Judaizers, even after the *limpieza de sangre* laws became no more than a bureaucratic formality, the fixation on Jewish taint, promoted by the Church, would remain alive in all strata of society. The effects of this prejudice are particularly visible in Spanish historiography where, until recently, the converso was either treated as a crypto-Jew or ignored completely.

CHAPTER 7

The Converso Returns

The Colombina archive in Seville houses a copy of a discourse written by Fray Agustín Salucio at the end of the sixteenth century in which the Dominican friar examines, with a good measure of irony, the question, 'Who is an Old Christian?'[1] While there were no studies available on the subject, Salucio observes, the obvious answer to the question is that an 'Old Christian' was the person who converted to Christianity before the 'New Christian.' However, to appreciate fully the term 'Old Christian,' it was necessary to understand that Spaniards of his own day stemmed from four different social groups: the conquerors, the conquered, those who were neither conquerors nor conquered, and a mixture of some or all of the above. The conquerors were those people who initially fled north during the Moors' invasion of Spain in 711, preferring to live in the Asturian and Vizcayan mountains than to exist under the yoke of Muslim rule. From their mountain retreat, these valiant Christians waged war on the Muslims and, in the first wave of the Reconquest, wrested Spanish territory from the invaders.

The second group of Spaniards, 'the conquered,' were those Moors and Jews who, reluctant to abandon their farms and businesses after the northern Christian forces had reconquered the southern territory (from the twelfth century onward), remained in Christian Spain. These *vil* (base) individuals later converted to Christianity, preferring apostasy to the constant attacks from their Christian neighbors. These were known as 'New Christians.'

© The Author(s) 2018
K. Ingram, *Converso Non-Conformism in Early Modern Spain*,
https://doi.org/10.1007/978-3-319-93236-1_7

The third group of Spaniards were those Christians—the vast majority—who remained in Moorish territory after the Muslim invasion. Resisting the call of their co-religionists in the north, these Christians—Mozarabs as they became known—preferred to cohabit with the Moors, whom they found much more acceptable than the tyrannical Visigothic king, whom the invaders had deposed. Like the New Christians, these were *vil* (base) people, who were referred to by their Arab hosts as *marranos*, a term meaning apostate or deserter [clearly a jibe by Salucio at sixteenth-century Old Christian society, who used the derogatory term *marrano*, which they associated with swine, to refer to New Christians]; the northern resistance movement referred to these Mozarabs as *mixtos*, in reference to their religion, which was mixed with that of the Moors. For their part the collaborationists—Mozarabs—labeled the northern Christians 'rebels,' and depicted their king, Don Pelayo, as a charlatan who took up arms against the Moor, not for the Christian faith, but for his own political interests.

At the end of the first wave of reconquest, then, Christian Spain was made up of New Christians (converts from Judaism and Islam), Mozarabs, who had for centuries practiced an ersatz or tainted form of Christianity, and a group of Christian (or 'Old Christian') conquerors from the north. This last group of Spaniards were not only pure Christians, they were also, according to Salucio, Spain's true nobility (here the author seemingly panders to the Spanish *hidalgos*' conceit that their ancestors were Vizcayan nobles who moved south with the armies of the Reconquest); however, Salucio goes on to inform us that the names of these noble northerners were now lost to history; the present-day Old Christian society, nobles and commoners alike, had no idea who their distant ancestors were. It was highly probable, indeed, that the Old Christians of his own day came from one of two groups: base Jewish and Muslim converts to Christianity, or base Mozarabs. Regrettably, Salucio writes, in recent times laws had been passed (*limpieza de sangre* statutes) banning New Christians from positions in the Church and other institutions, on the grounds that they were of an inferior status. These laws were illogical. There was only one difference between present day Old- and New Christian Spain: Old Christian Spain had no idea who its ancestors were.

No doubt a more prudent converso apologist than Fray Agustín would have written a study indicating how the New Christian could be the equal to his Old Christian neighbor in moral probity and in the sincerity of his Christian beliefs. However, in Salucio's account the Old and the New

Christians are united not in virtue but in self-interest and moral turpitude. The author also notes—in a seemingly gratuitous aside—that the Moors were able to conquer Spain so easily because they were considered an improvement on Visigothic rule (Old Christians, as Salucio well knew, lauded the 'virtuous, Christian' Visigoths, whom they regarded as their ancestors). Furthermore, he notes, the head of the Christian resistance movement, King Pelayo (an Old Christian icon), may well have been motivated more by political ambition than by Christian fervor.

Allowing for a certain converso combativeness, Salucio's account is an honest attempt to present Spanish history in its less than glorious reality, and a bold challenge to the anti-converso legislation that was undermining his society. Unfortunately, Old Christian Spain was in no mood to countenance either historical realism or attacks on its *limpieza de sangre* legislation, as Salucio discovered when, in 1599, he circulated a discourse urging that the laws be drastically curtailed. The work was soon ordered to be destroyed, and the author reprimanded for his audacity.[2]

For three centuries after Salucio wrote the above study, Spain continued to turn its back on its historical reality, or to stifle reality with national myth. In the popular consciousness, the Spaniard remained a pure-blooded product of the Vizcayan mountains, a member of a warrior race who swept south to rid the peninsula of the infidel in the *Reconquista* and re-establish Spain's purity of race and religious purpose. From this warrior caste there sprang magically, like Athena from Zeus' head, the brilliant literary works of the Spanish Golden Age: melancholic and mystical testaments to the Spaniard's intensity of faith and his singularity of religious vision. In this historical interpretation, the Jews and Muslims became a nefarious miasma that was purged from Spain in 1492, leaving no cultural legacy of any importance. As for the converso, after being exposed by the Inquisition for his Judaizing ways, he headed for Spain's historical backwoods, rarely to show his face. Nevertheless, the threat of Jewish taint remained, ready to corrupt society the moment its good Catholic members relaxed their vigilance.

For the majority of Spaniards, the conversos had become, in the course of the sixteenth and seventeenth centuries, the embodiment of alien attitudes and beliefs, the corruptors of Spanish tradition, and thus, by some perverse syllogism, anyone who promoted religious or social renovation was likely to be branded a Jew. Charles III's chief minister, the Italian Marquis of Esquilache, expelled from Spain in 1766 for his attempts at reforming the Spanish Church and nobility, was accused of being both a heretic and a Jew. Likewise, the Crown's representative in Seville, Pablo de Olavide, who found himself in an Inquisition prison for his non-conformist views, became the subject of a popular song in which his crimes were described as Masonic and Jewish.[3] It was, indeed, normal for Spain's reformers to be pronounced both Freemasons and Jews, the two groups being regarded as secret, hermetic societies that were bent on destroying the Catholic faith and, by extension, Spanish society.

Aware of the Catholic Church's hold on the Spanish psyche, eighteenth-century reformers were generally careful to temper their religious non-conformism. Even those radical liberals who framed Spain's first constitution in 1812 decided against including a freedom of conscience clause; not that this made their document any more palatable to the Church or Crown, which conspired, on Ferdinand VII's return from exile in 1814, to outlaw the constitution's authors and their supporters. Significantly, these malefactors were labeled 'new Jews.'[4]

After Ferdinand VII's death in 1833, the liberal (*Progresista*) faction once again found themselves in a position of power, this time as de facto policy makers at the regent Maria Cristina's court. Once again they declined to separate Church and State, although their respect for tradition did not extend to the Inquisition and *limpieza de sangre* statutes, both of which were soon abolished. The architect of these liberal reforms, Juan Álvarez Mendizábal, who was believed to have converso roots, was soon attacked as a representative of sinister Jewry, the conservative broadsheet *La Posdata* referring to him as 'Juanon el rabino' and caricaturing him as a rat with an enormous tail, an allusion to the popular belief that Jewish men were born with a tail-like appendage.[5]

The first attempt to assess the Jews contribution to Spanish history with a degree of objectivity came in 1848 with *Estudios históricos, políticos y literarios sobre los judíos en España*, in which the author, José Amador de los Ríos, lamented his country's ignorance of the Sephardic culture:

> It would be easy to present here a large catalogue of work in which persons of that race were presented, sometimes truthfully, sometimes falsely, in which they have been attributed actions to some extent correct, to some extent hateful. But it is difficult to find a work on the descendants of the prophet king [David] during their long period in Spain, which examines their customs and relationship with Christians.[6]

Thirty years after publishing *Estudios historicos*, Amador returned to the same theme in his three-volume *Historia social, política y religiosa de los judíos de España y Portugal* (1875–1876), this time including a more detailed account of the conversos and their treatment at the hands of the Inquisition. He even mentioned briefly the vicissitudes of an intellectual elite, those 'illustrious cultivators of science, letters and the arts, who attracted the terrible suspicions and insatiable ire of the Holy Office.'

> Neither the most refined virtues [Amador continued, grandiloquently] nor the highest merits were respected; next to a Hernando de Talavera and a Bartolomé de Carranza, clear geniuses of the Church and of learning; next to an Arias Montano and a Francisco Sánchez de la Brozas, everlasting glories of classical and oriental philology, next to a Pablo de Céspedes and a Fray Luis de León, envied ornaments of archeological science and the divine arts of painting and poetry, the inexorable hand of the inquisitors placed, with more than a little extravagance, the names of another thousand eminent geniuses, to whose foreheads it attached the stigma of Judaism.[7]

In 1876, the year in which the last volume of Amador's *Historia social* appeared in print, the liberal scholar Gumersindo de Azcárate published an article on Spain's political situation in which he singled out intolerance as the villain behind his country's political and economic stasis. This article soon gave rise to a heated debate among a number of conservative and liberal scholars on Spain's intellectual insularity. For the liberal group, Spain's decline in fortune was the direct result of an obscurantist Church and its reactionary watchdog, the Inquisition. For the group of Catholic apologists, led by Marcelino Menéndez Pelayo, the Inquisition was blame-free; the country had declined not through closed-mindedness but through embracing, on certain occasions in its history, foreign, pagan views. There was some disagreement among the Catholic apologists as to when the rot had set in. Some believed that it had arrived with the Renaissance, while others, including Menéndez Pelayo, laid the blame at the Enlightenment's door. They all agreed on one thing, however, and in this they concurred with their liberal opponents: Spain needed to recover its unique spiritual identity before it could once again triumph in the world.[8]

For Miguel Unamuno, writing at the turn of the century, his country's spiritual essence was a subterranean stream that moved stealthily through history, surfacing occasionally to leave its mark on an age.[9] This 'intra-historic' spiritual current, according to Unamuno, had surged up in the Golden Age, manifesting itself in the likes of Cervantes' knight, Don Quijote; in the Spanish mystics, Juan de Ávila, John of the Cross, and Teresa of Ávila; and in the mystical art of El Greco.[10] Ironically, it would appear that four of Unamuno's emblems of Spanish essentialism were conversos, and the fifth was a Greek expatriate whose mystical vision mirrored that of his converso humanist patrons.[11] Those characteristics that Unamuno had attributed to atavistic Iberian spiritual traits were more likely the result of New Christian disquiet.

Spain's regenerationists had taken refuge in fables to explain the Spanish national character. This was the view of the émigré Spanish historian and philologist Américo Castro, who argued that his country's identity was a product not of prehistory but of a medieval landscape in which three socio-religious groups converged. In this arena the Christians may have been the all-powerful political force, but they relied heavily on the Muslim (Mudéjar) and Jewish minorities, who controlled urban life as traders, artisans, and administrators. The Jews were also prominent as royal advisors, as were the conversos, who dominated scholarship in the Spanish Golden Age. Reacting to an increasingly powerful converso minority, Old Christian society introduced the *limpieza de sangre* statutes, creating in the process a culture so sensitive to Jewish taint that its members distanced themselves from everything that might suggest a Jewish background, including intellectual pursuits. According to Castro, it was this neurosis, born of fear and hatred, that was behind Spain's decline, and not the loss of some intra-historic spiritual force.

Castro first presented his views on Spain's three-caste culture in *España en su historia*, published in 1948, at a time when the Franco regime was attempting to shed its fascist image and ingratiate itself with its Western democratic neighbors. As part of this campaign, the regime's propagandists had begun to depict Spain as a defender of the Jews during World War II, claiming that it provided a safe haven for thousands of Jews on the run from Nazism.[12] This was a gross exaggeration. The government's aid to the Jews was little and late, undertaken with a view to impressing the Allied powers, who had now gained the upper hand against Hitler. In truth, the Francoist regime was no less anti-Semitic than the conservative, Catholic, traditionalist forces that supported it. It was thus to be expected that the Francoist academy would react adversely to Castro's 'Jewish' book. Surprisingly, however, one of Castro's earliest and most vitriolic critics was his fellow Republican émigré, Claudio Sánchez-Albornoz.

A medievalist whose historical vision, like that of Menéndez Pelayo, was informed by his fervent Catholicism, Sánchez-Albornoz regarded Castro as a Spanish apostate, willfully and perversely intent on undermining Spain's true culture; and he set out, in his *España, un enigma histórico*, to expose the treachery.[13] The Jews, he opined, had no visible influence on Spanish ('Hispano') culture. The Spanish people had graciously allowed this minority group into their country, but instead of showing their appreciation, they had continually plotted to overthrow their hosts. They had become moneylenders, tax farmers, and merchants in order to finance their revolution, which would be signaled, they believed, by the arrival of their Messiah. Unable to tolerate the Jewish subterfuge any longer, the Spanish had expelled them from the country in 1492. As far as Sánchez-Albornoz was concerned, there was a Jewish mentality and a Christian mentality, and these remained separate throughout Spain's history.[14]

As a corrective to Castro's vision of Spanish cultural development, Sánchez-Albornoz offered his own interpretation—a theory that harked back to Unamuno's intra-historic Spanish spirit. In Sánchez-Albornoz's opinion the Spanish character was strongly influenced by its *herencia temperamental*, a *volksgeist* which evolved in prehistoric times and traversed history in an all but pristine state of preservation. This prehistoric genetic force was particularly visible in Spain's heroes: those men and women who had appeared at propitious moments to inspire the nation.[15] Spanish history (that is to say, the history of the 'Hispanos,' as opposed to the Moors and Jews) was formed by its heroes, the *herencia temperamental* of the people, and the nation's destiny, or 'as believers would see it, the marvellous projection of the supreme will of God, whose infinite mysteries cannot be captured by our human reason, both slow and miserable.'[16]

Despite his ideological prejudice for a Spanish (Hispanic) culture free from Jewish and Muslim influence, Sánchez-Albornoz presented *España, un enigma historico* as the work of a rigorous scholar who, unlike his rival Américo Castro, would not allow himself to be carried away by an 'ungainly eagerness to dazzle his readers with clever but frail fantasies.'[17] This image of Sánchez-Albornoz as the professional, dispassionate historian contesting Américo Castro, the philologist out of his element, was readily embraced by members of the Francoist academy, who shared the medievalist's historical vision.[18] For although Sánchez-Albornoz was, like Castro, a Republican exile, his views on Spanish historiography conformed, in many ways, to those of the Franco regime. Like Sánchez-Albornoz, Franco's ideologues propounded an essentialist vision of Spain in which a pure Hispanic race had honed its unique character while triumphing over alien cultures. For Sánchez-Albornoz, this character refinement had taken place during the *Reconquista*, when Christian Spain had confronted the Arab interloper. For the ideologues, the *Reconquista* and the Spanish Civil War were engagements in the same conflict against anti-Hispanic forces, in the latter case represented by communists, freemasons, and an international Jewish conspiracy. According to this version of recent history, the Nationalist forces, like the Catholic Monarchs, had liberated Spain of divisive elements, and were now in the process of creating a new society based on 'those virtues of our great captains and politicians of the Golden Age, educated in the Catholic Theology of Trent.'[19] However, in order to carry out this counter-reformation, it was first necessary to purge the university system of non-conformist elements. By 1944, 155 of Spain's 278 departmental chairs had changed hands. The majority of the new men, like their colleagues who had managed to hold on to their positions, subscribed to a conservative, Catholic ideology.[20]

Obviously, this cleansed environment was not conducive to a historiographical account that assigned the Jews and conversos an important place in medieval and early modern Spanish culture. Nonetheless, a number of studies did begin to appear, albeit by Spanish scholars on the margins of the Francoist academy, which lent support to Castro's views on the importance of the converso to sixteenth-century Spanish society.[21] These studies indicated that conversos were prominent in artisanal occupations, especially textile and leather production, and silversmithing; they were conspicuous as merchants, doctors, printers, notaries, and lawyers; they were university professors, civil and clerical bureaucrats, and advisors to royal and noble courts. Indeed, conversos predominated in all those positions that called for an intellectual formation—the administrative office for trade with the Indies, the *Casa de Contratación*, was, for example, controlled by men from converso backgrounds. Conversos may have been a social minority, but they held a prominent place in the professional and economic life of Spain's most important urban centers, as studies on a number of early modern Spanish cities began to attest.

José Carlos Gómez-Menor's study of sixteenth-century Toledo indicated a large population of conversos who controlled the city's commerce.[22] Many of these New Christians had used their wealth to enter into marriage alliances with members of the lower nobility, forming what Gómez-Menor termed a '*mestizo*' urban elite, with a powerful presence in Toledo's cathedral chapter and city council. Ruth Pike's studies of sixteenth-century Seville also emphasized the importance of the city's conversos as artisans, merchants, and professionals. Like their Toledo counterparts, Seville's wealthy conversos also used their money to gain access to the nobility, either through marriage alliances or through the purchase of positions on the city council, which conferred an *hidalgo* status. Seville's conversos also formed important endogamous alliances, strengthening their position in the commercial and political life of the city.[23]

Meanwhile, other studies by Francisco Márquez Villanueva and Stephen Gilman appeared, which, in examining the converso backgrounds of important late-medieval literary figures, also presented a picture of an intellectual environment dominated by New Christians.[24] The conversos had, at last, entered Spanish Golden Age history as significant protagonists; however, not everyone chose to recognize the extent of their presence, as Stephen Gilman stated in his 1972 biography of Fernando de Rojas:

> The Jewish origins of many important Spaniards of the past are first of all denied (in the case of Rojas, as recently as 1967); and then, if the denial cannot stand up in the face of the evidence, they are ignored [...] The belief that only the caste of Old Christians was truly Spanish and truly honorable was so in-rooted that it has endured over four centuries. There even seems to prevail among some of our colleagues, peninsular and otherwise, the tacit notion that to bring to light the background of a Rojas or a Diego de San Pedro (not to speak of a Saint Teresa of Ávila) is an unpatriotic act, a virtual deletion of their works from the national Honor Roll.[25]

Writing in 1967, after several of the above works had been published, Eugenio Asensio was unable to deny that a number of Golden Age figures were from converso backgrounds. However, these figures, he asserted, were few; moreover, it was they who had been influenced by Spanish Old Christian culture, and not vice versa.[26] Saint Teresa's mysticism, Luis Vives' pacifism, and Luis de León's stoicism were the products not of their converso condition but of the intellectual milieux (Old Christian, according to Asensio) in which they moved. Fray Luis, for example, may have been technically speaking a converso, but it was not unusual for the people in the world in which he moved—Salamanca University and the Augustinian religious order—to have a drop of Jewish blood in their veins; Fray Luis' own drop of Jewish blood did not affect his religious writings, which, in fact, revealed a man every bit as orthodox as that 'sublime Old Christian' Arias Montano.[27]

Asensio's comparison of Luis de León with Benito Arias Montano is an apt one, but not for Old Christian orthodoxy. For although Montano's family roots remain somewhat opaque, everything about the Spanish humanist points to a converso background: his birthplace, Fregenal de la Sierra, renowned for its large converso community; his adoptive converso parents; his close friendship with the converso merchant Diego Núñez Pérez, whom he referred to as his cousin; his equally close relationship with the Antwerp converso merchant-banker, Luis Pérez; his choice of academic studies—Hebrew—in a period in which Old Christian Spain was careful to avoid any intimation of Jewish roots; his interest in Old Testament exegesis; and his indifference to the works of the Church Fathers—most unusual for a Catholic theologian. These characteristics may not have impressed Eugenio Asensio; they did, however, impress Montano's contemporaries, including Lope de Vega, who, in a much cited poem, made a clear allusion to Montano's Jewish roots.[28] Benito Arias Montano and his friend Fray Luis de León certainly shared certain characteristics, but Old Christian orthodoxy was not among them. Both men were, to use their Old Christian antagonist León de Castro's term, '*hebreazantes*,' that is to say, scholars interested in emphasizing the importance of the Hebrew Bible and Jewish culture to Christianity. This interest led to Fray Luis' imprisonment, from 1570 to 1575. Montano was luckier: certain friends in high places were able to protect him, although his image as a Judaizer remained with him throughout his life.

The Spanish academy's predilection for a *castizo* Golden Age, free from converso influence, continued into the post-Franco period, maintained by older, conservative academics, who remained potent political forces in their universities, where they were able to dictate the character of their junior colleagues' scholarship. Resistance to change was particularly evident among historians of early modern Spanish history, who continued to treat the Golden Age as the creation of Old Christian talent. As José-Carlos Gómez-Menor wrote in 1994, 'I am aware that normally converso roots are hidden in the biographies of well-known people: this is the case of Juan Luis Vives, Juan de Ávila, Teresa de Jesús (de Ahumada), Fray Luis de León and many others.'[29] But not only did scholars continue to circumvent the backgrounds of those writers whose Jewish roots were incontrovertible; they also often protested the Old Christian character of figures whose social identities were, to say the least, ambiguous. In my own investigations into a group of Andalusian scholars I have come across a number of these protestations by local historians who clearly feel the need to guard the reputations of their cities' Golden Age luminaries. For example, the author of *Córdoba y su provincia* writes of the fifteenth-century Córdoban poet Juan de Mena: 'Although for some time critics have speculated on [Mena's] possible descent from a family of conversos, this hypothesis has been definitively dismissed by Professor Eugenio Asensio. It seems that, on the contrary, according to the study of a number of ancient and noble Castilian lineages—*a work attributed to Mena* (my italics)—his family was from the mountains.'[30]

It would seem, as Stephen Gilman noted, that some biographers of Golden Age figures believe that they have a patriotic duty to protest their subjects' pure, Old Christian blood. A number of the editors of the Castalia and Cátedra editions of Golden Age literary works appear to be particularly prone to this 'sanitization' process. In the Introduction to Luis de Granada's *Introducción del símbolo de la fe,* José María de Balcells writes, 'In 1504, the same year that Isabel the Catholic died in Medina del Campo, Luis de Sarría was born in Granada, into a very poor family of Old Christians, or of "pure" blood.'[31] And several lines later, he returns to Luis' Old Christian background, stating that the friar graduated from the Dominican college of San Gregorio in 1529 'not without having substantiated, with maximum rigor, his *limpieza de sangre*.'[32] This rigorous *limpieza* examination is, however, a figment of Balcells' imagination. We have no idea whether Fray Luis' *limpieza* inquiry was rigorous or a mere formality, his *expediente* having gone missing in the 1836 monastic dissolution process. Indeed, the only evidence we have that Fray Luis was *castizo* comes from a seventeenth-century hagiography, in which the author states formulaically: 'The parents of Fray Luis were not wealthy or landed, nor of illustrious lineage, but poor and humble, although Old Christians, clean and free of all trace of Jews and Moors, and without mixture of bad blood.'[33] Fray Luis himself wrote almost nothing about his family background; we do know, however, that the family surname was taken from a Spanish town (Sarria, in Galicia), which is suggestive of converso roots.[34] As for the fact that Fray Luis passed the *limpieza de sangre* tests for the Dominican college, this, as Balcells must surely know, is no proof of Old Christian origins; sixteenth-century *limpieza de sangre* statutes were often sidestepped by conversos, who were prominent among church intellectuals. One of the most celebrated Dominicans of the early sixteenth century was the converso Francisco de Vitoria (his name taken from the northern Spanish town), who, between 1529 and 1546, occupied the prime chair in theology at Salamanca University; another was Fray Agustín Salucio, author of the famous *limpieza de sangre* treatise, whom we met earlier in this chapter.

Another Golden Age figure who continues to be portrayed as Old Christian, despite important circumstantial evidence suggesting otherwise, is the sixteenth-century Seville humanist Pedro Mexía. In the Introduction to the Cátedra edition of Mexía's *Silva de varia leccion*, Antonio Castro writes:

> The *Sevillian* humanist Pedro Mexía came, according to all the references of his contemporaries, from a lineage originating in Galicia, which was uprooted and expanded through all of Andalusia, especially in the zones of Córdoba and Seville, from the time that these two capitals were re-conquered in the thirteenth century by King Fernando III, the Saint. Among the remote ancestors of Pedro Mexía we find high-ranking knights and clergy who participated with Ferdinand III in the conquest of Córdoba and Seville (like Don Juan de Arias Mexía and Don Juan Arias, Archbishop of Santiago), important representatives of the military orders (like Don Gonzalo Mexía, Master of the Order of Santiago, who was actively involved in the civil war between Pedro I and Enrique II of Castile) and titled nobility (like don Gonzalo Mexía, Lord of La Guardia and Marquis of Santofamia).[35]

Antonio Castro's claim that Mexía came from a northern (and by implication Old Christian) *hidalgo* family is, in fact, based on the genealogical studies by Mexía's Seville contemporary, Gonzalo Argote de Molino, whose information, at least in part, came from Pedro Mexía himself. Argote used Mexías' study in his *Nobleza de Andalucia* to fabricate a noble lineage for the maternal (Mexía) branches of his own family.[36] Neither he nor Mexía belonged to noble clans; they were, rather, the sons of successful *letrados* who used their family wealth to buy themselves noble status (in Mexía's case conferred through the position of city councillor). In his Silva de *Varia Leccion*, Mexía appears to justify his own parvenu status by extolling those who achieve nobility through merit, comparing them to the great Roman orator Cicero, a man he clearly identifies with:

> [I]n his *Oration on the Agrarian Law* [Mexía writes], Cicero confessed that he himself had no coat of arms as he was a man of new lineage; however, through his personal excellence (that is to say through his eminence in letters, as well as his discretion and extreme eloquence), he occupied a high position in Rome of that time and merited these and other noble and patrician privileges.[37]

Whether or not a Galician nobleman named Mexía took part in the first Reconquest drive is a moot point; it is, however, a fact that the name Mexía was prominent among sixteenth-century Seville's converso-dominated merchant and professional groups, as an examination of that city's notarial records attests. Indeed, a Pedro Mexía figures among a group of converso tax collectors who fled Seville in 1481, on the arrival of the Inquisition, creating a grave financial crisis in the city.[38] Mexía's intellectual formation, both humanist and scientific (he was employed as a cosmographer in the *Casa de Contratacion*), also suggests a converso background, as does his interest in an Erasmian clerical reform program. Furthermore, in his works Mexía not only demonstrates a much greater interest in the Old Testament than the New Testament, he also presents the Jewish culture as the intellectual equal of the Greek and Roman cultures—a prominent concern among converso humanists.[39] In other words, we have no reason to take Mexía's Old Christian provenance as an established fact.

The predilection for a *castizo* Golden Age pantheon has led many Spanish scholars in Franco's Spain and after to affirm, often on the slimmest evidence, the Old Christian roots of Spain's great artistic and literary figures. Curiously, however, this ingenuousness is often transformed into rigid skepticism when sources indicate Jewish origins. In her articles examining the converso backgrounds of the playwright Diego Jiménez de Enciso and the poet Juan de Jáuregui, both from Seville, Ruth Pike calls our attention to this phenomenon. Pike notes that in his 1914 study of Enciso, the eminent Spanish scholar Emilio Cotarelo y Mori presented the Enciso family as Old Christian and noble, 'despite evidence to the contrary in the documents that he [Cotarelo] utilized, namely, the inquiries conducted in 1624 and 1626 into the qualifications of two of the dramatist's nephews for entrance into the Order of Santiago.' Pike further notes that 'Cotarelo's description of the noble and Old Christian ancestry of the Encisos has been generally accepted, even though it was based on a purely subjective interpretation of the facts.' Pike's own investigation into the playwright's background reveals that members of his family appeared in early sixteenth-century *composiciones*, or contracts drawn up between the Crown and groups of conversos, under the terms of which the king returned to those condemned by the Inquisition or their heirs all confiscated property, in return for a large contribution to the royal treasury.[40]

In her article on the converso lineage of the Seville poet Juan de Jáuregui, Ruth Pike notes that Jáuregui's biographer, José Jordan de Urries y Azara, concluded, 'despite substantial information to the contrary, that the poet's family, on all sides, was of Old Christian and *hidalgo* origin.' In fact, as Pike points out, Jáuregui's mother, Isabel Hurtado de Sal, was a member of a wealthy and influential Sevillian converso clan.[41] Unfortunately, the editor of the 1993 Cátedra edition of Juan de Jáuregui's collected poems, Juan Matas Caballero, appears not to have been aware of Pike's article; thus his introduction to the compilation perpetuates Jordan de Urries' bias for an Old Christian Jáuregui. Matas writes:

> His [Jáuregui's] distinguished origins are endorsed by the rank of his parents, the Riojan Don Miguel Martínez de Jáuregui—who was an alderman in Seville from 1586, and whose noble origins go back to the middle of the fifteenth century in the jurisdiction of Vergara, where the estate of the Lizarraldes and Jáureguis was situated—and the Sevillian Doña Isabel de Sal, of elevated Seville lineage, among whose ancestors was Pedro González de la Sal, who in 1472 was the 'Judge' of Seville, and among whose close family was her cousin, the famous physician and poet Juan de Salinas y Castro. However, neither was his paternal family free of problems concerning its [claim to] noble status, nor the maternal branch free of accusations of [lack of] *limpieza de sangre*; serious questions which finally were resolved in favor of both families.[42]

The implication is that Jáuregui's *limpieza de sangre* examination successfully resolved the matter in favor of an Old Christian lineage. In fact, the poet underwent a long, expensive, and enormously painful *probanza*, which began in 1616, when he applied for entry into the noble Order of Calatrava, and ended 23 years later with the coveted title. In the intervening period, Jáuregui was subjected to four separate genealogical inquiries, each of which brought forth new denunciations, and, in 1628, 13 years into the investigation process, a humiliating rejection by the council of the military orders. Nine years later, a new committee reversed the earlier decision, for reasons that are not altogether clear, although it appears that Jáuregui, like his friend Diego Velázquez, received his noble insignia only through the intervention of a benevolent Philip IV.[43]

Spanish academics of the post-Franco period have often been reluctant to explore the extent and implications of the converso presence in early modern high culture. I do not mean to suggest that they have always avoided this exploration willfully, as adherents to a *castizo* outlook promoted earlier by Claudio Sánchez-Albornoz or Eugenio Asensio. I would suggest, however, that they have been formed in environments in which *castizo* views have often prevailed and in which variant ideas have not been encouraged. Happily, this situation has now begun to change, although, as I noted in the preface to this book, the converso's involvement in Spain's intellectual and reform environments remains underexplored. It would seem that the bias for an early modern Spanish high culture in which the conversos were all but invisible has been replaced by a preference for shelving the issue altogether. The argument, it seems, is that while the conversos were undoubtedly significant in early modern Spain as intellectuals and religious activists, it is neither possible nor, indeed, necessary to explore further the extent of this involvement. While this view is presented as a rational solution to an old academic conflict, it is based, I would argue, on political rather than scientific considerations: the need to gain a degree of closure on a debate that began and evolved in Franco's Spain, and which became associated with the political divisions in Spanish society.

Those who subscribe to this solution tend to argue that the earlier debate on the conversos' prominence in Spanish culture took place against a background of early twentieth-century nationalism and national essentialism, in which scholars were influenced not only by their political prejudices but also by certain dubious intellectual ideas of their day, now thankfully rejected by contemporary academics. The message is that the earlier scholarship is flawed and not to be taken too seriously.

Américo Castro himself seems to take the brunt of the criticism, although others who entertain views similar to those of Castro are also singled out for attack. For example, in her recent essay 'Creating Converos,' the Spanish historian Mercedes García-Arenal takes issue with the scholarship of Ángel Alcalá, who, she argues, continues to essentialize the converso and exaggerate his place in Spain's early modern reform environment.[44] García-Arenal attributes Alcalá's shortcomings to his political background—the son of Republicans who spent much of his professional career outside of Spain—and his attachment to the Américo Castro school of Spanish historiography. Castro himself, she admits, was a gifted scholar; however, 'his training as a philosopher [*sic*] (his reliance on Dilthey) and maybe his own personal vital trajectory led him to define "essences" in a way which has dented his reputation and current standing among historians.'[45] In contrast, García-Arenal states, recent scholarship, untainted by personal and political rivalries, and unburdened by essentialist arguments, has arrived at a more nuanced and balanced view of converso identity.

The observation that converso identity has become more nuanced as a result of recent scholarship is undoubtedly true. However, García-Arenal also claims that this recent scholarship has successfully challenged the view that the converso predominated in an early modern Spanish reform environment. In support of this assertion, she makes reference to scholarly works on the European Counter-Reformation outside of Spain, which have demonstrated that the Church's social discipline created tension throughout society, among all social groups and strata. She thus extrapolates from this scholarship that spiritual concern, skepticism, and religious dissidence were also to be found in all areas of post-Tridentine Spanish society 'without there being any direct connection with their origin. It happened whether their origin was converso or Old Christian.'[46] And to emphasize her point, she notes that most people prosecuted by the Inquisition for religious transgressions in Counter-Reformation Spain were Old Christians.

There are two evident problems with this argumentation. First, unlike the rest of Europe, Spain had a converso issue; any conclusion we make as to the general character of Counter-Reformation religious dissidence in France or Italy should be applied to Spain with a good degree of caution. Second, we should be careful not to confuse or conflate those people who after Trent suddenly found themselves prosecuted for common misdemeanors, which a pre-Tridentine Church had turned a blind eye to, with advocates for religious transformation. And thus while it is indisputable that most of those prosecuted by the Inquisition after Trent were Old Christians, the vast majority of these offenders were reprimanded for their ignorance of Tridentine policy. They were the hapless casualties of a Church that wished to create greater awareness of official dogma and orthodox practice; they were not religious dissidents or reformers.[47]

Spain's bona fide reformers, on the other hand, formed a much smaller group of offenders. If we wish to discover the character of their religious activism, either in pre- or post-Tridentine Spanish society, then the obvious place to begin is in Spain itself, with the movement's leading figures, for whom we already have a good deal of background information on which to build: Alonso de Oropesa, Pedro de Osma, Antonio de Nebrija,

Hernando de Talavera, Alonso Fernández de Madrid, Pedro de Lerma, Juan Luis Vives, Juan de Valdés, Alfonso de Valdés, Juan de Vergara, Juan de Cazalla, María de Cazalla, Bartolomé de las Casas, Bernabé de Palma, Francisco Ortiz, Francisco de Osuna, Alonso de Madrid, Antonio de Ciudad Real, Juan de Ávila, Juan Gil (Egidio), Constantino Ponce de la Fuente, García Arias, Casiodoro de Reina, Cipriano de Valera, Antonio del Corro, Juan Pérez, Pedro de Cazalla, Agustín de Cazalla, Carlos de Seso, Bartolomé de Carranza, Cipriano de la Huerga, Benito Arias Montano, Luis de Granada, Luis de León, Gaspar de Grajal, Martín Martínez de Cantalapiedra, Francisco Sánchez de las Brozas (El Brocense), Juan de Malara, Pedro de Valencia, Agustín Salucio, Ambrosio de Morales, Juan de Mariana, Teresa of Ávila, John of the Cross, Pedro Fernández de Navarrete, and so on. Let us begin here, and see where our investigations take us. Above all, let us be sensitive to our protagonists' hidden messages. For if we are not alert to their secrets, we simply won't uncover them.

NOTES

CHAPTER 1: INTRODUCTION

1. See Kevin Ingram, 'Diego Velázquez's Secret History,' *Boletin del Museo del Prado*, 35 (1999), pp. 69–85. It is my view that Velázquez's contemporaries at court, unlike modern Velázquez scholars, suspected that the painter was from a converso background.
2. Converso, the Spanish term for convert, was applied by Old Christian society to both the converts from Judaism to Christianity and their heirs, who had been born inside the Catholic Church. When I refer to someone as 'converso' in the following pages, I do so in the belief that he was a direct descendant of Jews on at least one side of his family, had grown up in an environment among people who were also descendants of Jews, and had been marked psychologically by that experience. When I use the term 'humanist,' I apply it broadly to mean men and women with an inclination toward humanist studies and Erasmian principles, whether expressed in Latin or in the vernacular.
3. *El Alboraique*, described in an anti-converso pamphlet of the same name, written around 1465, is the legendary hybrid animal *al-Burāq* that, according to Muslim tradition, took Mohammad from Mecca to the Dome of the Rock in Jerusalem, from where he ascended to heaven. The anonymous author of the pamphlet wished to emphasize the conversos' bestial and hybrid characteristics, neither Christian nor Jew, but some kind of religious aberration. For an examination of the work, see

Jeremy Lawrence, 'Alegoría apocalipsis en *El Aboraique*,' *Revista de poética medieval* 11 (2003), pp. 11–39.
4. The *Sapienta*, or books of wisdom, were especially favored by converso humanists, in particular the *Song of Songs*, which revealed a religious union founded on love rather than on doctrine, and Ecclesiastes and Job, which appealed to their own self-doubts and uncertainties.
5. In his picaresque work *Guzmán de Alfarache*, Mateo Aleman wrote two introductions, one for 'el lector discreto,' the other for 'el vulgo.' In *The Lost Lexicon*, Sanford Shepherd examines in some detail the hidden messages contained in converso authors' works. The majority of these double entendres are found in picaresque fiction, a literary genre created and dominated by conversos fully aware of their marginal status. Sanford Shepard, *The Lost Lexicon: Secret Meanings in the Vocabulary of Spanish Literature During the Inquisition* (Miami, FL: Ediciones Universal, 1982).
6. For Ambrosio de Morales' converso background, see Chap. 3.
7. Francisco Pacheco, *Libro de descripción de verdaderos retratos de ilustres y memorables varones* (Sevilla: Diputación Provincial de Sevilla, 1985), p. 357. For an examination of Juan de Malara's converso background and its influence on his *Philosophia vulgar*, see Kevin Ingram, 'El humanista converso Juan de Malara (1524–1570),' in Ruth Fine, Michèle Guillemont and Juan Diego Vila eds., *Lo converso: orden imaginario y realidad en la cultura española (siglos XIV–XVII)* (Madrid: Iberoamericana, 2013), pp. 307–24.
8. Francisco Pacheco, *El arte de la pintura* (Madrid: Cátedra, 1990), p. 202.
9. See Victoriano Roncero López, 'El tema del linaje en el Estebanillo González: la 'indignitas hominis,' *Bulletin of Hispanic Studies*, LXX (1993), p. 416. Sanford Shepherd notes that the terms Portuguese, Gallego, Asturiano, and Montañes were used by converso authors as euphemisms for New Christians of Jewish descent. See Sanford Shepard, *The Lost Lexicon*, pp. 78–80, 101–4 and 135–7.
10. *Memorias de algunas linajes antiguas e nobles de Castilla*, Biblioteca Nacional ms. 3390, cited in Florence Street 'La Vida de Juan de Mena,' *Bulletin Hispanique*, 55. 2 (1953), p. 151, note 2. Mena claimed that his ancestors came south to take part in the thirteenth-century *Reconquista*.
11. The surname Arias figures prominently in the Llerena Inquisition tribunal's prosecution of the large converso population of Fregenal de la Sierra. For Francisco Pacheco's and Arias Montano's family backgrounds, see Chap. 5.

12. Miguel Cervantes, *Don Quijote de La Mancha*, Barcelona, 2002, p. 43. Unless stated, all translations from Spanish to English are my own.
13. Cervantes perfectly captures his society's prejudice for pure blood in Sancho Panza's remark: 'I'm an Old Christian, and that is enough ancestry for a count.' To which Don Quijote replies, 'And more than enough' (*Don Quijote*, Part 1, Chap. 21). Here Cervantes draws the reader's attention not only to the ridiculous conceit of the blood purity laws but also, in Don Quijote's throwaway line, to the culturally impoverished society that supported the prejudice. Later in the book, when Sancho finds himself the governor of Barataria, Cervantes returns to the blood issue, making a similar jibe against his vacuous, seriously underachieving, society:

    Sancho asked: Who here is my secretary?

    And one of those standing by answered: 'I, sir, for I can read and write, and I'm a Basque.'

    'With the last qualification,' said Sancho, 'you could well be secretary to the Emperor himself. Open this envelope and see what it says.' (*Don Quijote*, Part 2, Chap. 47)

    Not for the first time Cervantes takes the opportunity to poke fun at the Basques, satirizing their overweening pride in their Old Christian noble status, which he contrasts with their reputation for being barely literate. Although old-school *Cervantistas* continue to insist upon Cervantes' Old Christian provenance, many of their colleagues now acknowledge that his family background (medical and mercantile) strongly suggests converso roots, and that this assessment is corroborated by his works, which reveal pro-Erasmian and anti-*limpieza* sentiments. See Alberto Sánchez, 'Nuevas Orientaciones en el Planteamiento de la Biografía de Cervantes,' in *Cervantes* (Madrid: Centro de Estudios Cervantinos, 1995) pp. 19–40.
14. Alonso Núñez de Reinoso, *Los amores de Clareo y Florisea y los trabajos de la sin ventura Isea*, ed. Miguel Angel Teijeiro Fuentes (Badajoz: Universidad de Extremadura, 1991), p. 196, note 145. Constance Hubbard Rose has argued convincingly that Núñez de Reinoso's work is an allegory of the Jews' suffering in exile after the 1492 expulsion and the conversos' situation in Spain. See Constance Hubbard Rose, *Alonso Nuñez de Reinoso: The Lament of a Sixteenth-Century Exile* (Rutherford N.J.: Fairleigh Dickinson University Press, 1971).
15. Juan Pérez de Moya, *Philosofía secreta*, ed. Carlos Clavería (Madrid: Cátedra, 1995), Book 2, Chap. 28.
16. See Chap. 6.

Chapter 2: From Toledo to Alcala

1. On the extent of Jewish conversion, see Heim Beinart, 'The converso Community in Fifteenth-Century Spain,' in R.D. Barnett ed., *The Sephardic Heritage* (London: Mitchell Valentine, 1971), p. 425. The 1391 pogrom was followed by an intense proselytizing campaign, led by the Dominican friar Vicente Ferrer, that resulted in the 1412 Valladolid Laws and the 1413 Disputation of Tortosa. The Valladolid Laws aimed at undermining the Jewish *aljamas* through strict prohibitions on dress, work, and physical movement. The Disputation was a stage-managed event at which leading rabbis were required to prove that the Messiah had not already arrived. Intimidated into contradicting themselves, the Jewish leaders cut poor figures; several even converted to Christianity soon after the event, promoting further conversions among the rank-and-file Jewry. For an account of the Ferrer proselytizing campaign and the Disputation of Tortosa, see Yitzhak Baer, *A History of the Jews in Modern Spain*, Vol. II (Philadelphia: Jewish Publication Society, 1978), pp. 166–243.
2. All three of these families prospered as a result of their support of the successful pretender to the throne, Enrique de Trastamara. See Helen Nader, *The Mendoza Family in the Spanish Renaissance* (New Brunswick, N.J.: Rutgers University Press, 1979), Chapter 2.
3. For a detailed examination of the Toledo uprising, see Eloy Benito Ruano, *Toledo en el siglo XV* (Madrid: CSIC, 1961), pp. 33–81.
4. For an account of the converso reaction to the Toledo statute, see Albert A. Sicroff, *Los estatutos de limpieza de sangre. Controversias entre los siglos XV y XVII* (Madrid: Taurus, 1985), Chapter 2; and the introduction to Guillermo Verdín-Díaz, *Alonso de Cartagena y el Defensorium unitatis christianae* (Oviedo: Universidad de Oviedo, 1992), a Castilian translation of the original Latin text. For an examination of Díaz de Toledo's reply to the statute, the *Instrucción del Relator*, see Nicholas G. Round, 'Politics, Style and Group Attitudes in the Intrucción del Relator,' *Bulletin of Hispanic Studies* 46.4 (1969), pp. 280–319.
5. Cartagena's father was Pablo de Santa Maria, Bishop of Burgos, who before converting to Christianity, in 1390 or 1391, was an eminent rabbi. The Santa Maria family became both wealthy and influential through attaining important positions in the Church. Pablo's eldest son, Gonzalo, was Bishop of Azorga, Plasencia, and Sigüenza; while his third son, Alonso, succeeded him as Bishop of Burgos. For accounts of the family, see Luciano Serrano y Pineda, *Los conversos Don Pablo de Santa María y Don Alfonso de Cartagena. Obispos de Burgos, gobernantes, diplomatos y escritores* (Madrid: Escuela de Estudios Hebraicos, 1942), and

Francisco Cantera Burgos, *Alvar García de Santa María y su familia de conversos: Historia de la Judería de Burgos y sus conversos más egregios* (Madrid: Instituto Arias Montano, 1952). See also Luis Fernández Gallardo, *Alonso de Cartagena (1385–1456): una biografía política en la Castilla del siglo XV* (León: Junta de Castilla y León, 2002).

6. E. Michael Gerli, 'Performing Nobility: Mosén Diego de Valera and the Poetics of converso Identity,' *La corónica* 25.1 (1996), p. 26.
7. Quoted from Gregory B. Kaplan, 'Towards the Establishment of a Christian Identity: the Conversos and Early Castilian Humanism,' *La corónica* 25.1 (1996), pp. 53–68. In his article Kaplan examines the theme of nobility through virtue in the works of Gato, Guillén, Cota, and Poeta. For a discussion of these converso writers and their involvement in Archbishop Alfonso Carrillo's literary circle, see Carlos Moreno Hernández, 'Algunos aspectos de la vida y la poesía de Pero Guillén de Segovia,' *Anales de Literatura Española* 5 (1986–1987) pp. 329–356. See also Francisco Márquez Villanueva, *Investigaciones sobre Juan Álvarez Gato* (Madrid: Real Academia Española, 1960).
8. Gregory B. Kaplan, 'Towards the Establishment of a Christian Identity,' p. 63.
9. Archbishop Carrillo's mother's family, the Ayalas, was linked through marriage to the family of Alonso de Cartagena, author of the *Defensorium unitatis christianae*.
10. Fernando de Pulgar, *Claros Varones de Castilla*, ed. Robert Brian Tate (Oxford: Oxford University Press, 1971), p. 10. While Tate's study provides a useful historical backdrop to Pulgar's work, it sidesteps his converso background and its implications for his writing. For a discussion of Pulgar's defense of the conversos, see Francisco Cantera, 'Hernando de Pulgar y Los conversos,' *Sefarad* 4.2 (1944), pp. 295–348. Pulgar was an outspoken critic of the Inquisition and its attacks on the converso community. For these opinions he was dismissed, at least temporarily, from the royal court. In 1482 Pulgar wrote to his friend and patron Cardinal Pedro González de Mendoza, complaining about a *limpieza de sangre* ordinance in Guipúzcoa that prohibited conversos from entering the territory. 'Isn't it risible,' wrote Pulgar, 'that all of them, or most, send their sons down here to serve us, and many of them are young hidalgos [*mozos de espuelas*], yet do not care to be the in-laws of those they wish to serve' (cited from Albert A. Sicroff, *Los estatutos de limpieza de sangre*, p. 125, note 102).
11. For an account of humanism as a middle-sort socio-political movement, see Quentin Skinner, *The Foundations of Modern Political Thought*, Vol. I (Cambridge: Cambridge University Press, 1979), Chapters 4 and 8.

12. For the humanists' influence on the courts of Mantua, Ferrara, and Urbino, see Alison Cole, *Art of the Renaissance Courts* (Upper Saddle River, NJ: Prentice Hall, 2005). See also Lisa Jardine's comments on Federigo da Montefeltro, the Duke of Urbino, in *Worldly Goods: A History of the Renaissance* (New York: Doubleday, 1996), pp. 183–198.
13. For converso double entendres and secret references, see Sanford Shepherd, *Lost Lexicon*. These references are mostly taken from Spanish picaresque fiction. There are, however, other converso topoi: for example, *la envidia del vulgo*. In Spanish humanist works, the *vulgo* often signifies an ignorant and prejudiced Old Christian society, its *envidia* (envy) directed against a successful converso community.
14. While the great figure of Christian humanism, Erasmus, appreciated the need to study Hebrew for biblical exegesis, he paid relatively little attention to the Hebrew Scriptures. In fact, he wrote, 'I wish it were that the Christian Church did not place such importance on the Old Testament.' Natalio Fernández Marcos y Emilia Fernández Tejero, *Biblia y Humanismo* (Madrid: Fundación Universitaria, 1997), p. 20.
15. Juan de Malara, *Philosophia vulgar* (Madrid: Biblioteca Castro, 1996), p 29.
16. The anonymous author of the *Refundición*, generally considered to have been a converso from Toledo, links the post-diluvium colonization of Spain not to Túbal, who was of the Gentile line of Noah's son Japhet, but significantly to a certain Rocas, the descendant, so the chronicler informs us, of Noah's eldest son Shem or Sem, the founding father of the Semitic or Hebrew nation. Thus the author promotes the view that these first Spaniards were a branch of the Jewish family. Furthermore, he tells us, at the time of the destruction of the first temple, the Spanish ruler Pirrhus, an ally of the Babylonian King Nebuchadnezzar, brought a large group of Jews to Spain, who, he emphasizes, were also of the line of Shem. These wise Jews went on to build, populate, and ennoble the city of Toledo, at that time known as Ferrezola. Such was the standing of the Jews within Toledo that they were later granted exemption from the 30 coins annual tax placed upon the Peninsula's Jewry as a punishment for the Jerusalem Jews' rejection of Jesus as the Messiah. BNM ms 7594, pp. 1–13. Ramon Menéndez Pidal briefly examines the *Refundición* in *Crónicas generales* (Madrid: Real Biblioteca, 1918). For more recent analyses, see Aengus Ward, '*El Arreglo toledano de la Crónica de 1344*: Antiguas tradiciones y nuevos usos,' in Aengus Ward ed., *Teoría y práctica de la historiografía hispánica medieval* (Birmingham: University of Birmingham Press, 2000) pp. 59–79, and Mercedes Vaquero, 'Horizonte Ideológico del Arreglo Toledano de la Crónica de 1344,' *La Corónica* 32.3 (2004), pp. 249–277.

17. See Haim Beinart, '¿Cuando llegaron los judíos a España?' *Estudios*, 3, Inst. Central de Relaciones Culturales Israel-Iberoamerica, España y Portugal, 1962, pp. 5–18.
18. For an examination of Montano's *In Abdias*, see Francisco Javier Perea Siller, 'Benito Arias Montano y la identificación de Sefarad: exegesis poligrafica del Abdias 20,' *Helmántica: Revista filología, clásica y hebrea* 154 (2000), pp. 199–218.
19. Among Higuera's claims was that 500 of Jesus' Judean followers arrived in Spain soon after the Messiah's death, where they successfully converted many of the peninsular Jews to Christianity. Thus, according to Higuera's fallacious account, the Sephardim formed the first Christian communities in Spain. See Juan Gil, 'Judíos y conversos en los falsos cronicones,' in A. Molinié and J. P. Duviols eds., *Inquisition d'Espagne* (Paris: Presses de l'Université de París-Sorbonne, 2003), pp. 21–43. For an examination of Higuera's works in the context of post-Tridentine Spanish nationalism, see Katrina B. Olds, *Forging the Past: Invented Histories in Counter-Reformation Spain* (New Haven and London: Yale University Press, 2015). A cursory examination of the backgrounds of Spain's most prominent fifteenth- and sixteenth-century chroniclers (Alfonso de Cartagena, Rodrigo Sánchez de Arévalo, Diego de Valera, Florián de Ocampo, Ambrosio de Morales, and Juan de Mariana) indicates that all were from New Christian backgrounds. For Florián de Ocampo's converso roots, see Emilio Cotarelo, 'Varias noticias nuevas acerca de Florián de Ocampo,' *Boletin de la Real Academia Española* 13 (1926), pp. 259–268, and Julio Caro Baroja, *Los judíos en la España moderna y contemporánea*, Vol. II (Madrid: Ediciones Istmo, 1986), p. 370; for Morales New Christian family background, see Chap. 3 of the present work; and for Mariana's converso maternal line, see Juan Blázquez Miguel, *Herejía y heterodoxia en Talavera y su Antigua tierra* (Talavera de la Reina: Ediciones Hierba), pp. 206–208. In his *La crónica general de España*, Ocampo, following the false chronicler Annio da Viterbo, stated that Chaldean was the language spoken throughout the peninsula before the Celtibero invasion, and that an expeditionary force of Spain's early Semitic colonists founded Rome, a name often given to Jewish women. See *La crónica general de España*, Madrid, 1791 [BNM. 1/9022], Chapter 20.
20. An example of a noble and converso union is the marriage of Diego Hurtado de Mendoza and Juana de Cartagena, which produced the court poet Fray Iñigo de Mendoza, author of 'Coplas de vita christi,' an attack on the court society of Henry IV. See Julio Rodríguez Puértolas, *Fray Íñigo de Mendoza y sus 'Coplas de vita christi,'* (Madrid: Gredos, 1968).

21. For the Spanish nobility's lack of interest in letters, see Nicholas G. Round, 'Renaissance Culture and its Opponents in Fifteenth-Century Castile,' *Modern Languages Review* 57.2 (1962), pp. 204–215. Round writes (p. 205), 'In fact, the enthusiasm of the king [Juan II] and the erudition of several contemporaries did not succeed in creating a class of nobles either literate in Latin or favorably disposed to learning even when it was profitable morally and enlightening spiritually.' In the late fifteenth century, the Italian humanist Peter Martyr wrote: 'The youth of Spain from the time of their grandfathers and great grandfathers to the present day have mistakenly believed that those interested in letters should be despised, because up until now they have considered letters an impediment to warfare, which is the only thing they believe is honorable enough to employ their zeal and effort.' Cited in Luis Gil Fernández, *Panorama social del Humanismo español (1500–1800)* (Madrid: Editorial Tecnos, 1995), p. 293. Martyr had been invited to Spain by the Archbishop of Seville, Pedro González de Mendoza, who encouraged the humanist to establish a school for Letters in his nephew Iñigo López de Mendoza's court at Granada. It is possible that the Spanish mystic Luis de Granada was one of Martyr's pupils. See Fray Luis de Granada, *Introducción del Símbolo de la Fe*, ed. José María Balcells (Madrid: Cátedra, 1989), p. 15.

22. In *The Mendoza Family*, Helen Nader puts forward the thesis that humanism grew up among the Spanish nobility as a political response to a Trastamaran state-centralization program. As Nader views it, on one side of this political divide were the noble humanists, on the other side the *letrados*—men of scholastic inclination in the service of the Crown. However the *letrados*—that is to say, professional men trained at university—are not so easily categorized. Some followed traditional (scholastic) precepts, others were drawn toward the new, humanist ideas, which they came into contact with either through studying in Italy (often in the Spanish college at Bologna) or through their contact with men who had done so. *Letrados* who inclined toward humanism entered both the royal court and those few noble households that were disposed toward intellectual inquiry. The scenario was similar to that of quattrocento Italy, where humanists were able to galvanize some of the new nobility with the view that noble status was one that was achieved through a combination of arms and letters, and not passively inherited through a bloodline. Spanish humanism, like Italian humanism, was not per se a noble phenomenon, although a handful of noble families promoted its study.

23. Pérez de Guzmán also maintained close relations with Cartagena's brother, the historian Alvar García de Santa María. See Fernan Pérez de Guzmán, *Generaciones y Semblanzas*, ed. R.B. Tate (London: Támesis, 1965), p. xi.

24. See Francisco López Estrada, 'La Retórica en las 'Generaciones y Semblanzas' de Fernán Pérez de Guzmán,' *Revista de Filología Española* 30 (1946), pp. 346–349.
25. Noel Fallows, 'El 'Doctrinal de los Cavalleros' de Alfonso de Cartagena, segun el ms. Gaml. Kongl. Saml. 2219 de la Real Biblioteca de Copenhague,' *Hispania* 188 (1994), pp. 1107–1135.
26. For the converso character of Santillana's cultural circle, see Ángel Gómez Moreno, 'Judíos y conversos en la prosa castellana,' in *Judíos en la literatura española*, ed. I. M. Hassán and R. Izquierdo Benito, Cuenca, 2001, pp. 57–86. Luis Girón Negrón notes that Santillana maintained a close relationship with Jewish scholars in the *aljama* of Carrion de los Condes, the town in which he was born. See Luis Girón Negrón, 'Huellas hebraicas en la poesia del Marqués de Santillana,' in *Encuentros y Desencuentros. Spanish Cultural Intersection Throughout History*, ed. Carlos Carrete Parrondo, Marcelo Dascal et al. (Tel Aviv: University Publishing Projects, 2000), pp. 161–211. For the converso presence in Guadalajara, see Francisco Cantera Burgos & Carlos Carrete Parrondo, 'Las juderías medievales en la provincia de Guadalajara,' *Sefarad* 34.1 (1974): 43–78; and 34.2 (1974): 313–386; and Pedro Luis Lorenzo Cadarso, 'Esplendor y decadencia de las oligarquias conversas de Cuenca y Guadalaljara (siglos XV y XVI),' *Hispania* 186 (1994), pp. 53–81.
27. For Pedro Díaz de Toledo's relationship with Santillana and his contribution to fifteenth-century scholarship, see Maria Laura Giordano, *Apologetas de la fe: elites conversas entre inquisición y patronazgo en España (siglos XV y XVI)* (Madrid: Fundación Universitaria Español, 2004), pp. 39–57. Giordano notes that most fifteenth-century translations of Latin works, both religious and profane, were made by converso *letrados*. Ibid. p. 38. For a longer account of Pedro Díaz's life and work, see Nicholas G. Round, 'Pero Díaz de Toledo: a study of a fifteenth century converso translator in his background,' diss. University of Oxford, 1966.
28. The first part of the *Diálogo* is a philosophical-theological examination of life, which leans heavily on a Senecan stoicism. Díaz assumes the role of mentor, Santillana the curious disciple. Ottavio Di Camillo, *El Humanismo Castellano del Siglo XV* (Valencia: Fernando Torres, 1976), p. 126, note 18.
29. Ibid. p.125, note 17.
30. Cardinal González Mendoza's close connections to the converso community are also evident in Rodrigo de Cota's parody of the wedding between Mendoza's niece and the son of the converso royal accountant Diego Arias Dávila. Cota, probably upset at not being invited to the nuptials, likens the occasion to a Jewish wedding. See Julio Caro Baroja,

Los judíos en la España moderna y contemporánea, Vol. I, p. 30. It was the Cardinal who was responsible for inviting the Italian humanist Peter Martyr to his nephew's court at Granada to attempt to educate Spanish youth, who 'from the time of their grandfathers and great grandfathers to our days have incorrectly believed that men of letters should be disparaged.'

31. Talavera replied to the anonymous author's attack in his *Católica impugnación*, which he used to defend the Christian faith while subtly introducing arguments for its reform. See Hernando de Talavera, *Católica impugnación*, ed. Francisco Márquez Villanueva. A new edition of the work was published in 2012 with a foreword by Stefania Pastore. An opponent of the Inquisition in Seville and later Granada, where he was archbishop, Talavera clashed with the vicious Córdoba inquisitor Lucero, who accused him and his family of Judaizing. The accusation led to the arrest of his sister and nieces and their trial for heresy. After fighting the accusation for three years, Talavera finally witnessed his family's acquittal and release, in April 1507, several weeks before his death. For the trial, see Tarsicio Herrero del Collado, 'El proceso inquisitorial por delito de herejía contra Hernando de Talavera,' *Anuario de historia del derecho español* 39 (1969), pp. 671–706.

32. Helen Nader, *The Mendoza Family in the Spanish Renaissance*, p. 187.

33. See Alberto Vázquez and R. Selden Rose eds., *Algunas cartas de Don Diego Hurtado Mendoza, escritas 1528–1552* (New Haven: Yale University Press, 1935), pp. 119–120.

34. Pedro Manrique de Lara, the first Duke of Nájera, maintained close ties with the Jewish *aljamas* in his *señorio*, providing them with favorable conditions for expansion. The duke's *mayordomo* (estate manager) was a rabbi. See José Luis Lacave, *Juderias y Sinagogos Españoles* (Madrid: Editorial Mapfre, 1992), p. 232.

35. For accounts of the Manriques' involvement in the Carrillo circle, see John G. Cummins, 'Pero Guillén de Segovia y el ms. 4.114 El Cancionero,' *Hispanic Review* 41.1 (1973), pp. 28–32; and Antonio Serrano de Haro, *Personalidad y destino de Jorge Manrique* (Madrid: Gredos, 1966).

36. Benito Ruano, *Toledo en el siglo XV*, Madrid, 1961, p. 136. Gómez Manrique was married to Juana Mendoza, who was the patron of Alonso de Cartagena's erudite niece, Teresa de Cartagena, and the dedicatee of two of Teresa's works, *Arboleda de los enfermos* and *Admiraçión Operum Dei*. A number of Teresa's brothers married into the Mendoza family. See Maria Laura Giordano, *Apologetas de la fe*, p. 58.

37. Julio Caro Baroja, *Los judíos en la España moderna y contemporánea*, Vol. I, p. 313. In a letter to Antonio Manrique de Lara, second Duke of Nájera, the converso Francisco López de Villalobos stated: 'If any good comes from your house, it is owing to us [the Jews] who are genus electum, regale sacerdotium.' Cited in Antonio Domínguez Ortiz, *La Clase Social de Los conversos en Castilla en la Edad Moderna* (Granada: Universidad de Granada, 1991), p. 163, note 21.
38. Luis Gil Fernández, *Panorama Social del Humanismo Español (1500–1800)*, p. 457.
39. For Averroist ideas among the Jews and conversos, see Yitshak Baer, *A History of the Jews in Christian Spain*, pp 253–259; and Eric Lawee, 'Sephardic Intellectuals: Challenges and Creativity (1391–1492),' in Eric Lawee ed., *The Jew in Medieval Iberia: 1100–1500* (Boston: Academic Studies Press, 2012), pp. 352–394.
40. Here the great Maimonides set a precedent. Confronting the Almohads' twelfth-century Jewish pogrom, the Jewish rabbi and philosopher opined that Jews could convert to Islam in exceptional circumstances, provided that they continued to observe their own religion in private. See Jane S. Gerber, *The Jews of Spain: A History of the Sephardic Experience* (New York: The Free Press, 1994), p. 81. Contemporaneous accounts—both those of detractors and sympathizers—concur that substantial numbers of conversos continued to Judaize two and three generations after their ancestors had converted to Christianity. It is instructive to note that while the converso writers Alfonso de Palencia, Fernando de Pulgar, and Juan de Lucena berated the Inquisition for its inhumanity toward the New Christians, all three men recognized that Judaizing was prevalent in the converso community, especially in Andalusia, where, Palencia noted, 'it had become widespread among the conversos the belief that the fallacious messiah's arrival was at hand.'
41. On the subject of the converso skeptics, Francisco Márquez Villanueva writes: 'What we observe in fact much more among the conversos is a heretical attitude of denying every supernatural perspective, Jewish as well as Christian ... In the inquisitorial lawsuits these are accused of maintaining that "we live and die as the beasts," or of various similar expressions of disbelief or a crude Epicureanism. We may regard this attitude as a consequence of enforced conversion and of the demoralization produced through it, although there, too, old trends of Averroism can be detected and the survival of a Sadducean attitude.' See Francisco Márquez Villanueva, 'The Converso Problem: An Assessment,' *Collected Studies in Honor of Américo Castro's Eightieth Year* (Oxford: Lincoln Lodge Research Library, 1965), pp. 317–333.

The terms 'Sadducean' and 'Epicurean' were often applied in contemporary accounts to those people who did not believe in the immortality of the soul, and thus rejected the idea of Jesus as Savior. It appears that Alonso de Cartagena himself entertained such notions, at least according to his contemporary Juan de Lucena. See Alejandro Medina Bermúdez, 'Los inagotables misterios de Juan de Lucena,' *Dicienda, Cuadernos de Filología Hispanica,* 1999, 17, p. 307.

42. Cited from Yosi Yisraeli, 'Constructing and Undermining Converso Jewishness: Porfiat Duran and Pablo Santa Maria,' in Ira Katznelson and Miri Rubin eds., *Religious Conversion: History, Experience and Meaning* (Abingdon, Oxon: Routledge, 2016), p. 202.

43. See Ottavio Di Camillo, *El Humanismo Castellano del Siglo XV*, pp. 156–166. Di Camillo notes that while Cartagena's father, Pablo de Santa Maria, converted to Christianity in 1391, his mother remained Jewish. Di Camillo speculates (p. 166): 'The intimate contact with two distinct beliefs could have led him to consider the relativity of God, who it was necessary to reach through an act of faith. Whatever the case, it is evident that his idea that knowledge cannot be attained disguises an attitude of empathy and toleration, implying that the differences between sects do not involve God but the ways in which He has revealed himself to men.' See also Francisco López Estrada, 'La Retórica en las 'Generaciones y semblanza' de Fernán Pérez de Guzmán,' pp. 339–349. For Alonso de Cartagena's interest in St. Paul, see María Laura Giordano, *Apologetas de la fè*, Chapter 1.

44. The work was begun in 1450, a year after the *Sentencia-Estatuto* was introduced in Toledo. Oropesa appears to have been influenced by Cartagena's *Defensorium*, which refers to Jewish law as a spiritual light that was intensified with the arrival of Christ, at which point it was also made available to the Gentiles. See Chap. 9 of the *Defensorium*, translated into Spanish by Guillermo Verdín-Díaz in *Alonso de Cartagena y el Defensorium unitatis christianae.*

45. For an examination of *Lumen*, in which Oropesa, like his contemporaries Alonso de Cartagena and Diego de Valera, also emphasizes the Jews' importance to Christianity, see Albert Sicroff, 'Anticipaciones de Erasmismo Español en *Lumen ad revelationem gentium* de Alfonso de Oropesa,' *Nueva Revista de Filología Hispanica,* 30.2 (1981). For an account of the Jewish cell in the Jeronymite monastery at Guadalupe, see Albert Sicroff, 'Clandestine Judaism in the Hieronymite Monastery of Nuestra Señora de Guadalupe,' in Izaak A. Langas and Barton Sholod eds., *Studies in Honor of Mair J. Bernardete* (New York: Las Americas, 1965), pp. 89–125. On the same subject, see Gretchen D. Starr-LeBeau, *In the Shadow of the Virgin: Inquisitors, Friars, and Conversos in Guadalupe, Spain* (Princeton: Princeton University Press,

2003). See also Stefania Pastore, 'Fake Trials and Jews with Old-Fashioned Names: Converso Memory in Toledo,' *La corónica* 41.1 (2012) pp. 235–262, in which Pastore relates how Old Christians within the Jeronymite Order exaggerated converso Judaizing to oust a converso governing body.

46. See John Edwards, *Ferdinand and Isabella: Profiles in Power* (Harlow, UK: Routledge, 2004), pp. 140–142. Edwards singles out paeans to Isabel's virtue and restorative powers by the conversos Fray Iñigo de Mendoza, Diego San Pedro, and Antón de Montoro (*el ropero*). It is also evident that Montoro's outrageously hyperbolic poem comparing the Queen to the Virgin Mary is a brilliantly irreverent work that surreptitiously attacks Christian and Isabeline pretensions—a typical piece of converso doublespeak.

47. Luis Enrique Rodríguez-San Pedro Bezares ed., *Historia de la Universidad de Salamanca: Vol. III.I Saberes y confluencias* (Salamanca: Universidad de Salamanca, 2006), p. 532.

48. See Henry Kamen, *The Spanish Inquisition: An Historical Revision* (London: Weidenfeld and Nicolson, 1997), pp. 89–91.

49. This comparison of ritual-obsessed monks to Jews is found in a number of Erasmus' works, including his *Enchiridion* and *Praise of Folly*. Of the *Enchiridion* (translated into Castilian in 1527 by the converso Alonso Fernández de Madrid), Erasmus wrote to the English humanist John Colet, 'I composed it not in order to show off my cleverness or my style, but solely in order to counteract the error of those who make religion in general consist in rituals and observances of an almost more than Jewish formality, but who are astonishingly indifferent to matters that have to do with true goodness.' Quoted from Erika Rummel ed., *The Erasmus Reader* (Toronto: University of Toronto Press, 1990), p. 138. The conversos conveniently ignored the anti-Semitic aspect of Erasmus' comparison. For Erasmus' Judeophobia, see Shimon Markish, *Erasmus and the Jews* (Chicago: University of Chicago Press, 1996). It is possible that Erasmus was aware that his following in Spain was predominantly converso, and that this group was utilizing him in its own parallel reform campaign. In a reply to attacks from Spanish scholars on his *Enchiridion*, Erasmus wrote: 'Let Zuñiga and Carranza fling themselves after heretics of another sort, who have already littered the fields of the Lord more than enough. Certain Jews, half-Jews, and quarter-Jews are getting even stronger, pushing their way among us, bearing the name of Christian but carrying all Moses in their souls' (Shimon Markish, *Erasmus and the Jews*, p. 77).

50. This may have been the case of the illuminist María de Cazalla. See Alastair Hamilton, *Heresy and Mysticism in Sixteenth-Century Spain: The Alumbrados* (Toronto: University of Toronto Press, 1992), p. 87.

51. The conversos at Charles' court also hoped to recruit supporters for their struggle against the Inquisition, as the Inquisitor General, Cardinal Cisneros, was aware. In 1516 he had his Brussels agent point out to Charles who the court conversos were, a group which he believed were in league against him. E. González González, 'Vives: Un humanista judeoconverso en el exilio en Flandes,' in Luc Dequeker, Werner Verbeke eds., *The Expulsion of the Jews and the Emigration to the Low Countries (15th/16th C)* (Leuven: Leuven University Press, 1998), pp. 35–82 (p. 43).

52. Vives regarded Jesus as the exemplary stoic, his crucifixion the ultimate in stoical self-sacrifice. See Marcia L. Colish, 'The *De veritate fidei christianae* of Juan Luis Vives,' in *Christian Humanism: Essays Offered to Arjo Vanderjagt on the Occasion of His Sixtieth Birthday*, ed. Alasdair A. MacDonald, Zweder von Martels, and Jan R Veenstra (Leiden: Brill, 2009), pp. 188–189. He also stated: 'I do not think, in fact, that there is any truer Christian than the Stoic sage.' *Opera Omnia*, ed. G. Mayans y Siscar, 8 vols., Valencia, 1782–1790, reprinted London, 1964, Vol. III, p. 17.

53. A number of Vives' immediate family, including his mother and father, were convicted of Judaizing and burnt at the stake. Vives' father was first prosecuted for Judazing in 1500. A year later his aunt Castellana and cousin Miguel were convicted of using their home as a clandestine synagogue, a crime for which both were executed. Whether Juan Luis Vives was brought up as a Jew is a matter of conjecture. He would certainly have grown up aware of his converso condition and the dangers attached to it. For the Vives' family prosecutions, see Miguel de la Pinta Llorente and Jose Maria de Palacio y de Palacio, *Procesos inquisitoriales contra la familia judía de Juan Luis Vives* (Madrid: Instituto Arias Montano, 1964).

54. Juan Luis Vives, *Epistolario*, ed. José Jiménez Delgado (Madrid: Editorial Nacional, 1978), no. 62, pp. 314–316.

55. Vives attacked the scholastics in one of his first works, *In psuedodialecticos* (*Against the Pseudo-Dialecticians*), published in 1519. He extends this attack to the *vulgo* in *Introductio ad sepientiam* (*Introduction to Wisdom*), where he calls on the virtuous man to separate himself from the *vulgo*'s opinion, for the worst thing in life is not poverty, nor prison, but lack of judgment and understanding.

56. Marcia L. Colish, 'The veritate fidei christianae of Juan Luis Vives,' p. 191.

57. *Introductio ad sapientiam*, Chapter 8.

58. Ibid.

59. Cited in Catherine Curtis, 'The Social and Political Thought of Juan Luis Vives: Concord and Counsel in the Christian Commonwealth,' in Charles Fantazzi ed., *A Companion to Juan Luis Vives* (Leiden: Brill, 2008), pp. 113–164 (p. 157).
60. Juan Luis Vives, *De la concordia y de la discordia. De la pacificación*, trans. and ed. Enrique Rivera (Madrid: Ediciones Paulinas, 1978), p. 401.
61. For the Valladolid conference, see Marcel Bataillon, *Erasmo y España*, pp. 227–278. Lu Ann Homza also discusses the conference in Chapter 2 of *Religious Authority in the Spanish Renaissance* (Baltimore: Johns Hopkins University Press, 2000).
62. Alfonso de Valdés, *Diálogo de Mercurio y Carón*, ed. Rosa Navarro (Madrid: Cátedra, 1999).
63. For the *alumbrados*' influence on Juan de Valdés, see José C. Nieto, *Juan de Valdés y los orígenes de la Reforma en España e Italia* (Mexico D.F.: Fondo de Cultura Económica, 1979), pp. 108–139. For the Valdés brothers' converso background, see Miguel Jiménez Monteserín, 'Los hermanos Valdés y el mundo judeoconverso conquense,' in P. Fernández Albaladejo, J. Martínez Millán and V. Pinto Crespo eds., *Politica, religión e inquisición en la España moderna. Homenaje a Joaquín Pérez de Villanueva* (Madrid: Universidad de Autónoma de Madrid, 1996), pp. 379–400. The brothers' maternal uncle was burnt at the stake in 1484 for Judaizing. In 1513 their father, Hernando, and elder brother, Andrés, were prosecuted for attempting to resist Inquisition investigations. During his hearing, Andrés announced his pride in being a converso, because the converso condition made him a liberal, noble, and honorable man. Ibid., p. 387, note 20.
64. Juan de Valdés, *Diálogo de doctrina cristiana*, ed. Emilio Monjo Bellido (Madrid, Cátedra, 2007), p. 88.
65. The archbishop offered the Holy Office the enormous sum of 50,000 ducados to secure his release. See Charles Henry Lea, *A History of the Inquisition of Spain*, Vol. III (New York: Macmillan, 1908), p. 417.
66. See Haim Beinart, 'Ines of Herrera del Duque. The Prophetess of Extremadura,' in Mary E. Giles ed., *Women in the Inquisition: Spain and the New World* (Baltimore: Johns Hopkins University Press, 1999), pp. 42–52.
67. Manuel Serrano y Sanz, 'Pedro Ruiz de Alcaraz, iluminado alcarreño del siglo XVI,' *Revista de Archivos, Bibliotecas y Museos* 1 (1903), p. 3.
68. Jose C. Nieto argues that Alcaraz was a major influence on the young Valdés. See José C. Nieto, *Juan de Valdés y los orígenes de la Reforma en España y Italia*, pp. 108–139.

69. Manuel Serrano y Sanz, 'Pedro Ruiz de Alcaraz, iluminado alcarreño del siglo XVI,' p. 11.
70. Ibid. p. 12. Not all the *alumbrados* were indifferent to Jesus. Others, like María de Cazalla, placed their faith in a Pauline Christ that unified a Gentile and Jewish community.
71. José C. Nieto, *Juan de Valdés y los orígenes de la Reforma en España y Italia*, p. 127.
72. Bataillon, *Erasmo y España*, p. 181.
73. For the converso presence in the comunero revolt, see Juan Ignacio Gutiérrez Nieto, 'Los conversos y el movimiento Comunero,' *Hispania* 94 (1964), pp. 237–261. For Ferdinand's attack on the conversos as regent of Spain, see Benzion Netanyahu, *The Origins of the Inquisition in Fifteenth Century Spain* (New York: Random House), pp. 1035–1040.
74. The scant biographical details available on Francisco de Osuna are presented by Melquiades Andrés in his introduction to Osuna's *Tercer abecedario spiritual* (Madrid: Biblioteca de Autores Cristianos, 1972). Bernabé de Palma's biography is even sketchier than Osuna's, almost all of the information coming from a sixteenth-century hagiography by Fray Andrés de Guadalupe, contained in his *Historia de la Santa Provincia de Los Angeles*, Madrid, 1662, pp. 311–322. Fray Andrés also refers to Bernabé de Palma as Bernabé de Sicilia, and states that his ancestors were from Sicily. However, his family's occupation, they were *hortaleros* (vegetable gardeners), suggests that they may have belonged to the town's large Mudéjar population, introduced to the area from Aragon in the fourteenth century by the local lord, Egidio Bocanegra. Bernabé de Palma and Francisco de Osuna formed part of a triumvirate of early sixteenth-century Franciscan mystics. Bernardino de Laredo, the third member of the group, is usually described, on no evidence whatsoever, as coming from a noble family. In fact his father was a physician, and he himself took up medicine before deciding to join the Franciscan Order, choosing the small Franciscan community of San Francisco del Monte, close to Seville. It was here that he wrote his mystical work *Subido del Monte Sión* and attacked the Inquisition. See Jessica A. Boon, 'A Mystic in the Age of the Inquisition: Bernardino de Laredo's converso Environment and Christological Spirituality,' *Medieval Encounters* 12. 2 (2006), pp. 133–152.
75. Prologue to the *Primer abecedario*.
76. Promulgated by the Inquisitor General Alonso Manrique, the Edict of Faith listed 48 heretical propositions, most taken from recent *alumbrado* trials. It seems Manrique was worried about the increase in prosecutions against Spain's non-conformists, and wished to distinguish between good non-conformists, the Erasmians, and bad ones, the radi-

cal *alumbrados*. In reality, however, the Erasmians and *alumbrados* held certain reform ideas in common, and leading Erasmians were often drawn to illuminist practice. In his *Tercer abecedario*, published two years after the Edict, Francisco de Osuna worked hard to disguise his more radical reform views. 'His words,' writes Melquiades Andrés, 'are often carefully, not to say Sibillinely, short and adjusted.' (Melquíades Andrés, introduction to the *Tercer abecedario*, p. 39). And in examining Osuna's views on mystical communion, Marcel Bataillon notes that he 'made ingenious strides to suggest the preponderance of divine grace in the most elevated spiritual life, without denying the value of human efforts' (Marcel Bataillon, *Erasmo en España*, p. 168).
77. Melquiades Andrés, 'Los alumbrados de Toledo en el Cuarto Abecedario Espiritual, o ley de amor, de Francisco de Osuna (1530),' *Archivo Iberoamericano* 41 (1981), pp. 459–480 (p. 466).
78. Ibid.
79. Cited from Marcel Bataillon, *Erasmo y España*, p. 176.
80. The increasing obsession with Jesus' suffering had serious repercussions for the Jewish communities, who found themselves more than ever the target of organized violence during Holy Week, with the result that Jews were usually confined to their homes while local priests attacked them from the pulpit and ordinary citizens repeated these views in popular anti-Jewish folk songs. David Nirenberg notes that in parts of Spain 'killing the Jews' was incorporated into the Holy Thursday liturgy during the Middle Ages, and that the practice continued into modern times: 'In modern Asturias the children would shake their rattles and sing a song ... : "Marranos Jews: you killed God, now we kill you. Thieving Jews: first you kill Christ and now you come to rob Christians."' David Nirenberg, *Communities of Violence: Persecution of Minorities in the Middle Ages* (Princeton: Princeton University Press, 1996), pp. 202–203. For an examination of the Holy Week attacks on Jews in Aragon, see ibid., Chapter 7.
81. It was reported in the trial of the *alumbrada* Isabel de la Cruz that she whipped her maid for crying on Maunday Thursday, while she herself made merry, disregarding the solemnities of the tragic day. See John E. Longhurst, *Luther's Ghost in Spain (1517–1546)* (Lawrence, Kansas: Coronado Press, 1964), p. 94. The view that the conversos, like the Jews, rejoiced in the death of Jesus was widespread in late medieval and early modern Spain. The authors of the 1449 *Sentencia-Estatuto* listed the conversos' Easter malpractice as one of the reasons for banning them from public positions within Toledo: 'and also on Maunday Thursday, while the holy oil and chrism were sanctified and the Body of our Redeemer placed on the Monument [platform], the said conversos

slit lambs' throats and eat them and celebrate other types of burned offerings and Jewish sacrifices.' See Alonso de Cartagena, *Defensorium unitatis christianae*, Latin transcription by Padre Manuel Alonso (Madrid: CSIC, 1947), apéndice III, p. 360.

82. 'You will be judged by what you eat and how you dress ... and if they can't find anything here, they will begin to attack your lineage.' Francisco de Osuna, *Tercer abecedario*, p. 568.

83. Ibid.

84. For Martín de Licona, see Darío de Aretillo, 'Nuevos datos sobre el abuelo materno de san Ignacio de Loyola,' *Archivum Historium Societatis Iesu* 26 (1957), pp. 219–229.

85. Juan Velázquez de Cuéllar, like his father, Gutiérrez, was a chief accountant (*contador mayor*) at court, a position usually occupied by conversos (See Julio Caro Baroja, *Los judíos en la España moderna y contemporánea*, Vol. I, p. 30). The most famous of Spain's converso *contadores mayores* was Diego Arias Dávila, the *contador mayor* of Enrique IV, whose son became the Count of Puñonrostro. Ávila was also the name of the Velázquez de Cuéllar family before they changed it to that of their later place of residence, Cuellar, near Segovia—a town, like Ávila, with a large converso merchant community. The seventeenth-century historian and genealogist Jose Pellicer stated that the family were Old Christian minor nobility. However, it is likely that he was employed specifically to launder the family's background. Pellicer was, in fact, a pen for hire, who had few scruples about mixing authentic documents with false ones to present glowing genealogies for those families who bought his services. See M. Serrano y Sanz, *Noticias y documentos historicos del condado de Ribagorza* (Madrid: Centro de Estudios Históricos), Chapters 2 and 3. Serrano y Sanz describes Pellicer's *Historia genealógica de la Gran Casa de Alagon* as 'extremely suspicious.' With few other options open to them, modern scholars of the Velázquez de Cuéllar family have relied on Pellicer's work for information on the family's genealogy. See Luis Fernández Martín, 'El hogar donde Iñigo de Loyola se hizo hombre 1506–1517,' *Archivum Historia Societatis Iesu* 49 (1980), pp. 21–85; and Máximo Diago Hernando, 'Los Velásquez de Cuellar, tenientes de Arévalo, en el horizonte político a fines de a edad media,' *Cuandernos Abulenses* 16 (1991), pp. 11–40. Pellicer's genealogical studies are contained in his *Elogio del licenciado Gutierre Velázquez de Cuéllar* in RAH, Colección Salazar y Castro, B-35, fols. 46–87, and *Memorial de la casa y servicios de don Andrés Velázquez de Velasco, cavallero de la orden de Santiago, conde de Escalante i de Tahalí, señor del estado de Villabaquerín i Sinova*, BNE, R/23906(8).

86. For the *Mancebo*, see L.P. Harvey, *Muslims in Spain 1500 to 1614* (Chicago and London: University of Chicago Press, 2005), pp. 169–193 and *passim*. Harvey believes that Arévalo was an important center of an early sixteenth-century crypto-Islamic movement. See ibid., pp. 110–113; and Serafín Tapia Sánchez, *La comunidad morisca de Ávila* (Salamanca: Universidad de Salamanca, 1991), p. 227. See also Teresa Narvaez's long introduction to her edited edition of the work: *Mancebo de Arévalo, Tratado [Tafsira]* (Madrid: Trotta, 2003).
87. *Fontes Narrativi de S. Ignatio de Loyola et de Societatis Jesu initis. Vol. I, Narraciones sciptae ante Nahum 1557*, Rome, 1947, cited in Ignatius of Loyola, *A Pilgrim's Journey: The Autobiography of Ignatius of Loyola*, trans. and ed. Joseph N. Tylenda (San Francisco: Ignatius Press, 2001), p. 73.
88. For the Velázquez de Cuéllar library, see Luis Fernández Martín, 'El hogar donde Iñigo de Loyola se hizo hombre 1506–1517,' pp. 21–84 (pp. 62–67).
89. Cazalla was not only an agent for Velázquez de Cuéllar, organizing loans to the Treasury through his extensive client network; he was also a close friend of his and his wife, Maria Velasco, even acting as executor for Maria's will. This friendly relationship between the two families may have been reinforced by Maria Velasco's relationship with Pedro de Cazalla's wife, Leonor de Vivero. The Vivero family, descendants of Juan II's converso accountant Alonso Pérez de Vivero, were linked to the Velasco family through marriage. For the relationship between Juan Velázquez de Cuéllar and Pedro de Cazalla, see David Alonso García, 'La financiación de las Guardas de Castilla a principios de la Edad Moderna,' in Enrique García Hernán and David Maffi eds., *Guerra y Sociedad en la Monarquia Hispanica: política, estrategia y cultura en la Europa Moderna (1500–1700)*, Vol. I (Madrid: CSIC, 2006), pp. 793–796.
90. See Luis Fernández, 'Iñigo de Loyola y los Alumbrados,' *Hispania Sacra* 35 (1983), p.41.
91. Antonio's father, Pedro Manrique de Lara, the first Duke of Nájera, also maintained a close relationship with Jewish merchants. His estate manager (*mayordomo*) was a certain Rabi Yuce. See Francisco Cantera Burgos, 'La administración judia del duque de Nájera en las palatinas de Amusio,' in *Homenaje à Georges Vajada. Études d'histoire et de pensé juives*, ed. Gérard Nahon and Charles Truati (Louvain: Peeters, 1980), pp. 309–321.
92. Inés Pascual's son Juan Sagrista Pascual revealed in his deposition for Loyola's beatification process that his mother met Loyola while on her way with a group of friends to the Montserrat monastery, something they did every Saturday. Why they chose Saturday rather than Sunday

for the visit to the monastery, Juan Sagrista does not say, although it does appear to have set their own religious visits apart from regular religious practice.

93. Ricardo García-Villoslada, *San Ignacio de Loyola: Nueva Biografía* (Madrid: Biblioteca de Autores Cristianos, 1988), p. 205.
94. Testimony of Juan Pascual in Ignatius of Loyola's beatification process, 1582. Ibid., p. 259.
95. See Francisco de Borja Medina, 'Iñigo de Loyola y los mercaderes castellanos del norte de Europa. La financiación de sus estudios en la Universidad de Paris,' *Hispania Sacra* 103 (1999), pp. 183–186. It is possible that Loyola had been familiar with members of the Cáceres family and with Don Fadrique de Portugal (Bishop of Segovia from 1508 to 1511) while at Arévalo. Two of Loyola's devotees while he was in Barcelona were Don Juan de Zúñiga and his wife, Estafanía de Requesens, who were also attracted to the lay preacher Juan de Castillo, later executed as a Lutheran heretic. See Bataillon, *Erasmo y España*, p. 185.
96. Although Loyola always denied having any connection with the *alumbrados*, this was clearly untrue. Both Miona and Eguía formed part of his close circle, as did Beatriz Ramírez, who was denounced in 1532 to the Toledo tribunal of the Inquisition as an active participant in the illuminist movement of Alcalá. See John E. Longhurst, 'Saint Ignatius at Alcalá 1526–1527,' *Archivum Historicum Soceitatis Iesu* 26 (1957), pp. 252–256. Loyola also denied having been influenced by Erasmus. However, the Erasmus scholars Marcel Bataillon, A.H.T. Levi, and James McConica seriously question this denial. Both Bataillon and McConica note that the Spiritual Exercises were influenced by Erasmus' *Enchiridion*, which was published in a vernacular version by Eguía in 1527, the same year that Loyola produced an early draft of his own work. A.H.T. Levi notes that the preface to Erasmus' commentary on Saint Matthew's Gospel, published in 1522, 'contains all the major features of Ignatius's spirituality embryonically, including the principle of the *discretio spirituum* (the discernment of the spirits) and, among much else taken by Ignatius, the idea of imaginatively reconstructing the episodes of Jesus' life for meditative prayer that was to form the body of the Spiritual Exercises.' See A.H.T. Levi's introduction to Erasmus, *Praise of Folly* (London: Penguin, 2004), pp. xxxii–xxxiii; see also Bataillon, *Erasmo y España*, pp. 212–214 and 590–592; and James McConica, *Erasmus* (Oxford: Oxford University Press, 1991), p. 60.
97. In the thirteenth century Estella rivaled Burgos as an important mercantile center, its wealth generated by its Jewish merchants and bankers (*cambianistas*). However, in 1328 the town's Christians attacked and

massacred the Jewish inhabitants, as a result of which its economy declined. By the sixteenth century Estella lagged far behind Burgos as a commercial center; nevertheless, it did maintain a strong mercantile community which, like its Burgos counterpart, had grown rich on the wool trade. Miguel Eguía's father was himself head of Estella's wool guild. This community, like the larger merchant community of Burgos, was dominated by conversos, as was the printing business, Miguel Eguia's chosen profession. After his imprisonment for heretical belief, Eguia returned to Estella and his merchant background, trading in cloth and spices. For the Eguía family, see 'El impresor Miguel de Eguía procesado por la Inquisición (c. 1495-1546).' For the Jewish and converso involvement in early printing, see J. Rubio's introduction to José Maria Madurell's *Historia de la Imprenta y Libreria en Barcelona* (Barcelona: Gremios de Editores, 1955).

98. In reply, Loyola stated that in his country [Guipúzcoa] there were no Jews. This was perfectly true. In 1527 there were no Jews anywhere in Spain, at least officially. However, Loyola was not reminding Rodríguez of the 1492 expulsion, but rather of the Guipúzcoans' reputation for legislating against Jewish and converso settlement in their territory. Nevertheless, it is odd that he chose to answer the vicar's question indirectly, rather than merely stating that he was an Old Christian.

99. The family was also linked through marriage with another converso clan, the Castillos. For the Ulloas' converso roots, see *El tizón de la nobleza de España* ed. Armando Mauricio Escobar (Mexico DF: Frente de Afirmación Hispanista, 1999), pp. 138-144. In her study of the Fonseca family, Adelaida Sagarra notes that certain genealogists have indicated that the Fonsecas were from a Jewish background, but she does not identify these sources. See Adelaida Sagarra Gamazo, 'El protagonismo de la familia Fonseca, oriunda de Portugal y asentado en Toro, en la política castellana hasta el descubrimiento de América,' *Anuario del Instituto de Estudios Zamoranos Florián de Ocampo* 10 (1993), p. 422. Another member of the family, Alonso Ulloa de Fonseca, also occupied important positions within the Church. As Bishop of Cuenca (1485-1493), he became closely involved with a group of powerful converso town councillors, led by Hernando de Valdés, father of the humanist Alfonso de Valdés, who were resisting the Inquisition's investigations into the city's New Christian business community. See Miguel Jiménez Monteserín, 'Los hermanos Valdés y el mundo judeoconverso conquense.'

100. Ottavio Di Camillo, *El Humanismo Castellano del Siglo XV*, p. 249.
101. The college was opened in 1528. See Ricardo Espinosa Maeso, 'El maestro Fernan Pérez de Oliva en Salamanca,' *Boletín de la Real*

Academia Española XIII (1926), p. 456. For Pérez de Oliva's part in this enterprise, see Chap. 3. The Fonseca clan was a powerful presence in Salamanca. This power base had been established over the course of three generations in which Fonsecas, as Bishops of Santiago de Compostela, also wielded power over Salamanca, which, by some quirk, formed part of the Archbishop of Santiago's ecclesiastical jurisdiction. In 1523 Fonseca demonstrated his authority in the city by intervening in the trial of the converso illuminist Antonio Medrano, gaining his release from Salamanca's diocesan authorities. See Luis Fernández, 'Iñigo Loyola y los alumbrados,' pp. 596–597. The archbishop may have felt that he could have been more protective of Loyola in Salamanca than in Alcalá.

102. For Loyola's connection to the Spanish merchant communities of Amsterdam and Bruges, see Francisco de Borja Medina, 'Iñigo de Loyola y los Mercaderes Castellanos del Norte de Europa,' pp. 159–206.

103. For an exposition of these early Jesuits' certain or likely converso backgrounds, see Robert A. Maryks, *The Jesuit Order as a Synagogue of Jews: Jesuits of Jewish Ancestry and Purity of Blood Laws in the Early Society of Jesus* (Leiden: Brill, 2009), Chapter 2.

104. In 1547 Silíceo introduced a *limpieza* requirement into the Toledo Cathedral chapter. The archbishop's action promoted increased interest in *limpieza* legislation in other religious and civil institutions. For an account of the battle between the archbishop and his converso opponents within the cathedral, see Albert A. Sicroff, *Los estatutos de limpieza de sangre*, pp. 135–191.

105. John W. O'Malley, *The First Jesuits*, pp. 294–295. The Jesuit Order was continuously attacked during these early years for its Jewish composition. In 1572, for example, the rector of the Jesuit college at Córdoba wrote to the new general Francisco Borja, stating that all the boys in the city who believed they had a religious vocation entered the city's Dominican monastery, as the Jesuit college had the reputation of attracting only Jews. Ibid., p. 190.

106. One of the most ardent supporters of a *limpieza de sangre* statute within the order was Antonio Araoz, the nephew of Loyola's sister-in-law, Magdalena de Araoz. Araoz continually called for a *limpieza* statute, citing the court's displeasure at the Society's reluctance to impose this ban. In reply to these demands, Loyola told his relative categorically that under no circumstances would the Society exclude New Christians on grounds of race. William V. Bangert S.J. *Claude Jay and Alfonso Salmerón: Two Early Jesuits* (Chicago: Loyola University Press, 1985), p. 247.

107. A *limpieza de sangre* statute was finally introduced in 1593, provoking a number of conversos within the Jesuit leadership to protest the New Christians' service to Christianity and to the Jesuit Order. See Chap. 5.

CHAPTER 3: FROM ALCALA TO SEVILLE AND BEYOND

1. Cited from Benzion Netanyahu, *The Origins of the Inquisition in Fifteenth Century Spain*, p. 853.
2. The social tension in Córdoba was the result of a large and powerful converso community that controlled the city's economic and political life. Regarding the relationship between Old and New Christians in Córdoba, the chronicler Diego de Valera, also a converso, wrote: 'Among them [Old Christians and conversos] there was great animosity and envy, as the New Christians of that city were very wealthy, and they were seen to be continuously buying bureaucratic positions, which they used arrogantly, something the Old Christians could not tolerate.' Cited from Francisco Márquez Villanueva, 'Conversos y cargos concejiles en el siglo XV,' *Revista de Archivos, Bibliotecas y Museos* 63.2 (1957). For the Córdoba uprising, see Manuel Nieto Cumplido, 'La revuelta contra los conversos de Córdoba en 1473,' in José Valverde Madrid et al, *Homenaje a Antón de Montoro en el V centenario de su muerte* (Montoro: Ayuntamiento de Montoro, 1977), pp. 31–49. For the violent clashes in Úbeda, Baeza, Andujar, and Jaén, see Luis Coronas Tejada, *Judíos y judeoconversos en el reino de Jaén* (Jaén: Universidad de Jaén, 2003), pp. 69–92.
3. For the Portocarrero family's links to Toledo's converso patricians, see Antonio Blanco Sanchez, *Entre Luis y Quevedo. En busca de Francisco de la Torre* (Salamanca: Atlas, 1980), p. 232, note 4.
4. The Bocanegra-Portocarrero union was formed with the marriage of Egidio's grandson Gilio Bocanegra and Francisca Portocarrero in 1410. For a history of Palma del Rio under the Bocanegra and Portocarrero families, see Manuel Nieto Cumplido, *Palma del Río en la edad media (855–1503)* (Córdoba: Archivo Catedral de Córdoba, 2004).
5. Biographical information on Bernabé de Palma is contained in Fray Andrés de Guadalupe, *Historia de la santa provincia de Los Angeles* (Madrid, 1662), pp. 311–322. Bernabé's family were *hortelanos* or vegetable gardeners, and he himself, Fray Andrés tells us, was a keen gardener. This suggests that he formed part of the town's Morisco community.
6. Juan de Cazalla published his own mystical manual, *Lumbre del alma*, in 1528. See Juan de Cazalla, *Lumbre de alma*, ed. Jesús Martínez de Bufanda (Madrid: FUE, 1974).

7. Álvaro Castro Sánchez, *Las noches oscuras de María de Cazalla* (Madrid: la linterna sorda, 2011), p. 93. For the Cazalla family's extensive financial network and transactions, see David Alonso García, 'La financiación de las Guardas de Castilla a principios de la Edad Moderna,' in Enrique García Hernán and David Maffi eds., *Guerra y sociedad en la monarquia hispánica: política, estrategia y cultura en la Europa moderna (1500-1700)*, Vol. I (Madrid: CSIC, 2006), pp. 787-796.
8. According to the *Enciclopedia heráldica y genealógica*, the Priego family descended from one 'Muño o Nuño Fernández, Ricohombre de Galicia, Señor de Témez y de Chantada y Conquistador de Córdoba y Sevilla.'
9. Antonio Domínguez Ortiz, *Los judeoconversos en España y América* (Madrid: Ediciones Istmo, 1978), p.26. Fernández de Córdoba personally confronted the Old Christian ringleader, a blacksmith, running him through with a lance.
10. A *composición* was a list of converso families whose ancestral crimes were absolved. To enter this list conversos paid a sum of money to the Crown.
11. Joseph Pérez, *Crónica de la Inquisción en España* (Barcelona: Martínez Roca, 2002), p. 110 and note 50; and Juan Gil, *Los conversos y la Inquisición Sevillana*, Vol. I (Sevilla: Universidad de Sevilla, 2000), p. 57. Another member of the Fernández de Córdoba family, el Gran Capitán, protested the order for Jewish expulsion from the Kingdom of Naples while military governor of the territory in 1504. As a result of his action, the order was suspended. It was not until 1534 that it was reintroduced. See Antonio Domínguez Ortiz, *Los judeoconversos en España y America*, p. 47.
12. For Ambrosio de Morales' family background, see Rafael Ramírez de Arellano, *Ensayo de un catálogo biográfico*, Madrid, 1922, pp. 349-351. Enrique Redel, *Ambrosio de Morales* (Córdoba: Imprenta del Diario, 1909), also contains some useful information on the humanist's immediate family background, although the Morales' noble Old Christian ancestry outlined by Redel in the first pages of his biography is pure fiction.
13. This work was cited by William Atkinson in his 1927 monograph of the humanist Fernán Pérez de Oliva, attributing it, inaccurately, to Pérez de Oliva's father (the real author's maternal grandfather). Atkinson had undoubtedly viewed the poem, and yet, curiously, he makes no mention of its theme. He uses it only as proof of its author's literary pretensions, stating tersely that Pérez de Oliva senior [sic] exchanged verse correspondence with a Diego López 'arising out of a gift from López to the doctor of "unas pocas cerdas y esta copla,"' and that 'its sprightly

quintillas abound in good-humoured personalities.' William Atkinson, 'Hernan Pérez de Oliva, a Biographical and Critical Study,' *Revue Hispanique* 71 (1927), p. 311. The poem is found in 'Poesias del Doctor Oliva y de Diego López,' BNM mss/17932. This is a 1795 copy of the original work (now lost), although there is no indication who the copyist was or for whom it was transcribed. The copy eventually found its way into the collection of the Spanish writer and antiquarian Pascual de Gayangos, which was acquired by the Biblioteca Nacional de Madrid at the end of the nineteenth century. The poem is one of a number of informal epistolary or dialogue poems by Agustín de Oliva included in the octavo volume. I assume that these were all copied from a previous volume similarly structured. Besides the Oliva-López poem, the volume contains several poems to a Diego de Sosa, written from Montilla, where Oliva is spending his summer away from the Córdoba heat; a dialogue with a book Oliva left at a friend's house; and another dialogue with his stomach. A reference to the Marquis of Carpio in the Oliva-López poem allows us to date the work to a period between 1559, when Diego López de Haro became the first Marquis of Carpio, and 1579, when Agustín de Oliva died.

14. This Diego López was probably the same Diego López, 'master who teaches young men to read,' who appears as the executor of the playwright Lope Rueda's will, written on 21 March 1565. The will was dictated by Rueda while staying in López's house in Córdoba. Luis Astrana Marin, *Vida ejemplar y heroica de Miguel de Cervantes Saavedra*, Vol. I (Madrid: Editorial Reus, 1948), Chapter 11. López was also something of a writer, and this may have led to a local literary rivalry between himself and Agustín de Oliva that inspired the vindictive poetic dialogue. The close relationship between López and Rueda indicates that the playwright, like the majority of Spain's early sixteenth-century dramatists, was also from a converso background. For an examination of the conversos as early modern Spanish dramatists, see Elaine C. Wertheimer, *Honor, Love, and Religion in the Theater Before Lope de Vega* (Newark, Delaware: Juan de la Cuesta, 2003).

15. See the inventory of Ambrosio de Morales' possessions in Rafael de Ramírez de Arellano, *Ensayo de un Cátalogo Biografico*, Madrid, 1922, p. 380. The entry reads: 'Eleven pounds of bacon in two pieces. Two small moth-eaten hams weighing five pounds.'

16. The work was possibly written to entertain a literary group associated with Luis de Portocarrero's court at Palma del Rio, and thus the count was made one of the protagonists.

17. The Portocarrero family were said to stem from Portugal. The count's grandmother's family, the Velascos, maintained close ties with Jewish

and, subsequently, converso, *letrados*, and merchants. However, their own noble estate was located not in Aragon, as López states, but in the northern Castilian province of Rioja.
18. M.E. Cotarelo ed., *Cancionero de Antón de Montoro (el Ropero de Córdoba) Poeta del siglo XV* (Madrid: José Perales y Martínez, 1900), p. 165.
19. Julio Caro Baroja, *Los judíos en la España moderna y contemporánea*, Vol. I (Madrid, 1986), p. 308, note 50. Baroja also notes that the converso Francisco López de Villalobos maintained a long, bantering correspondence with the Admiral of Castile, both men making humorous references to the other's Jewish roots. See Julio Caro Baroja 'Un perfil renacentista: el doctor Francisco López de Villalobos,' *Tiempo de historia* VI.70 (1980) pp. 108–121. For the conversos in the Cancioneros, see Francisco Cantera Burgos, 'El cancionero de Baena: Judíos y conversos en él,' *Sefarad*, 27.1 (1967) pp. 71–111. For Anton Montoro's converso poetry, see Yirmiyahu Yovel, 'Converso Dualism in the First Generation: The Cancioneros,' *Jewish Social Studies, New Series*, 14. 3 (1998), pp. 1–28.
20. The physician who was sent for by Philip II in 1561 to cure his son, Don Carlos, of a head injury was a Morisco from Valencia (Henry Kamen, *Philip of Spain* [New Haven and London: Yale University Press, 1997], p. 92). Alonso de Castilla and Miguel de Luna, the two translators of the Sacramonte Lead Books, who were also probably involved in the fraud, were physicians from Granada.
21. Rafael Ramírez de Arellano, *Ensayo de un catálogo biográfico*, p. 350.
22. Ibid.
23. Ibid., p. 351.
24. For information on Pérez de Oliva senior's relationship with Cervantes' grandfather, see Margarita Cabrera Sánchez, *La medicina en Córdoba durante el siglo XV* (Córdoba: Diputación Provincial, 2002), pp. 63, 66, 88, 90–94. For an account of Columbus' relationship with the Córdoba business community, see the same author, 'Los amigos cordobeses de Cristóbal Colon,' in *Ordenanzas de limpieza de Córdoba (1498) y su proyecto* (Córdoba: Universidad de Córdoba, 1999), pp. 97–104. Ambrosio de Morales wrote of Fernán Pérez de Oliva senior: 'I also profited from my grandfather Fernán Pérez de Oliva's studies in his book *Image of the World*, written with great diligence and knowledge of Geography.' Rafael Ramírez de Arellano, *Ensayo de un catálogo biográfico*, p. 350. The biographical information on the humanist Fernán Pérez de Oliva, unless otherwise stated, is taken from William Atkinson, 'Hernan Pérez de Oliva, a Biographical and Critical Study,' *Revue Hispanique* 160 (1927) pp. 309–483.

25. William Atkinson, p. 321. Juan Martínez Silíceo, later Archbishop of Toledo, was responsible for the famous (or infamous) 1547 *limpieza de sangre* statute, banning all conversos from clerical office in his cathedral.
26. For Cristóbal Villalón's converso background, see Joseph J. Kinkaid, *Cristóbal de Villalon* (New York: Twayne, 1973), pp. 137–141 and 150. Francisco de Bobadilla y Mendoza was the author of *El tizón de la nobleza española*, written after his family was accused of having Jewish ancestry. Circulating in private until it was finally published in the nineteenth century, the work presents many of Spain's nobility as tainted to some extent by genealogical links to Jews. Alonso de Osorio was the grandson of Enrique IV's converso *contador mayor* (chief accountant), Alonso Pérez de Vivero, who was also grandfather to Leonor de Vivero. Leonor, along with her husband, Pedro de Cazalla, was investigated for *alumbrado* and Protestant beliefs around the time that Villalón's scholarly discussion took place. The scholarly gathering occurred almost a year to the day after the commencement of the famous Valladolid conference of 1527 that examined Erasmus' religious orthodoxy. At the Valladolid conference, the University of Valladolid professors formed most of the prosecution panel. In *El Scholastico* Villalón reverses the situation. Here an Erasmian group, led by Pérez de Oliva, places Salamanca's scholastics on trial for intellectual barbarism.
27. Cristóbal de Villalón, *El scholastico*, ed. Richard J. A. Kerr (Madrid: CSIC, 1967), p. 64.
28. There were four foundation members of the Colegio del Arzobispo, two of whom, Antonio and Juan, were members of the archbishop's family, the Fonsecas. The fact that Oliva formed part of this familial body indicates that he was on close terms with Fonseca and of a similar reformist bent.
29. Espinosa Maeso, 'El maestro Fernán Pérez de Oliva en Salamanca,' p. 456.
30. William Atkinson, p. 328. Oliva was interested in correct Latin and in providing guidelines for the correct use of the Spanish language. This interest was shared by his friend Villalón and his nephew Morales, both of whom wrote works on Castilian grammar.
31. William Atkinson, p. 352.
32. Silíceo appears to have restricted his tutorage to impressing upon Philip correct Catholic doctrine; otherwise his educational philosophy and methods were generally agreed to be archaic and inadequate. Finally, in 1541 Philip's custodian, the nobleman Juan de Zúñiga, maneuvered the theologian out of the position, replacing him with a young Erasmian humanist, Juan Cristóbal Calvete de Estrella. See Jose Luis González Sánchez-Molero, 'El erasmismo y la educación de Felipe II,' diss. Complutense, Madrid, 1997, pp. 364–373.

33. Fernán Pérez de Oliva, *Diálogo de la dignidad del hombre. Razonamiento. Ejercicios*, ed. María Luisa Cerrón Puga (Madrid: Cátedra, 1995), pp. 188–204.
34. There has been much written on Diego Rodríguez de Lucero's reign of terror in Córdoba. See, for example, José Amador de los Rios, *Historia social, política y religiosa de los judíos de España y Portugal*, Vol. III (Madrid: Fortanet, 1876), pp. 480–488; Francisco Márquez Villanueva, *Investigaciones sobre Juan Álverez Gato*, Madrid, 1960, pp. 131–140; and Benzion Netanyahu, *The Origins of the Inquisition in Fifteenth Century Spain*, pp. 135–140.
35. Fernán Pérez de Oliva, *Diálogo de la dignidad del hombre*, pp. 217–233.
36. At the *colegio mayor* of the University of Valladolid, for example, it was a Good Friday custom for the rector to read the biblical account of the Passion, before asking those students present, 'What do you think of those traitors who crucified Our Lord on this day?' He then turned to the student body and told them that all present had the duty to reveal a name of someone they believed to be from a tainted background so that everyone could be on their guard against them. Fray Francisco de Torrejoncillo, *Centinela contra judíos*, 1674, Chapter 5. Cited by José Amador de los Ríos, *Historia social, politica y religiosa de los judíos de España y Portugal*, Vol. III, p. 506. Pérez de Oliva's sermon for toleration may have been delivered in reaction to this custom.
37. Fernán Pérez de Oliva, *Diálogo de la dignidad del hombre*, p. 219.
38. 'Gloria a Dios en el cielo, y en la tierra paz a los hombres de buena voluntad.' Ibid., p. 223.
39. Ibid.
40. Psalm 85, 8. The correct Spanish version would be: 'Escucharé lo que hablará el Dios Jehová, porque hablará paz a su pueblo y a sus píos, *para que no se convierten a la locura*.'
41. Ibid., p. 224.
42. Pérez de Oliva had noted at the beginning of his sermon that the Romans in their victory celebrations used olive branches to signify peace and palm fronds to signify victory.
43. Fernán Pérez de Oliva, *Diálogo de la dignidad del hombre*, pp. 115–168.
44. Ibid., p. 155
45. Ibid., p. 151.
46. The belief that spiritual perfection was approached by rationality and self-control was one that Pérez de Oliva's nephew Ambrosio de Morales took to heart. Soon after his uncle died in 1531, Morales entered the San Jerónimo of Valparaiso Monastery, an institution supported financially by the Morales family, where he devoted himself to study and

meditation. However, unable to achieve the self-control necessary for quiet contemplation, he attempted to emasculate himself, nearly dying in the process. As a result he was found guilty of the sin of Origin and expelled from the institution. Morales dedicated the rest of his life to humanist pursuits in a secular environment. His ideas, similar to those of his uncle, are contained in his *Quince discursos* (published in 1586), a work that also includes a number of his uncle's essays, including his *Diálogo de la dignidad del hombre*. The emasculation incident is recounted in *Casos raros de Córdoba. Lib 2, XXI, Vida de Ambrosio de Morales Corenista de Phelipe II*, fol 123 vto.

47. There is no record of Ávila's date of birth; however, from information presented in Luis de Granada's biography and from other sources, it is believed that he was born in 1499. See Juan de Ávila, *Obras completas del santo maestro Juan de Ávila*, eds. Francisco Martín Hernández y Luis Sala Balust, Vol. I (Madrid: Biblioteca de Autores Cristianos, 1970), pp. 16–18.
48. 'de los más honrados y ricos.' Cited by Francisco Martín and Luis Sala Balust in their introduction to *Obras completas*, Vol. I, p.19.
49. Cited by Francisco Martín and Luis Sala Balust, ibid., p.19, note 23.
50. In 1509 the Inquisitorial tribunal of Valladolid informed the university that it was not to award degrees to persons recently converted from Judaism. Ibid., p. 27, note 77.
51. Cited by Francisco Martín and Luis Sala Balust, p.30.
52. For Contreras' likely converso roots, see Juan Gil, *Los conversos y la Inquisición Sevillana*, Vol. III (Sevilla: Universidad de Sevilla, 2001), p. 526. For Cristóbal Mosquera's converso background, see Ruth Pike, *Aristocrats and Traders* (Ithaca, New York: Cornell University Press, 1972), pp. 77–78.
53. Francisco Martín and Sala Balust, p. 39. Valtanás' attack on the *limpieza de sangre* statutes is contained within his *Apologías sobre ciertas materias morales en que hay opinión*, in which he advances an evangelical reform program. For a short summary of his *limpieza* essay, 'De la discordia de los linajes,' see Albert A. Sicroff, *Los estatutos de limpieza de sangre*, pp. 198–203. For studies on Valtanás' religious reformism, see Domingo de Baltanás, *Apología sobre ciertas materias morales en que hay opinión y Apología de la comunión frecuente*, estudio preliminar y edición de A. Huerga y P. Sainz Rodríguez (Barcelona: Juan Flors, 1963); and more recently, Gianclaudio Civale, 'Domingo de Baltanás, monje solicitante en la encrucijada religiosa Andaluza: confesión, Inquisición y compania de Jesús en la Sevilla del Siglo de Oro,' *Hispania Sacra* 119 20079, pp. 197–241.
54. *Obras*, I, p.42.
55. Ibid.

56. Ibid., p. 537.
57. Ibid.
58. Ibid.
59. Ibid., p. 523.
60. Ibid.
61. Ibid., p. 471.
62. Ibid., p. 870.
63. Ibid., p. 841.
64. *Obras*, Vol. V, carta no. 179. For an account of Ávila's evangelical mission in Granada, see David Coleman, *Creating Christian Granada: Society and Religious Culture in an Old World Frontier City, 1492–1600* (Ithaca, New York: Cornell University Press, 2003), pp. 137–153, and *passim*.
65. According to the Dominican friar Alonso de la Fuente, of the 70 priests in Zafra, 60 were 'Judíos,' that is to say, conversos. See Alastair Hamilton, *Heresy and Mysticism*, p. 121. For a history of Zafra, see Francisco Croche de Acuña, *Zafra, una leccion de historia y de arte* (Zafra: Caja de Ahorros de Badajoz, 1980), *La familia de los Mesa en la Zafra del siglo XVI* (Zafra: Caja Rural de Extremadura, 1996), and *Páginas de la historia Zafrense* (Zafra: Firmas de la contra portada, 1999).
66. See Chap. 5, note 3.
67. Alastair Hamilton, *Heresy and Mysticism*, p. 117. Fuente also attacked the two recent bishops of Badajoz, Juan de Ribera and Cristóbal de Rojas y Sandoval, both closely linked to Ávila and the Jesuits, who, according to the Dominican friar, were turning a blind eye to *alumbrado* activity in the region. It appears that these Extremadura illuminists also rejected Jesus as the Messiah. The leader of the sect, Hernando Álvarez, supposedly stated that Jesus Christ was good for nothing except to be a gypsy. See Henry Kamen, *The Spanish Inquisition*, p. 129. For a biographical study of Alonso de la Fuente, see Álvaro Huerga, *Historia de los Alumbrados, I: Los Alumbrados de Extremadura (1570–1582)* (Madrid: Fundación Universitaria Española, 1978), pp. 49–97.
68. Alastair Hamilton, *Heresy and Mysticism*, pp. 102 and 112. For an in-depth examination of the *alumbrados* in the University of Baeza, see Álvaro Huerga, *Los alumbrados de Baeza* (Jaén: Diputación Provincial, 1978).
69. 'Many New Christians follow him, not only those who ask for his advice, from many stations of society, but also those who follow him in ways similar to our order, and who have suffered a number of persecutions; and right now in Córdoba the Inquisition has detained a Dr. Carnaval [*sic*], and it is to be feared that this will all be recorded.' *Obras*, Vol. I, p. 166. Although probably from a New Christian background himself, Nadal was sensitive to the Jesuits' converso image, seeing it as an

impediment to successful growth. He was not in favor of banning conversos from the order, merely of disguising their presence within it. Loyola's relative, Antonio Araoz, was also sensitive to the order's converso image, although his views were based on a vehement hatred of the Jews and their New Christian descendants, typical of the Basques. Araoz infuriated Ávila by what the maestro discerned as anti-Semitic views.

70. According to Ávila, Catholicism, like Judaism, was marred by Pharisees. 'Who is the Pharisee? A man who prides himself with a lot of fasting, paying his tithes, with following the Law, lowering his eyes, observing ceremonies; a man who, if saintliness consists in this, is saintly indeed.' Ibid., p. 171. This same view was expressed by Erasmus in his *Enchiridion*. However, coming from a converso, Ávila's observation is also a rebuttal to Old Christian attacks on the conversos' falsity of faith. According to Ávila, the real Judaizers are an Old Christian faithful who observe the Law without true devotion to the precepts of the faith.

71. Ibid., p. 406.
72. Ibid., p. 199.
73. *Obras completas*, Vol. V, carta no. 5. In the early published editions of the letters 'en la cama' was cut, as was the name Erasmus among the list of authors Ávila recommended to Arias. In the trial of the Valladolid Protestants, one witness stated that Cristóbal Padilla, later burnt as a heretic, had read out to them a letter from Juan de Ávila, or so he claimed, in which the *beato* had stated that there was no need for penance because Jesus had already done penance for everyone. *Obras completas*, Vol. I, p. 201.
74. In the population census of 1494, 2000 conversos were registered out of a total population of 40,000. However, this census took place after 14 years of Inquisition activity, during which time hundreds of conversos had been burnt at the stake, and several thousand had fled the city. The chronicler Juan Bernal stated that in 1481 over 8000 conversos fled Seville to the territory of Rodrigo Ponce de León, Marquis of Cádiz, and that Ponce de León was only one of several nobles who offered the conversos refuge. Juan Gil, *Los conversos y la Inquisición sevillana*, Vol I, p. 21.
75. Ibid., p. 55. Juan Gil notes that King Ferdinand vacillated between threatening and bribing the nobles into cooperating in the prosecution of wealthy conversos. For allowing the Inquisition to prosecute conversos in his territory, Ferdinand offered the Duke of Medina Sidonia a third of the confiscated property. It becomes patently clear when one examines the Inquisition activity in its early years that this was a cynical organization, driven as much by avarice and political power brokering as by religious zeal.
76. Ibid., pp. 133–134.

77. José Antonio Ollero Pina, *La Universidad de Sevilla en los siglos XVI y XVII* (Sevilla: Universidad de Sevilla, 1993), p. 61.
78. Ibid., p. 63. The *limpieza* examination was in practice easily circumvented. Indeed, it is likely that many converso scholars, including the humanist Juan de Malara, used the university merely to gain graduate papers after studying in other institutions where students were submitted to a much more rigorous *limpieza* test before graduation. It is probable that Navarro imposed the *limpieza* regulation only to protect the College from accusations of being a converso institution.
79. For the Alcázar family, see Ruth Pike, *Aristocrats and Traders*, pp. 34–52.
80. It is noteworthy, in this respect, that the house was previously owned by a wealthy converso merchant family. The property was requisitioned by the state when the merchant fled Seville in 1480 to avoid an Inquisition trial. It was subsequently sold to the Enriquez de Riberas, one supposes for a fraction of its worth.
81. For Ribera's converso roots, see Juan Gil, *Los Conversos y la Inquisición sevillana*, vol 3, p. 127. For the prelate's support of the mystical movement in Extremadura, see Alexander Hamilton, *Heresy and Mysticism*, pp. 117–118.
82. For Mendoza's support for Fray Hernando de Talavera's *Católica impugnación*, see Francisco Marquéz Villanueva's 'estudio preliminar' in Fray Hernando de Talavera, *Católica impugnación* (Córdoba: Almuzara, 2012).
83. Marcel Bataillon, *Erasmo y España*, pp. 183–184, 188–189, and 478–480.
84. Ibid., p. 523. Constantino was referring to the *limpieza de sangre* examination that the Archbishop of Toledo Martínez Silíceo had recently introduced into the cathedral in a bid to rid himself of his converso antagonists among its canonry. Constantino's reference to his ancestor's ashes would seem to indicate that members of the family, which issued from Cuenca, had been burnt at the stake. We have no information on his friend Juan Gil's ancestry, save that his family came from Olvés, near Calatayud, in Aragon.
85. ASCM, Actas Capitulares, libro 23, fol. 51v, cited by Stafford Poole, *Juan de Ovando: Governing the Spanish Empire in the Reign of Philip II* (Norman, Oklahoma: University of Oklahoma Press, 2004), p. 39.
86. Constantino Ponce de la Fuente, *Suma de doctrina cristiana* (Madrid, 1863), p. 53.
87. Ibid., p. 20.
88. Ibid., p. 126.
89. Ibid., prologue.
90. José C. Nieto, *El Renacimiento y la otra España: vision cultural socioespiritual* (Geneva: Droz, 1997), p. 243.

91. Diarmaid MacCulloch, *Reformation. Europe's House Divided 1490–1700* (London: Penguin, 2003), pp. 226–233. The *spirituali*'s contribution to the Italian evangelical movement is also examined in John Jeffries Martin, *Venice's Hidden Enemies: Italian Heretics in a Renaissance City* (Baltimore and London: Johns Hopkins University Press, 2003), pp. 35–48.
92. One of these apostates was the Aragonese scholar Dr. Juan Morillo, who, along with his compatriot Bartolomé de Carranza, later Archbishop of Toledo, formed part of Cardinal Reginald Pole's reform circle during the first Tridentine Council. Later Morillo created a Protestant, or quasi-Protestant, cell in Paris, from whence he promoted dissention among like-minded non-conformists in his native Aragon (see Chap. 4). Morillo eventually moved to the German city of Frankfurt-on-Main, where he became head of a Calvinist group. He was reported as saying that if he were a heretic, Carranza and Pole had made him one. He died in 1555, poisoned, so it was believed, by agents working for the Spanish Crown. A. Gordon Kinder, 'A Hitherto Unknown Group of Protestants in Sixteenth-Century Aragon,' *Cuadernos de Historia de Jerónimo Zurita* 51–52 (1985), pp. 131–160 (131–137).
93. There has been much written on the so-called Protestant cells of Seville and Valladolid since Marcel Bataillon disputed the view that the protagonists were Lutherans or Calvinists, in his *Erasme et Espagne* (1933), arguing rather that their reform program was based on Erasmian ideas. The debate still continues, with little chance, it seems, of resolution. The debate is examined in some detail in Michel Boeglin, *Inquisición y Contrarreforma: El Tribunal del Santo Oficio de Sevilla (1560–1700)* (Sevilla: Espuela de Plata, 2006).
94. For Reina's and Corro's problems in Protestant exile, see Paul J. Hauben, *Three Spanish Heretics and the Reformation* (Geneva: Libraire Droz, 1967). Reina's and Corro's predicament was not unlike that of the converso Miguel Servetus, who was burnt at the stake in Calvinist Geneva for heresy just three years before the Seville monks' escape from Spain. Servetus was executed for denying the existence of the Trinity.
95. Ruth Pike, *Aristocrats and Traders*, p.68.
96. P. J. Hauben, 'Marcus Pérez and Marrano Calvinism in the Dutch Revolt and the Reformation,' *Bibliotheque D'Humanisme et Renaissance* 29 (1967), pp. 121–132. Marcos Pérez's brother Luis Pérez, a member of the Family of Love religious sect, was a close friend of the Seville humanist Benito Arias Montano. For Luis Pérez, see Chap. 5. The illicit Protestant book trade had been operating since the 1520s. Luther's works were translated and printed in Antwerp and shipped to Spain by Spanish merchants. In 1521 the papal nuncio Jerome Aleander

wrote that it was 'through the efforts of the Marranos' that Spanish versions of Luther's works were being produced in the northern port. See Henry Charles Lea, *A History of the Inquisition of Spain* Vol III (New York: Macmillan, 1922), pp. 413, 421, 422; and John E. Longhurst, 'Julián Hernández Protestant Martyr,' *Bibliotheque D'Humanisme et Renaissance* 22.1 (1960), p. 94.

97. See Juan Gil, *Los conversos y la Inquisicion Sevillana*, Vol. I, Chapter 8. In a contemporary report on Constantino de la Fuente's heretical movement, housed in the Vatican, the author makes explicit reference to Constantino's large converso following, stating that his Christianity was little different to Judaism, and it was for this reason that Seville's conversos loved him so much: 'y así no es de maravillar que le amen y favorezcan tanto.' See Ignacio J García Pinilla, 'Más sobre Constantino Ponce de la Fuente y el *parecer* de la Vaticana,' *Cuadernos de investigación científica* 17 (1999), pp. 191–225 (221).

98. For Juan de Malara's converso background and religious reformism, see Kevin Ingram, 'El humanista converso Juan de Malara (1524–1570).' For Benitio Arias Montano, see Chap. 5.

99. See Ruth Pike, 'The Converso Origin of Sebastian Fox Morcillo,' *Hispania* 51.4 (1968), pp. 877–882; and the same author's *Aristocrats and Traders*, pp. 144–147. Sebastian's grandfather Hernando, a hosier, appeared in the Sevillian composition of 1510, forming part of a list of conversos who had been prosecuted by the Inquisition as crypto-Jews. For Sebastian Fox Morcillo's involvement in a heterodox circle at the University of Louvain, see J.L. Tellechea Idigoras, 'Españoles en Lovaina 1551–1558. Primeras noticias sobre el bayanismo,' *Revista Española de Teología* 23 (1963), pp. 28–29.

100. The Valladolid Inquisition trial documents have long gone missing. Fortunately, the Bartolomé de Carranza trial proceedings have been preserved and these offer a certain amount of information on the Valladolid Protestant group, with which the archbishop was linked. For an account of the Valladolid Protestants, see Marcelino Menéndez Pelayo, *Historia de los heterodoxos españoles*, Vol. I (Madrid: CSIC, 1992), pp. 1299–1350 (first published in 1880). For a more recent and more extensive examination of the Valladolid group, see José Ignacio Tellechea Idígoras, *El Arzobispo Carranza y su tiempo*, Vol. I (Madrid: Guadarrama, 1968), pp. 105–243.

101. Menéndez Pelayo, *Historia de los heterodoxos españoles*, Vol. I, pp. 1305–1307.

102. Agustín de Cazalla, Pedro's elder brother, graduated first in Arts from Alcalá de Henares University in 1533, in the same year as his fellow converso, the future Jesuit General, Diego Láinez, graduated second.

Cazalla later became a royal chaplain and accompanied Charles V on his visits to Germany, where his non-conformist ideas may have been reinforced. He returned to Spain and a canonry in Salamanca Cathedral in 1552. In 1559 he was burnt at the stake, along with his three siblings Pedro, Francisco and Beatriz. His mother, Leonor de Vivero, who had died before the Protestant trials commenced, was exhumed and also burnt at the stake. Two other siblings, Juan and Constanza, were sentenced to life imprisonment. For the Cazalla family's involvement in the Valladolid Protestant conventicle, see Tellechea Idigoras, *El Arzobispo Carranza y su tiempo*, Vol. I, pp. 105–168.

103. For the Baeza family's connections with the Cazallas, see John Longhurst, *Luther's Ghost in Spain*, p. 302. For the Baeza family's involvement in the Valladolid 'Protestant' cell, see Marcelino Menéndez Pelayo, *Historia de los heterodoxos españoles*, Vol. I, p. 1332 and pp. 1344–1345. The stigma of coming from a converso family of heretics appears not to have been an impediment for Catalina and Maria's brother Francisco Reinoso Baeza, who was Bishop of Córdoba from 1597 to 1601. The other two nuns burnt at the stake along with Catalina and Maria Reinoso were named Margarita Santisteban and Maria de Miranda, both of which were Bartolomé de Carranza's family surnames, suggesting that both were related to the archbishop. Unfortunately, we have no information on their family backgrounds.

104. In Fernán Díaz de Toledo's attack on the 1449 *Sentencia-Estatuto*, the *Instrucción del relator*, the author notes that the converso Cartagena family had already established marital ties with the Rojas family. See Guillermo Verdín-Díaz, *Alonso de Cartagena y el Defensorium unitatis christianae*, p. 36. For the Rojas clan's connection to the converso community of Toledo, see Linda Martz, *A Network of Converso Families in Early Modern Toledo: Assimilating a Minority* (Ann Harbor, Michigan: University of Michigan Press, 2003), *passim*. Fray Domingo de Rojas' sister, Elvira de Rojas, married the second Marquis of Alcañices, Juan Enríquez de Almanza. This noble family, like the Rojas, were parvenus who had made marriage alliances with wealthy converso professionals. The marquis' grandfather was the converso *contador mayor* Rodrigo de Ulloa, who had married Constanza de Castilla, the illegitimate daughter of the Bishop of Sigüenza, Pedro de Enríquez, and a Jewess or conversa, Isabel Droklin. See *El tizón de la nobleza de España*, p.13.

105. This did not include Carranza, who, in any case, was out of the country when Cazalla's proselytizing campaign began.

106. In 1554 the Seville canon Juan Gil made a trip to Valladolid with the intention, it seems, of making contact with the Cazalla conventicle.

107. For Sancho de Carranza, see Marcel Bataillon, *Erasmo y España*, pp. 122–124 and *passim*.
108. Alfonso de Burgos was a member of the Santa Maria family. He grew up in the household of the ex-rabbi Pedro Santa Maria. His cousin, or perhaps his half-brother, was Alfonso de Cartagena, author of the attack on *limpieza* legislation, *Defensorium unitatis christianae*, examined in Chap. 2. Burgos' religious reformism was very much in keeping with that of his other family members. For a brief biography of Burgos, see Leandro Martínez Peñas, *El confessor del rey en el antiguo régimen* (Segovia: Editorial Universidad Complutense, 2007), pp. 52–65.
109. Stefania Pastore, *Una herejía española: Conversos, alumbrados e Inquisición (1449–1559)*, pp. 263–264.
110. Marcel Bataillon, *Erasmo y España*, pp. 518–519.
111. For Carranza's own relationship with Valdés and his works, see José Ignacio Tellechea Idigoras, *El Arzobispo Carranza: 'Tiempos recios,'* Vol. III (Salamanca: Publicaciónes Universidad Pontificía/Fundación Universitaria Española, 2005).
112. Carranza's relationship with Pole is examined in some depth in José Ignacio Tellechea Idígoras, *El Arzobispo Carranza. 'Tiempos recios,'* Vol. II (Salamanca: Publicaciones Universidad Pontificía/Fundación Universitaria Española, 2003), pp. 399–496. For Carranza's period in England, see *El Arzobispo Carranza. 'Tiempos recios,'* Vol. III, pp. 282–358, and, by the same author, 'Fray Bartolomé Carranza: A Spanish Dominican in the England of Mary Tudor,' in John Edwards and Ronald Truman eds., *Reforming Catholicism in the England of Mary Tudor: The Achievements of Friar Bartolomé Carranza* (Aldershot: Ashgate, 2005).
113. Shortly before his death, Pole was attacked by Pope Paul IV, who called for his return to Rome to answer accusations of heresy.
114. '[A]ll the heresies in Germany, France and Spain have been sown by descendants of Jews, as we have seen and still see every day in Spain,' the king had stated in 1554. Cited from Henry Kamen, *Philip of Spain*, p. 83.
115. In *El tizón de la nobleza de España*, published in 1560, just months after the Valladolid trials, Cardinal Francisco Mendoza y Bobadilla states that information on the Marquis of Alcañices' stained bloodline was to be found in the Protestant trial documents of his son Luis de Rojas and Luis' uncles (Fray Domingo de Rojas and Pedro Sarmiento de Rojas). See *El tizón de la nobleza de España*, p. 13. Unfortunately, all these documents are now lost.

116. José Ignacio Tellechea Idígoras, *El Arzobispo Carranza. Tiempos recios*, Vol. III, p. 18.
117. It is quite possible that the *limpieza* investigation was rigged, with the Miranda notary selecting, with the Inquisitors' connivance, a small group of Carranza family friends to give evidence. It should be noted that Carranza's case had divided the Dominican Order between the archbishop and his prosecutor Valdés, and that the Dominican inquisitors of Navarre may well have been inclined to support the former, who was after all a native son. Furthermore, the Carranza family was well known in Calahorra. Carranza's uncle Sancho had been a canon in the Calahorra Cathedral and a member of the Inquisition tribunal before taking up his position as canon in Seville. This may also have affected the character and outcome of the inquiry. Regarding the Carranza family background, we do have another source of information, although it is equally vague. This is the certificate of *hidalguía* taken out in 1528 by Bartolomé's father, Pedro, and his uncle, Sancho, in which they stated that the family, whose name was Santisteban before being changed to Carranza, or Carranza de Miranda, were Old Christian hidalgos from the Vizcayan village of Santisteban, in the Valley of Carranza. This type of certificate was an expensive commodity, and thus only purchased by wealthy men whose hidalgo status and, very often, Old Christian status, was in doubt. Fortunately, as the candidates paid for the entire process they were allowed to select their own *procurador* (legal representative) and direct him in the genealogical inquiries. The result was therefore usually a positive one. This was the case of Pedro and Sancho de Carranza, who were awarded the certificate, although not before the fiscal at the Court of Chancery in Valladolid had raised serious doubts as to the family's hidalgo status. First, he noted that Pedro and his father Bartol were veterinarians (*albeitares*), a profession hardly in keeping with noble status. Moreover, he suspected that they did not originate from the Valley of Carranza, as the brothers claimed, which suggests that they had not produced witnesses from the village of Santisteban to corroborate their claim. For the Carranza family's application for the certificate of *hidalguía*, see José Ignacio Tellechea Idígoras, *Tiempos recios*, Vol. III, pp. 26–49. It is noteworthy that the surname Santisteban was a popular one among conversos, possibly because Saint Stephen, a Jewish convert to Christianity, was the first Christian martyr. My own view is that the Carranza family covered up their converso roots by presenting themselves as denizens of a Basque hamlet named Santisteban. Later, to complete the deception, they took the name of the valley in which the hamlet was located.

Chapter 4: The Road Out of Trent

1. A. Tovar y M de la Pinta, *Procesos inquisitoriales contra Francisco Sánchez de las Brozas* (Madrid; Instituto Antonio de Nebrija, 1941), pp. 31–33.
2. Francisco Martínez Cuadrado, *El Brocense: Semblanza de un humanista* (Badajoz: Diputación de Badjoz, 2003), pp. 23–25. For Brocense's temerity, the Valladolid tribunal recommended that his possessions be confiscated and that he be placed in prison; however, the Inquisition Council (*la Suprema*), now under the control of Gaspar de Quiroga, a man of moderate disposition, rejected their advice, issuing Brocense with nothing more than a warning to guard his tongue in future on pain of rigorous castigation. Unfortunately, the humanist did not heed the advice, and in 1600 he found himself again in front of the Valladolid tribunal, accused of another series of indiscretions, among which was the statement: 'Those who criticize Erasmus are either friars or madmen.' Brocense's death, occurring while the trial was still taking place, undoubtedly saved him from a prison sentence.
3. Fray Luis' great-great-grandfather was Fernán Sánchez de Villanueva 'Daviuelo,' whose remains were disinterred and burnt after he was posthumously tried and convicted of Judaizing by the Cuenca Inquisition tribunal in 1492. A number of Fernán's children were also tried and convicted of Judaizing; for some reason, Fray Luis' great grandfather, Pero Rodriguez de Villanueva, managed to escape Inquisition prosecution, although it appears that he too had been a willing Judaizer. The Villanueva family also formed marriage unions with the Mora family of Quintanar de la Orden, who were tried for Judaizing in trials held by the Cuenca tribunal from 1588 to 1592. See 'Proceso original que la Inquisición de Valladolid hizo al maestro Fr. Luis de León, religioso del órden de S. Agustín [1572–1577],' *CODOIN* 10 (Madrid, 1847), pp. 159–163. See also C. Carrete Parrondo and Maria F. García Casar, 'Las raíces judias de fray Luis de León,' *La Ciudad de Dios* 204 (1991), pp. 587–591; and Herman P. Salomón, 'Spanish Marranism Re-Examined,' *Sefarad* 67.1 (2007), pp. 111–154 (116–120).
4. Quoted from Emilia Fernández Tejero, 'Fray Luis de León, Hebraísta: El *Cantar de los Cantares*,' *Sefarad* 48.2 (1988), p. 273. The italics are mine.
5. Fray Luis de León, *De los nombres de Cristo* (Madrid: Cátedra, 1997), pp. 376–377. In 1609 Doctor Álvaro Piçario de Palacios denounced this passage to the Inquisition as a piece of Jewish propaganda against the king and the Holy Office. See Bataillon, *Erasmo en España*, p. 767, note 77.

6. Fray Luis de León, *Poesía* (Madrid: Cátedra, 1997), p. 186. Pedro Portocarrero was the second son of the Marquises of Villanueva del Fresno. He studied law at Salamanca, where he was rector on two occasions. In 1580 he became a member of the Royal Council and two years later a member of the Council of the Inquisition. In 1589 he was made Bishop of Calahorra and in 1596 Bishop of Córdoba.
7. Henry Kamen, *The Spanish Inquisition*, p. 125.
8. Francisco Márquez Villanueva, 'Santa Teresa y el linaje,' in his *Espiritualidad y literatura en el siglo XVI* (Madrid: Alfaguara, 1968), pp. 141-152. See also Stephen Clissold, *St Teresa of Avila* (London: Sheldon Press, 1979), p. 7.
9. Two copies (*traslados*) of the original *ejecutoria* are housed in the Archivo Silveriano of Burgos. Both official copies have been manipulated so that we now read that the hidalguia of Don Alonso and his brothers 'sea guardado ... *especialmente* en Ávila, Majalbálago y Hortigosa,' not '*solamente*' in these places, as specified in the original document. In 1540, Teresa's brother, now a successful merchant living in Peru, asked his sister to send him a copy of the hidalgo certificate. Teresa wrote back: 'I said I will send with Antonio Moran a copy of the certificate, which they say could not be bettered, and this I will do with great care.' Was this copy, which Teresa had made 'with great care,' also adulterated? For it to be of use to her brother living in Peru, it would surely have had to have been doctored. See P. Tomás Álvarez, 'Santa Teresa de Ávila en el drama de los judeo-conversos Castellanos,' in Ángel Alcalá ed., *Judíos. Sefarditas. Conversos: la expulsión de 1492 y sus consecuencias* (Valladolid: Ambito, 1995), pp. 611-612. All the case documentation is included in Teófanes Egido, *El linaje judeoconverso de Santa Teresa* (Madrid: Editorial Espiritualidad, 1986).
10. For Ávila's religious reform movement, see Jodi Bilinkoff, *The Avila of Saint Teresa: Religious Reform in a Sixteenth-Century City* (Ithaca, New York: Cornell University, 1989), pp. 78-107.
11. Teresa's principal backers in Ávila, Medina del Campo, and Toledo were all conversos. In Toledo, the convent's ties to converso money created serious problems for Teresa. See Jodi Bilinkoff, *The Avila of Saint Teresa*, p. 130 and p. 146.
12. The Ulloa clan was based in Toro, near Zamora. Guiomar was the daughter of Pedro de Ulloa, a town councillor (*regidor*) in Toro, and Aldonza de Guzmán. She was the widow of Francisco Dávila, *señor de Salobralejo*. For the Ulloa's converso background, see Chap. 1.
13. In the inquiry for Teresa of Ávila's beatification, the nun Ana de Jesús stated: 'At the time of the Cazalla family heresies, this group had wished to establish links with doña Guiomar de Ulloa and other religious widows, and realizing that [the Cazalla group] were people of different

religious views, they [the widows] stated that they did not wish to enter into a house with so many doors [meaning, presumably, a place impossible to guard] and they had nothing to do with them ... and they [the Cazalla group] also wanted to talk to the Mother [Saint Teresa] before they realized she was involved with so many others.' *Procesos de Beatificación y canonización*, ed. P. Silverio de Santa Teresa, O.C.D., Vol. I (Burgos: Monte Carmelo), 1935, pp. 471–472. Teresa was Doña Guiomar's house guest between 1556 and 1559. See Jodi Bilinkoff, *The Avila of Saint Teresa*, p. 141.
14. See, for example, Chap. 7 of her *Life*.
15. Rowan Williams, *Teresa of Avila* (London: Continuum, 1991), p. 49.
16. 'Certifico a V.P. que soy el hombre del mundo menos linajudo.' Antonio Domínguez Ortiz, *Los judeoconversos en España y America*, p. 90. For the Rojas family's converso background, see Linda Martz, *A Network of Converso Families*.
17. Instituto Valencia de Don Juan, leg. 89, no. 61.
18. Teresa was interviewed by the Jesuit father Rodrigo de Álvarez, who had gained some renown as a man able to differentiate false from errant mysticism. After a lengthy interview, Álvarez pronounced Teresa an orthodox Catholic. Ironically, Álvarez was the leader of a secret mystical sect, the Order of the Pomegranate, later investigated by the Holy Office. The sect is examined in Chap. 5 in relation to Diego Velázquez's father-in-law, Francisco Pacheco, who may have been a member. For Teresa of Ávila's Seville expedition, see Stephen Clissold, *St. Teresa of Avila*, pp. 176–193.
19. Instituto Valencia de Don Juan, leg. 89, no. 393.
20. Salucio's *Discurso acerca de la justicia y buen gobierno de España, en los estatutos de limpieza de sangre* is examined by Vicente Parello in 'Entre honra y dishonra: el discurso de fray Agustín Salucio acerca de los estatutos de limpieza de sangre (1559),' *Criticon* 8 (2000), pp. 139–153.
21. The Second Alpujarras Rebellion (1568–1571) began after Philip II decided to place restrictions on the Granada Moriscos' cultural practices. After the revolt was suppressed, about half the Morisco population of the province was either enslaved or forcefully relocated to other areas of Castile. For a recent account of the rebellion, see L. P. Harvey, *Muslims in Spain 1500 to 1614* (Chicago and London: Chicago University Press, 2005), pp. 204–237.
22. *El felicísimo viaje del muy alto y muy poderos principe Don Phelippe*, vol, 1 (Madrid: Sociedad de Bibliófilos Españoles, 1930), p. 422. For the growth in religious persecution in the Netherlands in the 1560s, see Geoffrey Parker, *The Dutch Revolt* (London: Penguin, 1988), pp. 58–67.

23. See Juan Rafael de la Cuadra Blanco, 'King Philip of Spain as Solomon the Second. The Origins of Solomonism of the Escorial in the Netherlands,' in Wim de Groot ed., *The Seventh Window. The King's Window donated by Philip II and Mary Tudor to Sint Janskerck (1557)* (Hilversum: Uitgeverij Verloren, 2005).

24. The humanist Juan Cristóbal Calvete de Estrella entered Philip II's employment in 1541, when he replaced Juan Martínez Silíceo as the Prince's tutor. This substitution appears to have been stage managed by Philip's custodian (*ayo*) Juan de Zúñiga, a nobleman of Erasmian sympathies, who had previously contracted Calvete as tutor to his own son, Luis de Requesens, later governor of the Netherlands. In recommending Calvete for the position, Zúñiga passed over the candidate's humanist education, merely emphasising his sound scholarship. He also avoided his family background, mentioning only that Calvete was an Old Christian, in deference to Silíceo's obsession with *limpieza de sangre* requirements. It is evident, however, that this was a glib assurance, made without prying into the candidate's ancestry, which may well have been converso: both Calvete's father and grandfather were physicians, generally considered a converso occupation. Calvete promoted irenic views within the young Prince Philip's court, introducing Philip to Erasmus' *Institutio principis christiani* and *Querela pacis*. Calvete's *Felicísimo viaje* was expurgated in later editions for its description of the convicted Protestant Constantino Ponce de la Fuente as 'a very great philosopher and a profound theologian.' For Calvete's Erasmian interests, see José Luis González Sánchez-Molero, 'El erasmismo y la educación de Felipe II,' diss., Complutense, Madrid, 1997, pp. 364–373, 410–417, and *passim*.

25. Pedro Jiménez was a member of an Andalusian converso merchant clan that had established itself in Middleburg, Zeeland, a commercial center and home to many converso merchants in the first decades of the sixteenth century. See Carlos Gilly, 'El influjo de Sébastien Castellion sobre los heterodoxos españoles del siglo XVI,' in M. Boeglin y D. Kahn eds., *Recepción de la Reforma y disidencias religiosas en la Península ibérica el siglo XVI* (Madrid: Casa de Velázquez, in press). Gilly writes: 'Pedro Ximénez had sympathized for many years past with a group of irenic humanists who had decided to side with neither the confessions of Rome nor the Reformed Church, looking for a third way in concordance and toleration...' Recently Peter A. Hauer has demonstrated that Jiménez was the author of *Dialogus de pace*, a work recommending that Philip II allow his Dutch subjects freedom of conscience in order to bring the war with the Dutch Calvinists to a close. See Peter A. Heuser, P. A. 2013. 'Kaspar Schetz von Grobbendonk oder Pedro Ximénez? Studien zum historischen Ort des "Dialogus de pace" (Köln

und Antwerpen 1579),' in G. Braun y A. Strohmeyer eds., *Frieden und Friedenssicherung in der Frühen Neuzeit. Das Heilige Römische Reich und Europa. Festschrift für Maximilian Lanzinner* (Münster: Aschendorff, 2013), pp. 387-41. For an examination of *Dialogus pace*, see Ignacio J. García Pinilla, 'Paz Religiosa, Libertad Religiosa: La apuesta por el pacisismo de Pedro de Ximénez en el Dialogus de Pace (1579),' *Hispania Sacra* 141 (2018), pp. 39–50.

26. Among the group were Fray Julian de Tudela, Juan Martín Cordero, Sebastián Fox Morcillo, Fray Cristóbal de Santotis, Fadrique Furió Ceriol, Felipe de la Torre, Tomás Padilla, and Diego de Astudillo (de Burgos). Several of these men had previously formed part of a Parisian non-conformist or Protestant cell led by the Aragonese scholar Dr. Juan Morillo. The Louvain cell was also connected to a group of converso non-conformists in Antwerp, led by the merchants Martín López and Marcos Pérez, who were responsible for much of the Protestant literature that entered Spain in the middle decades of the century. Much of our information on the Louvain non-conformists comes from investigations by Arthur Gordon Kinder and José Ignacio Tellechea Idígoras. See José Ignacio Tellechea Idígoras, 'Españoles en Lovaina en 1551–1558,' in *Revista Española de Teología* XXIII, 1963, pp. 21–45, and 'Españoles en Lovaina en 1557' in Werner Thomas and Robert A. Verdonk eds., *Encuentros en Flandes* (Louvain: Universitaire Pers Leuven, 2000), pp. 133–155; Ronald W. Truman, *Spanish Treatises on Government, Society and Religion in the Time of Philip II* (Leiden: Brill, 1999), pp. 35–116. See also José Luis González Sánchez-Molero, 'El Erasmismo y la educación de Felipe II,' diss.

27. A Gordon Kinder, 'A Hitherto Unknown Group of Protestants in Sixteenth-Century Aragon,' *Cuadernos de Historia de Jerónimo Zurita* (1985), pp. 131–160.

28. Morillo's native Biel formed part of the territory known as the Five Towns, an area that sustained large Jewish *aljamas* in the Middle Ages, the majority of whose inhabitants were involved in textile and shoe production. One of Morillo's most fervent supporters from Biel was his nephew Jaime Sánchez, who went to study with him in Paris. Sánchez, who was later burnt as a heretic, stated in his trial that he did not know the names of his grandparents, nor did he know if his parents were from Jewish backgrounds. However, the fact that both his parents' surnames were Sánchez, a common one among the converso community of Biel, and that his brother was a shoemaker, suggests that the family formed part of Biel's large converso community. Another of Juan Morillo's Biel adherents was his cousin Maria del Frago, whose surname, taken from the nearby town of El Frago, also indicates that she was from a con-

verso background, For the Jewish communities of Biel and the surrounding towns, see Miguel Angel Motis, 'Los judíos de Biel en la Edad Media,' *Suessetania*, 12 (1992), pp. 21–53; *Los Judíos de Uncastillo en la Edad Media* (Ejea de los Caballeros: Centro de Estudios de las Cinco Villas, 2007), and *Judíos y Conversos de Ejea de los Caballeros en la Edad Media (XII-XV)* (Ejea de los Caballeros: Centro de Estudios de las Cinco Villas, 2003). See also, by the same author, *Los Judíos de Tarazona* (Tarazona: Instituto Fernando el Catolico, 2007), which examines the important community of Jews in Felipe de la Torre's hometown. Many of the Jews from this area moved to Navarre in 1492, from where they were also expelled six years later. Most returned to their native towns, where they naturally became the object of their Old Christian neighbors' suspicion and Inquisition attention. In this tense atmosphere many led double lives, attempting to demonstrate an orthodox faith in public while following a personal one in private. This is the case, I would suggest, of de la Torre and Morillo, as it was of their fellow Aragonese heretics, Joan Pérez and Joan de Sanctangel, both from Calatayud, who also formed part of the Morillo Protestant circle. Joan de Sanctangel was a member of the wealthy converso Sanctangel clan, implicated in the assassination of the Inquisitor Pedro Arbues, sent to Zaragoza to head the first Aragonese Inquisition tribunal in 1485.
29. Felipe de la Torre, *Institución de un Rey Cristiano*, ed. R.W. Truman (Exeter: Exeter University Press, 1979). See also R.W. Truman, 'Felipe de la Torre and His *Institución de un Rey Cristiano* (Antwerp, 1556). The Protestant Connexions of a Spanish Royal Chaplain,' *Bibliothèque d'Humanisme et Renaissance* 46.1 (1984) pp. 83–93. Here Truman refers to Inquisition documents that reveal a close connection between de la Torre and the wealthy converso merchant Martín López (the great uncle of Michel de Montaigne). López was the brother-in-law of the Calvinist Marcos Pérez, and like Pérez suspected of heretical religious views.
30. Ibid., p. 32.
31. Ibid.
32. See, for example, Constantino de la Fuente, *Doctrina Christiana*, Antwerp 1554/55, fol. 199r. Cited from R. W. Truman's introduction to *Institución de un Rey Cristiano*.
33. Ibid., p. 33.
34. Ibid.
35. Fadrique Furió Ceriol, *El Concejo y Consejeros del Príncipe*, ed. Henry Méchoulan (Madrid: Tecnos, 1993), p. 50.

36. See Miguel Almenara Sebastía, 'Documentación testamentaria del Humanista Valenciana Fadrique Furió Ceriol (1527–1592). Edición y comentario,' pp. 89–112. For other biographical information on Ceriol, see Ronald W. Truman, *Spanish Treatises on Government*, pp. 89–114, and by the same author, 'Fadrique Furió Ceriol's return to Spain from the Netherlands, in 1564: further information on its circumstances,' in *Bibliothèque d'Humanisme et Renaissance* 41 (1979), pp. 360–364. See also, José Luis Gonzalo Sanchez-Molero, 'El Erasmismo y la educación de Felipe II,' diss, pp. 730–722, *passim*.
37. See Marcel Bataillon, *Erasmo en España*, pp. 552–554; see also Marco Antonio Coronel Ramos, 'Juan de Bolonia y Fadrique Furió Ceriol: La ortodoxia doctrinal frente a la ortodoxia evangélica,' *Minerva: Revista de filología clásica* 10 (1996), pp. 145–166.
38. In 1563 Furió was ordered to return to Spain, where he was questioned by the Inquisition on his Protestant sympathies. Despite his friendship with Juan Morillo and Juan Pérez de Pineda, both of whom had converted to Calvinism, Furió managed to avoid prosecution. In 1573, he found himself once more in the Netherlands, as an advisor, along with his friend Benito Arias Montano, to the governor Luis de Requesens. Both Furió and Montano counseled a prudent, tolerant attitude toward Spain's rebellious Dutch subjects.
39. Fadrique Furió Ceriol, *El concejo*, p. 29.
40. Ibid., p. 129.
41. Cited from Ben Rekers, *Benito Arias Montano* (London: Warburg Institute, 1972), p. 101. Saravia also wrote, 'At another time, when I heard him say that he disapproved of nothing in our religion, I asked him why he did not join us at our Sunday communion services. "Oh," he said, "you are a lucky man to have a wife who agrees with you in religious matters. Mine does not. I must be able to live at home in peace with my wife if I am to survive."'
42. Ibid., p. 99.

CHAPTER 5: FOUR HUMANISTS

1. See Pérez Zagorin, *Ways of Lying: Dissimulation, Persecution and Conformity in Early Modern Europe* (Cambridge, Mass: Harvard University Press, 1990), especially Chapter 5, 'Nicodemism in Italy,' and Chapter 6, 'Controversialists, Sectarians and Familists.' See also, Jon. R. Snyder, *Dissimulation and the Culture of Secrecy in Early Modern Europe* (Berkeley: University of California Press, 2009), Chapters 1 and 2. For the call for religious concord, see Randolph Head, 'Introduction: The Transformations of the Long Sixteenth Century,' Thomas

F. Mayer, "'Heretics be not in all things heretics," Cardinal Pole, His Circle, and the Potential for Toleration,' and Marion Leathers Kuntz, 'The Concept of Toleration in the *Colloquium Heptaplomeres* of Jean Bodin,' in John Christian Laursen and Cary J. Nederman eds., *Beyond the Persecuting Society: Religious Toleration before the Enlightenment* (Philadelphia: University of Pennsylvania Press, 1998). In *All Can be Saved* (New Haven and London: Yale University Press, 2009), Stuart Schwartz's challenges the view that tolerant attitudes entered society in a Counter-Reformation setting, promoted by disaffected humanists. Instead he argues that the phenomenon already existed at the grassroots level among common folk, who were often too fearful to express their views in public. As proof of this theory, Schwartz examines toleration in sixteenth-century Spain, scanning a number of Inquisition registers for evidence of tolerant views among the *vulgo*—usually expressed through the belief that all religions communed equally with God and that all righteous people would be saved. Schwartz notes that while these views were often expressed by New Christians, they were not peculiar to them. He then presents a number of examples taken from Inquisition depositions in which men and women who were not labeled converso expressed respect for other religions or socio-ethnic groups (the conversos and Moriscos). Schwartz takes these statements as examples of Old Christian toleration. However, this is a problematical assumption. While Inquisition tribunals normally asked those interviewed if they were from converso backgrounds, they generally accepted the person's answer, unless the charge was Judaizing. Thus we cannot assume that someone was Old Christian merely because he stated he was. There is no way of knowing if the people who Schwartz designates as Old Christian were in fact from Old Christian backgrounds, although the manner in which they express their toleration (often attacking Old Christian society) should warn us against making this assumption. For example: the *beata* Catalina Crespo, from Baeza, who stated that Old Christians should beware the apocalypse when their sins against conversos would be judged; or the Catalan tailor Hieronimo Querols, resident in Mallorca, who stated that there was more charity among Muslims and Lutherans than among Christians [*sic*]; or Antonio Manso, resident of Alcázar de Consuegra in Castile, who responded to the jibe that all Portuguese were Jews by stating that in that case they were relatives of the Lord who when he wished to be born chose a Jew as a mother. This is not to say that these persons were not, as Schwartz claims, tolerant Old Christians. However the fact that their converso status is not registered by the Inquisition officials is no proof of this.

2. Ben Rekers, *Benito Arias Montano.*

3. In the Middle Ages Fregenal de la Sierra contained a large Jewish *aljama*, many of whose occupants converted to Christianity in the first decades of the fifteenth century. Other conversos soon joined this community, taking advantage of the commercial activities that it offered, being close to the Portuguese border. An important leather and shoemaking industry grew up in the town during the fifteenth century, which drew many conversos. In 1491 the Lerida Inquisition tribunal turned its attention to Fregenal, calling on the town's crypto-Jews to come forward and confess their sins during a period of grace. Three hundred and sixty men and women appeared before the tribunal, confessed, and were reconciled to the Church with relatively light fines. The name Arias figures quite prominently among the reconciled Judaizers: Alonso Arias Serrano (shoemaker) and his wife Mayor González; Alonso Arias 'el viejo' (shoemaker) and his wife, also named Mayor González; Alonso Arias 'el vermajo' (shoemaker); Maria Arias (wife of Fernando Alonso); Pedro Arias (son of Alonso Arias); Maria Arias (daughter of Alonso Arias); Beatriz López (wife of Arias Alonso); Isabel López (wife of Gonzalo Arias Perales); Mayor López (wife of Pedro Arias); Beatriz Gómez (wife of Rodrigo Arias); Beatriz Márquez (wife of Hernando Arias, deceased); Leonor Márquez (wife of Fernando Arias); Marina Gómez (wife of Arias Alonso 'el Bermejo' (redhead) shoemaker); and Mayor Alonso (wife of Alonso Arias tanner and shoemaker). The list of the 1491 Fregenal converso penitents is included in Fermín Mayorga, 'La comunidad judía en Fregenal al finales del siglo XV,' *Alcántara* 67 (2007), pp. 25–88.
4. This was the information that Montano gave to the Council of the Orders in his application for entry into the Order of Santiago. Carlos Sánchez Rodríguez, *Perfil de un humanista: Benito Arias Montano* (Huelva: Diputación Provincial de Huelva, 1996), p. 31.
5. Juan Gil, *Los conversos y la Inquisición sevillana*, Vol. III, p. 206.
6. See Juan Gil, 'Benito Arias Montano en Sevilla' in *Arias Montano y su tiempo* (Badajoz: Junta de Extremadura, 1998), p. 102.
7. For Montano's relationship with the Núñez Pérez family, see Juan Gil, *Arias Montano en su entorno* (Badajoz: Editora Regional de Extremadura, 1998), pp. 130–141. For Marcos Pérez' secret Protestant book trade, see Chap. 3 of this study.
8. Juan Gil in *Arias Montano y su tiempo*, pp. 105–106.
9. While studying at Alcalá, Montano made two lists of his books. The complete works of Erasmus in nine volumes are found in both lists. Ben Rekers, *Benito Arias Montano*, p. 2.
10. Like the humanist Juan de Malara, Montano left Seville to study, yet he used the Seville University to graduate. One is tempted to speculate

that Seville's lax *limpieza de sangre* examination may have been influential in both scholars' decisions to graduate in their hometown.

11. Juan Gil believes Montano was being accused of sodomy, and it is for this reason that the chronicler is reluctant to state the charge clearly. 'Pecado etc' is a reference to 'pecado nefando' or sodomy. 'Arias Montano en Sevilla' in José María Maestre ed. *Humanismo y pervivencia del mundo clásico: Homenaje al profesor Antonio Fontán*, Vol. I (Madrid: CSIC, 2002), pp. 263–280.

12. It is significant that Montano chose the period of the Seville 'Protestant' trials to enter the order. It is equally significant that his brother Juan Arias de la Mota and his close friend Gaspar Vélez (son of Montano's adoptive parents Antonio Alcocer and Isabel Vélez), whom he also referred to as 'brother,' chose the same period to obtain licenses to move to Peru.

13. Alfredo Albar Ezquerra, 'Montano y El Concilio de Trento,' in *Arias Montano y su tiempo*, pp. 126–127. In his intervention on 19 June 1562, Montano stated, 'I confess that I am going to base my argument and speech on the Holy Scriptures and the truth revealed by God.'

14. *Arias Montano y su tiempo*, p. 106.

15. See Haim Beinart, *Los judíos en España* (Madrid: Mapfre, 1993), pp. 11–21, and Francisco Javier Perea Siller, 'Benito Arias Montano y la identificación de Sefarad: exégesis poligráfico de Abdías 20,' *Helmántica: Revista de filología clásica y hebrea* 154 (2000), pp. 199–218.

16. 'To me it is evident that the cause of this punishment is not only that the majority of the Christians are divided into sects, deceived and misled, but also swollen and arrogant in their errors; and the others that profess the communion of the Catholic faith and the true doctrine, I see, do so carelessly almost perverting it.' Pedro de Valencia *Obras IX/2 Escritos espirituales. La 'Lección Cristiana' de Arias Montano* (León: Universidad de León, 2002), p. 139. This is a translation of Montano's *Dictatum*, made by Valencia after the humanist's death.

17. Ibid., p. 169.

18. For the Escobeda murder, see Henry Kamen, *Philip of Spain*, pp. 162–168.

19. Zayas was tight-lipped about his family background. It seems evident, however, from his reference to certain family members in his official letters that he was from a middle-sort family in Écija. See Pedro Rodriguez, 'Gabriel de Zayas (1526–1593). Notas biográficas,' *Espacio, Tiempo y Forma, Serie IV, Historia Moderna* 4 (1991), pp. 57–70. In her article on the family network of the Santisteban family of Malaga, María Teresa López Beltrán suggests that the Zayas family of Écija, who

formed endogamous unions with the Santisteban family, were conversos. See Maria Teresa López Beltrán, 'El universo familiar de los Santisteban, regidores de Malaga en época de los Reyes Católicos. Una contribución desde la prosopografía,' *Baetica. Estudios de Arte, Geografía e Historia* 31 (2009), pp. 255–274.

20. Although not as scholarly as Montano, Zayas was himself recognized as a man of some learning. According to Plantin's Calvinist financier Goropio Becano, Zayas was 'homo literratissimus.' Vicente Bécares Botas ed. *Arias Montano y Plantino: El libro flamenco en la España de Felipe II* (León:Universidad de León, 2009), p. 244.

21. Gonzalo Pérez was a member of the same Aragonese converso merchant clan as Marcos Pérez, the leader of the Antwerp Calvinists. Gonzalo began his bureaucratic career as the secretary of Alfonso Valdés, whose Erasmian credo he shared. In 1543 he became secretary to Prince Philip and remained in the post until his death in 1567. Like Philip's tutor, Juan Cristóbal Calvete de Estrella, Pérez used his position to promote humanist (Erasmian) scholarship at court. He was himself an accomplished Greek scholar, who produced the first Castillian translation of the *Odyssey*, in 1547. In his introduction to the work he reminded Philip that good government was impossible without following the precepts of moral philosophy, and criticized the Spanish for being more interested in war than in letters. José Luis González-Molero, 'El Erasmismo y la educación de Felipe II,' diss. Complutense, Madrid, 1997, pp. 634–640. For Gonzalo Pérez's converso background, see Gregorio Marañon, *Antonio Pérez*, Vol. I (Madrid: Espasa-Calpe, 1963), pp. 11–22. For a detailed biography of Gonzalo Pérez, see Ángel González Palencia, *Gonzalo Pérez, secretario de Felipe II*, 2 vols., (Madrid: CSIC, 1946).

22. Colin Clair, *Christopher Plantin* (London: Plantin Press, 1987), p. 14.

23. Clair believes that Plantin's first print shop was established with financial aid from Gabriel de Zayas and Alexander Graphaeus, a businessman who was *greffier* (registrar) of the city. In 1567 a letter was found in the house of a Spanish merchant which contained a list of the city's prominent heretics. Both Christopher Plantin and Alexander Grapheus appear on the list. Also on the list are Marcos Pérez ('Spagnol. Juif de rache'), Fernando de Berny ('Spagnol. Juif de rache'), Cornelis van Bonbergue, Carle de Bonbergue, and Goropio Becano. The Bonbergues, Grapheus, and Becano were all associates of Plantin. All fled Antwerp when the Duke of Alba's forces entered the city in 1567, as did Marcos Pérez, whose brother Luis was also closely associated with the Plantin print shop. See Colin Clair, *Christopher Plantin*, p. 58, note 2. In a letter written in 1608 to the Archbishop of Canterbury,

the Calvinist Adrianus Saravia, a friend of Plantin, provides us with an intimate glimpse at of the printer's religious views: 'Plantin's wife, and his servants and family, with the sole exception of the elder Raphelengius, his son-in-law [a Calvinist], were Papists. He [Plantin] seemed to me to think that that religion [Catholicism] was better adapted to uncultivated minds. At one time when Lipsius, Plantin and I were walking in the country, we talked a great deal about religion, and Plantin said: "There are, and always have been, many and various religions, all hostile to each other. They all have a lot of simulation and concealment but they are not to be despised, provided they involve no crime, since they are useful to feebler minds. The common people have need of such elementary aids; they cannot grasp the heavenly and divine in any other way. There is only one piety, which is simple and quite without show."' Ben Rekers, *Benito Arias Montano*, pp. 101–102. A source of much of our information on Plantin's affiliation with the Family of Love is a 160-page manuscript, titled *Cronika des Hüsgesinnes der Lieften*. The anonymous author of the chronicle writes: 'At that time—around the year 1550—he [Hendrik Niclaes, the founder of the sect] converted also to his manner of thinking a certain native of France named Christophe Plantin. This man was a bookbinder who earned his bread by the labor of his hands; for the rest, a man prudent and astute in business matters, from which he could reap certain advantages.' Colin Clair, p. 29. For an account of Plantin's involvement with the Family of Love, see Colin Clair, pp. 28–36.

24. Ibid., pp. 23–25.
25. The van Bomberghens' cousin, we are told, was Fernando de Bernuys, another of Plantin's partners. In a contemporary document listing Antwerp's heretics (see note 61) Bernuys, like Marcos Pérez, is described as 'Spagnol. Juif de Rache.' Daniel van Bomberghen (Cornelis' father) 'was renowned as a printer of Hebrew books and had owned a flourishing press in Venice until the decrees of the Inquisition and the open hostility of the nobility of Venice forced him to leave the city' (Colin Clair, p. 39). It was from the van Bomberghens that Plantin bought the Hebrew typeface with which he printed the Hebrew text of the Polyglot Bible.
26. Granvelle championed Plantin's Polyglot Bible project, gaining access to important Greek manuscripts in the Vatican and having them copied at his own expense for the Greek section of the work. He was also kept informed by Plantin and Montano of the project's development. Later, when Plantin was accused of Protestant heresy, Granvelle came to his defense. See M. Van Durme, *El Cardinal Granvela (1517–1586)* (Barcelona: Vicens Vives, 1955), p. 300. During Granvelle's period as

Philip's ambassador in Rome, he employed Justus Lipsius as his secretary of Latin letters, introducing the young scholar to an important group of humanists who would prove useful in advancing his career. Ibid., pp. 307-308.

27. Both Montano and Plantin wished to amend the Vulgate, using earlier Greek and Hebrew biblical texts as their authorities. Philip II was adamantly against the plan. He was, however, persuaded to countenance a separate, seventh volume of the work, offering the Hebrew Old Testament and Greek New Testament with an interlinear Latin translation by Santes Pagnini and Montano. See Baltomero Macías Rosendo, *La Biblia políglota de Amberes en la correspondencia de Benito Arias Montano (ms. Estoc. A 902)* (Huelva: Universidad de Huelva, 1998), p. xxv.
28. See Rekers, p. 51.
29. The philological work was completed by May 1570. It took another year to set up and print the texts. Rekers, p. 52.
30. Volume 7 contained interlinear Latin translations of the Hebrew Bible and the Greek New Testament. The Hebrew Bible translation was by Santes Pagnini; the interlinear Latin version of the Greek Bible was the Vulgate with certain amendments by Montano (Colin Clair, p. 71). The Louvain theologians were, to quote Eustacio Sanchez Salor, men 'impregnados del erasmismo.' See Sanchez Salor, 'La imprenta de Plantino' in *Arias Montano y su Tiempo*, p. 143.
31. Philip II to the Duke of Alba, 17 March 1572, in Rekers, p. 56.
32. Rekers, pp. 62-64.
33. Letter from Montano to Zayas, 28 August, 1571, *CODOIN* 41 (Madrid, 1862), p. 253.
34. Furió Ceriol's *memoria* is included in a 1952 edition of his *El concejo y los consejeros del Principe*, ed. Diego Sevilla Andrés, pp. 177-185.
35. Rekers, p. 28.
36. See note 3.
37. For an account of the Family of Love, see Alastair Hamilton, *The Family of Love* (Cambridge: James Clarke and Co., 1981).
38. Montano also makes note of this revelation in a Latin ode contained in his *Comentaria in duodeim prophetas*. In Sigüenza's Inquisition trial in 1592, a fellow Jeronymite friar, José de Ronda, noted that Fray Luis de León 'had told a monk of this order that everything that Montano knew [about religión] he had learnt within two weeks.' See Luis Gomez Canseco, *El humanismo después de 1600: Pedro de Valencia* (Sevilla: Universidad de Sevilla), p. 40. Montano also stated in his first intervention at the fourth Tridentine Council (19 June 1562): 'I was inspired by a divine breath and now I see everything clearly, and that is the way

I'm going to present it.' Alfredo Albor Ezquerra, 'Montano y El Concilio de Trento,' p. 127.
39. The passage is taken from Montano's foreword to his commentary on the Apocalypse, in B. Ariae Montani *Elucidationes in omnia S. Apostolorum script*, Antwerp 1588, translated by Ben Rekers in *Benito Arias Montano*, p. 92. For Barrefelt's interpretation of St. John's Book of Revelations and Montano's interest in the work, see Alaistair Hamilton, 'The Apocalypse Within: Some Inward Interpretations of the Book of Revelation from the Sixteenth to the Eighteenth Century,' in Jürgen Christian Hermann Lebram and Jan Willem van Henten eds. *Tradition and Re-Interpretation in Jewish and Early Christian Literature* (Leiden: Brill, 1986), pp. 269–283.
40. Juan Rafael de la Cuadra Blanco dates the replacement to 1584. For an extensive examination of the Escorial's Solomonesque character, see Cuadra Blanco's article, "Arquitectura e historia sagrada. Nuevas consideraciones sobre la idea de El Escorial y el Templo de Jerusalem," *Cuadernos de Arte e Iconografía* 43 (2013), pp. 11–258. Cuadra Blanco believes that Philip's Erasmian education propelled him toward associating his palace-monastery with the pacific King Solomon. Ibid., pp. 183–184.
41. The prior's canvas was painted for El Escorial by the Italian Francesco de Urbino, while Philip's *Judgement* was the work of the Dutchman Pieter Aertsen, who had painted the work some 20 years previously, at a time, after the Seville and Valladolid Protestant scare, when Philip's persecution of the Dutch heretics had grown tenfold.
42. In the library frescoes, Arithmetic is represented by Solomon, who solved the puzzle presented to him by the Queen of Sheba; Music by David playing his harp; Astronomy by the infirm King Ezequias, who is cured after moving into the shadow of the sun; Grammar by the tower of Babel and Nebucodonoser's school of grammar in Babylon, where Daniel studied. See Cornelia von der Osten Sacken, *El Escorial: Estudio iconológico* (Bilbao: Xarait Libros, 1984). At the same time the Italian painter Pellegrino Tibaldi was commissioned to decorate the Basilica's sagrario, or tabernacle, a chamber located behind the high altar, with scenes from the Old Testament foreshadowing the Last Supper. The frescoes represent the Israelites collecting manna in the wilderness, eating the lamb before the Passover; the priest Melchizedek blessing Abraham with bread and wine; and Elias given bread and water by the angel to sustain him on his journey across the desert to Horeb, the mount of God. While these themes, believed to have been chosen by Montano, present the Old Testament texts as foreshadowing the coming of Christ, they also underline once again the close relationship

between Christianity and Judaism. For the frescoes, see Rosemarie Mulcahy, *'A la mayor gloria de Dios y el Rey': La decoración de la Real Basilica del Monasterio de El Escorial* (Madrid: Patrimonio Nacional, 1992), Chapter 5.

43. 'Carta y Discurso del Maestro Fr. Luis de Estrada sobre la aprobación de la Biblia Regia y sus versiones; y juiçio de la que hizo del Nuevo Testamento Benito Arias Montano,' cited in Guy Lazure, 'Perception of the Temple, Projections of the Divine, Royal Patronage, Biblical Scholarship and Jesuit Imaginary in Spain 1580–1620,' in *Calamvs renascens. Revista de humanismo y tradición clásica* 1 (2000), p. 167. Along with Ambrosio de Morales and Pedro Serrano, Luis de Estrada had formed part of the Alcalá theological committee commissioned to examine Montano's Polyglot Bible. It was Estrada who had earlier warned Montano of León de Castro's campaign against the work: 'A certain person has tried to persuade, and unfortunately has persuaded Spain that the original Hebrew and Aramaic texts have been corrupted by Jews.' Cited in Gaspar Morocho y Gayo y otros, 'Cipriano de la Huerga, maestro de humanistas,' in Victor García de la Concha y Javier San José Lera eds., *Fray Luis de León: historia, humanismo y letras* (Salamanca: Universidad de Salamanca, 1996), p. 184.

44. 'Carta y discurso del Maestro Fr. Luis de Estrada ....'

45. *Hieranymi Pradi et Ioannis Baptistae Villalpandi e Societate Iesu in Ezechielem explanationes et Apparatus Urbis, ac Templi Hierosolymitani*, Roma, 1596–1605.

46. *El Templo de Salomón según Juan Bautista Villalpando. Comentarios de la profecía de Ezekiel*, ed Juan Antonio Ramírez, trad. José Luis Oliver Domingo, vol II libro I, cap. 10, p. 41. This is a Spanish translation of the second volume of *In Ezechielem. El Templo de Salomón según Juan Bautista Villalpando. Comentarios a la profecía de Ezequiel*, ed. Juan Antonio Ramírez, trad. José Luis Oliver Domingo (Madrid: Siruela, 1991).

47. For the background of the Torreblanco family, see Francisco I. Quevedo Sánchez, 'Francisco de Torreblanco Villalpando: jurista, religioso, escritor, patron,...converso,' in Félix Labrador Arroyo ed., *II Encuentro de Jovenes Investigadores en Historia Moderna. Líneas recientes de investigacion en Historia Moderna* (Madrid: Ediciones Cinca, 2015), pp. 273–290. Franciso de Torreblanco Villalpando was the nephew of Juan Bautista Villalpando. Like his uncle he was also interested in Solomon's Temple and the Solomonic Arts, as witnessed in his work *Discurso en defensa de los libros católicos de magia*. In a *memorial*, dated 9 October 1622, Torreblanco Villalpando wrote of the Jewish expulsion of 1492: '[A]fter over a million households left, there were still infinite numbers who remained, spontaneously receiving baptism and mixing with

Christians such that today we do not know who these people were.' See Julio Caro Baroja, *Los judíos en la España moderna y contemporánea,* Vol. I, p. 202. Like his uncle, it seems, Francisco was interested in promoting a message of converso integration.

48. The circumstances of Villalpando's meeting with Herrera were described by the physician Andrés de Morales y Padilla in his *Historia general de la muy leal ciudad de Córdoba y de sus nobilisimas familias* (1604), cited in Juan Antonio Ramírez, René Taylor et al. eds., *Dios Arquitecto: Juan Bautista Villalpando y el Templo de salomón* (Madrid: Siruela, 1991), p. 345.

49. According to the *Diccionario Histórico de la Compañia de Jesús: Biografico-Tematico* IV, p. 3212, Prado taught Scripture at the University of Baeza in 1570, and continued teaching in that institution after he joined the Jesuits in 1572. For the attack on the Baeza University faculty, see Álvaro Huerga, *Historia de los Alumbrados, tomo II: Los alumbrados de la alta Andalucia (1575–1590)* (Madrid: Fundación Universitaria Española, 1978), pp. 175–201 and Juan de Ávila, *Obras completas,* I, p. 44 and pp. 343–356.

50. ARSI, cod. Epist. Hisp. XVIII, fol. 314, cited from John W. O'Malley, *The First Jesuits,* p. 190.

51. For the division among the Jesuits with regard to *limpieza de sangre* legislation in the last decades of the sixteenth century, see Robert. A. Maryks, *The Jesuits as a Synagogue of Jews,* Chapters 3 and 4.

52. Ibid., p. 177.

53. Haim Beinart, '¿Cuando llegaron los judíos a España?'.

54. See Juan Gil, 'Judíos y conversos en los falsos cronicones.' For a detailed examination of Higuera's false chronicles in the context of Counter-Reformation Spain, see Katrina B. Olds, *Forging the Past.*

55. Villalpando wrote: 'Sagunto was also a thriving city [of Jews] before the reign of Solomon, the wisest of kings, and in this city, in 1480, a stone tomb was discovered next to the castle gate. Adonirán, the representative of Solomon, died in the city where he had previously asked to be buried in a Stone tomb. Thus the tomb's Hebrew script reads: "This is the tomb of Adonirán, Solomon's minister who came here to collect taxes and died on this day." Unfortunately, owing to the damage, the date has been completely erased, and thus impossible to know.' Villalpando noted that he was not personally able to find the headstone on his visit to Sagunto. Juan Antonio Ramírez ed., *El Templo de Salomón según Juan Bautista Villalpando. Comentarios de la profecía de Ezekiel,* vol 2, trans José Luis Oliver (Madrid: Editorial Siruela, 1991), p. 463.

56. Ibid.

57. Vaughn Hart, *Art and Magic in the Courts of the Stuarts* (London: Routledge, 1994), p. 71. In Chapter 3 of the book, Hart examines the influence of Villalpando's work on James I's court.
58. For Philip's interest in the hermetic arts, see René Taylor, *Arquitectura y magia: consideraciones sobre la 'idea' de El Escorial* (Madrid: Siruela, 2006). In 1595 Luna sent a report on the Lead Books to Philip II, stating that they were written in a pre-Koran Arabic script known as Salomonic. He knew this to be true because he had come across the term in old books like *Clavícula de Salomon*, which he had read in the Escorial library. See Mercedes García-Arenal and Fernando Rodríguez Mediano, *Un oriente español* (Madrid: Marcial Pons, 2010), p. 182.
59. Cited in Mercedes García-Arenal, 'The Religious Identity of the Arabic Language and the Affair of the Lead Books of the Sacromonte de Granada,' *Arabica* 56 (2009), pp. 495–528 (497).
60. The story is outlined in Manuel Sotomayor, 'Los fundamentos histórico-eclesiástico del Sacromonte: de Santiago y sus varones apostólicos a los hallazgos de valparaíso,' in Manuel Barrios Aguilera and Mercedes García-Arenal eds., *¿La historia inventada? Los libros plúmbeos y el legado sacramontano* (Granada: Universidad de Granada, 2008), pp. 29–43.
61. Mercedes García-Arenal and Fernando Rodríguez Mediano, 'Miguel de Luna, Cristiano Arábigo de Granada,' in Manuel Barrios Aguilera and Mercedes García-Arenal eds., *¿La historia inventada?* p. 85. The Lead Books fraud is brilliantly parodied in Miguel de Cervante's *Don Quijote*. On the Cervantes' parody, see Thomas E. Case, 'Cide Hamete Benengeli y los Libros plúmbeos,' *Cervantes* 22.2 (2002), pp. 9–24, See also Gerard Wiegers, 'The Granada Lead Books Translator Miguel de Luna as a Model for the Toledan Translator of Cide Hamete Benengeli in Cervantes' Don Quijote,' in Kevin Ingram ed., *The Conversos and Moriscos in Late Medieval Spain and Beyond, Vol III: Displaced Persons* (Leiden: Brill, 2015), pp. 150–163.
62. For a comparison of Luna's false chronicle with those of Román de la Higuera, see Mercedes García-Arenal and Fernando Rodríguez Mediano, 'Jerónimo Román de la Higuera and the Lead Books of Granada,' in Kevin Ingram ed., *The Conversos and Moriscos in Late Medieval Spain and Beyond, Vol I: Departures and Change* (Leiden: Brill, 2009), pp. 243–269.
63. Ibid., pp. 106–107.
64. Ben Rekers, *Benito Arias Montano*, p. 160.
65. Ibid.
66. For an examination of Montano's substantial estate and his relationship with the Núñez Pérez family, see Juan Gil, *Arias Montano en su entorno*.

67. For the Lisbon merchant affair, see Alfredo Alvar Ezquerra, 'Bentio Arias Montano en Portugal,' in *Arias Montano y su tiempo*, pp. 197–204. Alvar relates the story as if Arias Montano was a dispassionate intermediary. It seems he is unaware of Montano's close ties to the Núñez López merchant clan.
68. See Manuel José de Lara Ródenas, 'Arias Montano en Portugal. La Revisión de un Tópico sobre la Diplomacia Secreta de Felipe II,' in Luis Gómez Canseco ed. *Anatomía de Humanismo. Benito Arias Montano 1598–1998* (Huelva: Diputación Provincial de Huelva, 1998), p. 365.
69. Letter to Zayas in *CODOIN* 41, p. 407.
70. The verse is cited in 'Epístola a don Gaspar de Barrionuevo,' *Biblioteca de Autores Españoles*, 36, p. 427.
71. Montano to Zayas, 31 May, 1577, in *CODOIN* 41, p. 346.
72. Montano chose a psalm to introduce each of his friends and explore their character. The list of dedicatees included Luis Pérez (the Antwerp merchant), Gabriel de Zayas, Justus Lipsius, the Licentiate Francisco Pacheco, and Pedro de Valencia. See Benito Arias Montano, *Comentario a los treinta y un primeros salmos de David* (León: Universidad de León, 1999).
73. See Juan Gil, *Arias Montano en su entorno*, p. 35, note 71. We also know that several years previously, the abbot of Seville University, Francisco de Medina, uncle of the humanist of the same name, spent his last moments attended by Ana Núñez. Were both Medina and Montano being prepared for death in a customary Jewish fashion by a fellow converso?
74. Archivo Catedral de Sevilla, 'Pruebas de Sangre,' Leg. F, no. 7.
75. See Francisco Cantera, 'La judería de Miranda de Ebro,' *Sefarad* 2 (1942), pp. 325–375.
76. Alfonso Franco Silva y Rafael Cruz Mariño, 'Juan Pacheco, privado de Enrique IV, y el oficio de Corregidor de Jerez de la Frontera,' *En la España Medieval* 35 (2012), pp. 285–313.
77. For an examination of Jerez de la Frontera's large converso community, see Gonzalo Carrasco García, 'Judeoconversos de Jerez de la Frontera y el obispado de Cádiz a fines del siglo XV,' *En la España Medieval* 29 (2006), pp. 311–345.
78. Francisco Rodríguez Marín, *Nuevos datos para las biografías de cien escritores de los siglos XVI y XVII* (Madrid: Revista de Archivos, Bibliotecas y Museos, 1923), p. 457, pp.464–465, and 466–467. The biographical information comes from another *limpieza de sangre* examination, undertaken by the painter Francisco Pacheco and his brothers between 1595 and 1601. It seems that they wished to create their own *limpieza de sangre* document, possibly with the view of entering the Inquisition as *familiares*.

79. 'Sátira apologética en defensa del divino Dueñas,' ll 1–3, in 'Una sátira sevillana del Licenciado Francisco Pacheco,' *Revista de Archivos, Bibliotecas y Museos* 11 (1907). Surprisingly, there is no critical edition of the satire. In 1907, Rodriguez Marin published the poem with some brief notes, promising a fuller analysis in the future. This never materialized, one assumes because the material was too racy for the Seville scholar to handle.
80. 'Una Sátira Sevillana del Licenciado Francisco Pacheco,' p. 5.
81. Ibid., ll 692–693.
82. Ibid., ll 523–525.
83. Ibid., ll 88–91.
84. Pedro Vélez de Guevara, a witness in 1569 at Pacheco's examination for his university degree, was a canon in the Seville Cathedral and a legal consultant for the Sacro Colegio de la Iglesia of Seville. He was also a relative of Benito Arias Montano's adoptive mother, Isabel Vélez, and a close friend of Montano.
85. Bartolomé Pozuelo Calero, *El Licenciado Francisco Pacheco: Sermones sobre la instauración de la libertad del espíritu y lirica amorosa* (Sevilla-Cádiz: Universidad de Sevilla, 1993), p. 99. Pozuelo Calero's work is a modern Spanish translation and edited edition of Pacheco's Latin original.
86. Ibid., p. 121.
87. Ibid., p. 117.
88. 'And for having violated countries' rights and the divine concord of mother earth in wars, profaning sacred things and devastating everything with acts of rapine, the stupid vulgo believes them to be illustrious.' Ibid.
89. Ibid., p. 129.
90. Ibid., p. 131. Juan de Ovando (?–1575) was a successful *letrado*. His relationship with Pacheco probably began in the 1550s when the absentee Archbishop of Seville, Fernando de Valdés, nominated him his agent (*juez provisor*). Later he became president of the Council of the Indies, where he commissioned a number of important studies on the Spanish American colonies and instituted a series of far-reaching financial and legal reforms. The Ovando family maintained close ties with the Indies. One of its members, Pedro Mexía de Ovando, was responsible for 'La Ovandina,' a genealogical work, published in Lima in 1621, in which the Ovandos are presented with an immaculate noble trajectory from Visigoths of Vizcaya and Galicia. The work, as Marquéz Villanueva has pointed out (*Investigaciones sobre Juan Álvarez Gato*, p. 77, note 104), was the creation of a man who saw the profitability of selling false genealogical studies to wealthy Indies merchants and offi-

cials whose true ancestry was best kept a secret. For Juan de Ovando's relationship with the Indies, see Stafford Poole, *Juan de Ovando*. For his relationship with a converso humanist and bureaucratic circle, see by the same author, 'The Politics of *Limpieza de Sangre*: Juan de Ovando and his Circle in the Reign of Philip II,' *The Americas*, 55.3 (1999), pp. 359–389. The other *letrado* mentioned by Pacheco, Juan López de Velasco, was born in Vinuesa, Soria, in 1530, and died in Madrid in 1598. He is known primarily as the Royal Cosmographer and author of *Geografía y descripción universal de las Indias*. He was first and foremost a humanist, however, whose interest in philological reform is demonstrated in his work *Ortografía y pronuncia castellana*. Pacheco probably got to know López in Seville while the latter was compiling information on the Indies. For López's philological interests, see José Maria Pozuelo Ivancas, *López de Velasco en la teoría gramatical del siglo XVI* (Murcia: Universidad de Murcia, 1981).
91. Pozuelo Calero, p. 139.
92. Ibid., p. 169.
93. Ibid., p. 177.
94. Ibid., p. 181.
95. Ibid., p. 191.
96. Ibid., p. 189.
97. Ibid.
98. Rubio Lapaz writes that Céspedes' historical works 'tend to demonstrate the direct relationship between the earliest Spanish history and the prestigious episodes of the first books of the Old Testament in an ideal program of Counter-Reformation legitimization of Spanish imperial preeminence.' Jesús Rubio Lapaz, *Pablo de Céspedes y su círculo: humanismo y contrarreforma en la cultura andaluza del Renacimiento al Barroco* (Granada: Universidad de Granada, 1993), p. 164.
99. Ibid., p. 41. In his *Libro de descripción de verdaderos retratos*, Francisco Pacheco noted that Céspedes never said mass and often opposed received opinion in an amusing, paradoxical fashion that gave rise to witty anecdotes. In his *Sales españolas o agudezas del ingenio nacional*, Paz y Melia includes two anecdotes on Céspedes' irreverent attitude to Catholic ceremony and dogma. In the first, Céspedes finds himself among a group of fellow prebendaries in the cathedral when the party comes across a priest holding up the host at mass, at which point all of the group kneel except Céspedes, who says that he has a bad leg. When the priest raises the wine cup, however, Céspedes makes an attempt to kneel, stating that he has always had a greater attraction to the 'sanguis' (wine) than to the 'corpus' (bread). On another occasion he is holding forth on some subject when he hears loud voices in the street com-

mending souls to heaven from purgatory, a usual practice. Angered, Céspedes raised his hands in the air, saying, 'Blessed art thou Algiers where there are no souls in purgatory nor people in the street commending them to heaven, disturbing those that are speaking about that which they can fulfil.'

100. Of the 265 books listed in an inventory of Céspedes' property, taken after his death, barely 20 are religious works. Among these are two Greek bibles (given Céspedes' interest in the Old Testament, one of these was probably a Septuagint, the other almost certainly Erasmus' Greek New Testament), Benito Arias Montano's *Biblia regia* (the Antwerp Polyglot Bible published by Plantin in 1572), Erasmus' *Enchiridion*, a breviary, a book of psalms, and three works, listed as the *Life of Christ* by Juarez, Maluenda's *Love of Christ*, and Rivera on *the Apocalypse*. These works suggest a strong evangelical, or Erasmian, Christianity. Among the other works listed are Ambrosio de Morales *Crónica general de España*; Juan de Mariana's *Historia general de España* (probably the 1601 Toledo edition) and his *De ponderibus* (1599), in which he attacks the Crown's disastrous monetary policy; Josephus' *History of the Jews*; three accounts of trips to or sojourns in Jerusalem; a Jewish grammar; an 'arte hebreo'; a 'libro hebreo'; and an Arabic alphabet. Many of the works are by classical Roman writers, among whom are Ovid, Cicero, Plutarch, Juvenal, Martial, Virgil, and Salust. See Rafael Ramírez Arellano, 'Pablo de Céspedes. Pintor, escultor, arquitecto, literato insigne y ¿musico?' in *Boletin de la Sociedad Español de Excursiones* 132 (1904), pp. 34–37.

101. Archivo de la Catedral de Córdoba, *Actas Capitulares*, libro 23. Pablo de Céspedes' representative in Alcolea was his maternal uncle Pedro Martínez de Arroyo. In Ocaña he was represented by an Alonso de Céspedes, who was clearly a member of his family, although the nature of this relationship is not stated, and a Francisco Álvarez, who is described as a regidor (councilman) on the Ocaña town council. Alonso de Céspedes may have been the member of the Ocaña town council who formed part of a committee to construct a magnificent fountain in the town, finished in 1578, a year after Pablo de Céspedes' *limpieza* inquiry. See Miguel Díaz Ballesteros, Benito de Lariz, and Justo García Suelto, *Historia de la villa de Ocaña*, Vol. II (Ocaña: Agustín Puigrós, 1873), p. 30.

102. All *limpieza de sangre* examinees with something to hide would prepare the ground prior to the investigations taking place, often at great cost. This appears to have been the case in the Céspedes investigation. Just prior to the investigation, Pablo's Uncle Pedro, who was passing on his prebendary to his nephew, borrowed over a thousand ducados on the strength of his property in Córdoba. This money, I believe, funded

Pablo's successful *limpieza* process. Some 20 years later, on Pedro's death, the loan was still outstanding, with the result that Pablo, who was Pedro's sole heir, was forced to sell the family home to relinquish the debt. This information appears in the records of the Córdoba notary Alonso Rodríguez de la Cruz, on 17 June 1597. Rafael Ramírez de Arellano includes the entry in his article on Céspedes for the *Boletin de la Sociedad Española de Excursiones* 126–128 (1903), pp. 204–236 (207–212).

103. For the Mora family of Quintanar de la Orden, see Vincent Parello, 'Inquisition and Crypto-Judaism: The 'Complicity of the Mora Family of Quintanar de la Orden (1588–1592),' in Kevin Ingram ed., *The Conversos and Moriscos in Late Medieval Spain and Beyond. Vol I: Departures and Change*, pp. 187–210.

104. See Justo García Suelto, *Historia de la villa de Ocaña*, Vol. II, p. 163. Céspedes' grandfather Alonso was the son of this Alonso, born in Ocaña in the late fifteenth century. One of the witnesses in Céspedes' *limpieza* investigation noted that everyone referred to this Alonso Céspedes as *el Viejo* (*Actas capitulares*, libro 23, fol. 751 (v)).

105. The name Hervás suggest that the person's ancestors came from the small Extremadura town of Hervás, renowned for its large population of Jews in the fifteenth century. The town has since become synonymous with crypto-Judaism, even being the subject of a local rhyme: '*En Hervás, judíos los más; en Aldeanueva, la judería entera; en Bejar, hasta las tejas; en Baños, judíos y tacaños*' ['In Hervás, mainly Jews; in Aldeanueva, entirely Jewish; in Bejar full to the roof; in Baños Jews and skinflints'] José Ramón y Fernández Oxea, 'Nuevos dictados tópicos cacereños,' *Revista de Estudios Extemeños* 5 (1949), p. 398. Jews often took the name of the town in which they were baptized as their Christian surname.

106. The concurrence once again of the surnames Céspedes and Mora suggests that the two families formed close social bonds during the period. The practice of office sharing was not unusual in cathedral chapters, where canons and other officials attempted to pass their lucrative positions to family members. The official holder would thus apply to Rome for a license to share the responsibilities with another, usually younger man, who would later, on the elder man's death, take full control of the position and its generous salary. Pablo de Céspedes received his Córdoba prebendary through the same stratagem, sharing the position with Pedro de Céspedes, who was purportedly his uncle, although he may have been his father.

107. Amador de los Ríos notes that this Pedro de Céspedes was one of ten canons who protested Archbishop Silíceo's 1547 statute. See José Amador de los Rios, *Historia social, política y religiosa de los judíos de España y Portugal*, Vol. III, p. 500, note 1. Céspedes' opposition to the

earlier *limpieza de sangre* statute is recorded in the 'Relacion del estatuto de limpieza de la capilla de los reyes nuevos,' located in the Archivo Capitular de Toledo. Secretaria Capitular.

108. In Pablo de Céspedes' *limpieza de sangre* investigation, the man said to be his father, Alonso de Céspedes, is a nothing more than a specter. The people interviewed in Pablo's mother's village never mention him. As for the witnesses in Ocaña, only two refer to Alonso, but as a child, not as an adult. It is possible, of course, that he died soon after Pablo's birth, but strangely no one mentions this. On the other hand, many of the witnesses refer to Pablo's uncle, who himself notes that Pablo was born and raised in his Córdoba home. I would suggest that Alonso de Céspedes died in childhood, and was resurrected briefly to play the role of father in Pablo's genealogical inquiry. Pablo's real father was probably the Córdoba prebendary Pedro de Céspedes, who may have met and maintained a relationship with Aulalia de Arroyo, Pablo de Céspedes' mother, while studying at Alcalá, a few miles away from her village, in the early 1540s.

109. See Priscilla E. Muller, 'Pablo de Céspedes: A Letter of 1577,' *The Burlington Magazine* 1115 (1996), pp. 89–91. Pacheco has also been challenged by modern scholars over Céspedes' date of birth. The consensus is that Céspedes was born some time before 1548, possibly as early as 1538. Maria Angeles Raya Raya notes that in his will of 11 July 1547, Francisco López Aponte bequeathed 100,000 maravedis to Pablo for his education. This would seem to confirm that Pablo was born at least a year before 1548. Unfortunately, Raya does not include a reference to the notarial document from which the information was taken. See Maria Angeles Raya Raya, *Catálogo de la pintura de la Catedral de Córdoba* (Córdoba: Monte de Piedad y Caja de Ahorros de Córdoba, 1988), p. 43.

110. Simancas was in fact the Bishop of Ciudad Rodrigo, not Zamora, when Céspedes knew him in Rome. He was later awarded the Zamora bishopric for his services to the Crown, although he probably had his sights set on the Córdoba see, where his family were already politically powerful. His autobiography, in which he dwells on the Carranza trial, is included in Serrano y Sanz, *Autobiografías y memorias* (Madrid: Biblioteca de Autores Españoles, 1905), pp. 151–210.

111. Juan de Simancas, the absentee Bishop of Cartagena de Indias, resident in Córdoba, was in a position to help Céspedes gain his prebendary in the cathedral. The *juro* may have been payment for this help. The *juro* is mentioned in a 1597 notarial document, included by Rafael Ramírez de Arellano in his article, 'Pablo de Céspedes,' *Boletin de la Sociedad Española de Excursiones* 126–128 (1903), pp. 204–236 (207–212).

112. It is clear from Simancas' autobiography that he felt Philip II had let him down by offering him the lesser see of Zamora. See Diego de Simancas, *Vida y cosas notables del señor de Zamora don Diego de Simancas*, in M. Serrano y Sanz ed., *Autobiografías y memorias*, pp. 151–210. See also Macarena Moralejo, 'El obispo Diego de Simancas y su papel como Virrey de Napoles,' Librosdelcorte.es. no. 4, año 4, invierno-primavera, 2012, p. 152.
113. Licentiate Céspedes' interview with the Inquisition on 29 December 1559 is included in J. Ignacio Tellechea Idigoras, *Fray Bartolomé Carranza. Documentos históricos* (Madrid: Real Academia de la Historia, 1962), pp. 211–215. Juan Antonio Llorente's reference to Pablo de Céspedes appears in his *Historia crítica de la Inquisicion de España*, Vol. I (Barcelona: Juan Pons, 1870), pp. 511–512.
114. In his 1576 *memorial* 'Prision de el Arzobispo de Toledo D. Fray Bartolomé de Carranza...' Morales presents Carranza as a victim of political intrigue. Morales reserves his sharpest barbs for Carranza's arresting officer, Rodrigo de Castro, later Archbishop of Seville, whom he paints as a devious and manipulative careerist. Castro's malice is nicely indicated by Morales when he states that the mule presented to the archbishop to convey him from Alcalá de Henares to the Inquisition prison at Valladolid was not provided with reins: 'strange and amazing to see a great prelate, no one higher than him in Spain, reduced to such deplorable misery either by lack of fortune, or the blind envy of his enemies.' See 'Prision de el Arzobispo de Toledo D. Fray Bartolomé de Carranza...' *CODOIN* 5 (Madrid, 1844), pp. 465–494.
115. We know that Céspedes was in contact with the papal agent Juan Rubio Herrera while in Rome. Rubio, whose family were from the city of Córdoba, was one of many converso agents in Rome who helped their clients, often conversos themselves, to gain papal approval for church benefices, including dispensations in the case of *limpieza de sangre* impediments. Ironically, in 1583 Rubio was himself requested by the Córdoba Cathedral to provide evidence for his own *limpieza de sangre* in connection with the prebend he held in the cathedral. In the same year Céspedes was sent to Rome to discuss this matter and others with Rubio. See David García Cueto, 'Sobre las relaciones de Velázquez y Don Juan de Córdoba tras el regreso del segundo viaje a Italia,' *Archivo Español de Arte* 334 (2011), pp. 177–180.
116. The Jewish ancestry of the Seville poet Fernando de Herrera is alluded to by Licentiate Francisco Pacheco in his poem, 'La sátira apologética en defensa del divino Dueñas,' discussed in this chapter. The converso background of the Córdoba poet Luis de Góngora is examined in Enrique Soria Mesa, *El origen judío de Góngora* (Córdoba: Ediciones Hannover, 2015). Bernardo de Fresneda, Bishop of Córdoba from

1572 to 1577, referred to Salucio's converso roots in a letter to Philip II in 1575, describing him as 'hijo de Genoves y no buena madre.' 'No buena' signified 'converso.'

117. 'Discurso sobre la antiguedad de la cathedral de Córdoba y como antes era templo del dios Jano,' in Jesús Rubio Lapaz and Fernando Moreno Cuadro, *Escritos de Pablo de Céspedes, Córdoba. Edición Critica* (Córdoba: Diputación Provincial de Córdoba, 1998), pp. 79–133.

118. 'Tratado sobre el topónimo de Córdoba y otros lugares cercanos y sobre hijos ilustres cordobeses,' ibid., pp. 49–71.

119. The Islamic city of Córdoba produced two of the most outstanding philosophers of the Middle Ages—the Muslim Averroes and the Jewish Maimonides, both of whom were concerned with the task of reconciling Greek rationalism with received religious wisdom, a mission later assumed by Thomas Aquinas in a Christian context. Among the city's great physicians was Hasdai ibn Shaprut, the head of al-Andaluz' Jewish community and the famous advisor to the Caliph of Córdoba, Abd-al-Rahman III. It was ibn Shaprut who was reputed to have cured the Christian King Sancho of obesity.

120. The Fernández de Córdobas were 'descendants of those first leaders who with animated courage managed at the cost of their own blood to release this noble city from the intolerable yoke of the Moors' barbarous tyranny and restore its ancient liberty, freeing it from their accursed superstition.' 'Tratado sobre el topónimo de Córdoba...' *Escritos*, p. 68.

121. See Chap. 3.

122. In his 'Tratado sobre el toponimo de Córdoba...' (*Escritos*, p. 60), Céspedes refers to discussions he had with Miguel de Luna on his theories. Céspedes describes Luna as 'a distinguished man, both in his professions of philosophy and medicine and for his service to this language [Arabic] which is seen in his translations of certain Arab histories into Spanish and the holy books found in Granada in 1594 and 95.'

123. Rubio Lapaz writes, 'The attempt to legitimize the classical orders by offering them an earlier principle of biblical or Christian origin shows a clear wish to overcome the discordance or criticisms in a period of maximum Counterreformation rigor.' *Escritos de Pablo de Céspedes*, p. 312.

124. The baptismal document was first published by M. Serrano y Sanz in *Pedro de Valencia. Estudio biográfico-critico* (Badajoz: Arqueros, 1910). Much of our information on Valencia comes from a short anonymous biographical study written in the seventeenth century. This is now located in the Biblioteca Nacional de España, Ms. 5781. The biography was found in the papers of Juan de Fonseca y Figueroa, the friend and patron of Diego Velázquez, who, like Valencia, was from Zafra. From

an examination of the script, Jaime Sanchez Romeralo argues that the biography was the work of Valencia's cousin and brother-in-law Juan Moreno Ramírez. See Jaime Sánchez Romeralo, 'Pedro de Valencia y Juan Ramírez (La hermandad de ambos humanistas),' *AIH Actas* III (1968), p. 804. Recently the biographical information has been augmented by Francisco Croche de Acuña: 'Datos ordenados para una biógrafia de Pedro de Valencia,' *Revista de Estudios Extremeños* 40 (1984), pp. 35–99. There have been two modern biographical/literary studies of Valencia: Luis Gómez Canseco, *El humanismo despues de 1600: Pedro de Valencia*, and Grace Magnier, *Pedro de Valencia and the Catholic Apologists of the Expulsion of the Moriscos* (Leiden: Brill, 2010). Gomez-Canseco's work attempts to situate Valencia within a Spanish post-Tridentine humanist movement, while Magnier's study concentrates on the humanist's works related to moral statecraft. Since 1994 the University of León has edited a number of Valencia's works, with useful scholarly introductions to each volume.

125. Segura de León contained a sizeable Jewish *aljama* prior to the Expulsion in 1492. Its most famous occupant was the rabbi Isaac Abravanel, who established his residence there in 1483, when he moved to Spain from Portugal. An enormously wealthy merchant and financier, Abravanel worked for the Catholic Monarchs as a treasurer and tax collector, positions he had previously held in Portugal. In 1492 he and his family left Spain for Italy, which became his base for a successful merchant network, stretching throughout the Mediterranean. Abravanel's son, the physician León Hebreo, was the author of the Neoplatonic work *Diálogos de Amor*.

126. See Joaquín de Estrambasaguas y Peña, 'Una Familia de Ingenios, Los Ramírez de Prado,' *Revista de Estudios Extremeños* 3.2 (1929), pp. 241–257, which examines two *limpieza de sangre* tests undertaken by Pedro de Valencia's second cousin and godson, Lorenzo Ramírez de Prado. Lorenzo was the son of Alonso Ramírez de Prado, an official in the royal treasury who, along with a group of accomplices, defrauded the Crown out of a small fortune in the early years of Philip III's reign. In 1607 Alonso was imprisoned for his crimes, where he died a year later. At his trial a number of witnesses noted that he was from a converso background. In 1625 his son Lorenzo Ramírez de Prado applied to become a *familiar* of the Inquisition in Zafra, which he subsequently gained with the support of his friend, the Inquisitor General Andrés Pacheco, despite the fact that the majority of the witnesses interviewed stated that his father's family were renowned conversos. Three years later, in 1628, Lorenzo applied for entry into the Military Order of Santiago, and once again the majority of those interviewed stated that

he was from a converso background. In response to this, Lorenzo conducted a parallel investigation in which he found over 200 people who swore that he was an Old Christian. This information was presented to the Council of the Orders in 1631, who rejected the earlier report in favor of the new one, awarding him a knighthood. Reading between the lines, it is evident that as a middle-aged man, Lorenzo wished to restore his family's honor, blemished by his father's crimes and the revelations that his ancestors were Jews. The best way of gaining an honorable image was through entry into the Inquisition as a familiar and membership of a prestigious noble order. Lorenzo must have realized that both applications would bring forth accusation of tainted blood, but he counted, correctly, on some friends in high places and what was left of the family fortune to achieve his ends. One of these friends was the Count-Duke of Olivares, who during the period that Ramírez de Prado was applying for his knighthood was also helping a number of Portuguese conversos gain noble titles, putting pressure on the Council of the Orders to achieve his ends. The Ramírez family's Jewish background is also indicated in a report from the Llerena Inquisition tribunal, in 1592. In that year the Llerena inquisitors visited Zafra to examine the state of the faith in the town and its surrounding districts. One of the people brought before the Inquisitors was Alonso Núñez Ramírez from Segura de León, accused of denying the existence of Hell. In his hearing it was noted that he was a notorious converso (*notoriamente confeso*) and that his wife had previously been prosecuted for Judaizing. AHN Inquisición. Leg. 1988, n.40.

127. Francisco Croche de Acuña: 'Datos ordenados para una biógrafia de Pedro de Valencia,' p. 39.
128. Of course, Valencia justified this prejudice on practical grounds: 'There is no food that mixes with others worse than milk. Thus it should be taken alone, without mixings, so that it does not turn one's stomach.' Letter to Fray José de Sigüenza, in Guillermo Antolin, 'Cartas inéditas de Pedro de Valencia al P. José de Sigüenza,' *La Ciudad de Dios* 42 (1896), p. 494.
129. Pedro de Valencia maintained a close relationship with both Pablo de Céspedes and José Sigüenza, their friendship preserved in a number of letters. For the correspondence between Valencia and Céspedes, see J. Martínez Ruiz, 'Cartas inéditas de Pedro de Valencia a Pablo de Céspedes,' *Boletin de la Real Academia Española* 59 (1979), pp. 371–397, and Jesús Rubio Lapaz, 'La relación epistolar entre Pedro de Valencia y Pablo de Céspedes,' *Cuadernos de arte de la Universidad de Granada* 26 (1995), pp. 371–383. For Valencia's correspondence with Fray José de Sigüenza, see Guillermo Antolin, 'Cartas inéditas de Pedro

de Valencia al P. José de Sigüenza, *La Ciudad de Dios* 41 (1897), pp. 341–350, 491–502; 42 (1897), pp. 127–135; 43 (1897) pp. 364–368 and 436–441.
130. Pedro de Valencia, *Obras completas III: Academica* (León: Universidad de León, 2006), p. 209.
131. Ibid., p. 229.
132. Ibid., p. 445.
133. Luis Gómez Canseco, *El humanismo despues de 1600: Pedro de Valencia*, p. 61.
134. For the *limpieza de sangre* legislation within the Jesuit Order, see Albert A. Sicroff, *Los estatutos de limpieza de sangre*, pp. 361–385. Sicroff examines Ribadeneira's response to the 1593 statute on pages 376–378. For a recent examination of the Jesuit *limpieza* statute, see Robert A. Maryks, *The Jesuit Order as a Synagogue of Jews*, Chap. 4.
135. In his *Nobleza de Andalucia* (Sevilla, 1588), Gonzalo Argote y Molina stated that Salucio's ancestors were the Saluzzi and Adorno families, both of which were Italian merchants. This information has been repeated by modern scholars, including Álvaro Huerga in his introduction to Salucio's *Avisos para los predicadores del Santo Evangelio* (Barcelona: Juan Flors, 1956). However, it is clear that Argote used his *Nobleza* to sanitize his own and his friends' backgrounds. Another contemporary of Salucio, the Bishop of Córdoba, Bernardo de Fresneda stated in a letter to Philip II, in 1575, that the friar was '*hijo de Genoves y no de buena madre*' (Instituto Valencia de Don Juan, leg. 89, no. 61). In other words, his mother's family were conversos.
136. *Discurso hecho por Fray Agustin Salucio maestro en santa teologia de la Orden de Santa Domingo acerca de la justicia y buen gobierno de España en los estatutos de limpieza de sangre y si conviene o no alguna limitación en ellas*, p. 26v.
137. Ibid.
138. The work was dedicated to the Archbishop of Toledo, who had earlier supported Salucio's anti-*limpieza* discourse.
139. Pedro de Valencia, 'Para la declaracion de un gran parte de la estoria apostolica...,' BNE Ms 464, Chapter 4. Curiously, Valencia writes of the Old Christians, '*you* that were far from God,' seemingly excluding himself from this group.
140. Ibid., p. 43.
141. Ibid.
142. *Arbitristas* were men who peddled solutions to Spain's economic, social, and political problems to the court. Some of these studies were quite astute analyses of Spain's woes, and plausible ideas for recovery; others were more fanciful nostrums. See Jean Vilar, *Literatura y*

Economia: La figura satirica del arbitrista en el Siglo de Oro (Madrid: Selecta de Revista de Occidente, 1973). In his short story, 'The Dog's Colloquy,' Cervantes presents us with an *arbitrista* whose idea for enriching the Spanish treasury is through one day's compulsory fasting a month for subjects between the age of 14 and 60. The money saved by each person was then to be handed over to the state.

143. Martín González Cellorigo, *Memorial de la política necesaria y útil restauración de España y estados de ella, y desempeño universal de estos*, ed. José de Ayala (Madrid: Sociedad Estatal Quinto Centenario, 1991).
144. 'Discurso sobre el acrecimiento de la labor de la tierra,' BNE ms. 5586.
145. The first obligation of kings, like that of shepherds, is to make their flock 'strong, healthy, and fat.' Cited from a letter to Diego Mardones, Philip III's confessor, BNE Ms 11160, fol. 17 r°.
146. Cited from Grace Magnier, p. 239.
147. For an examination of Velázquez's canvas in the context of the Count-Duke of Olivares' political program and the tensions it created at Philip IV's court, see Chap. 6.
148. Pedro de Valencia, "Tratado acerca de los moriscos de España," in *Obras completas* IV/2 (León: Universidad de León, 1999), p. 117.
149. Ibid., p. 125.
150. Ibid., p. 127. Valencia cites Isaiah 33, 1.
151. Ibid., pp. 413–415.
152. 'El discurso de Pedro de Valencia sobre el pergamino y láminas de Granada,' in Pedro de Valencia, *Obras completas* IV/2, p. 438.
153. Ibid., p. 444.
154. Ibid., pp. 454–455.
155. It was Pedro de Castro who had requested this brief from the partisan Clement VIII to prevent criticism of the works.
156. *Obras completas* IV/2, p. 332. The Lead Books were only sent to Rome for analysis a year after Pedro de Castro's death, in 1624. They were declared anathema in 1682.

Chapter 6: Diego Velázquez and the Subtle Art of Protest

1. Blunt believed that Poussin's philosophy, expressed through his classical, rationalist canvases, was influenced by the view of the *libertines*, a group of French humanists 'who saw in the teachings of ancient philosophy a moral code on which to base their lives,' and whose rationalist outlook 'tended on occasion to be in conflict with the orthodox teachings of the Roman Catholic Church.' Anthony Blunt, *Poussin* (London: Pallas Athene, 1995), p. 211.

2. See Una Roman D'Elia, *The Poetics of Titian's Religious Paintings* (Cambridge: Cambridge University Press, 2005). D'Elia uses the singularly inappropriate term 'decorum' to describe Titian's dissimulative practice. This implies that the painter was driven by prudish conservatism, not canny self-preservation. A better term, one that was used by Titian's humanist contemporaries, is prudence.
3. Augusto Gentili, 'Tiziano e la religione,' in Joseph Manca ed., *Titian 500* (Hanover, New Hampshire: National Gallery of Art, Center for Advanced Studies in Visual Arts, 1993), pp. 147–165. Nicodemus was the Pharisee who visited Jesus in secret. Calvin used the term Nicodemite to describe secret adherents of the Reformed Church in Catholic lands.
4. David Davies, 'The Ascent of the Mind to God: El Greco's Religious Imagery and Spiritual Reform in Spain' in *El Greco: Identity and Transformation* (Madrid: Skira, 1999), pp. 187–215.
5. Antonio Palomino de Castro y Velasco, *El museo pictórico y escala óptica*, p. 265. First published in 1726, *El museo pictórico* consists of 226 short biographies of Spanish artists and 'those illustrious foreigners who have collected in these provinces.' Palomino did not know Velázquez personally; he was, however, a friend of Juan de Alfaro, who spent some time in Velázquez's workshop and provided information for his study. Palomino also relied upon Francisco Pacheco's *El arte de la pintura* (1649) for background information on Velázquez, scant though this is. The major nineteenth-century work on Velázquez is Carl Justi's *Diego Velázquez und sein Jahrhundert* (1888). For his account of Velázquez's background, Justi borrows from Pacheco's and Palomino's works, besides making use of the painter's *probanza* for the Order of Santiago. He also repeats Palomino's unfounded assertion that Velázquez's paternal and maternal family lines were noble. In 1960, to commemorate the 300th anniversary of Velázquez's death, the Dirección General de Bellas Artes published the two-volume *Varia Velazqueña*, edited by Antonio Gallego Burin, which included much of the documentation on the painter's life available up to that point. The essays in Michael Clarke ed. *Velázquez in Seville* (New Haven and London: Yale University Press, 1996) present useful background information on the social and cultural environment of the young Velázquez. This picture was amplified in 1999 with the catalogue to the exhibition *Velázquez y Sevilla*, to commemorate the 400th anniversary of Velázquez's birth. In the same year I published an article titled 'Velázquez's Secret History' in the *Boletín del Museo del Prado* 35 (1999), with new documentation on Velázquez's family, discovered in the Seville Provincial Archive. Part of the present chapter incorporates information first presented in that article.

6. For Velázquez's *probanza* for the Order of Santiago, see *Varia Velazqueña*, Madrid, 1960, pp. 301–377.
7. Witness no. 23.
8. Witness no. 64.
9. Witness nos. 84 and 86.
10. See *Varia Velazqueña*, p. 213, doc. 2.
11. Ibid., doc. 1.
12. Meat tax exemption was given to nobles, churchmen, university degree holders, and *familiares* (honorary members) of the Inquisition. Diego Ortiz de Zúñiga, in his *Anales eclesiásticos de Sevilla (año 1515)*, writes, 'Returning the the blanca coin for meat purchases is absolutely no proof of hidalgo status.' Quoted from Carl Justi, *Velázquez y su siglo* (Madrid: Espasa Calpe, 1953), p. 760.
13. Antonio Palomino, *El museo pictórico*, pp. 265–266.
14. Ibid., p. 266.
15. To understand better the Council's reaction to the Velázquez candidacy, one needs to examine it against the Council's ongoing dispute with the Crown. The relationship between Philip IV and the Council, and between the king's privado, the Count-Duke of Olivares, and the Council, was often fractious. The Council resented the Crown presenting it with dubious candidates for titles and then interfering in its decision-making; the Crown objected to the Council's stringent regulations regarding a candidate's noble ancestry and *limpieza de sangre*, which too often created difficulties (although not insurmountable ones) for Crown favorites. Olivares was particularly incensed by the Council's *limpieza de sangre* regulations, and introduced the *patria común* measure to bypass them. This stated that the court was a historical unity equal to a candidate's country of origin, and could thus be a substitute for the true *patria* in investigation proceedings for the noble orders. Portuguese *conversos* in particular took advantage of the *patria común* privilege to avoid in-depth inquiries into their ancestry. It was this privilege that Velázquez was referring to in his letter to the king of 29 June 1658. For a description of the Council of the Orders and its relations with Philip IV, see Elena Postigo Castillanos, *Honor y Privilegio en la Corona de Castilla: El Consejo de los Ordenes y los Caballeros de Habito en el Siglo XVII* (Valladolid: Junta de Castilla y León, 1988), pp. 138–180.
16. In June 1602 Fernando Velázquez, the painter's uncle, submitted himself to a *limpieza de sangre probanza*. One of the *probanza* witnesses, Juan Fernández Román, noted that Juan Velázquez Moreno and his wife, Ana Mexía, had died of *landres* (bubonic plague) in 1599. See Archivo de Protocolos de Sevilla (APS) Oficio 13, 1602, libro 5, fols.

255-257. This *probanza* is 1 of 24 notarial documents that I have discovered in Seville's Archivo de Protocolos which relate to Velázquez's maternal family. The documents are contained in the registers of the notarial offices 1, 11, 13, and 21, and span the period 1566–1602.
17. Diego Velázquez's parents' marriage certificate states that the bride's mother was Juana Mexía (and not Catalina de Zayas, as the painter claims in his *probanza*). This is confirmed by documents that I have discovered in Seville's Archivo de Protocolos.
18. Antonio Domínguez Ortiz, *Los judeoconversos en España y America*, p. 202. The number of successful converso families in Seville seeking noble titles had created a situation in the early seventeenth century in which deception and bribery were inevitable. A particularly unsavory product of this environment was the *linajudo*, a man who examined the family lineages of suspected conversos with the intention of either stymieing a candidate's petition for a noble title or, more often, extorting money in return for favorable testimony. See Ruth Pike, 'The Dramatist Diego Jiménez de Enciso and the *Linajudos* of Seville,' *Bulletin of Hispanic Studies* 70 (1993), pp. 115–119; and Elena Postigo Castellanos, *Honor y privilegio en la corona de Castilla*, p. 149.
19. Ruth Pike, 'The Dramatist Diego Jiménez de Enciso.'
20. In the first years of the sixteenth century, the Crown, strapped for funds, gave conversos the opportunity to buy back property taken from their ancestors in Inquisition prosecutions. Lists were then made of the interested parties; later these lists were used by *linajudos* to unmask New Christian candidates for noble titles, or by the Inquisition in proceedings against alleged Judaizers. See Claudio Guillén 'Un padrón de conversos sevillanos (1510)' *Bulletin Hispanique* 65.1–2 (1963), pp. 49–98.
21. Ruth Pike, '*Converso* Lineage and Tribulations of the Sevillian Poet Juan de Jáuregui,' *Romance Quarterly* 38.4 (1991) pp. 423–429. For a longer account of Jáuregui's petition for entry into the Military Order of Calatrava, see José Jordán de Urríes y Azara, *Bibliografía y estudio crítico de Jáuregui* (Madrid: Real Academia Española, 1899). Jordán de Urríes concluded, despite what Ruth Pike states was 'substantial information to the contrary,' that Jáuregui's family, on all sides, was Old Christian and of *hidalgo* origin. The biographer of Enciso, Emilio Cotarelo y Mori, writing in 1914, also stated that his subject was an Old Christian hidalgo, again ignoring substantial evidence to the contrary. See Emilio Cotarelo y Mori, 'Don Diego Jiménez de Enciso y su teatro,' *Boletín de la Real Academia Española* 1 (1914), pp. 208–248, 385–415, 510–550.

22. Despite the evidence that Enciso's two nephews and Jáuregui were from Jewish backgrounds, all three men eventually received their noble titles. It is likely that the Count-Duke of Olivares, a friend of both Jáuregui and Enciso, and himself vehemently opposed to the *limpieza de sangre* statutes (see note 11), was instrumental in gaining the candidates their knighthoods. Philip IV personally intervened on Jáuregui's behalf. See Pike, '*Converso* Lineage and Tribulations of the Sevillian Poet Juan de Jáuregui,' and 'The Dramatist Diego Jiménez.'
23. Julián Gállego, *Velázquez en Sevilla* (Sevilla: Universidad de Sevilla, 1994), pp. 20–21.
24. Antonio Domínguez Ortiz, *La clase social de los conversos*, p. 82.
25. Edward Glaser, 'Referencias Antisemitas en la Literatura Peninsular de la Edad de Oro,' *Nueva Revista de Filología Hispanica* 8.1 (1954), p. 49.
26. See *Varia Velazqueña*, p. 302.
27. Julio Caro Baroja, *Los judíos en la España moderna y contemporánea*, Vol. I, pp. 218–221.
28. Ibid., p. 206. See also Pilar Huerga Criado, *En la raya de Portugal: solidaridad y tensiones en la comunidad judeoconverso* (Salamanca: Universidad de Salamanca, 1993), pp. 36–37.
29. In the Simón de Pineda notarial register for 1597 (1597, libro 3, fol. 1054) we find a *confeccionario* (pharmacist), Diego Rodríguez, entering into a business agreement with a Fernando Vallejo. Diego Rodríguez describes himself as a resident of Seville, in the San Salvador neighborhood, and the son of Manuel Rodríguez and Leonor Díaz, residents of Mora (Moura?, 140 kilometers northwest of Seville) in the kingdom of Portugal. He is also, he informs us, the husband of Maria de Silva, the daughter of Pedro Hernandez and Isabel de Silva, residents of Seville. Is this a description of Velázquez's paternal grandparents? Certainly the names fit. Unfortunately, the Simón de Pineda notarial registers have yielded no further information; the document thus presents us with no more than an intriguing possibility.
30. The information on the Velázquez Moreno family comes from the research I undertook in the notarial records of Seville's *Archivo de Protocolos*, from 1998 to 1999. I discovered 20 references to the tailor and businessman, taking his story back to the year 1566. Velázquez Moreno made his breeches from velvet, for the quality end of the clothes market. The velvet was very probably woven by Juan's brother, Francisco, a velvet weaver based in the city of Granada. For a more expansive account of Velázquez Moreno's merchant activities, see Kevin Ingram, 'Velázquez's Secret History,' in the *Boletín del Prado* 35 (1999), pp. 78–84. For the converso presence in the textile trade, see

Domínguez Ortiz, *Los Judeoconversos en España y America*, pp. 202–203; and *La clase social de los conversos*, pp. 149–151. See also Caro Baroja, *Los judíos en la España moderna*, Vol. I, pp. 353–357.

31. For Jews and conversos in the notarial profession, see Caro Baroja, *Los judíos en la España moderna*, Vol. I, p. 353; and Domínguez Ortiz, *La clase social de los conversos*, p. 149.
32. For the incidence of the Mexía surname in Seville's converso community, see Juan Gil, *Los conversos y la Inquisición sevillana*, Vol. IV (Sevilla: Universidad de Sevilla, 2001), pp. 461–467.
33. In 1589 Ana Velázquez was already married and Fernando was working as a notary in the notarial office of his father's friend, Simón de Pineda. I assume therefore that both Ana and Fernando were born around 1570, and certainly no later than 1573. Gerónima Velázquez gave birth to her sixth child, Francisco, in 1617. I therefore estimate that she was born no earlier than 1577.
34. The ceremony was, however, recorded in the San Pedro church registers. See *Varia Velazqueña*, p. 213, doc. 1. There were three witnesses to Juan and Gerónima's wedding ceremony in December 1597: a music teacher, Juan de Vargas, and two notaries, Antonio de Ripa and Simón de Pineda. Pineda figures prominently in Velázquez Moreno's story; he was the merchant's preferred notary during the last 12 years of his life; he was also the employer of Velázquez Moreno's son, Fernando, and a witness to the baptism of Juan Rodríguez and Gerónima Velázquez's second child, Juan (named after the maternal grandfather; the first child, Diego, having been named after the paternal one).
35. Francisco Rodríguez Marín, *Nuevos datos para las biografías de cien escritores de los siglos XVI y XVII*, p. 457, pp. 464–465, and 466–467. The documents do not explain why Pacheco and his three brothers carried out this do-it-yourself *limpieza de sangre probanza*. It was not, however, an unusual occurrence in a city so obsessed with *limpieza*. Perhaps the four wished to have a certificate of purity ready in case of problems. Pacheco would surely have used it to enter the Inquisition as a *familiar* in 1618.
36. This is also the surname she gives on her 1618 wedding certificate. *Varia Velazqueña*, p. 218.
37. For this informal academy, see Jonathan Brown, *Images and Ideas in Seventeenth-Century Spanish Painting* (Princeton: Princeton University Press, 1978), Chapter 1; and Bonaventura Bassegoda's introduction to Francisco Pacheco, *Arte de la Pintura*, Madrid, 1990, pp. 22–32.
38. Pacheco maintained close links to the Society all his life. His confessor for 24 years was the Jesuit father Gaspar de Zamora (d. 1621). Luis de

Alcázar was a member of a wealthy and influential family of conversos. His father was the poet Baltasar Alcázar, who was secretary to the first Duke of Alcalá. We know nothing about Juan de Pineda's background; however, his interest in Hebrew, his commentaries on the Old Testament Job and Ecclesiastes, and his elaborate study of King Solomon, suggest that he too may have been one of the early Jesuits' large contingent of conversos. Both Alcázar and Pineda shared with Pacheco a devotion to the *Inmaculada*.

39. Jáuregui and Fonseca y Figueroa had Jewish ancestors. Francisco de Rioja's parents were Anton García of Alcalá Mayor and Leonor Rodríguez of Seville. In his application for a royal chaplaincy in 1617, Rioja stated first that he was 'hijo a padres muy honrados,' then corrected it to 'padres bien nacidos.' He did not state, as was usual practice, that they were *cristianos viejos* or *limpios*. See Francisco de Rioja, *Poesía*, ed. Begoña López Bueno (Madrid: Cátedra, 1984), p. 15.

40. For Catalina de Jesús, see Álvaro Huerga, *Historia de los alumbrados IV: Los alumbrados de Sevilla* (Madrid: Fundación Universitaria Española, 1988), Chapter 4. Catalina's maestro, Pedro de Hojeda, was rector of the University of Baeza, an educational establishment which Juan de Ávila helped found. For the *alumbrado* movement in the University of Baeza, see Álvaro Huerga, *Los alumbrados de Baeza*. Huerga believes that the attack on the *alumbrados* in Seville came as a direct result of the reform-minded Count-Duke of Olivares taking control of the Spanish government at this time, and notes that Olivares nominated Andrés Pacheco as Inquisitor General in 1622, with greater vigilance in mind. This is most unlikely. Olivares was no friend of the Inquisition. He dismissed the Inquisitor General Luis de Aliarga in 1621 because he was a corrupt careerist and a member of the Lerma faction. He replaced him with Andrés Pacheco, a Franciscan and a man of humanist education. The attack on the Seville *alumbrados* was engineered not by Pacheco but locally, by Dominican inquisitors, who were both disturbed by the growth of clandestine mystical sects in the city and offended by the way one of these sects, the Congregation of the Pomegranate, promoted the cult of the Immaculate Conception, a concept that the Dominicans vehemently resisted.

41. For my information on the Congregation I have relied on the following works: Álvaro Huerga, *Historia de los alumbrados*, Vol. IV, Chap. 8; Vicente Lleó Cañal, 'La Sevilla del Siglo de Oro: ortodoxias y heterodoxias, in Javier Portús Pérez ed., *Fábulas de Velázquez: Mitología e historia sagrada en el Siglo de Oro* (Madrid: Museo Nacional del Prado, 2007), pp. 95–113; Fernando J. Campese Gallego, 'Gómez Camacho: Un profeta paradójico en el Siglo de Oro,' *Investigaciones históricas* 28

(2008), pp. 11–28, and by the same author, 'Rodrigo Álvarez, SJ (1523–1587), el sucesor del profeta,' *Revista de Historia Jerónimo Zurita* 85 (2010), pp. 207–228; Antonio González Polvillo, 'La Congregación de la Granada, el Inmaculismo sevillano y los retratos realizados por Francisco Pacheco de tres de sus principales protagonistas: Miguel Cid, Bernard de Toro y Mateo Vázquez de Leca,' *Atrio*, 15–16 (2009–2010), pp. 47–72.
42. Fernando J. Cámpese Gallego, 'Gómez Camacho,' p. 14.
43. Ibid. While confined to his Inquisition cell, Camacho requested that Juan de Ávila examine his visions, believing no doubt that the *beato*'s mission and his own were similar. However, Ávila, who had been imprisoned in the same building some years previously, was not prepared to support Camacho's more eccentric path toward change, and classified his prophesies as *vanidades*. Ibid., p. 15.
44. The Revelation of St. John the Divine, 12: 1–3.
45. See Miguel Jiménez Monteserín, 'Los hermanos Valdés y el mundo judeoconverso conquense,' p. 389, note 27.
46. According to Álvarez's early Jesuit biographer, Juan de Santibáñez, his father was a Portuguese physician who gained a doctorate at the University of Salamanca. See Fernando J. Campese Gallego, 'Rodrigo Álvarez' p. 208, note 7.
47. Ibid., pp. 216–218.
48. Antonio González Polvillo, 'La Congregación de la Granada,' p. 53.
49. '...fue concebido como vos, y como yo y como Martín Lucero,' Vicente Lleó Cañal, 'La Sevilla del Siglo de Oro,' p. 102.
50. Cited from Susan L. Stratton, *The Immaculate Conception in Spanish Art* (Cambridge: Cambridge University Press, 1994), p. 72. I have maintained the Spanish word *religiosos*, which from the context I believe is to be used ironically for a lay religious community. Stratton translates the word as 'monks.'
51. According to the Morisco translator of the Lead Books, Miguel de Luna (who was also, probably, one of the forgers), the cryptic Arabic text revealed the prophetic teachings of the Virgin Mary, addressed chiefly to Saint Peter. It also revealed that these teachings had been translated into Arabic by Cecilius, a first-century Arab evangelist who accompanied Saint James on his apostolic mission to Spain, and was martyred in Granada. Among the books' revelations was Mary's disclosure that she had been immaculately conceived. The Virgin also stated her love for the Arab people and their language. For a comparison of the Lead Books forgery with converso assimilationist propaganda of the late sixteenth century, see Chap. 4.

52. Antonio González Polvillo, 'La Congregación de la Granada,' pp. 69–72.
53. For Pacheco's possible membership of the Congregation, see Vicente Lleó Cañal, 'La Sevilla del Siglo de Oro,' pp. 95–113; and Antonio González Polvillo, 'La Congregación de la Granada,' pp. 9–26.
54. Cited from Lleó Cañal, p. 107.
55. Ibid., p.108.
56. Ibid., p. 104.
57. Antonio González Polvillo refers to this strange comment in 'La Congregación de Granada,' p. 10, note 25.
58. We only have information on two of the bodegones' early owners, both of whom were members of Pacheco's humanist circle. These were Juan de Fonseca y Figueroa, owner of The Waterseller, and the third Duke of Alcalá de los Gazules, owner of Christ in the House of Martha and Mary. For the provenance of the latter painting, see Jonathan Brown and Richard Kagan, 'The Duke of Alcalá: His collection and its Evolution,' in *Art Bulletin*, 2, 1987, pp. 231–55. The Alcalá family was closely linked to both a humanist and a religious reform movement in Seville. The first duke's administrator, Gaspar Zapata (a converso), was accused of Lutheranism in the Seville Protestant trials of 1557–1559, and fled to France. The first duke's sister, Doña María Enríquez, Marchioness of Villanueva del Fresno, was herself intimately connected with this group of 'Protestant' clerics, although she managed to escape prosecution. See Juan Gil, *Los Conversos y La Inquisición Sevillana*, vol. 1, pp. 353–66.
59. Francisco Pacheco, *El arte de la pintura*, p. 614.
60. Velázquez's daughter Francisca was baptized on Easter Sunday (18 May) 1619. Her godfather was Esteban Delgado of the San Lorenzo neighborhood of Seville. See *Varia Velazqueña*, Vol. I, pp. 218–219. It is possible that Velázquez's young Magus is a reference to Delgado.
61. Pérez Lozano calls attention to the fig in the glass as a reference to Fonseca y Figueroa in 'Velázquez y los gustos concepcionistas: el Aguador y su destinatario,' in *Boletin del Museo e Instituto Camón Aznar* 54 (1993), pp. 9–10. For Velázquez's connection to Fonseca, see José López Navío, 'Velázquez tasa los cuadros de su protector D. Juan de Fonseca,' *Varia Velazqueña*, Madrid, 1960.
62. José López Navío, 'Don Juan de Fonseca, canónigo maestrescuela de Sevilla,' *Archivo Hispalense*, 126–127 (1964), pp. 83–103 (85–86). López Navío mentions that Fonseca's grandmother was the conversa Ana de Ulloa. What he does not mention is that the Fonseca family formed endogamous marriages with the Ulloas for generations. The two families are intimately linked in all their branches.

63. Olivares' mother was María Pimentel de Fonseca, daughter of the fourth count of Monterrey. J.H. Elliott, *The Count-Duke of Olivares: The Statesman in an Age of Decline* (Newhaven and London: Yale University Press, 1986), p. 12. This branch of the Fonseca family also entered into marriage alliances with the Ulloas.
64. Ibid., p. 22.
65. Cited from J.H. Elliott, *The Count-Duke of Olivares*, pp. 10–11.
66. For Olivares' converso background, see ibid. In 1623, the same year that he entered the Order of Alcántara, Olivares directed the Inquisitor General to collect and burn all copies of the *Libro verde*, a work which presented an Aragonese nobility infiltrated by converso patrician families, like the Conchillos, his own ancestors. For the censorship of the *Libro verde*, see Antonio Domínguez Ortiz, *La clase social de los conversos*, p. 205.
67. J.H. Elliott, *The Count-Duke of Olivares*, pp. 300–304. For Olivares' relationship with the Portuguese converso merchants, see also James C. Boyajian, *Portuguese Bankers at the Court of Spain, 1626–1650* (New Brunswick: Rutgers University Press, 1983), pp. 103–132.
68. J.H. Elliott, *The Count Duke of Olivares*, p. 10.
69. For Quevedo and the co-patronage issue, see Pablo Jauralde Pou, *Francisco Quevedo (1580–1645)* (Madrid: Castalia, 1998), pp. 541–572.
70. J.H. Elliott, *Spain and its World 1500–1700* (New Haven and London: Yale University Press, 1992), p. 195.
71. In 1633 Quevedo produced a pamphlet, *Execracion de los judíos*, attacking the Portuguese converso community in Madrid and their benefactor, the Count-Duke.
72. 'La isla de los monopantos,' written sometime in the 1530s, was eventually published in *La hora de todos y la fortuna con seso* (Zaragoza, 1650), after Olivares had been ousted from power. In the tale, Chinchollas (Olivares) is the leader of a group of conversos, *los monopantos*, who meet with members of the Jewish community of Salonica to hatch a plot to destabilize Christian Europe.
73. For the San Plácido affair, see Charles Lea, *A History of the Inquisition of Spain*, Vol. III, pp. 133–157; Mercedes Agullo y Cobo, 'El Monasterio de San Plácido y su fundador, el madrileño don Jerónimo de Villanueva, Protonotario de Aragón,' *Villa de Madrid* 45–46 (1975), pp. 59–68; and Carlos Pujol Buil, *Inquisición y política en el reinado de Felipe IV: los procesos de Jerónimo de Villanueva y las monjas de San Plácido, 1628–1660*, Madrid, 1993.
74. For an extensive examination of the Degradation of the Cross affair and its socio-religious implications, see Juan Ignacio Pulido Serrano,

Injurias a cristo: Religión, política y antijudaismo en el siglo XVII (Alcalá: Universidad de Alcalá, 2002), pp.109–343. The affair is also examined in some detail by Yosef Hayim Yerushalmi in *From Spanish Court to Italian Ghetto: Isaac Cardoso, a Study in Seventeenth-Century Marranism and Jewish Apologetics* (New York and London: Columbia University Press, 1971), Chapter 7.

75. Claude Stuczynski, 'Providentialism in Early Modern Catholic Iberia,' *Hebraic Political Studies* 3.4 (2008), p. 391.
76. J. H. Elliott, *The Count-Duke of Olivares*, pp. 641–642.
77. Two of these were by Francisco Camilo. In the first, four adults and three girls hold thorny rose branches, ready to whip the crucified Christ icon, while three women and a man take the enormous icon from its secret hiding place in a chimney. In the second canvas the crucified Christ, hanging by a rope from the ceiling, is whipped by a group of Judaizers. In the third canvas, by Francisco Fernandez, the Judaizers drag the cross across the floor while continuing to whip it. The fourth canvas, by Andrés Vargas, depicts two scenes from the ritual murder: in the first the group tries to burn the cross without success, in the second they chop it up to throw into a fire. The fifth canvas, by Francisco Rizi, the most important of the four painters, has not survived; however, it appears to have been a depiction of the 1632 *auto de fe*, in which the group was paraded in Madrid's Plaza Mayor, before being burnt at the stake. See Juan Ignacio Pulido Serrano, *Injurias de Cristo*, pp. 328–329.
78. *Christ after the Flagellation* has long posed a problem for art historians. Its sophisticated rendition of the human form and domination of light and space appear to place it in the period after Velázquez's first trip to Italy in 1629, and yet the background preparation, using a red-brown tint, is reminiscent of an earlier period of the painter's works. López-Rey and Jonathan Brown favor a pre-1629 dating, while Enriqueta Harris suggests a slightly later date. However, none of these scholars have related the painting to the Degradation affair. I would suggest 1632 as the probable date, sometime after the July *auto de fe*, when the Degradation became the subject of religious processions, poetic competitions, and socio-political tracts. Who commissioned the work remains a mystery. It may have been a commission from a religious house to paint a flagellation scene in commemoration of the Jewish treachery, which Velázquez transformed into something altogether different. It may also have been commissioned by someone close to the Olivares circle, whose views ran counter to the euphoria that accompanied the Portuguese conversos' executions.
79. See Gabriele Finaldi, 'Pintura y devoción,' in Javier Portús Pérez ed., *Fábulas de Velázquez*, pp. 175–201 (181).

80. Jonathan Brown, *Velázquez: Painter and Courtier* (New Haven and London: Yale University Press, 1986), p. 60.
81. Ibid.
82. The contest judges were Fray Juan Bautista Maino and Giovanni Battista Crescenzi. For Maino's and Crescenzi's support for a modern approach to painting demonstrated by Velázquez, see Jonathan Brown, *Velázquez: Painter and Courtier*, pp. 60–61. For the painters' close relationship with Olivares, see Jonathan Brown and J.H. Elliot, *A Palace for a King*, revised and expanded edition (New Haven and London: Yale University Press, 2003), p. 44.
83. Antonio Palomino, *El museo pictórico*, p. 217.
84. It is now apparent that many of the Aragonese and Valencian nobility who voted for expulsion viewed it as a profitable economic transaction. By the beginning of the seventeenth century these men were heavily in debt, their profligate lifestyles financed by loans in the form of *juros* and *censos*, which were now costing them a third or more of their annual income. By evicting their Morisco laborers from increasingly unprofitable fixed-rent lands they could sell off the terrain and pay their debts. Henry Kamen, *Spain 1469–1714: A Society in Conflict* (London: Routledge, 2005), pp. 233–234.
85. See Ruth Pike, '*Converso* Lineage and Tribulations of the Sevillian Poet Juan de Jáuregui,' *Romance Quarterly* 38.4 (1991), pp. 423–429.
86. For the many interpretations of *Los Borrachos*, see Steven N. Orso, *Velázquez, Los Borrachos, and Painting at the Court of Philip IV* (Cambridge: Cambridge University Press, 1993), Chap. 1.
87. In his *Philosofía secreta*, which Velázquez consulted for his mythological paintings, Pérez de Moya refers to Bacchus as a 'captain of great bravery who was esteemed by God for his great deeds, like pacifying discord and building cities.' Peréz de Moya, p. 305. Spanish humanists were drawn to the story that Bacchus had visited Spain in antiquity, where he founded the city of Nebrija (Lebrija). See Steven N. Orso, *Velázquez, Los Borrachos...*, pp. 97–108. See also Rosa López Torrijos, *La mitología en la pintura española del Siglo de Oro* (Madrid: Cátedra, 1995), pp. 337–349. The fact that Bacchus represented a link between Spain and the classical Greek world would have further inspired Velázquez to use this god as a symbol of the humanist credo. Orso's view is that the Bacchus canvas is an analogy for the compassionate rule of Philip IV. Velázquez may indeed be alluding to Philip, but Orso ignores the fact that his Bacchus is sitting in judgment of something. If we wish to penetrate the mysteries of the canvas we first need to take this into account.

88. To my knowledge all previous interpreters of *Los Borrachos* have viewed the men that surround Bacchus as a homogeneous, peasant group. This is a natural enough mistake, one that the artist has deliberately provoked by bunching the figures together and by placing the cloaked figure within the peasant group, on the right-hand side of the canvas.
89. Velázquez may have based his peasant tableau on the *autos sacramentales*— the fanciful and often elaborate Eucharist dramas that were popular in post-Tridentine Spain, presented at Easter and Corpus Christi. For Calderon de la Barca's famous auto sacramental, *El nuevo palacio del Retiro*, see Jonathan Brown and John H. Elliott, *A Palace for a King*, pp. 240–241.
90. *Los Borrachos* was painted sometime between September 1628 and June 1629, when the painting is first mentioned as forming part of the collection of Philip IV. Steven N. Orso, *Velázquez, Los Borrachos*, p. 35. Jáuregui's epic poem *Orfeo* was published in 1624. For an examination of Jáuregui's poem, see Juan de Jáuregui, *Poesía*, pp. 63–76. Velázquez was well acquainted with Jáuregui, who collaborated on Francisco Pacheco's *Arte de la pintura* and his *Libro de descripción de verdadero retratos*. In the *Retratos*, Jáuregui provides poetic accompaniments to Pacheco's portraits of Benito Arias Montano and Baltasar de Alcázar. In his elegy to Alcázar, Jáuregui refers to the '*blasón del arte*' [art's noble crest], and to the artist's ability to immortalize both his subject and himself. In 1629, around the time that *Los Borrachos* was painted, Jáuregui formed part of a group of painters who petitioned the royal exchequer for exemption from the *alcabala* (sales) tax, on the grounds that their artistic status conferred noble standing upon them, and thus relieved them of tax payments. Juan de Jáuregui, *Poesía*, ed. Juan Matas Caballero (Madrid: Cátedra, 1993), pp. 29–30.
91. Ovid, *Metamorphoses*, trans. A. D. Melville (Oxford: Oxford University Press, 1986), p. 251.
92. In a recent radiograph of *Los Borrachos* it was established that this figure and the begging man in the opposite corner of the canvas were added at a later stage in the painting process. As the art historian Jonathan Brown notes, the two men 'are painted with thinner color layers and seem to float on the surface.' According to Brown, these late additions were made after Velázquez 'sensed a certain inertia in the composition' See Jonathan Brown and Carmen Garrido, *Velázquez. The Technique of Genius* (New Haven and London: Yale University Press, 1998), pp. 34–35. However, I would suggest that the laureled silhouette was always an important component of Velázquez's design, deliberately added at a later stage in the composition, and thus with thinner color layers, to convey the fact that he was physically distanced from the

other protagonists, observing the scene but not involved in the action. The other figure was also painted at a later stage in the process to give the composition a tonal as well as a geometrical balance.

93. Several days after Fonseca died, on 16 January 1627, Velázquez was called upon to evaluate his paintings. See José López Navio, 'Velázquez tasa los cuadros de su protector D. Juan de Fonseca,' *Archivo Español de Arte* 34 (1961), pp. 53–84. Velázquez valued his *Aguador* at 400 ducados, by far the highest price he placed on any of the canvases. Among the lot was a portrait of the father of Neostoicism, Justus Lipsius. We also know from this document who bought some of the works. The principal buyers were Gaspar de Bracamonte, later third Duke of Peñaranda, and Manuel Cortizos, the Portuguese converso merchant and financier who founded a wealthy financial dynasty in the capital. Cortizos bought a landscape, eight paintings of hermits, and a Veronica. In 1641 Manuel and two of his brothers entered the Order of Alcántara, despite their evident converso background. Several years later, members of the clan were investigated by the Inquisition for Judaizing. See Julio Caro Baroja, *Los judíos en la España moderna y contemporanea*, Vol. II, pp. 115–134; and Carmen Saintz Ayán, 'Consolidación y destrucción de patrimonios financieros en la edad moderna: Los Cortizos (1630–1715),' in Ricardo Robledo ed., *Fortuna y negocios: formación y gestión de los grandes patrimonios (siglos XVI–XX)* (Valladolid: Universidad de Valladolid, 2002), pp. 73–98.

94. Alejandro Vergara, 'El universo cortesano de Rubens,' in Jonathan Brown ed. *Velázquez, Rubens y Van Dyck* (Madrid: Museo Nacional del Prado, 1999), p. 84.

95. For Peter Paul Rubens' Neostoical beliefs, see Frances Huemer, *Rubens and the First Roman Circle: Studies of the First Decade* (New York: Garland Publishing, 1996), pp. 55–85.

96. For Marcos Pérez, see Chap. 3. He was the brother of Luis Pérez, the close friend of Benito Arias Montano. For Montano's relationship with Luis Pérez, see Chap. 5.

97. It is also noteworthy that from 1596 to 1600 Peter Paul Rubens studied under Otto Van Veen (Vaenius), a painter scholar and a friend of Lipsius. Like Lipsius, Van Veen had also moved across the Protestant-Catholic divide. In fact, the two men had met in Calvinist Leiden. Later they renewed their friendship in Antwerp. Peter Paul Rubens' childhood friend Francisco Raphelengius later married the daughter of the famous Antwerp printer and member of the Family of Love, Christophe Plantin.

98. Frances Huemer, *Rubens and the First Roman Circle*, pp. 56–57.

99. Alejandro Vergara, 'El universo cortesan de Rubens,' p. 82.

100. The visit to El Escorial is referred to by Francicco Pacheco in *El Arte de la Pintura*. He writes: '[Rubens] communicated little with painters, only making friends with my son-in-law [Velázquez] (with whom he had corresponded prior to his visit) and favored his paintings for their modesty, and they went together to vist El Escorial.' *El Arte de la Pintura*, p. 202.
101. Cited from Jonathan Brown, *Velázquez: Painter and Courtier*, p. 69.
102. 'un poco pin di portiere, e meno di agiutante di camera.' Letter from Flavio Atti, the Palma Embassador, to the Duchess of Palma regarding Velázquez's visit to Italy, 26 July 1629, in *Varia Velazqueña*, Vol, I, doc. 43.
103. See note 15.
104. We now know that during his second trip to Rome, from 1549 to 1551, Velázquez was in contact with the converso papal agent Juan de Córdoba, who aided him in the purchase of art for the royal collection. However, Córdoba was more than an art agent; he was one of many converso agents at the papal court who dealt with financial matters, in particular the purchase of religious offices and papal dispensations. Many of these agents' clients were fellow conversos who needed papal approval for church benefices, including dispensations in the case of *limpieza de sangre* impediments. While in Rome Velázquez painted one of the most important of these converso facilitators, Ferdinando Brandani, possibly as a favor for gaining Pope Innocent X's consent to sit for him. When Velázquez returned to Spain he maintained contact with the agent Juan de Córdoba, acting as his representative on private business transactions. On Velázquez's death, in 1660, Córdoba wrote to the painter's executors, reminding them that Velázquez still owed him money for some non-specified transaction. Was this transaction, perhaps, related to Velázquez's application to the papacy for dispensation in the matter of his Santiago knighthood? We also know that Velázquez applied, unsuccessfully, to Philip IV for permission to return to Rome in 1657, at the time that the Council of the Orders was conducting its investigations into his family background. Was Velázquez interested in returning to Italy to make doubly sure that he secured the new Pope Alexander VII's support for his noble venture? For Velázquez's relationship with Juan de Córdoba, see David García Cueto, 'Sobre las relaciones de Velázquez y Don Juan de Córdoba tras el regreso del segundo viaje a Italia,' *Archivo Español de Arte* 334 (2011), pp. 177–180. For Spain's converso agents at the papal court, see Antonio J. Díaz Rodríguez, 'Papal Bulls and Converso Brokers: New Christian Agents at the Service of the Catholic Monarchy in the Roman Curia (1550–1650),' *Journal of Levantine Studies* 6 (2016) pp. 205–223.

105. 'Even after death, envy pursued [Velázquez]. Because certain malevolent people had tried to turn his Monarch against him, with slanderous words sinisterly conveyed, it was necessary for Don Gaspar de Fuensalida, as a friend, an executor of his will, and as a court official, to satisfy the king, in a private audience with His Majesty, that these charges were untrue, and to assure him that Velázquez was faithful, legal [lawful], and upright in everything he did.' Antonio Palomino, *El museo pictórico*, p. 271.
106. Jonathan Brown, *Velázquez: Painter and Courtier*, pp. 216–217; Javier Cordero y Ricardo J. Hernández, *Velázquez un logístico en la corte de Felipe IV*, Vol. I (Madrid: Díaz de Santos, 2000), pp. 149–151.
107. The first scholar to identify the noble artist theme in *Las Meninas* was Charles de Tolnay. See Charles de Tolnay, 'Velázquez's *Las Hilanderas* and *Las Meninas* (An Interpretation),' *Gazette de Beaux-Arts* 35 (1949), pp. 21–38 (36).
108. Again, Tornay was first to point out that the two canvases on the back wall addressed the theme of noble artistry, although he identified the painting on the right, erroneously, as *Apollo and Marsyas*. Tornay believed that these paintings were 'myths which symbolize the victory of divine art over human craftsmanship, or the victory of true art over unskillfulness.' This view of the noble-artist-god defeating lesser beings has been repeated by other scholars, who, unlike Rubens and Jordaens, miss the ambivalence of Ovid's tales. Rubens and Jordaens are not empathizing with the gods (why would they?), but with the exceptionally gifted human and satyr (half-human, half-goat) who compete with them and, arguably, triumph. This is also the theme of Titian's *Apollo and Marsyas*, in which Titian presents himself as Midas contemplating the fate of the satyr Marsyas (he is flayed alive) for challenging the god. In fact, Midas is not present in this Ovidian drama; he is, however, present in the contest between Pan and Apollo, in which he judges in favor of the faun. For this temerity, Apollo transformed his ears into those of a donkey. Despite the consequences, Titian sides with the judge Midas, not with Apollo.
109. Henry Kamen, *The Spanish Inquisition*, p. 293.
110. The fear that the conversos would taint society with their Jewish malfeasance is virulently expressed by Francisco de Torrejoncillo in his popular *Centinela contra judíos*, published in Madrid in 1674 and reprinted in 1674 and 1678. For an examination of Torrejoncillo's work against the background of seventeenth-century Spanish anti-Semitism, see François Soyer, *Popularizing Anti-Semitism in Early Modern Spain and its Empire* (Leiden: Brill, 2014).

Chapter 7: The Converso Returns

1. *Tratado del origen de los villanos, a quienes llaman cristianos viejos en Castilla*. Biblioteca Capitular y Colombina (Sevilla) Ms. 28-7-33. A number of studies exist on Fray Agustín Salucio: see, for example, Hipólito Sancho, 'El Maestro Fray Agustín Salucio, O.P. Contribución a la Historia Literaria Sevillana del siglo XVI,' in *Archivo Hispalense*, XVI (1952) 9–47; and Álvaro Huerga's introduction to Fray Agustín Salucio, *Avisos para los predicadores del santo evangelio*. All of these studies skirt the issue of Salucio's heterodox views and his converso background. It is likely, however, that the maternal side of the prelate's family were conversos. See Chap. 4, note 162. In 1570 the Bishop of Córdoba, Bernardo de Fresneda, wrote to the king informing him of a widespread alumbrado (heretical) movement in his diocese that was centered on the *converso* community, and he linked Salucio, '*hijo de Genoves y no de buena madre*,' to the movement (Instituto Valencia de Don Juan no. 89-393). Salucio was a close friend of Juan de Ávila and Fray Luis de Granada, and shared their views on spiritual reform. He also maintained close ties with the Seville group of humanists which formed in the 1570s and 1580s around Fernando de Herrera and Licenciado Francisco Pacheco.
2. *Discurso hecho por fray Agustín Salucio, Maestro en santa Teología, de la Orden de Santo Domingo, acerca de la justicia y buen gobierno de España en los Estatutos de limpieza de sangre: y si conviene, o no, alguna limitación de ellos*. BNE sig. R/29.688. In his *discurso*, Salucio proposed a 100-year moratorium on the limpieza statutes, at which point everyone would be an Old Christian (that is to say, their ancestors would have converted more than four generations previously). In this way Spanish society could avoid the 'scandals and nightmares' that the *limpieza* laws caused. See Antonio Domínguez Ortíz, *Los judeoconversos en España y América*, pp. 89–90.
3. Gonzalo Álvarez Chillida, *El anti-semitismo en España: La imagen del judío (1812–2002)* (Madrid: Marcial Pons, 2002), p. 55.
4. Ibid., p. 111.
5. Ibid., pp. 116–117. Mendizabal came from a family of merchants based in Cádiz. The family was almost certainly of converso origin, a background the politician and financier attempted to disguise by changing his surname from Méndez, one closely associated with a Spanish and Portuguese converso merchant community, to Mendizabal, which suggested Basque, Old Christian origins. He even lied about his place of birth, replacing Cádiz with Bilbao, capital of the northern province of Vizcaya.
6. Amador de los Rios, *Estudios sobre los judíos de España* (Madrid: D. M. Díaz, 1848), x.

7. José Amador de los Ríos, *Historia social, política y religiosa de los judíos de España y Portugal*, Vol. III, p. 506.
8. For the debate, see Antonio Santoveña Setién, 'Una alternativa cultural católica para la España de la Restauración.' *Investigaciones Historicas* 12 (1992), pp. 237–253.
9. Unamuno's views on Spain's 'intra-historic' spiritual force, which he termed '*la tradición eterna*,' were put forward in his work *En torno al casticismo* (1895). The theory is mostly an amalgam of Hegel's *volksgeist* and William James' 'stream of consciousness.' See Gayana Jurkevich, *The Elusive Self: Archetypal Approaches to the Novel of Miguel de Unamuno* (Columbia, Missouri: University of Missouri Press, 1991).
10. '[El Greco] came to Spain,' Unamuno wrote in 1914, 'to give us, better than anyone else, the pictorial and graphic expression of the Castilian soul; and he revealed, with his brushes, our spiritual naturalism. I say spiritual nationalism and not idealist realism, because the Castilian soul of Don Quijote and the mystics is not, in effect, idealist, but spiritualist ... Idealism is of this world, it is pagan, platonic, of the Renaissance. Our Castilian spiritualism is mystical, of another world, medieval.' Quoted from José Álvarez Lopera, *De Cean a Cossio: La fortuna crítica del Greco en el siglo XIX* (Madrid: Fundación, 1987), p. 98.
11. For Juan de Ávila's and Teresa of Ávila's backgrounds, see, respectively, Chaps. 3 and 4. For Juan de la Cruz's ancestry, see José-Carlos Gomez-Menor, *El linaje familiar de Santa Teresa y de San Juan de la Cruz. Sus parientes toledanos*, Toledo, 1970, and 'Los antepasados judaizantes de Juan de Yepes. Nuevos documentos útiles para la biografía de San Juan de la Cruz,' *Boletín de la Real Academia de la Historia*, 190 (1993), pp. 13–30. El Greco's close association with Toledo's converso community and his heterodox religious views are examined by David Davies in his article 'The Ascent of the Mind to God: El Greco's Religious Imagery and Spiritual Reform in Spain' in José Álvarez Lopera ed., *El Greco: Identity and Transformation. Crete. Italy. Spain.* Madrid, 1999. pp. 187–215.
12. The Spanish government made overblown claims about its support of the Jews in World War II, with the view to getting its post-war sanctions lifted. Meanwhile, in Spain itself the government launched a campaign against the new Jewish state of Israel, which had been one of the United Nations states to vote against lifting sanctions. See Gonzalo Álvarez Chillido, *El antisemitismo en España*, p. 425. For an account of Spain's Jewish policy in World War II, see Haim Avni, *Spain, the Jews and Franco* (Philadelphia: Jewish Publication Society, 1982).
13. Claudio Sánchez Albornoz, *España, un enigma histórico*, 2 vols. (Buenos Aires: Editorial Sudamericana, 1956).

14. For Sánchez-Albornoz's anti-semitic views, see his chapter 'Lo judaico en la forja de lo hispanico,' in *España, un enigma historico*. Benzion Netanyahu examines these pages in 'Una visión española de la historia judía en España: Sánchez Albornoz,' in Ángel Alcalá ed. *Judíos. Sefarditas. Conversos*, pp. 89–121.
15. Claudio Sánchez-Albornoz, *España, un enigma historico*, Vol. I., 2nd edition (Buenos Aires: Editorial Sudamerican, 1962), p. 57. Sánchez-Albornoz believed that both the Roman and Visigothic cultures influenced Spanish culture; however, the influence was always tempered or guided by the Hispanic *herencia temperamental*. As for the Muslim influence on the Spanish character, he took the view that this, like that of the Jews, was negligible. In his opinion, Islamic culture, or the culture of the East, did not begin to penetrate al-Andalus before the eleventh century, at the time when Christian forces began to overtake much of the peninsula. The majority of Muslims, that is to say, the Neo-Muslims of Hispano Roman descent, and all of the Mozarabs, who later found themselves subjects in a Christian realm, were immunized against Arab acculturation through their 'temperamental inheritance' as well as through their physical separation from the real Arab world for the first three hundred years of Islamic rule. See ibid., pp. 157–175. The view that Arab culture barely penetrated Iberian society during the first three centuries of Islamic occupation is described by the Islamist and Hispanist Thomas F. Glick as 'simply and clearly wrong.' See the introduction to Thomas F. Glick, *Islamic and Christian Spain in the Early Middle Ages* (Princeton: Princeton University Press, 1979).
16. Claudio Sánchez-Albornoz, *España, un enigma histórica*, p. 61.
17. Ibid., Prologue.
18. This comparison was later championed by a group of conservative Spanish scholars whose works obfuscated Sánchez-Albornoz's ideological bias for a *castizo* Spain. This is the case of Jose Luis Gómez-Martínez's *Américo Castro y el origen de los Españoles: historia de una polémica*. Writing in 1975, at the beginning of the Transition period, Gómez-Martínez purports to present a disinterested essay on the Castro Sánchez-Albornoz debate while situating the medievalist on the moral and academic high ground. Gómez-Martínez writes: 'Sánchez-Albornoz, *in some ways representing historians* [my emphasis], made it a personal issue to challenge Castro's theories, not only refuting those that seemed erroneous, but also presenting his own version of the Spanish past' (p. 52), and several pages later he notes: 'The most systematic and most comprehensive attack on Castro's work was without a doubt that of Sánchez-Albornoz. His work, and in particular the two

voluminous tomes of *España, un enigma histórico* should have been sufficient, given the intensity and acuteness with which they were written, to end a polemic that was barely started. The result, however, was quite different. *España, un enigma histórico* gave rise to an energetic and determined counteroffensive by Castro [and his disciples] ... who, taking sides with Castro, began to publish numerous articles, the great majority of which were of a strong polemic character ... The disciples of Sánchez-Albornoz, as was to be expected, took it upon themselves to defend their master, who in general remained faithful to his maxim: "only engage in combat with worthy opponents [*No toreo sino miuras*]."' See José Luis Gómez-Martínez, *Américo Castro y el origin de los Españoles: historia de una polémica*, Madrid, 1975. More recently, José Andrés-Gallego has dismissed Castro's *España en su historia* by citing a note written in a copy of the work by a certain Rafael Altamira. Andrés-Gallego writes: 'Striking are the lines written by Rafael Altamira in the front of his personal copy of Castro's work: "A book full of prejudices against Spain, clearly defeatist, and an exaggerated tribute to his new friends, who are also defeatists, because they proclaim themselves the most worthy Spaniards."' And Andrés-Gallego continues: 'In 1957, Claudio Sánchez-Albornoz, also an academic chair in the Central University and a radical republican—in reality Azañista—minister of state in 1933, ambassador to Portugal in 1936 and president of the Republican Government in exile since 1939, replied to Américo Castro with *España, un enigma histórico*, in which he demonstrated documentarily the primordial weight of Christian Rome [on Spain].' See José Andrés-Gallego, *Historia de la historiografía española* (Madrid: Ediciones Encuentros, 2003), pp. 344–345. In his autobiographical *Mi testamento histórico-político* (1975) Sánchez-Albornoz stated, without offering any proof, that Castro was himself of Jewish background, and that was why he spoke 'the voice of the blood.' See Gonzalo Álvarez Chillida, *Antisemitismo en España*, p. 434.

19. Cited from the 1938 *Ley de Reforma de la Enseñanza Secundaria*. See Rafael Valls Montes, 'El bachillerato universitario de 1938.' in *La universidad española bajo el régimen de Franco. Actas del Ccongreso celebrado en Zaragoza el 8 y 11 noviembre de 1989*, dirigido por Juan José Carreras Ares (Zaragoza: Institución Fernando el Católico, 1991), p. 198.
20. Alicia Alted Vigil, 'Bases político-ideológicos y jurídicos de la universidad franquista,' ibid., p. 117.
21. I am referring, in particular, to Antonio Domínguez Ortiz, *La clase social de los conversos*, and Julio Caro Baroja, *Los judíos en la España moderna y contemporánea*.

22. José Carlos Gomez-Menor Fuentes, 'La sociedad conversa toledana en la primera mitad del siglo XVI' in *Simposio Toledano Judaico* (Toledo 20–22 Abril, 1972) (Toledo:Centro Universitario de Toledo, 1972). Gomez-Menor believes it was the converso community's size that made Toledo's Old Christian society fearful of it, and that this fear led to the bloody uprising against the conversos in 1457. In a more recent study, Linda Martz cites a contemporary document which reveals that 2300 of Toledo's conversos were reconciled by the Inquisition in 1486. As these figures were taken from only 17 of the city's 21 parishes, Martz estimates that the true number of reconciled conversos was around 3000, or 17–20 percent of the city's population, estimated to be between 15,000 and 18,000 in the late fifteenth century. Linda Martz, 'Converso Families in Fifteenth- and Sixteenth-Century Toledo: The Significance of Lineage,' *Sefarad* 63.1 (1988). It is evident, therefore, that the total number of conversos—both reconciled and non-reconciled—represented more than 20 percent of the population of Toledo. A census for Talavera de la Reina, taken between 1477 and 1487, reveals that Jews alone made up 20 percent of the of the town's population. See Maria Jesús Suárez, *La Villa de Talavera y Su Tierra en la Edad Media (1369–1504)* (Oviedo: Universidad, 1982), p. 118. It is thus very likely, given the fact that by the late fifteenth-century urban conversos were more numerous than Jews, that around 40 percent of the population of Talavera was of Sephardic origin. Cuenca, Segovia, Trujillo, Ocaña, Soria, Ávila, Zamora, and Murcia were also home to large converso communities. Seville's converso community was also very visible up until the arrival of the Inquisition in 1480, when many fled the city. This community recovered rapidly in the early sixteenth century, dominating commerce and the city guilds. See Antonio Domínguez Ortíz, *La clase social de los conversos*, p. 14.

23. See Ruth Pike, *Aristocrats and Traders*. A number of important studies have appeared subsequent to the works by Gomez Menor and Ruth Pike, examining the converso presence in specific areas of Spain. See, for example, Haim Beinart, *Conversos on Trial: The Inquisition in Ciudad Real* (Jerusalem: Magnes Press, Hebrew University, 1981); Stephen Haliczer, *Inquisition and Society in the Kingdom of Valencia 1479–1834* (Berkeley: University of California Press, 1990); Máximo Diago Hernando, 'Los judeoconversos en Soria después de 1492,' *Sefarad* 51.2 (1991), pp. 259–297; Pilar Huerga Criado, *En la raya de Portugal: Solidaridad y tensiones en la comunidad judeoconverso*, Salamanca: Universidad de Salamanca, 1993; Pedro Luis Lorenzo Cadalso, 'Esplendor y decadencia de las oligarquías conversas de Cuenca y Guadalajara (Siglos XV y XVI),' *Hispania* 186 (1994), pp. 53–94; Linda Martz, *A Network of converso Families in Early mod-*

ern *Toledo: Assimilating a Minority* (Ann Harbor: University of Michigan Press, 2003).
24. Francisco Márquez Villanueva, *Investigaciones sobre Juan Álvarez Gato* (Madrid: Real Academia Española, 1960). Stephen Gilman, *The Spain of Fernando de Rojas* (Princeton: Princeton University Press, 1972). See also the more recent biographies, Y.H. Yerushalmi, *From Spanish Court to Italian Ghetto: Isaac Cardoso, a Study in Seventeenth-Century Marranism and Jewish Apologetics* (New York and London: Columbia University Press, 1971); and Y. Kaplan, *From Christianity to Judaism: Isaac Orobio de Castro* (Oxford: The Littman Library of Jewish Civilization, 1989).
25. Stephen Gilman, *The Spain of Fernando de Rojas*, p. 27.
26. Eugenio Asensio, 'La peculiaridad literaria de los conversos,' *Anuario de Estudios Medievales*, no. 4, (1967), pp. 327–351.
27. 'Su biblismo, si le hace blanco de malsines, también le vincula a excelsos cristianos viejos, como Arias Montano.' Ibid., p. 331.
28. See Chap. 4.
29. José-Carlos Gómez-Menor, 'Linaje judío de escritores religiosos y místicos españoles del siglo XVI' in Ángel Alcalá ed. *Judíos. Sefarditas, Conversos*, p. 596.
30. Marcel Guarinos Cánovas, *Córdoba y su provincia* (Córdoba: Gever, 1986), p. 34. Juan de Mena was born in Córdoba into a professional family. Accused by his contemporaries of Jewish ancestry, he claimed that his family came from the Valley of Mena, in the province of Burgos, 'in the land they call the Mountains.' See Florence Street, 'La Vida de Juan de Mena.' Maintaining that their ancestors were from the mountains (i.e. the north of Spain) was a typical device used by conversos to bolster their claims to Old Christian status (see Chap. 1).
31. Fray Luis de Granada, *Introducción del símbolo de la fé*, pp. 13–14: 'En 1504, el mismo año de la muerte de Isabel la Católica en Medina del Campo, nació Luis de Sarria en Granada, en el escenario de una familia modestísima de cristianos viejos, o de sangre pura.'
32. Ibid., p. 16: '*no sin haber sido atestiguada, con el máximo rigor, su limpieza de sangre.*'
33. Ibid., p. 14, note 3: '*Los padres de Fray Luis no fueron ricos o hacendados, ni de esclarecido linaje, sino pobres y humildes aunque cristianos viejos, limpios y libres de toda raça de Judíos como Moros, y sin mezcla de mala sangre.*'
34. Conversos often took their surnames from the town in which they converted to Christianity. For example, an examination of the census taken in 1510 of conversos in Seville reveals numerous surnames taken from towns of substantial medieval Jewish communities: Sevilla, Jerez, Toledo, Córdoba, Carmona, Llerena, Marchena, Gibraleón, Zafra,

Tarifa, Sanlucar, Palencia, Palma, Aguilar, Burgos, and Écija. See Claudio Guillén, 'Un padrón de conversos sevillanos (1510),' *Bulletin Hispanique*, 65 (1963), pp. 49–98. In his *Libro de Oración* (III parte, Tratado Segundo, II, I), having recommended a frugal diet, Fray Luis de Granada makes the comment that in his experience New Christians live longer than Old Christians because they eat less. It seems to me that Granada is not only making a subtle allusion here to Old Christian greed; he is also linking himself to a more spiritually correct converso population.

35. Pedro Mexía, *Silva de varia lección*, Vol. I, ed. Antonio Castro (Madrid: Cátedra, 1989), p. 9.
36. Mexía wrote a study of his surname, which his son, Francisco, gave to Argote de Molina. See Juan Gill, *Los conversos y la Inquisición Sevillana*, Vol. IV, p. 461. The extent to which Andalusia's converso elite covered up its problematic ancestry has recently been revealed by a Córdoban investigative group led by Professor Enrique Soria Mesa. See, for example, Enrique Soria Mesa, *El cambio inmóvil. Transformaciones y permanencias en una elite de poder (Cordoba, siglos XVI–XIX)* (Córdoba: Ayuntamiento de Cordoba, 2000), and by the same author, *La nobleza en la España moderna. Cambio y continuidad* (Madrid: Marcial Pons, 2007).
37. Pedro Mexía, *Silva de varia lección*, Vol. II, p. 329.
38. Juan Gil, *Los Conversos y la Inquisición Sevillana*, Vol. I, p. 134. The painter Diego Velázquez's maternal grandmother was also a Mexía.
39. For example, in Silva III, 3, Mexía writes, 'The first books and libraries in the world it would seem were those of the Jews; thus as they were first to have writing and the use of it, they also took care to save what they wrote.' In associating the first written words with the Jews, Mexía was, I believe, giving them a central place in his humanist credo. In both his *Silva de varia leccion* and in his *Coloquios*, Mexía demonstrates a much greater interest in the Old Testament than in the New Testament. Of the *Coloquios*, Antonio Castro notes 'a strong inequality in the citations of the Old and New Testaments, with numerous references to the first and very few to the second,' without commenting on why this was so. See Castro's introduction to the *Silva de varia lección*, Vol. I, p. 52.
40. Ruth Pike, 'The Converso Origins of the Sevillian Dramatist Diego Jiménez de Enciso,' *Bulletin of Hispanic Studies* 67.2 (1990), pp. 129–135.
41. Ruth Pike, 'Converso Lineage and the Tribulations of the Sevillian Poet Juan de Jáurequi,' *Romance Quarterly* 38 (1991), pp. 423–429. The paternal side of Jáuregui's family came from Nájera, Logroño, where they were involved in the iron trade.

42. Juan de Jáuregui, *Poesia*, ed. Matas Caballero, pp. 11–12.
43. Ruth Pike, 'Converso Lineage' p. 427.
44. Mercedes García-Arenal, 'Creating Conversos: Genealogy and Identity as Historiographical Problems (after a recent book by Ángel Alcalá),' *Bulletin for Spanish and Portuguese Historical Studies* 38.1 (2013), pp. 1–19. Of Ángel Alcalá's *Los judeoconversos en la cultura y sociedad españolas* (Madrid: Trotta, 2011), García-Arenal writes: 'Finally, it seems to be Alcalá's view that there is not a single reformer or radical thinker in early modern Spain who, if his genealogy is examined closely enough, does not turn out to be a judeoconverso.' This does not accurately reflect Alcalá views. What he does say, rather awkwardly, is the following: 'It seems, astonishingly, that writers and mystics of the Golden Age from converso backgrounds—the biggest paradox being mystics also—are in the majority in respect to those who come from the triumphant caste of Old Christians, and what's more are the best ones. We cannot fail to notice that many of the classic writers and greatest Spanish saints of the age come from recent converso origins.' Ángel Alcalá, *Los judeoconversos en la cultura y sociedad españolas*, pp. 265–266.
45. Mercedes García-Arenal, 'Creating Conversos,' p. 8. The German philosopher Wilhelm Dilthey's theory of 'lived experience' influenced many early twentieth-century Spanish intellectuals, including Castro, Ortega y Gassett, and Sánchez-Albornoz. However, to suggest that Castro's ideas on the conversos stand or fall on the respectability of Dilthey's philosophical theories, as some of Castro's earlier antagonists have done, is to seriously misrepresent Castro's scholarship and, by implication, a generation of liberal scholars who, inspired by Castro, entered the archives to confront the received wisdom on Golden Age Spain. For Castro's interest in Dilthey, see José L. Gómez-Martínez, 'Dilthey en la obra de Americo Castro,' *Abside* 37 (1973), pp. 461–471.
46. Meredes García-Arenal, 'Creating Conversos,' p. 16.
47. In *God in La Mancha*, Sarah Nalle examines the effects of Tridentine policy on the city of Cuenca and its archdiocese. She notes that the most important result of Trent was a greater sensitivity to comportment among both the priesthood and laity, with over half of the Inquisition defendants being charged with 'blasphemy or bigamy or for making erroneous statements about sex, marriage, and celibacy.' Sara T. Nalle, *God in La Mancha: Religious Reform and the People of Cuenca, 1500–1650* (Baltimore: Johns Hopkins University Press, 1992), p. 121.

Select Bibliography

Works Cited

There is a very large and growing body of work examining all aspects of the converso phenomenon in Spain and beyond. In this select bibliography I have chosen to list only those works that I have found relevant to my own research on converso non-conformism, or ones that I believe the reader may find useful in exploring this subject further.

Primary Sources

Arias Montano, Benito, *Comentrario a los treinta y un primeros salmos de David* (León: Universidad León, 1999).
Arias Montano, Benito, 'Lección Cristiana,' in Pedro de Valencia, *Obras IX/2 Escritos Espirituales. La 'Lección Cristiana' de Arias Montano* (León: Universidad de León, 2002).
Ávila, Juan de, *Obras Completas del Santo Maestro Juan de Ávila*, 6 vols., Francisco Martín Hernández y Luis Sala Balust (Madrid: Biblioteca de Autores Cristianos, 1970).
Baltanás, Domingo de, *Apología sobre ciertas materias morales en que hay opinión y Apología de la comunión frecuente*, estudio preliminar y edición de A. Huerga, y P. Sainz Rodríguez (Barcelona: Juan Flors, 1963).
Calvete de Estrella, Juan Cristóbal, *El felicismo viaje del muy alto y muy poderos príncipe Dom Phelippe*, 2 vols. (Madrid: Sociedad de Bibliófilos Españoles, 1930).

Cartagena, Alonso de, *Defensorium unitatis christanae*, trans. Guillermo Verdin-Díaz (Oviedo: Universidad de Oviedo, 1992).
Cazalla, Juan de, Lumbre de alma, ed. *Jesús Martínez de Bufanda* (Madrid: FUE, 1974).
Díaz de Toledo, Fernán, 'Instrucción del relator por el obispo de Cuenca a favor de la nación hebrea,' in *Alonso de Cartagena, Defensorium unitatis christianae*, ed. P. Manuel Alonso (Madrid: CSIC, 1943), pp. 343–356.
Erasmus, Desiderius, *Praise of Folly*, ed. A.H.T. Levi, trans. Betty Radice (London: Penguin, 2004).
Furió Ceriol, Fadrique, *El concejo y consejeros del príncipe*, ed. Henry Méchoulan (Madrid: Editorial Tecnos, 1993).
González Cellorigo, Martin, *Memorial de la política necesaria y útil restauración de España y estados de ella, y desempeño universal de estos*, ed. José Luis Pérez de Ayala (Madrid: Sociedad Estatal Quinto Centenario, 1991).
Granada, Fr. Luis de, *Introducción del símbolo de la fe*, ed. José María Balcells (Madrid: Cátedra, 1989).
Jáuregui, Juan de, *Poesía*, ed. Juan Matas Caballero (Madrid: Cátedra, 1993).
León, Fray Luis de, *Poesía* (Madrid: Cátedra, 1997a).
León, Fray Luis de, *De los nombres de Cristo* (Madrid, Cátedra, 1997b).
Loyola, Ignatius of, *A Pilgrim's Journey: The Autobiography of Ignatius of Loyola*, ed. and trans. Joseph N. Tylenda (San Francisco: Ignatius Press, 2001).
Malara, Juan de, *Philosophia vulgar*, ed. Manuel Bernal Rodríguez (Madrid: Biblioteca Castro, 1996).
Mexía, Pedro, *Silva de varia lección*, 2 vols., ed. Antonio Castro (Madrid: Cátedra, 1989 and 1990).
Montoro, Anton de, *Cancionero de Antón de Montoro (el ropero de Córdoba) poeta del siglo XV*, ed. Emilio Cotarelo y Mori (Madrid: José Perales y Martínez, 1900).
Morales, Ambrosio de, 'Prision de el Arzobispo de Toledo D. Fray Bartolomé de Carranza…' CODOIN, Vol. V (Madrid, 1844), pp. 465–494.
Núñez de Reinoso, Alonso, *Los amores de Clareo y Florisea y los trabajos de la sin ventura Isea*, ed. Miguel Angel Teijeiro Fuentes (Badajoz: Universidad de Extremadura, 1991).
Oliva, Agustín, 'Poesias del Doctor Oliva y de Diego Lopez,' BNM mss/17932.
Ovid, *Metamorphoses*, trans. A. D. Melville (Oxford: Oxford University Press, 1986).
Pacheco, Francisco, *Libro de descripción de verdaderos retratos de ilustres y memorables varones* (Sevilla: Diputación Provincial de Sevilla, 1985).
Pacheco, Francisco, *El arte de la pintura* (Madrid: Cátedra, 1990).
Pacheco, Francisco (Licentiate), 'La sátira apologética en defensa del divino Dueñas,' in 'Una satira sevillana del Licenciado Francisco Pacheco,' *Revista de Archivos, Bibliotecas y Museos* 11 (1907), pp. 1–25.
Pacheco, Francisco (Licentiate), 'Dos sermones sobre la instalación de la libertad del espíritu para vivir recta y felizmente dedicados al muy noble y muy docto Pedro Vélez de Guevara,' in Bartolomé Pozuelo Calero trans. and ed., *El*

Licenciado Francisco Pacheco: Sermones sobre la instauración de la libertad del espíritu y lírica amorosa (Cádiz and Sevilla: Universidad de Sevilla, 1993).

Palomino de Castro y Velasco, Antonio, *El museo pictórico y escala óptica*, Vol. III (Madrid: Alianza Editorial, 1986).

Pérez de Moya, Juan, *Philosofía secreta*, ed. Carlos Clavería (Madrid: Cátedra, 1995a).

Pérez de Oliva, Fernán, *Diálogo de la dignidad del hombre. Razonamientos. Ejercicios*, ed. María Luisa Cerrión Puga (Madrid: Cátedra, 1995b).

Ponce de la Fuente, Constantino, *Suma de doctrina cristiana*, ed. Luis Uso y Rio (Madrid, 1863).

Pulgar, Fernando de, *Crónica de los Reyes Católicos* ed. Juan de Mata Carriazo (Madrid: Espasa-Calpe, 1943).

Pulgar, Fernando de, *Claros varones de Castilla*, ed. Robert Brian Tate (Oxford: Oxford University Press, 1971).

Quevedo, Francisco, 'La isla de los monopantos,' in *La hora de todos y la fortuna con seso* (Zaragoza: Herederos de Pedro Lanaja, 1650).

Rioja, Francisco de, *Poesía*, ed. Begoña López Bueno (Madrid: Cátedra, 1984)

Salucio, Agustín, *Tratado del origen de los villanos, a quienes llaman cristianos viejos en Castilla*. Biblioteca Capitular y Colombina (Sevilla) Ms. 28-7-33.

Salucio, Agustín, *Discurso hecho por fray Agustín Salucio, Maestro en santa Teología, de la Orden de Santo Domingo, acerca de la justicia y buen gobierno de España en los Estatutos de limpieza de sangre: y si conviene, o no, alguna limitación de ellos*. BNE sig. R/29.688.

Salucio, Agustín, *Avisos para los predicadores del santo evangelio*, ed, Alvaro Huerga (Barcelona: Juan Flors, 1956).

Simancas, Diego de, *Vida y cosas notables del señor de Zamora don Diego de Simancas*, in M. Serrano y Sanz ed., *Autobiografías y memorias* (Madrid: Biblioteca de Autores Españoles, 1905).

Talavera, Hernando de, *Católica impugnación*, ed. Francisco Marquez Villanueva, foreword by Stefania Pastore (Córdoba: Almuzara, 2012).

Torre, Felipe de la, *Institución de un rey cristiano*, ed. R.W. Truman (Exeter: Exeter University Press, 1979).

Unamuno, Miguel de, *En torno al casticismo*, ed. Jean-Claude Rabaté (Madrid: Cátedra, 2005).

Valdés, Alfonso de, *Diálogo de Mercurio y Carón*, ed. Rosa Navarro (Madrid: Cátedra, 1999).

Valdés, Juan de, *Diálogo de doctrina cristiana*, ed. Emilio Monjo Bellido (Madrid, Cátedra, 2007).

Valencia, Pedro de 'Discurso sobre el acrecimiento de la labor de la tierra,' BNE ms. 5586.

Valencia, Pedro de, 'Para la declaración de una gran parte de la estoria apostólica...,' BNE ms. 464.

Valencia, Pedro de, 'Tratado acerca de los moriscos de España,' in *Obras completas* IV/2, ed. Rafael González Cañal and Hipólito B. Riesco Álvarez (León: Universidad de León, 1999a).

Valencia, Pedro de, 'El discurso de Pedro de Valencia sobre el pergamino y láminas de Granada,' in Pedro de Valencia, *Obras completas* IV/2, eds. Rafael González Cañal and Hipólito B. Riesco Álvarez, León: Universidad of León, 1999b).

Valencia, Pedro de, 'Academica,' in *Obras completas III: Academica* (León: Universidad de León, 2006).

Villalón, Cristóbal, *El Scholastico*, ed. Richard J. A. Kerr (Madrid: CSIC, 1967).

Villena, Enrique, *Obras completas* (Madrid: Turner/Fundación Antonio Castro, 1994).

Vives, Juan Luis, *Epistolario*, ed. José Jiménez Delgado (Madrid: Editorial Nacional, 1978a).

Vives, Juan Luis, *De la concordia y de la discordia. De la pacificación*, trans. and ed. Enrique Rivera (Madrid: Ediciones Paulinas, 1978b).

Secondary Sources

Agulló y Cobo, Mercedes, 'El Monasterio de San Plácido y su fundador, el madrileño Jerónimo de Villanueva, protonotario de Aragón,' *Villa de Madrid* 46 (1975), pp. 59–68 and 47 (1975), pp. 37–50.

Alvar Ezquerra, Alfredo, 'Montano y el Concilio de Trento' in *Arias Montano y su tiempo* (Badajoz: Junta de Extremadura, 1998), pp. 113–128.

Almenara Sebastiá, Miguel, 'Documentación testamentaria del humanista valenciano Fadrique Furio Ceriol (1527–1592). Edición y comentario,' *Estudis* 21 (1995), pp. 89–111.

Alonso García, David, 'La financiación de las Guardas de Castilla a principios de la Edad Moderna,' in Enrique García Hernán and David Maffi eds., *Guerra y Sociedad en la Monarquía Hispánica: política, estrategia y cultura en la Europa moderna (1500–1700)*, Vol. I (Madrid: CSIC, 2006), pp. 787–804.

Alted Vigil, Alicia, 'Bases político-ideológicas y jurídicas de la universidad franquista,' in *La universidad española bajo el régimen de Franco. Actas del Congreso celebrado en Zaragoza el 8 y 11 noviembre de 1989*, dirigido por Juan José Carreras Ares (Zaragoza: Institución 'Fernando el Católico,' 1991).

Álvarez, Tomás, 'Santa Teresa de Ávila en el drama de los judeoconversos castellanos,' in Ángel Alcalá ed., *Judíos. Sefarditas. Conversos: La expulsión de 1492 y sus consecuencias* (Valladolid: Ambito, 1995), pp. 609–630.

Álvarez Chillida, Gonzalo, *El antisemitismo en España, Madrid: La imagen del judío (1812–2002)* (Madrid: Marcial Pons, 2002).

Álvarez Lopera, José, *De Cean a Cossío: La fortuna crítica del Greco en el siglo XIX* (Madrid: Fundación Universitaria Española, 1987).

Amador de los Ríos, José, *Estudios sobre los judíos de España* (Madrid: D.M. Díaz, 1848).

Amador de los Ríos, José, *Historia social, política y religiosa de los judíos de España y Portugal*, 3 vols. (Madrid: Fortanet, 1876).

Amelang, James, *Historias paralelas: Judeoconversos y moriscos en la España moderna* (Madrid: Ediciones Akal, 2012).

Andrés, Melquíades, 'Los alumbrados de Toledo en el Cuarto Abecedario Espiritual, o ley de amor, de Francisco de Osuna (1530),' *Archivo Iberoamericano* 163–164 (1981), pp. 459–480.
Andrés-Gallego, José, *Historia de la historiografía española* (Madrid: Ediciones Encuentro, 2003).
Antolín, Fray Guillermo, 'Cartas inéditas de Pedro de Valencia al P. José de Sigüenza,' *La Ciudad de Dios* 61 (1896) pp. 341–350, 490–503; 62 (1897) pp. 127–135, 292–296, 360–441; 64 (1897) pp. 354–358.
Aretillo, Darío de, 'Nuevos datos sobre el abuelo materno de san Ignacio de Loyola,' *Archivum Historium Societatis Iesu* 26 (1957), pp. 227–230.
Asensio, Eugenio, 'La peculiaridad literaria de los conversos,' *Anuario de Estudios Medievales* 4 (1967), pp. 327–351.
Astrana Marín, Luis, *Vida ejemplar y heroica de Miguel de Cervantes Saavedra*, Vol. I (Madrid: Editorial Reus, 1948).
Atkinson, William, 'Hernán Pérez de Oliva, a Biographical and Critical Study,' *Revue Hispanique* 71 (1927), pp. 310–482.
Avni, Haim, *Spain, the Jews and Franco* (Philadelphia: Jewish Publication Society, 1982).
Baer, Yitshak, *A History of the Jews in Christian Spain*, 2 vols. (Philadelphia: Jewish Publication Society, 1978).
Bangert, William V. *Jerome Nadal, S.J. 1507–1580* (Chicago: Loyola University Press, 1992).
Bangert, William V. *Claude Jay and Alfonso Salmerón: Two Early Jesuits* (Chicago: Loyola University Press, 1985).
Beinart, Haim, '¿Cuándo llegaron los judíos a España?' *Estudios* 3 (1962), pp. 1–31.
Beinart, Haim, 'The Converso Community in Fifteenth-Century Spain,' in R. D. Barnett ed. *The Sephardic Heritage* (London: Mitchell Valentine, 1971), pp. 425–456.
Beinart, Haim, *Records of the Trials of the Spanish Inquisition in Ciudad Real*, 2 vols. (Jerusalem: Israel National Academy of Sciences and Humanities, 1974).
Beinart, Haim, *Conversos on Trial: The Inquisition in Ciudad Real* (Jerusalem: Magnes Press, Hebrew University, 1981).
Beinart, Haim, 'Inés of Herrera del Duque. The Prophetess of Extremadura,' in Mary E. Giles ed., *Women in the Inquisition: Spain and the New World* (Baltimore: Johns Hopkins University Press, 1999), pp. 42–52.
Benito Ruano, Eloy, *Toledo en el siglo XV* (Madrid: CSIC, 1961).
Bilinkoff, Jodi, *The Avila of Saint Teresa: Religious Reform in a Sixteenth-Century City* (Ithaca, New York: Cornell University Press, 1989).
Blanco Sánchez, Antonio, *Entre Fray Luis y Quevedo. En busca de Francisco de la Torre* (Salamanca: Atlas, 1980).
Blunt, Anthony, *Poussin* (London: Pallas Athene, 1995).
Boeglin, Michel, *Inquisición y contrarreforma: El Tribunal del Santo Oficio de Sevilla (1560–1700)* (Sevilla: Espuela de Plata, 2006).

Boon, Jessica A., 'A Mystic in the Age of the Inquisition: Bernardino de Laredo's *converso* Environment and Christological Spirituality,' *Medieval Encounters* 12. 2 (2006), pp. 133–152.

Borja Medina, Francisco de, 'Iñigo de Loyola y los mercaderes castellanos del norte de Europa. La financiación de sus estudios en la Universidad de Paris,' *Hispania Sacra* 51 (1999), pp. 159–206.

Boyajian, James C., *Portuguese Bankers at the Court of Spain, 1626–1650* (New Brunswick: Rutgers University Press, 1983).

Brown, Jonathan, *Images and Ideas in Seventeenth-Century Spanish Painting* (Princeton: Princeton University Press, 1979).

Brown, Jonathan, *Velázquez: Painter and Courtier* (New Haven and London: Yale University Press, 1986).

Brown, Jonathan, and Kagan, Richard, 'The Duke of Alcalá: His Collection and Its Evolution,' *Art Bulletin* 69.2 (1987), pp. 231–255.

Brown, Jonathan and Garrido, Carmen, *Velázquez. The Technique of Genius* (New Haven and London: Yale University Press, 1998).

Brown, Jonathan and Elliot, J.H., *A Palace for a King*, revised and expanded edition (New Haven and London: Yale University Press, 2003).

Cabrera Sánchez, Margarita, 'Los amigos cordobeses de Cristóbal Colón,' in *Ordenanzas de limpieza de Córdoba (1498) y su proyecto* (Córdoba: Universidad de Córdoba, 1999), pp. 97–104.

Cabrera Sánchez, Margarita, *La medicina en Córdoba durante el siglo XV* (Córdoba: Diputación Provincial, 2002).

Cámpese Gallego, Fernando J., 'Gómez Camacho: Un profeta paradójico en el Siglo de Oro,' *Investigaciones históricas* 28 (2008), pp. 11–28.

Cámpese Gallego, Fernando J., 'Rodrigo Álvarez, SJ (1523–1587), el sucesor del profeta,' *Revista de historia Jerónimo Zurita* 85 (2010), pp. 207–228.

Cantera Burgos, Francisco, 'La judería de Miranda de Ebro (1350–1402),' *Sefarad*, 2.2 (1942), pp. 325–375.

Cantera Burgos, Francisco, 'Hernando de Pulgar y los conversos,' *Sefarad* 4.2 (1944), pp. 295–348.

Cantera Burgos, Francisco, *Álvar García de Santa María y su familia de conversos. Historia de la judería de Burgos y sus conversos más egregios* (Madrid: Instituto Arias Montano, 1952).

Cantera Burgos, Francisco, 'El Cancionero de Baena: Judíos y conversos en él,' *Sefarad* 27.1 (1967), pp. 71–111.

Cantera Burgos, Francisco, and Carrete Parrondo, Carlos, 'Las juderías medievales en la provincia de Guadalajara,' *Sefarad* 33.1 (1973), pp. 3–44; 34.1 (1974), pp. 43–78; and 34.2 (1974), pp. 313–386.

Caro Baroja, Julio, *Los judíos en la España moderna y contemporánea*, 3 vols. (Madrid: Ediciones Istmo, 1986).

Carrasco García, Gonzalo, 'Judeoconversos de Jerez de la Frontera y el obispado de Cádiz a fines del siglo XV,' *En la España Medieval* 29 (2006), pp. 311–345.
Carrete Parrondo, C. and García Casar, María F. 'Las raíces judías de fray Luis de León,' *La Ciudad de Dios* 204 (1991), pp. 587–591.
Case, Thomas E., 'Cide Hamete Benengeli y los libros plúmbeos,' *Cervantes* 22.2 (2002), pp. 9–24.
Castro, Américo, *La realidad histórica de España*. 9th edn. (México: Editorial Porrúa, 1987).
Castro, Américo, *España en su historia. Ensayos sobre historia y literatura* (Madrid: Editorial Trotta, 2004).
Castro Sánchez, Álvaro, *Las noches oscuras de María de Cazalla: mujer, herejía y gobierno en el siglo de oro* (Madrid: La linterna sorda, 2011).
Childers, William, *Transnational Cervantes* (Toronto: University of Toronto Press, 2014).
Civale, Gianclaudio, 'Domingo de Baltanás, monje solicitante en la encrucijada religiosa Andaluza: confesión, Inquisición y Compañía de Jesús en la Sevilla del Siglo de Oro,' *Hispania Sacra* 59 (2007), pp. 197–241.
Clair, Colin, *Christopher Plantin* (London: Plantin Publishers, 1987).
Clarke, Michael, ed. *Velázquez in Seville* (New Haven and London: Yale University Press, 1996).
Clissold, Stephen, *St Teresa of Avila* (London: Sheldon Press, 1979).
Cole, Alison, *Art of the Renaissance Courts* (Upper Saddle River, NJ: Prentice Hall, 2005).
Coleman, David, *Creating Christian Granada: Society and Religious Culture in an Old World Frontier City, 1492–1600* (Ithaca, New York: Cornell University Press, 2003).
Colish, Marcia L., 'The *De veritate fidei christianae* of Juan Luis Vives,' in *Christian Humanism: Essays Offered to Arjo Vanderjagt on the Occasion of His Sixtieth Birthday*, eds. Alasdair A. MacDonald, Zweder von Martels, and Jan R. Veenstra (Leiden: Brill, 2009), pp. 178–198.
Cordero Javier and Hernández, Ricardo J., *Velázquez un logístico en la corte de Felipe IV* (Madrid: Díaz de Santos, 2000).
Coronas Tejada, Luis, *Judíos y judeoconversos en el reino de Jaén* (Jaén: Universidad de Jaén, 2003).
Coronel Ramos, Marco Antonio, 'Juan de Bolonia y Fadrique Furió Ceriol: La ortodoxia doctrinal frente a la ortodoxia evangélica,' *Minerva: Revista de filología clásica* 10 (1996), pp. 145–165.
Cotarelo y Mori, Emilio, 'Don Diego Jiménez de Enciso y su teatro,' *Boletín de la Real Academia Española* 1 (1914), pp. 209–550.
Croche de Acuña, Francisco, *Zafra, una lección de historia y de arte* (Zafra. Caja de Ahorros de Badajoz, 1972).
Croche de Acuña, Francisco, 'Datos ordenados para una biografía de Pedro de Valencia,' *Revista de Estudios Extremeños* 60 (1984), pp. 35–99.

Croche de Acuña, Francisco, *Páginas de la historia Zafrense* (Zafra: Firmas de la Contraportada, 1999).
Cuadra Blanco, Juan Rafael, 'King Philip of Spain as Solomon the Second. The Origins of Solomonism of the Escorial in the Netherlands,' in Wim de Groot, *The Seventh Window. The King's Window donated by Philip II and Mary Tudor to Sint Janskerck (1557)* (Hilversum: Uitgeverij Verloren, 2005), pp. 169–180.
Cuadra Blanco, Juan Rafael, 'Arquitectura e historia sagrada. Nuevas consideraciones sobre la idea de El Escorial y el Templo de Jerusalén,' *Cuadernos de Arte e Iconografía* 43 (2013), pp. 11–258.
Cummins, John G., 'Pero Guillén de Segovia y el ms. 4.114 El Cancionero,' *Hispanic Review* 41 (1973), pp. 6–32.
Curtis, Catherine, 'The Social and Political Thought of Juan Luis Vives: Concord and Counsel in the Christian Commonwealth,' in Charles Fantazzi ed., *A Companion to Juan Luis Vives* (Leiden: Brill, 2008), pp. 113–176.
Davies, David, 'The Ascent of the Mind to God: El Greco's Religious Imagery and Spiritual Reform in Spain,' in José Alvarez Lopera ed., *El Greco: Identity and Transformation. Crete. Italy. Spain* (Madrid: Skira, 1999), pp. 187–215.
D'Elia, Una Roman, *The Poetics of Titian's Religious Paintings* (Cambridge: Cambridge University Press, 2005)
Di Camillo, Octavio, *El Humanismo Castellano del Siglo XV* (Valencia: Fernando Torres, 1976).
Diago Hernando, Máximo, 'Los judeoconversos en Soria despues de 1492,' *Sefarad* 51. 2 (1991), pp. 259–297.
Diago Hernando, Máximo, 'Los Velázquez de Cuéllar, tenientes de Arévalo, en el horizonte político a fines de edad media,' *Cuadernos Abulenses* 16 (1991), pp. 11–40.
Díaz Ballesteros, Miguel, Lariz, Benito et al., *Historia de la villa de Ocaña*, 2 vols. (Ocaña, 1873).
Díaz Rodríguez, Antonio J., 'Papal Bulls and Converso Brokers: New Christian Agents at the Service of the Catholic Monarchy in the Roman Curia (1550–1650),' *Journal of Levantine Studies* 6 (2016), pp. 205–223.
Domínguez Ortiz, Antonio, *Los judeoconversos en España y América* (Madrid: Ediciones Istmo, 1978).
Domínguez Ortiz, Antonio, *La clase social de los conversos de la edad moderna* (Granada: Universidad de Granada, 1991).
Drayson, Elizabeth, *The Lead Books of Granada* (New York and Basingstoke, U.K.: Palgrave Macmillan, 2013).
Edwards, John, 'Trial of an Inquisitor: the dismissal of Diego Rodríguez de Lucero, Inquisitor of Córdoba, 1508,' *Journal of Ecclesiastical History* 37 (1986), pp. 240–257.
Edwards, John, 'Religious Faith and Doubt in Late Medieval Spain: Soria Circa 1450–1500,' *Past and Present* 70 (1988), pp. 3–25.

Edwards, John, *Ferdinand and Isabella: Profiles in Power* (Harlow, United Kingdom: Routledge, 2004).
Egido, Teófanes, *El linaje judeoconverso de Santa Teresa* (Madrid: Editorial Espiritualidad, 1986).
Elliott, J.H., *The Count-Duke of Olivares: The Statesman in an Age of Decline* (New Haven and London: Yale University Press, 1986).
Elliott, J.H., *Spain and its World 1500–1700* (New Haven and London: Yale University Press, 1992).
Espinosa Maeso, Ricardo, 'El Maestro Fernán Pérez de Oliva en Salamanca,' *Boletín de la Real Academia Española* 13 (1926), pp. 433–473.
Estrambasaguas y Peña, Joaquín, 'Una familia de ingenios, los Ramírez de Prado,' *Revista de Estudios Extremeños* 3.2 (1929), pp. 241–257.
Fallows, Noel, 'El "Doctrinal de los cavalleros" de Alfonso de Cartagena, según el ms. Gaml. Kongl. Saml. 2219 de la Real Biblioteca de Copenhague.' *Hispania: Revista Española de Historia* 54 (1994), pp. 1107–1035.
Fernández Marcos, Natalio, and Fernández Tejero, Emilia, *Biblia y humanismo* (Madrid: Fundación Universitaria, 1997).
Fernández Martín, Luis, 'El hogar donde Iñigo de Loyola se hizo hombre 1506–1517,' *Archivum Historia Societatis Iesu* 49 (1980), pp. 21–85.
Fernández Martín, Luis, 'Iñigo de Loyola y los alumbrados,' *Hispania Sacra* 35 (1983), pp. 585–680.
Fernández Tejero, Emilia, 'Fray Luis de León, hebraísta: El *Cantar de los Cantares*,' *Sefarad* 48.2 (1988), pp. 271–292.
Finaldi, Gabriele, 'Pintura y devoción,' in Javier Portús Pérez ed., *Fábulas de Velázquez* (Madrid: Museo del Prado, 2007), pp. 175–201.
Fine, Ruth, Guillemont, Michèle and Vila, Juan Diego eds., *Lo converso: Orden imaginario y realidad en la cultura española (siglos XIV–XVII)* (Madrid: Iberoamericana, 2013).
Firpo, Massimo, *Juan de Valdés and the Italian Reformation (Catholic Christendom 1300–1700)* (London: Routledge, 2016).
Franco Silva, Alonso and Cruz Mariño, Rafael 'Juan Pacheco, privado de Enrique IV, y el oficio de Corregidor de Jerez de la Frontera,' *En la España Medieval* 35 (2012), pp. 285–313.
Gállego, Julián, *Velázquez en Sevilla* (Sevilla: Universidad de Sevilla, 1994).
García de la Concha, Víctor, and San José Lera, Javier, eds., *Fray Luis de León: Historia, humanismo y letras* (Salamanca: Universidad de Salamanca, 1996).
García-Arenal, Mercedes, 'The Religious Identity of the Arabic Language and the Affair of the Lead Books of the Sacromonte de Granada,' *Arábica* 56 (2009), pp. 495–528.
García-Arenal, Mercedes and Rodríguez Mediano, Fernando, 'Miguel de Luna, Cristiano Arábigo de Granada,' in Barrios Aguilera, Manuel and García-Arenal, Mercedes, eds., *¿La historia inventada? Los libros plúmbeos y el legado sacromontano* (Granada: Universidad de Granada, 2008).

García-Arenal, Mercedes and Rodríguez Mediano, Fernando, 'Jerónimo Román de la Higuera and the Lead Books of Granada,' in Kevin Ingram ed., *The Conversos and Moriscos in Late Medieval Spain and Beyond, Volume I: Departures and Change* (Leiden: Brill, 2009) pp. 243–268.

García-Arenal, Mercedes and Rodríguez Mediano, Fernando, *Un oriente español* (Madrid: Marcial Pons, 2010).

García Cueto, David, 'Sobre las relaciones de Velázquez y Don Juan de Córdoba tras el regreso del segundo viaje a Italia,' *Archivo Español de Arte* 334 (2011), pp. 177–180.

García Pinilla, Ignacio J., 'Paz Religiosa, Libertad Religiosa: La apuesta por el pacisismo de Pedro de Ximénez en el Dialogus de Pace (1579),' *Hispania Sacra* 141 (2018), pp. 39–50.

García-Villoslada, Ricardo, *San Ignacio de Loyola: Nueva biografía* (Madrid: Bibioteca de Autores Cristianos, 1988).

Gerber, Jane S. *The Jews of Spain: A History of the Sephardic Experience* (New York: The Free Press, 1994).

Gentili, Augusto, 'Tiziano e la religione,' in Joseph Manca ed., *Titian 500* (Hanover, New Hampshire: National Gallery of Art, Center for Advanced Studies in Visual Arts, 1993), pp. 147–165.

Gerli, E. Michael, 'Performing Nobility: Mosén Diego de Valera and the Poetics of Converso Identity,' *La corónica*, 25.1 (1996), pp. 19–36.

Gil Fernández, Luis, *Panorama social del humanismo español (1500–1800)* (Madrid: Editorial Tecnos, 1995).

Gil, Juan, *Arias Montano en su entorno* (Badajoz: Editora Regional de Extremadura, 1998a).

Gil, Juan, 'Benito Arias Montano en Sevilla,' in *Arias Montano y su tiempo* (Badajoz: Junta de Extremadura, 1998b).

Gil, Juan, *Los conversos y la Inquisición sevillana*, 8 vols. (Sevilla: Universidad de Sevilla, 2000–2004).

Gil, Juan, 'Arias Montano en Sevilla' in J. M. Maestre, J. Pascual Barea et al., eds., *Humanismo y pervivencia del mundo clásico: Homenaje al profesor Antonio Fontán*, Vol. I (Madrid: Laberinto, 2002), pp. 263–280.

Gil, Juan, 'Judíos y conversos en los falsos cronicones,' in A. Molinié and J. P. Duviols eds., *Inquisition d'Espagne* (París: Presses de l'Université de Paris-Sorbonne, 2003) pp. 21–43.

Gilly, Carlos, 'El influjo de Sébastien Castellion sobre los heterodoxos españoles del siglo XVI,' in M. Boeglin y D. Kahn eds., *Recepción de la Reforma y disidencias religiosas en la Península ibérica el siglo XVI* (Madrid: Casa de Velázquez, 2018).

Gilman, Stephen, *The Spain of Fernando de Rojas: The Intellectual and Social Landscape of La Celestina* (Princeton: Princeton University Press, 1972).

Gilman, Stephan, 'A Generation of Conversos,' *Romance Philology* 33 (1979), pp. 87–101.

Giordano, María Laura, *Apologetas de la fe: elites conversas entre inquisición y patronazgo en España (siglos XV y XVI)* (Madrid: Fundación Universitaria Española, 2004).

Giron Negrón, Luis, 'Huellas hebraicas en la poesía del Marqués de Santillana,' in *Encuentros y Desencuentros. Spanish Cultural Intersection Throughout History*, ed. Carlos Carrete Parrondo, Marcelo Dascal et al. (Tel Aviv: University Publishing Projects, 2000), pp. 161–211.

Glaser, Edward, 'Referencias antisemitas en la literatura peninsular de la Edad de Oro,' *Nueva Revista de Filología Hispánica* 8 (1954), pp. 39–62.

Glick, Thomas F. *Islamic and Christian Spain in the Early Middle Ages* (Princeton: Princeton University Press, 1979).

Gómez Canseco, Luis, *El humanismo después de 1600: Pedro de Valencia* (Sevilla: Universidad de Sevilla, 1993).

Gómez Canseco, Luis, ed. *Anatomía del humanismo: Benito Arias Montano 1598–1998* (Huelva: Diputación Provincial de Huelva, 1998).

Gómez-Martínez, José-Luis, 'Dilthey en la obra de Américo Castro,' *Abside* 37 (1973), pp. 461–471.

Gómez-Martínez, José-Luis, *Américo Castro y el origen de los españoles: historia de una polémica* (Madrid: Editorial Gredos, 1975).

Gómez-Menor Fuentes, José Carlos, 'La sociedad conversa toledana en la primera mitad del siglo XVI,' in *Simposio Toledano Judaico* (Toledo 20–22 Abril, 1972) (Toledo: Centro Universitario de Toledo, 1972).

Gómez-Menor Fuentes, José Carlos, 'Linaje judío de escritores religiosos y místicos españoles del Siglo XVI,' in Ángel Alcalá ed. *Judíos. Sefarditas. Conversos* (Valladolid: Ambito Ediciones, 1995), pp. 587–600.

González Novalín, *El Inquisidor general Fernando de Valdés (1483–1568): Su vida y su obra* (Oviedo: Universidad de Oviedo, 1968).

Gonzáléz González, E., 'Vives: Un humanista judeoconverso en el exilio en Flandes,' in Luc Dequeker, and Werner Verbeke eds., *The Expulsion of the Jews and the Emigration to the Low Countries (15th/16th C)* (Leuven: Leuven University Press, 1998).

González Polvillo, Antonio, 'La Congregación de la Granada, el Inmaculismo sevillano y los retratos realizados por Francisco Pacheco de tres de sus principales protagonistas: Miguel Cid, Bernardo de Toro y Mateo Vázquez de Leca,' *Atrio* 15–16 (2009–2010), pp. 47–72.

González Sánchez-Molero, José Luis, 'El erasmismo y la educación de Felipe II,' diss., Complutense, Madrid, 1997.

Goñi Gaztambide, José, 'El impresor Miguel de Eguía procesado por la Inquisición,' *Hispania Sacra* 1 (1948), pp. 35–88.

Gutiérrez Nieto, Juan Ignacio, 'Los conversos y el movimiento comunero,' in *Collected Studies in Honor of Américo Castro's 80th Year*, ed. Marcel P. Hornik (Oxford: Lancombe Lodge Research Library, 1965), pp. 199–220.

Guillén, Claudio, 'Un padrón de conversos sevillanos (1510),' *Bulletin Hispanique* 65 (1963), pp. 49–98.

Haliczer, Stephen, *The Comuneros of Castile: The Forging of a Revolution, 1475–1521* (Madison: University of Wisconsin Press, 1981).

Haliczer, Stephen, *Inquisition and Society in the Kingdom of Valencia 1479–1834* (Berkeley: University of California Press, 1990).

Hamilton, Alastair, *The Family of Love* (Cambridge: James Clarke and Co, 1981).

Hamilton, Alastair, 'The Apocalypse Within: Some Inward Interpretations of the Book of Revelation from the Sixteenth to the Eighteenth Century,' in Hermann Lebram, Jürgen Christian and Jan Willem van Henten eds., *Tradition and Re-Interpretation in Jewish and Early Christian Literature* (Leiden: Brill, 1986), pp. 269–283.

Hamilton, Alastair, *Heresy and Mysticism in Sixteenth-Century Spain: The Alumbrados* (Toronto: University of Toronto Press, 1992).

Harris, Enriqueta, *Velázquez* (London: Pheidon Press, 1982).

Harris, Katy A., *From Muslim Spain to Christian Granada: Inventing a City's Past in Early Modern Spain* (Baltimore: Johns Hopkins University Press, 2007).

Hart, Vaughn, *Art and Magic in the Courts of the Stuarts* (London: Routledge, 1994).

Hauben, Paul J, *Three Spanish Heretics and the Reformation* (Geneva: Libraire Droz, 1967a).

Hauben, Paul J, 'Marcus Pérez and Marrano Calvinism in the Dutch Revolt and the Reformation,' *Bibliotheque D'Humanisme et Renaissance* 29 (1967b), pp. 121–132.

Herrero del Collado, Tarsicio, 'El proceso inquisitorial por delito de herejía contra Hernando de Talavera,' *Anuario de historia del derecho español* 39 (1969), pp. 671–706.

Heuser, Peter A. 'Kaspar Schetz von Grobbendonk oder Pedro Ximénez? Studien zum historischen Ort des "Dialogus de pace" (Köln und Antwerpen 1579),' in G. Braun y A. Strohmeyer eds., *Frieden und Friedenssicherung in der Frühen Neuzeit. Das Heilige Römische Reich und Europa. Festschrift für Maximilian Lanzinner* (Münster: Aschendorff, 2013), pp. 387–341.

Homza, Lu Ann, *Religious Authority in the Spanish Renaissance* (Baltimore and London: Johns Hopkins University Press, 2000).

Huemer, Frances, *Rubens and the First Roman Circle: Studies of the First Decade* (New York: Garland Publishing, 1996).

Huerga, Álvaro, *Los alumbrados de Baeza* (Jaén: Diputación Provincia, 1978a).

Huerga, Álvaro, *Historia de los alumbrados (1570–1630) Vol I: Los alumbrados de Exremadura (1570–1582)* (Madrid: Fundación Universitaria Española, 1978b).
Huerga, Álvaro, *Historia de los alumbrados (1570–1630), Vol. IV: Los alumbrados de Sevilla (1605–1630)* (Madrid: Fundación Universitaria Española, 1988).
Huerga Criado, Pilar, *En la raya de Portugal: Solidaridad y tensiones en la comunidad judeoconversa* (Salamanca: Universidad de Salamanca, 1993).
Hutcheson, Gregory S., 'Cracks in the Labyrinth,' *La corónica* 25.1 (1996), pp. 37–52.
Ingram, Kevin, 'Velázquez's Secret History: The Family Background the Painter was at Pains to Hide in His Application for Entry into the Military Order of Santiago,' *Boletín del Museo del Prado* 35 (1999), pp. 69–95.
Ingram, Kevin, 'The Converso Phenomenon and the Issue of Spanish Identity,' in M. Rozbicki and G. Ndege eds., *Cross-Cultural History and the Domestication of Otherness* (New York and Basingstoke U.K.: Palgrave Macmillan, 2012), pp. 15–38.
Ingram, Kevin, 'El humanista converso Juan de Malara (1524–1570),' in Ruth Fine, Michèle Guillemont, and Juan Diego Vila eds. *Lo converso: orden imaginario y realidad en la cultura española (siglos XIV–XVII)* (Madrid: Iberoamericana, 2013).
Ingram, Kevin, 'Philip II as the New Solomon: The Covert Promotion of Religious Tolerance and Synergism in Post-Tridentine Spain,' in Kevin Ingram ed. *The Conversos and Moriscos in Late Medieval Spain and Beyond, Volume III: Displaced Persons* (Leiden: Brill, 2015), pp. 129–149.
Jardine, Lisa, *Worldly Goods: A History of the Renaissance* (New York: Doubleday, 1996).
Jauralde Pou, Pablo, *Francisco Quevedo (1580–1645)* (Madrid: Castalia, 1998).
Jeffries Martin, John, *Venice's Hidden Enemies: Italian Heretics in a Renaissance City* (Baltimore and London: Johns Hopkins University Press, 2003).
Jiménez Monteserín, Miguel, 'Los hermanos Valdés y el mundo judeoconverso conquense,' in P. Fernández Albaladejo, J. Martínez Millán et al. eds., *Política, religión e inquisición en la España moderna. Homenaje a Joaquín Pérez de Villanueva* (Madrid: Universidad Autónoma de Madrid, 1996), pp. 379–400.
Jordán de Urríes y Azara, José, *Bibliografía y estudio crítico de Jáuregui* (Madrid: Real Academia Española, 1899).
Jurkevich, Gayana, *The Elusive Self: Archetypal Approaches to the Novel of Miguel de Unamuno* (Columbia, Missouri: University of Missouri Press, 1991).
Justi, Carl, *Velázquez y su siglo* (Madrid: Ediciones Istmo, 1999).
Kagan, Richard, *Clio and the Crown: The Politics of History in Medieval and Early Modern Spain* (Baltimore and London: Johns Hopkins University Press, 2009).
Kamen, Henry, *Philip of Spain* (New Haven and London: Yale University Press, 1997a).

Kamen, Henry, *The Spanish Inquisition: A Historical Revision* (London: Weidenfeld and Nicolson, 1997b).
Kaplan, Gregory B., 'Towards the Establishment of a Christian identity: the Conversos and Early Castilian Humanism,' *La corónica* 25.1 (1996), pp. 53–68.
Kaplan, Gregory B., *The Evolution of Converso Literature: The Writings of the Converted Jews of Medieval Spain* (Gainesville, Florida: University Press of Florida, 2002).
Kaplan, Yosef, *From Christianity to Judaism: Isaac Orobio de Castro* (Oxford: The Littman Library of Jewish Civilization, 1989).
Kinder, Gordon, 'A Hitherto Unknown Group of Protestants in Sixteenth-Century Aragon,' *Cuadernos de Historia de Jerónimo Zurita* 51–52 (1985), pp. 131–160.
Kinder, Gordon, 'Two previously unknown letters of Juan Pérez de Pineda, Protestant of Seville in the Sixteenth Century,' *Bibliothèque d'Humanisme et Renaissance* 49 (1987), pp. 111–120.
Kinkaid, Joseph J, *Cristóbal de Villalon* (New York: Twayne, 1973).
Lacave, José Luis, *Juderías y sinagogas españolas* (Madrid: Editorial Mapfre, 1992).
Lara Ródenas, Manuel José, 'Arias Montano en Portugal. La revisión de un tópico sobre la diplomacia secreta de Felipe II,' in Luis Gómez Canseco ed. *Anatomía del humanismo. Benito Arias Montano 1598–1998* (Huelva: Diputación de Huelva, 1998), pp. 343–366.
Laursen, John C. and Nederman, Cary J., eds., *Beyond the Persecuting Society: Religious Toleration before the Enlightenment* (Philadelphia: University of Pennsylvania Press, 1998).
Lawrence, Jeremy, 'Alegoría apocalipsis en *El Aboraique*,' *Revista de poética medieval* 11 (2003), pp. 11–39.
Lazure, Guy, 'Perceptions of the Temple, Projections of the Divine, Royal Patronage, Biblical Scholarship and Jesuit Imaginary in Spain 1580–1620,' in *Calamvs renascens. Revista de humanismo y tradición clásica* 1 (2000), pp. 155–188.
Lea, Charles Henry, *A History of the Inquisition of Spain*, 4 vols. (New York: Macmillan, 1906–1908).
Leathers Kuntz, Marion 'The Concept of Toleration in the *Colloquium Heptaplomeres* of Jean Bodin,' in John C. Laursen, and Cary J. Nederman eds., *Beyond the Persecuting Society* (Philadelphia: University of Pennsylvania Press, 1998), pp. 125–144.
Lleó Cañal, Vicente, 'La Sevilla del Siglo de Oro: ortodoxias y heterodoxias,' in Javier Portús Pérez ed., *Fábulas de Velázquez: Mitología e historia sagrada en el Siglo de Oro* (Madrid: Museo del Prado, 2007), pp. 95–130.
Longhurst, John E., 'Saint Ignatius at Alcalá 1526–1527,' *Archivum Historicum Soceitatis Iesu* 26 (1957), pp. 252–256.

Longhurst, John E. 'La beata Isabel de la Cruz ante la Inquisición 1524–1529,' *Cuadernos de historia de España* 25–26 (1957), pp. 279–303.
Longhurst, John E., 'Alumbrados, erasmistas y luteranos en el proceso de Juan de Vergara,' *Cuadernos de Historia de España* 27 (1958), pp. 99–163; 28 (1958), pp. 102–165; 29–30 (1959), pp. 266–292; 31–32 (1960), pp. 322–356; 35–36 (1962), pp. 337–353; 37–38 (1963), 356–371.
Longhurst, John E., 'Julián Hernández Protestant Martyr,' *Bibliotheque D'Humanisme et Renaissance* 22 (1960), pp. 90–118.
Longhurst, John E., *Luther's Ghost in Spain (1517–1546)* (Lawrence, Kansas: Coronado Press, 1964).
López Beltran, María Teresa, 'El universo familiar de los Santisteban, regidores de Málaga en época de los Reyes Católicos. Una contribución desde la prosopografía,' *Baetica. Estudios de Arte, Geografía e Historia* 31 (2009), pp. 255–74.
López Estrada, Francisco, 'La Retórica en las "Generaciones y semblanza" de Fernán Pérez de Guzmán,' *Revista de Filología Española* 30 (1946), pp. 346–349.
López Martínez, Celestino, 'Gonzalo Argote de Molina, historiador y bibliófilo,' *Archivo Hispalense* 18 (1953), pp. 187–208.
López Navío, José, 'Velázquez tasa los cuadros de su protector D. Juan de Fonseca,' *Archivo Español de Arte* 34 (1961), pp. 53–84.
López Navío, José, 'Don Juan de Fonseca, canónigo meastrescuela de Sevilla,' *Archivo Hispalense* 126–127 (1964), pp. 83–103.
López Torrijos, Rosa, *La mitología en la pintura española del Siglo de Oro* (Madrid: Cátedra, 1995).
Lorenzo Cadarso, Pedro Luis, 'Esplendor y decadencia de las oligarquías conversas de Cuenca y Guadalajara (siglos XV y XVI),' *Hispania* 186 (1994), pp. 53–94.
MacCulloch, Diarmaid, *Reformation. Europe's House Divided 1490–1700* (London: Penguin, 2003).
Macías Rosendo, Baltomero, *La Biblia políglota de Amberes en la correspndencia de Benito Arias Montano (ms. Estoc. A 902)* (Huelva: Universidad de Huelva, 1998).
Madurell, José María, *Historia de la imprenta y librería en Barcelona* (Barcelona: Gremios de Editores, 1955).
Maeso, Espinosa, 'El Maestro Fernán Pérez de Oliva en Salamanca,' *Boletín de la Real Academia Española* 13 (1926), pp. 433–473.
Maestre, José María, ed. *Humanismo y pervivencia del mundo clásico: Homenaje al profesor Antonio Fontón* (Madrid: Laberinto, 2002).
Magnier, Grace, *Pedro de Valencia and the Catholic Apologists of the Expulsion of the Moriscos* (Leiden: Brill, 2010).
Maíz, Ramón, 'Raza y mito celta en los orígenes del nacionalismo gallego,' *Revista Española de Investigaciones Sociológicas* 25 (1984), pp. 137–180.

Markish, Shimon, *Erasmus and the Jews* (Chicago: University of Chicago Press, 1996).
Márquez, Antonio, *Los alumbrados. Orígenes y filosofía (1525–1529)* (Madrid: Taurus, 1980).
Márquez Villanueva, Francisco, 'Conversos y cargos concejiles en el siglo XV,' *Revista de Archivos, Bibliotecas y Museos* 63 (1957), pp. 503–540.
Márquez Villanueva, Francisco, *Investigaciones sobre Juan Álvarez Gato* (Madrid: Real Academia Española, 1960).
Márquez Villanueva, Francisco, 'Santa Teresa y el linaje,' in Francisco Márquez Villanueva, *Espiritualidad y literatura en el siglo XVI* (Madrid: Alfaguara, 1968), pp. 141–152.
Martín, José Luis, 'Claudio Sánchez-Albornoz en la historiografía sobre la edad media hispana,' *Cuadernos de Estudios Gallegos* 107 (1995), pp. 171–205.
Martínez Cuadrado, Francisco, *El Brocense: Semblanza de un humanista* (Badajoz: Diputación de Badajoz, 2003).
Martínez Millán, José ed., *La corte de Felipe II* (Madrid: Alianza Editorial, 1994).
Martínez Ruiz, J. 'Cartas inéditas de Pedro de Valencia a Pablo de Céspedes,' *Boletín de la Real Academia Española* 207 (1979), pp. 371–398.
Martz, Linda, 'Converso Families in Fifteenth- and Sixteenth-Century Toledo: The Significance of Lineage,' *Sefarad* 48.1 (1988), pp. 117–196.
Martz, Linda, *A Network of Converso Families in Early Modern Toledo* (Ann Arbor, Michigan: University of Michigan Press, 2003).
Maryks, Robert A., *The Jesuit Order as a Synagogue of Jews* (Leiden: Brill, 2009).
Mayer, Thomas F. '"Heretics be not in all things heretics," Cardinal Pole, His Circle, and the Potential for Toleration,' in John C., and Cary Nederman eds., *Beyond the Persecuting Society* (Philadelphia: University of Pennsylvania Press, 1998).
Mayorga, Fermín, 'La comunidad judía en Fregenal a finales del siglo XV,' *Alcántara* 67 (2007).
McConica, James, *Erasmus* (Oxford: Oxford University Press, 1991).
Medina Bermúdez, Alejandro, 'Los inagotables misterios de Juan de Lucena,' *Dicenda, Cuadernos de Filología Hispánica* (1999), pp. 295–311.
Menéndez Pelayo, Marcelino, *Historia de los heterodoxos españoles:* 3 vols. (Madrid: CSIC, 1992).
Meyerson, Mark D. and Engish, Edward D. eds. *Christians, Muslims, and Jews in Medieval and Early Modern Spain. Interaction and Cultural Change* (Notre Dame: University of Notre Dame Press, 2000).
Moreno Hernández, Carlos, 'Algunos aspectos de la vida y la poesía de Pero Guillén de Segovia,' *Anales de Literatura Española* 5 (1986–1987), pp. 329–356.
Moreno Uclés, J., 'El humanista baezano Jerónimo de Prado,' *Boletín del Instituto de Estudios Giennenses* 141 (1990), pp. 9–80.

Motis, Miguel Ángel, 'Los judíos de Biel en la Edad Media,' *Suessetania* 12 (1992), pp. 21–53.

Motis, Miguel Ángel, *Judios y Conversos de Ejea de los Caballeros en la Edad Media (XII-XV)* (Ejea de los Caballeros: Centro de Estudios de las Cinco Villas, 2003).

Motis, Miguel Ángel, *Los Judíos de Tarazona en el siglo XIV* (Tarazona: Instituto Fernando el Católico, Tarazona, 2007a).

Motis, Miguel Ángel, *Los judíos de Uncastillo en la Edad Media* (Ejea de los Caballeros: Centro de Estudios de las Cinco Villas, 2007b).

Mulcahy, Rosemarie, *'A la mayor gloria de Dios y el Rey': La decoración de la Real Basílica del Monasterio de El Escorial* (Madrid: Patrimonio Nacional, 1992).

Muller, Priscilla E. 'Pablo de Céspedes: A Letter of 1577,' *The Burlington Magazine* 1115 (1996), pp. 89–91.

Nader, Helen, *The Mendoza Family in the Spanish Renaissance* (New Brunswick: Rutgers University Press, 1979).

Nalle, Sara T., *God in La Mancha: Religious Reform and the People of Cuenca, 1500–1650* (Baltimore: Johns Hopkins University Press, 1992).

Netanyahu, Benzion, *The Origins of the Inquisition in Fifteenth Century Spain* (New York: Random House, 1995a).

Netanyahu, Benzion, 'Una visión española de la historia judía en España: Sánchez Albornoz,' in Ángel Alcalá ed. *Judíos. Sefarditas. Conversos: La expulsión de 1492 y sus consecuencias* (Madrid: Ambito, 1995b), pp. 89–121.

Nieto, José C., *Juan de Valdés y los orígenes de la Reforma en España e Italia* (México D.F.: Fondo de Cultura Económica., 1979).

Nieto, José C., *El Renacimiento y la otra España: visión cultural socioespiritual* (Geneva: Droz, 1997).

Nieto Cumplido, Manuel, 'La revuelta contra los conversos de Córdoba en 1473,' in José Valverde Madrid et al, *Homenaje a Antón de Montoro en el V centenario de su muerte* (Montoro: Ayuntamiento de Montoro, 1977).

Nieto Cumplido, Manuel, *Palma del Río en la edad media (855–1503)* (Córdoba: Archivo Catedral de Córdoba, 2004).

Olds, Katrina B., *Forging the Past: Invented Histories in Counter-Reformation Spain* (New Haven and London: Yale University Press, 2015).

Ollero Pina, José Antonio, *La Universidad de Sevilla en los siglos XVI y XVII* (Sevilla: Universidad de Sevilla, 1993).

Orso, Steven N. *Velázquez, Los Borrachos, and Painting at the Court of Philip IV* (Cambridge: Cambridge University Press, 1993).

Osten Sacken, Cornelio von der, *El Escorial: Estudio iconolólico* (Bilbao: Xarait Libros, 1984).

Parello, Vincent, 'Inquisition and Crypto-Judaism: The "Complicity" of the Mora Family of Quintanar de la Orden (1588–1592),' in Kevin Ingram ed., *The*

Conversos and Moriscos in Late Medieval Spain and Beyond, Volume I: Departures and Change (Leiden: Brill, 2009), pp. 187–210.
Parker, Geoffrey, *The Dutch Revolt* (London: Penguin, 1988)
Pastore, Stefania, *Una herejía española. Conversos, alumbrados e Inquisición (1449–1559)* (Madrid: Marcial Pons, 2010).
Pastore, Stefania, 'Fake Trials and Jews with Old-Fashioned Names: Converso Memory in Toledo,' *La corónica* 41.1 (2012), pp. 235–262.
Perea Siller, Francisco Javier, 'Benito Arias Montano y la identificación de Sefarad: exégesis poligráfica del Abdias 20,' *Helmántica: Revista filología, clásica y hebrea* 154 (2000), pp. 199–218.
Pérez, Joseph, *La revolución de las Comunidades de Castilla (1520–1521)* (Madrid: Siglo XXI, 1999).
Pérez, Joseph, *Crónica de la Inquisición en España* (Barcelona: Martínez Roca, 2002).
Pérez Lozano, M., 'Velázquez y los gustos concepcionistas: el Aguador y su destinatario,' *Boletín del Museo e Instituto Camón Aznar* 54 (1993), pp. 25–48.
Pike, Ruth, 'The Converso Origin of Sebastian Fox Morcillo,' *Hispania* 51.4 (1968), pp. 877–882.
Pike, Ruth, *Aristocrats and Traders* (Ithaca, New York: Cornell University Press, 1972).
Pike, Ruth, 'The converso Origins of the Sevillian Dramatist Diego Jiménez de Enciso,' *Bulletin of Hispanic Studies* 57.2 (1990), pp. 129–135.
Pike, Ruth, 'Converso Lineage and the Tribulations of the Sevillian Poet Juan de Jáurequi,' *Romance Quaterly* 38 (1991), pp. 423–429.
Pinta Llorente, Miguel, and Palacio, José María, *Procesos inquisitoriales contra la familia judía de Juan Luis Vives* (Madrid: Instituto Arias Montano, 1964).
Poole, Stafford, *Juan de Ovando: Governing the Spanish Empire in the Reign of Philip II* (Norman, Oklahoma: University of Oklahoma Press, 2004).
Portús Pérez, Javier, ed., *Fábulas de Velázquez* (Madrid: Museo Nacional del Prado, 2007).
Postigo Castillanos, Elena, *Honor y privilegio en la corona de Castilla: El consejo de las órdenes y los caballeros de hábito en el siglo XVII* (Valladolid: Junta de Castilla y León, 1988).
Pulido Serrano, Juan Ignacio, *Injurias a cristo: Religión, política y antijudaísmo en el siglo XVII* (Alcalá de Henares: Universidad de Alcalá de Henares, 2002).
Quevedo Sánchez, Francisco I., 'Francisco de Torreblanco Villalpando: jurista, religioso, escritor, patrono…converso,' in Félix Labrador Arroyo ed., *II Encuentro de Jóvenes Investigadores en Historia Moderna. Líneas recientes de investigaciones e Historia Moderna* (Madrid: Fundación Española de Historia Moderna, 2015).
Rábade Obrado, *Una élite de poder en la corte de los Reyes Católicos. Los judeoconversos* (Madrid: Sigilo, 1993).

Ramírez, Juan Antonio ed., and Oliver Domingo, José Luis trans. *El Templo de Salomón según Juan Bautista Villalpando. Comentarios a la profecía de Ezequiel* (Madrid: Siruela, 1991).

Ramírez, Juan Antonio, Taylor, René et al. eds., *Dios arquitecto: Juan Bautista Villalpando y el Templo de Salomón* (Madrid: Siruela, 1991).

Ramírez Arellano, Rafael, 'Pablo de Céspedes. Pintor, escultor, arquitecto, literato insigne y ¿músico?' *Boletín de la Sociedad Española de Excursiones* 11 (1903), pp. 204–214 and 232–236; and 12 (1904), pp. 34–41 and 204.

Ramírez Arellano, Rafael, 'Ensayo de un catálogo biográfico de escritores de la provincia y diócesis de Córdoba,' *Revista de Archivos, Bibliotecas y Museos,* 2 vols. (1921–23).

Raya Raya, María Ángeles, *Catálogo de la pintura de la Catedral de Córdoba* (Córdoba: Monte de Piedad y Caja de Ahorros de Córdoba, 1988).

Redel, Enrique, *Ambrosio de Morales* (Córdoba: Imprenta del Diario, 1909).

Redondo, Agustín, 'El doctor Egidio y la predicación evangelista en Sevilla durante los años 1535–1549,' in Juan Luis Castellano and Francisco Sánchez-Montes González eds., *Carlos V. Europeísmo y universalidad* (Granada: Universidad de Granada, 2000), pp. 577–598.

Rekers, B., *Benito Arias Montano* (London: The Warburg Institute, 1972).

Robledo, Ricardo, ed., *Fortuna y negocios: formación y gestión de los grandes patrimonios (siglos XVI–XX)* (Valladolid: Universidad de Valladolid, 2002).

Rodríguez, Pedro, 'Gabriel de Zayas (1526–1593). Notas biográficas,' *Espacio, Tiempo y Forma, Serie IV, Historia Moderna* 4 (1991), pp. 57–70.

Rodríguez Marín, Francisco, 'Una sátira sevillana del Licenciado Francisco Pacheco,' *Revista de Archivos, Bibliotecas y Museos* 17 (1907), pp. 1–25 and pp. 433–454.

Rodríguez Marín, Francisco, *Nuevos datos para las biografías de cien escritores de los siglos XVI y XVII* (Madrid: *Revista de Archivos, Bibliotecas y Museos,* 1923).

Roncero López, Victoriano, 'El tema del linaje en el Estebanillo González: la "indignitas hominis,"' *Bulletin of Hispanic Studies* 70 (1993), pp. 415–423.

Round, Nicholas G., 'Renaissance Culture and its Opponents in Fifteenth-Century Castile,' *Modern Languages Review* 57 (1962), pp. 204–215.

Round, Nicholas G., 'Politics, Style and Group Attitudes in the *Instrucción del Relator,*' *Bulletin of Hispanic Studies* 46 (1969), pp. 289–319.

Rose, Constance Hubbard, *Alonso Nuñez de Reinoso: The Lament of a Sixteenth-Century Exile* (Rutherford N.J.: Fairleigh Dickinson University Press, 1971).

Rubio Lapaz, Jesús, *Pablo de Céspedes y su círculo: humanismo y contrarreforma en la cultura andaluza del Renacimiento al Barroco* (Granada: Universidad de Granada, 1993).

Rubio Lapaz, Jesús 'La relación epistolar entre Pedro de Valencia y Pablo de Céspedes,' *Cuadernos de Arte de la Universidad de Granada* 26 (1995), pp. 371–383.

Rubio Lapaz, Jesús and Moreno Cuadro, Fernando eds., *Escritos de Pablo de Céspedes, Córdoba*. Edición crítica (Córdoba: Diputación Provincial de Córdoba, 1998).

Sagarra Gamazo, Adelaida, 'El protagonismo de la familia Fonseca, oriunda de Portugal y asentado en Toro, en la política castellana hasta el descubrimiento de América,' *Anuario del Instituto de Estudios Zamoranos Florián de Ocampo* 10 (1993), pp. 421–458.

Saintz Ayán, Carmen, 'Consolidación y destrucción de patrimonios financieros en la edad moderna: Los Cortizos (1630–1715),' in Ricardo Robledo ed., *Fortuna y negocios: formación y gestión de los grandes patrimonios (siglos XVI–XX)* (Valladolid: Universidad de Valladolid, 2002), pp. 73–98.

Salomón, Herman P., 'Spanish Marranism Re-Examined,' *Sefarad* 67.1 (2007), pp. 111–154.

Sánchez, Alberto, 'Nuevas orientaciones en el planteamiento de la biografía de Cervantes,' in *Cervantes* (Madrid: Centro de Estudios Cervantinos, 1995), pp. 19–40.

Sánchez-Albornoz, Claudio, *España, un enigma histórico*, 2 vols. (Buenos Aires: Editorial Sudamericana, 1956).

Sánchez-Albornoz, Claudio, *Españoles ante la historia* (Buenos Aires: Losada, 1958).

Sánchez Rodríguez, Carlos, *Perfil de un humanista: Benito Arias Montano* (Huelva: Diputación Provincial de Huelva, 1996).

Sánchez Romeralo, Jaime, 'Pedro de Valencia y Juan Ramírez (La hermandad de ambos humanistas),' in *Actas de la Asociación de Hispanistas* (1968), pp. 795–806.

Sancho, Hipólito, 'El Maestro Fray Agustín Salucio, O.P. Contribución a la Historia Literaria Sevillana del siglo XVI,' *Archivo Hispalense* 16 (1952), pp. 9–47.

Santoveña Setién, Antonio, 'Una alternativa cultural católica para la España de la Restauración,' *Investigaciones históricas: Época moderna y contemporánea* 12 (1992), pp. 235–254.

Schwartz, Stuart B., *All Can be Saved: Religious Tolerance and Salvation in the Iberian Atlantic World* (New Haven and London: Yale University Press, 2008).

Selke, Angela, 'El iluminismo de los conversos y la Inquisición. Cristianismo interior de los alumbrados: resentimiento y sublimación,' in Joaquín Peréz Villanueva ed., *La Inquisición española. Nueva visión, nuevos horizontes* (Madrid: Siglos XXI, 1980), pp. 617–636.

Serrano, Luciano, *Los conversos D. Pablo de Santa María y D. Alfonso de Cartagena* (Madrid: C. Bermelo, 1942).

Serrano de Haro, Antonio, *Personalidad y destino de Jorge Manrique* (Madrid: Gredos, 1966).

Serrano y Sanz, Manuel, 'Pedro Ruíz de Alcaraz, iluminado alcarreño del siglo XVI,' *Revista de Archivos, Bibliotecas y Museos* 7 (1903), pp. 1–6 and 126–139.
Serrano y Sanz, Manuel, *Pedro de Valencia. Estudio biográfico-crítico* (Badajoz: Arqueros, 1910).
Shepherd, Sanford, *Lost Lexicon: Secret Meanings in the Vocabulary of Spanish Literature during the Inquisition* (Miami, Florida: Ediciones Universal, 1982).
Sicroff, Albert, "Clandestine Judaism in the Hieronymite Monastery of Nuestra Señora de Guadalupe," in Izaak A. Langas, Isaak A. and Sholod, Barton eds. *Studies in Honor of Mair J. Bernardete* (New York: Las Americas, 1965), pp. 89–125.
Sicroff, Albert, 'Anticipaciones de Erasmismo Español en *Lumen ad revelationem gentium* de Alonso de Oropesa,' *Nueva Revista de Filología Hispánica*, 30.2 (1981), pp. 315–333.
Sicroff, Albert, *Los estatutos de limpieza de sangre. Contraversias entre los siglos XV y XVII* (Madrid: Taurus, 1985).
Skinner, Quentin, *The Foundations of Modern Political Thought*, 2 vols. (Cambridge: Cambridge University Press, 1979).
Snyder, Jon R., *Dissimulation and the Culture of Secrecy in Early Modern Europe* (Berkeley: University of California Press, 2009).
Soria Mesa, Enrique, *El cambio inmóvil. Transformaciones y permanencias en una élite de poder (Córdoba, siglos XVI–XIX)* (Córdoba: Ayuntamiento de Córdoba, 2000).
Soria Mesa, Enrique, *La nobleza en la España moderna. Cambio y continuidad* (Madrid: Marcial Pons, 2007).
Soria Mesa, Enrique, *El origen judío de Góngora* (Córdoba: Ediciones Hannover, 2015).
Starr-LeBeau, Gretchen D., *In the Shadow of the Virgin: Inquisitors, Friars, and Conversos in Guadalupe, Spain* (Princeton: Princeton University Press, 2003).
Stratton, Susan L., *The Immaculate Conception in Spanish Art* (Cambridge: Cambridge University Press, 1994).
Street, Florence, 'La Vida de Juan de Mena,' *Bulletin Hispanique* 55.2 (1953), pp. 149–173.
Stuczynski, Claude, 'Providentialism in Early Modern Catholic Iberia,' *Hebraic Political Studies* 3.4 (2008), pp. 377–395.
Suárez Álvarez, María Jesús, *La villa de Talavera y su tierra en la Edad Media (1369–1504)* (Oviedo: Universidad de Oviedo, 1982).
Taylor, René, *Arquitectura y magia: consideraciones sobre la 'idea' de El Escorial* (Madrid: Siruela, 2006).
Tellechea Idigoras, José Ignacio, *Fray Bartolomé Carranza. Documentos históricos* (Madrid: Real Academia de la Historia, 1962).
Tellechea Idigoras, José Ignacio, 'Españoles en Lovaina 1551–1558. Primeras noticias sobre el bayanismo,' *Revista Española de Teología* 23 (1963), pp. 21–45.

Tellechea Idigoras, José Ignacio, *El Arzobispo Carranza y su tiempo*, 2 vols. (Madrid: Guadarrama, 1968)
Tellechea Idigoras, José Ignacio, 'Españoles en Lovaina en 1557,' in Werner Thomas and Robert A. Verdonk eds., *Encuentros en Flandes* (Louvain: Universitaire Pers Leuven, 2000), pp. 133-155.
Tellechea Idigoras, José Ignacio, *El Arzobispo Carranza. 'Tiempos recios,'* (Salamanca: Publicaciones Universidad Pontificia/Fundación Universitaria Española, 2003).
Tellechea Idigoras, José Ignacio, 'Fray Bartolomé Carranza: A Spanish Dominican in the England of Mary Tudor,' in John Edwards and Ronald Truman eds., *Reforming Catholicism in the England of Mary Tudor: The Achievements of Friar Bartolomé Carranza* (Aldershot: Ashgate, 2005).
Tolnay, Charles de, 'Velázquez's Las Hilanderas and Las Meninas (An Interpretation),' *Gazette de Beaux-Arts* 35 (1949), pp. 21-38.
Tovar, A, and de la Pinta, M., *Procesos inquisitoriales contra Francisco Sánchez de las Brozas* (Madrid: CSIC, 1941).
Truman, Ronald W., 'Fadrique Furió Ceriol's return to Spain from the Netherlands, in 1564: further information on its circumstances,' in *Bibliotheque d'Humanisme et Renaissance* 41 (1979), pp. 359-366.
Truman, Ronald W., *Spanish Treatises on Government, Society and Religion in the Time of Philip II* (Leiden: Brill, 1999).
Valls Montes, Rafael, 'El bachillerato universitario de 1938,' in *La universidad española bajo el régimen de Franco. Actas del Congreso celebrado en Zaragoza el 8 y 11 noviembre de 1989*, dirigido por Juan José Carreras Ares (Zaragoza: Institución Fernando el Católico, 1991), pp. 197-212.
Van Durme, M., *El Cardinal Granvela (1517-1586)* (Barcelona: Vicens Vives, 1955).
Verdín-Díaz, Guillermo, *Alonso de Cartagena y el Defensorium unitatis christanae* (Oviedo: Universidad de Oviedo, 1992).
Vergara, Alejandro, 'El universo cortesano de Rubens,' in Jonathan Brown ed., *Velázquez, Rubens y Van Dyck* (Madrid: Museo Nacional del Prado, 1999) pp. 67-89.
Vilar, Jean, *Literatura y Economía: La figura satírica del arbitrista en el Siglo de Oro* (Madrid: Selecta de Revista de Occidente, 1973).
Wertheimer, Elaine C., *Honor, Love, and Religion in the Theater before Lope de Vega* (Newark, Delaware: Juan de la Cuesta, 2003).
Wiegers, Gerard, 'The Granada Lead Books Translator Miguel de Luna as a Model for the Toledan Translator of Cidi Hamete Berengeli in Cervantes' Don Quijote,' in Kevin Ingram ed., *The Conversos and Moriscos in Late Medieval Spain and Beyond, Vol. III: Displaced Persons* (Leiden: Brill, 2015), pp. 150-163.
Williams, Rowan, *Teresa of Avila* (London: Continuum, 2003).

Yerushalmi, Y. H., *From Spanish Court to Italian Ghetto: Isaac Cardoso, a Study in Seventeenth-Century Marranism and Jewish Apologetics* (New York and London: Columbia University Press, 1971).

Yisrael, Yosi, 'Constructing and Undermining Converso Jewishness: Profiat Duran and Pablo de Santa Maria,' in Ira Katznelson and Miri Rubin eds., *Religious Conversion: History, Experience and Meaning* (Farnham: Ashgate, 2014) pp. 185–216.

Yovel, Yirmiyahu, 'Converso Dualism in the First Generation: The Cancioneros,' *Jewish Social Studies, New Series*, 14. 3 (1998), pp. 1–28.

Yovel, Yirmiyahu, *The Other Within: The Marranos: Split Identity and Emerging Modernity* (Princeton: Princeton University Press, 2009).

Zagorin, Perez, *Ways of Lying: Dissimulation, Persecution and Conformity in Early Modern Europe* (Cambridge, Mass: Harvard University Press, 1990).

Index[1]

A
Abravanel, Isaac, 17, 18, 305n125
Aguilar, 54, 329n34
Aguilar, Gonzalo de, 48
Aguilar, Lord of, *see* Fernández de Córdoba, Alfonso, Lord of Priego
Aguilar, Tello de, 69
Alboraique, 5, 51, 243n3
Alcalá, Ángel, x, xii, 239, 331n44
Alcalá de Henares, 46, 49, 71, 134, 155, 303n114
Alcalá de Henares, University of (Complutense), 8, 9, 27, 45, 68, 80, 100, 108, 120, 124, 127, 136, 157, 159, 276n102
Alcalá, dukes of, *see* Enríquez de Ribera
Alcañices, Marquis of, *see* Enríquez de Almanza, Juan, Marquis of Alcañices
Alcántara, Military Order of, *see* Military Orders
Alcaraz, Pedro, *see* Ruiz de Alcaraz, Pedro
Alcázar, Baltasar de, 77, 314n38, 320n90
Alcázar family, 77, 274n79
Alcázar, Luis de, 188, 313–314n38
Alcázar Palace, Madrid, 209, 216
Alcocer, Antonio de, 119
Alcocer family, 119
Alcolea de Torote, 155
Aldeanueva, 301n105
Alexander VII, Pope, 182, 322n104
Almodóvar del Campo, 67, 68
Almohads, vii, 253n40
Alpujarras rebellion (1568–1571), 21, 173, 282n21
alumbrados, 8, 31–40, 43, 44, 46, 53, 69, 74, 85, 99–102, 120, 189, 191, 199, 204, 205, 257n63, 258n70, 258–259n76, 262n96, 269n26, 272n67, 272n68, 314n40, 324n1
dejamiento, 33, 34, 37, 205
dejamiento compared to *recogimiento*, 33
Álvarez, Francisco, 156, 300n101

---

[1] Note: Page numbers followed by 'n' refer to notes.

© The Author(s) 2018
K. Ingram, *Converso Non-Conformism in Early Modern Spain*,
https://doi.org/10.1007/978-3-319-93236-1

Álvarez Gato, Juan, 13
Álvarez, Hernando, 272n67
Álvarez Mendizábal, Juan, 228, 324n5
Álvarez, Rodrigo, 190, 191, 193, 194, 199, 282n18, 315n46
Amsterdam, 264n102
Andalusia, 9, 10, 22, 23, 32, 36, 48, 51–84, 101, 102, 118, 120, 121, 146, 147, 186, 234, 236, 253n40, 330n36
Antwerp, 39, 48, 83, 86, 107–109, 118, 120, 123–125, 127, 129–131, 144, 147, 166, 215, 216, 275n96, 284n26, 290n23, 291n25, 321n97
    Calvinism in, 83, 125–126
Antwerp Polyglot Bible, *see* Polyglot Bibles
arbitristas, 170, 307n142
Arévalo, 42, 43, 260n86
Arias Dávila, Diego, 251n30, 260n85
Arias, García, 75, 241
Arias Montano, Benito, xi, xiii, 6, 10, 18, 84, 107, 111, 118–148, 153, 154, 163, 170, 174, 176, 217, 229, 233, 234, 241, 286n38, 289n11, 289n12, 320n90
    In abdias, 18, 122
    and Antwerp Polyglot Bible (*Biblia regia*), 124, 126–129
    Dictatum christianum, 122–123, 134, 289n16
    at El Escorial, 132–134, 142–144
    family background, 119–120
    and Lead Books of Granada, 141–142
Arias, surname in Fregenal de la Sierra, 244n11, 288n3
Asensio, Eugenio, 233–235, 239
Ávila, 42, 97, 98

Ávila, Juan de, xi, 9, 22, 36, 39, 48, 54, 55, 67–75, 78, 79, 81, 87, 92, 94, 98–102, 136, 161, 164, 189, 229, 234, 241
    Audi, filia, 70–71, 73, 74, 75, 92
    and University of Baeza, 73–74
Ávila, Saint Teresa of, *see* Teresa of Ávila
Ayala, noble family, 12, 247n9

B
Badajoz, 78, 100, 102, 272n67
Baena, Alonso de, 78
Baeza, 52, 136, 189, 287n1
Baeza family, 85, 277n103
Baeza, University of, 73–74
Barcelona, 45, 48
Barefoot Carmelites, *see* Teresa of Ávila
Bleda, Jaime, 172
Bobadilla, Nicolás, 49
Bobadilla y Mendoza, Francisco, 60
    El tizón de la nobleza española, 60, 268n26, 278n115
Bocanegra, Egidio, 52, 258n74
Bologna, 79
    Spanish college at, 250n22
Bomberghen family, 125, 126, 291n25
Borja, Francisco de, 136
Burgos, 48, 262n97, 329n34
Burgos, Alfonso de, 87, 278n108
Burgos, Diego de, 20

C
Cáceres, Lope de, 45
Cádiz, Marquis of, *see* Ponce de Leon, Rodrigo, Marquis of Cádiz
Cajés, Eugenio, 209, 210
Calahorra (Navarre), 88
Calatayud, 285n28

INDEX 359

Calatayud, Francisco, 201
Calatrava, Military Order of, *see* Military Orders
Calvete de Estrella, Juan Cristóbal, 107, 269n32, 282n24
  Felicisimo viaje del muy alto y muy poderoso Don Phelipe, 107
Calvinism in Spain, 9, 75, 82–86, 88, 120
  See also Antwerp; conversos; Protestantism
Camacho, Gómez, 189–191, 315n43
Cancioneros, see conversos
Cano, Alonso, 181
Caravaggio, Michelangelo Merisi da, *see* Velázquez, Diego
Carducho, Vicente, 209, 210, 214
Carleval, Bernadino, 73
Carmelites, 96, 98
  See also Teresa of Avila; Barefoot Carmelites
Carmona, 329n34
Carranza, Bartolomé de, 72, 85–89, 102, 107, 109, 158, 159, 229, 241, 275n92, 277n103, 279n117
Carranza, Sancho de, 87, 279n117
Carrillo, Alfonso de, 14, 22
Cartagena, Alonso de, 4, 12–15, 18, 19, 25, 254n41, 254n43
  Defensorium unitatis christianae, 12
Cartagena, Teresa de, 252n36
Castro, Américo, x, 230–232, 239, 327n18, 331n45
Castro, Juan de, 48
Castro, Leon de, 128, 129, 133, 134, 145, 146, 234
Castro, Pedro de, 141, 142, 175–177, 193
Castro, Ródrigo de, 303n114
Cazalla, Agustín de, 85, 241
Cazalla, Alfonso de, 53
Cazalla, Juan de, 36, 43, 53, 241

Cazalla, María de, 36, 43, 53, 241
Cazalla, Pedro de (father), 35, 36, 43, 84
Cazalla, Pedro de (son), 84–86, 241
Cazalla Molina, Leonor de, 135
Cecilius, Saint (first Bishop of Granada), 139, 140, 142, 315n51
Cervantes, Miguel de, 7, 59, 229, 245n13, 296n61
Charles V, 22, 27, 28, 30–32, 35, 61, 100, 104, 132, 202, 214, 218
Cicero, Marcus Tullius, 5, 15, 109, 165, 166, 236
Columbus, Christopher, 59
Columbus, Ferdinand, 59
Comuneros, revolt of, 35, 45
Contreras, Fernando de, 68
conversos
  agents in Rome, 303n115, 322n104
  cancioneros and, 56, 57, 151
  cultural synergism, 118, 133, 139
  endogamy, 47, 51, 96, 163, 233
  feigning Vizcayan roots, 6, 324n5
  ham, giving and receiving gifts of, 55–57, 145, 146
  humanism, xii, 4, 5, 16, 118
  and Jeronymite Order, 25, 75, 82
  and Jesuit Order, xi, 40, 49, 136, 137
  Judaizing or crypto-Judaism, ix, x, 20, 22, 25, 27–29, 36, 53, 54, 55–56, 92, 96, 102, 130, 134, 144–146, 156, 164, 206, 224, 227, 252n31, 253n40, 254–255n45, 256n53, 257n63, 280n3, 287n1, 301n105
  limpieza double entendre, blood purity *vs.* bodily and spiritual purity, 15–17
  Messianism and millenarianism, 26, 32–33, 253n40

Conversos (*cont.*)
  picaresque fiction, 6, 244n5, 248n13
  Portuguese conversos, 3, 10, 72, 144, 167, 174, 184, 185, 203, 206, 207, 211, 219–221, 224
  and Protestantism, 82–88
  Sadduceanism, 47, 253n41–42
Córdoba, 52, 53, 55–57, 59, 60, 62, 63, 72, 73, 101, 102, 135, 136, 140, 154, 155, 157
Corro, Antonio del, 82, 241
Cota, Alonso de, 12, 13
Cota, Rodrigo de, 13, 14, 251n30
Cotarelo y Mori, Emilio, 237
Count-Duke of Olivares, *see* Guzmán, Gaspar de, Count-Duke of Olivares
Cuenca, 102, 224, 263n99, 274n84, 280n3, 331n47

D
David, King of Israel, 37, 64, 70, 104, 111, 132, 147, 228, 293n42
dejamiento, *see alumbrados*
Devotio moderna, 16, 26, 34, 42, 98
Díaz Becerril, Diego, 119
Díaz de Montalvo, Alonso, 12
Díaz de Toledo, Fernán, 12, 14, 20, 277n104
Díaz de Toledo, Pedro, 20, 25, 251n27
Díaz de Torreblanco, Juan, 59
Dilthey, Wilhelm, 239, 331n45
Dominican Order
  opposes cult of the Immaculate Conception, 191–192
  proselytizing campaign among the Jews, viii, 23
  San Gregorio College, Valladolid, 87

E
Écija, 69, 124, 289n19, 329n34
Edict of Faith (1525), 37, 38, 258n76
Egidio, Doctor, *see* Gil, Juan (Doctor Egidio)
Eguía, Miguel de, 45, 262n96, 263n97
El Brocense, *see* Sánchez de las Brozas
El Greco, 180, 230, 325n10
Enríquez de Almanza, Juan, Marquis of Alcañices, 277n104
Enríquez de Ribera, Fadrique, 1st Marquis of Tarifa, 77, 78
Enríquez de Ribera, Fernando, 3rd Duke of Alcalá, 316n58
Enríquez de Ribera, María, 78, 95
Enríquez de Ribera, Per Afan, 1st Duke of Alcalá, 77
Enríquez Ribera family, 77–78
Epicureanism, 66, 151, 152, 154, 253n41
Erasmus, Desiderius, x, 19, 25–27, 29–32, 45–47, 61, 68, 75, 87, 110, 120, 248n14, 255n49, 262n96, 273n70
  Antibarbarorum liber, 61, 110
  conversos' interest in, 27, 255n49
  Enchiridion militis christiani, 25, 45, 255n49, 262n96, 300n100
  Institutio principis christiani, 283n24
  Praise of Folly, 255n49
  Querela pacis, 283n24
  Valladolid debate (1527), 30, 47, 87
Escorial, 10, 111, 118, 129, 132–139, 141, 142, 143, 215, 217
Esquilache, Marquis of, Leopoldo Gregorio, 227
Esteban, Inés, 32, 33
Estella (Navarre), 45, 262–263n97

Extremadura, 6, 9, 32, 33, 51, 73, 118, 163, 186, 272n67
Ezekiel, 134, 135, 137, 138

F
False chronicles, 18, 249n19
Family of Love, 107, 115, 118–120, 125, 130, 131, 147, 291n23
Ferdinand III, 236
Ferdinand VII, 228
Ferdinand the Catholic, King of Aragon, 17, 21, 26, 35, 54, 161, 273n75
Feria, 4th Count of, *see* Fernández de Córdoba, Pedro, 4th Count of Feria
Fernández Portocarrero, Luis, Lord of Palma, 52, 53, 76
Fernández Portocarrero, Luis 2nd Count of Palma, 56, 71
Fernández de Córdoba, Alfonso, Lord of Priego, 54
Fernández de Córdoba, Catalina, Marchioness of Priego, 72
Fernández de Córdoba family, 54, 55, 161, 162
Fernández de Córdoba, Pedro, 4th Count of Feria, 72
Fernández de Madrid, Alonso, 241, 255n49
Fernández de Navarrete, Pedro, 241
Flanders, 27, 48, 126, 127, 215
Fonseca, Alonso de (the third Alonso), 32, 46–47, 48, 61
  Fonseca College, Salamanca, 47, 61, 63
Fonseca family, 46–47
  endogamous unions with the Ulloas, 47, 98
Fonseca y Figueroa, Juan de, 177, 188, 200, 201, 213, 214

Franciscan Order
  and Immaculate Conception, 191
  mystical practice, 33, 36, 39, 53
  proselytizing campaign among the Jews, viii, 23
Franco, Francisco, regime, x, 230–232, 237, 298–299n90
Fresneda, Bernardo de, 101–103
Furió Ceriol, Fadrique, 108, 112–114, 130, 284n26, 286n38
  El concejo y consejeros del principe, 112–114

G
Galicia, 6, 140, 181, 235–237, 298n90
García-Arenal, Mercedes, 239–240, 331n45
García de Licona, Martín, 41
Genoese, 52, 168
Ghent, 104
Gil, Juan (Doctor Egidio), 79, 80, 83, 84, 241
Gilman, Stephen, 233, 235
Góngora, Luis de, 159
González de Cellorigo, Martín, 171
González de Mendoza, Pedro, Archbishop of Seville, 20, 79, 250n21
Gracián, Jerónimo, 101
Grajal, Gaspar de, 96, 108, 164, 241
Granada, 21, 22, 57, 62, 118, 139–142, 162, 175, 176, 190, 193
Granada, Fray Luis de, 67–69, 72–73, 78, 109, 235, 241
Granvelle, Antoine Perrenot de, 115, 126, 128, 130, 291n26
Grapheus, Alexander, 290n23
Gregory XIII, Pope, 128, 129
Guadalupe, 25, 254n45

Gudiel, Alonso de, 96
Guillén, Pero, 13, 14
Guipúzcoa, 40, 41, 43, 100, 247n10, 263n98
Guzmán, Enrique de, 2nd Duke of Medina de Sidonia, 76
Guzmán, Gaspar de, Count-Duke of Olivares, 3, 177, 180, 201–207, 209–211, 213, 214, 217, 219, 220, 306n126, 310n15, 311n22, 314n40

H
Hasdai ibn Shaprut, 304n119
Heere, Lucas de, 104, 105
Herrera, Fernando de, 151, 159
Herrera, Juan de, 136
Hervás, 301n105
Hervás, Francisco, 157
Hervás, María, 157
Hojeda, Pedro de, 189, 314n40
Horace, Quintus Horatius Flaccus, 5, 94, 150, 151
Huerga, Cipriano de la, 241
humanism, xii, 4, 5, 16, 61, 62, 73, 118, 163, 250n22
See also conversos

I
Immaculate Conception cult, 191–193, 314n40
painting by Diego Velázquez, 197
painting by Francisco Pacheco, 193–194
Indies trade and merchants, 62, 68, 76, 171, 187, 232, 298–299n90
Innocent X, Pope, 219, 322n104
Inquisition, ix, x, 10, 21–23, 26–28, 32–36, 38, 39, 42, 45, 46, 53, 54, 56, 63, 66, 69–71, 73–76, 79, 80, 82–89, 92–94, 96, 97, 101, 114, 117, 119, 129, 130, 136, 143, 144, 156, 158, 159, 161, 163, 174, 177, 184, 189–192, 197, 203, 205, 206, 224, 227–229, 237, 240, 247n10
Irenism, 118, 166
Isaiah, 71
Israel, 17, 109, 138, 160, 162
Spain as a New Israel, 71, 133
Italy, 158, 159, 217–219

J
Jáen, 52
Jansen van Barrefelt, Hendrik, 119, 131
Jáuregui, Juan de, 8, 184, 188, 201, 204, 211, 213, 214, 237, 238, 311n21, 312n22, 320n90
Jerez de la Frontera, 73, 118, 148, 149, 187
Jerónimo de Torreblanco, Miguel, 136
Jeronymite Order, 25, 75, 82, 84, 118, 133, 142, 143
See also conversos
Jesuit Order, xi, 40, 43, 49, 55, 74, 100, 102, 115, 136, 137, 167, 188, 190, 191, 193
and Immaculate Conception, 191
limpieza de sangre statute, 49
See also conversos
Jews, vii, viii, ix, 6, 11–13, 17, 18, 21, 23, 24, 27, 37, 38, 52, 63, 64, 70, 71, 72, 75–78, 88, 93, 110–112, 114, 120, 122, 127, 129, 133, 136–138, 149, 150, 156, 169, 170, 173, 175, 176, 204, 225, 227, 228, 230–232, 235, 248n16, 249n19, 255n49, 259n80, 259n81, 273n69, 285n28, 295n55, 301n105,

325n12, 326n15, 328n22, 330n39
pogrom of 1391, vii, 3, 11, 23, 52, 75, 76, 246n1
Jiménez de Enciso, Diego, 237
Jordaens, Jacob, *Apollo as Victor over Pan*, 223, 323n108
Josephus, Titus Flavius, 17, 21, 300n100

L

Láinez, Diego, 48, 49, 136, 276n102
Lazarillo de Tormes, 22
Lead Books of Granada, 139–142, 175–177, 193
Lebrija, 189, 190, 319n87
Leiden, 115
León, Fray Luis de, 93–96, 108, 127, 164, 168, 229, 233–234, 241, 280n3
   Los nombres de cristo, 95, 168
Lerma, Duke of, *see* Sandoval y Rojas, Francisco, Duke of Lerma
limpieza de sangre statutes and investigations, ix, 3–6, 8, 12, 14, 18, 25, 41, 49, 67, 68, 73, 77, 79, 80, 81, 88, 89, 94, 98, 100, 103, 121, 136, 137, 148, 149, 155–157, 159, 167–169, 187, 201–203, 211, 219, 224, 226–228, 230, 235, 238, 247n10, 264n106, 271n53, 300n102, 303n115, 310n15, 322n104
limpieza doublé entendre, *see* conversos
Lipsius, Justus, 108, 114–117, 126, 165, 166, 179, 215, 216, 291n23, 291n26, 297n72
   Neostoicism, 179, 215
Lisbon, 120, 144, 145, 164, 203

Llorente, Juan Antonio, 159
Lope de Vega, Félix, 145, 234
López, Diego, 55–59
López, Martín, 284n26, 285n29
López, Rodrigo, 73
López Aponte, Francisco, 157
López Pacheco, Diego, 2nd Marquis of Villena, 31, 34
López de Miranda, Elvira, 148, 149, 187
López de Soria, Pero, 33
López de Úbeda, Francisco, 6
López de Velasco, Juan, 152
López de Villalobos, Francisco, 253n37, 268n19
Louvain, University of, 84, 108, 109, 113, 115, 127, 128
Loyola, Ignatius of, 8, 40–49, 55, 60, 73, 74, 136, 155
   and Alcalá de Henares, 45–47
   and *alumbrados*, 46, 262n96
   and converso merchants, 48
   at Manresa, 44–45
Lucena, Juan de, 253n40
Luna, Miguel de, 139, 141, 162, 296n58, 304n122

M

Machiavelli, Niccolo, 114
Madrid, 3, 10, 84, 112, 130, 136, 171, 174, 177, 181, 185, 189, 201, 203, 204, 206–208, 212, 214–217, 219, 224
Madrid, Alonso de, 241
Maimonides, Moses, 253n40, 304n119
Maino, Juan Bautista, 319n82
Malara, Juan de, 6, 17, 84, 120, 151, 188, 241
Maluendo, Pedro, 48
Mancebo de Arévalo, 42

Manrique, de Lara, Alonso (Archbishop of Seville and Inquisitor General), 9, 22, 30–32, 39, 46, 48, 61, 68, 79, 87
Manrique de Lara, Antonio, 2nd Duke of Nájera, 43, 253n37
Manrique de Lara, Gómez, 18
Manrique de Lara, Jorge, 18
Manrique de Lara noble family, 8, 12, 22, 55
Manrique de Lara, Pedro, 1st Duke of Nájera, 252n34
Manrique de Lara, Rodrigo, 22
Marchena, 329n34
Mardones, Diego de, 170, 172, 173
Mariana, Juan de, 129, 137, 241
Mármol del Carvajal, Luis, 141
Márquez Villanueva, Francisco, 233
Martínez, Jusepe, 209
Martínez Montañes, Juan, 191, 194
Martínez de Arroyo, Pedro, 156
Martínez de Cantalapiedra, Martín, 96, 127, 164, 241
Martínez de Jáuregui, Miguel, 238
Masius, Andreas, 127, 128, 129, 153, 174
Medina del Campo, 42, 83, 98, 235
Medina Sidonia, 2nd Duke of, see Guzmán, Enrique de, 2nd Duke of Medina de Sidonia
Medina Sidonia, noble house of, 54, 187
Mendoza, Diego de, 3rd Count of Priego, 34
Mendoza, Fray Iñigo de, 249n20, 255n46
Mendoza, Pedro González de, 20, 79, 247n10, 250n21
Mendoza, Diego Hurtado de, 21, 249n20
Mendoza, Iñigo López de, Marquis of Santillana, 18–20

Mendoza, Iñigo López de, 2nd Count of Tendilla, 21
Mendoza, noble house of, 8, 12, 20, 22, 34, 55
Menéndez Pelayo, Marcelino, ix, 159, 229, 230
Messianism, see conversos
Mexía, Juana (or Ana), 183, 186
Mexía, Pedro, 236–237
Mexía de Ovando, Pedro, 298n90
Military Orders, 121, 180, 183, 214, 219
 Council of the Military Orders, 180, 185, 238
 Order of Alcántara, 201, 202, 317n66, 321n93
 Order of Calatrava, 184, 211, 238, 311n21
 Order of Santiago, 1, 2, 121, 122, 180, 181, 182, 183, 201, 203, 220, 222, 224, 226, 236, 237, 305n126
millenarianism, see conversos
Miona, Manuel, 45, 262n96
Miranda del Ebro, 187
Montalvo, Alonso de, 43
Montilla, 55, 72, 266n13
Mora, conversos of Ocaña, 156
Mora, Francisca de, 155–157
Mora, Francisco de, 157
Morales, Ambrosio de, 5, 55, 56, 58–60, 124, 127, 159, 160, 241, 270n46, 294n43, 303n114
Morales, Antonio de, 55, 58
Morillo, Juan, 109, 113, 275n92, 284n28
Moriscos, 4, 21, 22, 42, 57, 58, 72, 103, 118, 139–142, 169, 172, 173, 176, 193, 209, 211, 282n21
Mosquera, Cristóbal, 68
Mozarabs, 226, 326n15
Mudéjares, 52, 56, 230, 258n74

INDEX 365

Murcia, 51, 328n22
Muslims, 21, 37, 52, 161, 173, 176, 225, 227
  See also Mudéjares
Mysticism, 8, 25, 26, 31, 33–40, 44, 52–53, 73, 96, 98, 99, 102, 107, 119, 131, 135, 180, 189, 190, 191, 199, 201, 205
  See also alumbrados

N
Nadal, Jerónimo, 42, 49, 74, 272n69
Nájera, 43
Nájera, dukes of, see Manrique de Lara
Naples, Kingdom of, 12, 43, 45, 88, 279n117
Nardi, Angelo, 209
Navarre, Kingdom of, 266n11
Nebrija, Antonio de, 26, 47, 61, 153, 240
Negrón, Luciano de, 116, 119, 146
Neoplatonism, 66, 305n125
Neostoicism, 108, 114, 117, 179, 215
Niclaes, Hendrik, 107, 125, 131, 290n23
Nicodemism, 108
Noah, 7, 17, 137, 160, 248n16
Noblejas, 156, 157
Numancia, 137
Núñez, Ana, 147
Núñez Pérez, Diego, 146, 147, 234
Núñez Pérez, merchant family, 83, 120, 144
Núñez de Reinoso, Alonso, Los amores de Clareo y Florisea y los trabajos de la sin ventura Isea, 7, 245n14

O
Ocampo, Florián de, 249n19
Ocaña, 155–157, 328n22

Ocaña, Fray Francisco de, 35
Oliva, Agustín de, 55–58
Olivares, Count-Duke of, see Guzmán, Gaspar de, Count-Duke of Olivares
Oropesa, Alonso de, 25, 240
Orpheus, 213
Ortega y Gassett, José, 331n45
Osorio, Alonso, 60, 269n26
Osorio, Álvaro, 60
Osorio, María, 95
Osuna, Fray Francisco de, 36–40, 98, 241, 259n78
Ottoman Empire, 167, 169
Ovando family, 298–299n90
Ovando, Juan de, 152, 298n90
Ovid, *Metamorphoses*, 7, 213

P
Pacheco, Andrés, 305n126, 314n40
Pacheco, Francisco (painter), 6, 157, 158, 184, 187–189, 191, 193, 194, 197, 201, 214, 217, 218
Pacheco, Francisco (Licentiate), 6, 116, 118, 119, 146, 148–154, 159, 165, 168
Pacheco, Juan, 1st Marquis of Villena, 149
Padilla, Cristóbal, 273n73
Padilla, Tómas, 284n26
Pagnini, Santes, 127, 292n27, 292n30
Palma del Rio, 36, 52, 53, 56, 58, 71, 72
Palma del Rio, Count of, see Fernández Portocarrero
Palomino, Antonio, 180, 182, 210, 220, 309n5
Paris, 39, 48, 59, 60, 62, 83, 109, 113, 125, 275n92
Pastrana, 37, 44
Paul V, Pope, 175, 176, 193

Pelayo, Asturian king, 6, 226, 227
Pellicer, José, 260n85
Pereira, Vasco, 191, 194
Pérez, Antonio, 124
Pérez, Baltasar, 108
Pérez, Gonzalo, 124, 290n21
Pérez, Julián, invented chronicler, *see*
   Román de la Higuera, Jerónimo
Pérez, Luis, 120, 127, 129, 130, 144,
   234, 297n72
Pérez, Marcos, 83, 109, 120, 125,
   284n26, 285n29, 290n21,
   290n23
Pérez de Ayala, Martín, 122
Pérez de Guzmán, Fernán, 18, 19
Pérez de Guzmán, Juan Alonso, 3rd
   Duke of Medina Sidonia, 203
Pérez de Guzmán, Juan Alonso, 6th
   Duke of Medina Sidonia, 77
Pérez de Moya, Juan, *Philosophia
   secreta*, 7, 211, 319n87
Pérez de Oliva, Fernán, 55, 58–66
   Dialogo de la dignidad del hombre,
      65–66
   *Razonamiento para la navegación
      del rio Guadalquivir*, 62–63
   Triunfo de Cristo en Jerusalén,
      63–65
Pérez de Pineda, Juan, 286n38
Pérez de Vivero, Alonso, 261n89,
   269n26
Pharisees, compared to churchmen
   immersed in law, 27, 110,
   273n70
Philip I, 35
Philip II, 9, 10, 62, 84, 86, 87, 88,
   100–109, 111, 122–124,
   126–139, 142, 144, 154, 155,
   158, 159, 166, 168, 177
   as the New Solomon, 103–107,
      111, 132–142
   suspicious of conversos, 88, 103

Philip III, 169, 171–173, 175, 177,
   202, 210, 211, 305n126
Philip IV, 2, 3, 169, 177, 180, 201,
   202, 206, 207, 214, 215, 219,
   220, 238, 310n15, 312n22,
   319n87, 322n104
Phoenicians, vii
picaresque fiction, *see* conversos
Pineda, Juan de, 188, 194, 314n38
Pineda, Simón de, 312n29, 313n33,
   313n34
Pius V, Pope, 128
Plantin, Christophe, 107, 118,
   124–126, 127, 128, 129, 130,
   142, 143, 146, 290n23, 291n25
Plantin Press, 122, 123, 125, 127,
   128, 166
pogrom of 1391, *see* Jews
Polanco, Juan Alfonso de, 49, 136
Pole, Cardinal Reginald, 87, 88, 104,
   109, 275n92
politique, 9, 10, 22, 117, 126
Polyglot Bibles
   Antwerp Polyglot Bible (*Biblia
      regia*), 107, 118, 120, 123,
      124, 126, 127, 129, 134, 144,
      153, 164, 174, 291n26,
      294n43
   Complutensian Polyglot Bible, 27,
      123
Ponce de la Fuente, Constantino,
   78–81, 107, 109, 119, 241
   Suma de doctrina Christiana, 80–81
Ponce de Leon, Rodrigo, Marquis of
   Cádiz, 54, 76, 273n74, 274n84,
   276n97, 283n24
Portocarrero, Francisca, 265n4
Portocarrero, Pedro (Inquisitor
   General), 95, 169
Portocarrero, Pedro, Marquis of
   Villanueva del Fresno, 78
Portugal, 3, 147, 163, 180, 181, 185

Poussin, Nicolas, 179, 308n1
Prado, Jerónimo de, 134–137
Protestantism, 9, 22, 27, 32, 36, 49,
   75, 78–89, 91–93, 95, 98, 99,
   104, 105, 107–110, 112, 113,
   115, 117, 119–121, 123–126,
   129, 167, 201, 215, 216
   See also conversos
Pulgar, Fernando de, 14, 15, 21,
   247n10, 253n40
   Claros varones de Castilla, 14, 15

Q
Quevedo, Francisco de, 204, 207
   Execración contra los judíos, 207
   La isla de los monopantos, 204
Quiroga, Gaspar de, 95, 129, 280n2

R
Ramírez, Beatriz, 262n96
Ramírez family of Segura de León,
   163, 306n126
Ramírez, Isabel, 163
Ramírez, Juan, 163
Ramírez Moreno, Juan, 174, 175, 177
Ramírez de Prado, Alonso, 305n126
Ramírez de Prado, Lorenzo, 305n126
Reconquista, viii, 16, 54, 161, 227,
   232
Refundición de la crónica de 1344, 17,
   248n16
Reinoso, Catalina, 85, 277n103
Reinoso, María, 85, 277n103
Reinoso y Baeza, Francisco, 277n103
Requesens, Estefanía de, 262n95
Requesens y Zúñiga, Luis de, 112,
   128–130
Ribadeneira, Pedro de, 41, 49, 167
Ribera, Catalina de, 78
Ribera, Juan de, 78

Rioja, Francisco de, 188, 201,
   314n39
Rizi, Francisco, 318n77
Rodríguez de Figueroa, Juan, 46
Rodríguez de Lucero, Diego, 54, 63,
   161, 252n31
Rodríguez de Silva, Diego, 180, 181,
   182
Rodríguez de Silva, Juan, 180, 182,
   186
Roelas, Juan de, 208, 209
Rojas, Domingo de, 85, 86
Rojas family of Toledo, 277n104,
   278n115
Rojas, Fernando de, 233
Rojas, Luis de, 278n115
Rojas y Sandoval, Cristóbal de,
   100–103, 272n67
Román de la Higuera, Jerónimo,
   137–138, 296n62
Rubens, Jan, 215–216
Rubens, Peter Paul, 179, 214–218,
   323n108
   and Diego Velázquez, 215, 217
Rubens, Philip, 216
Rueda, Lope, 267n14
Ruiz de Alcaraz, Pedro, 31, 34, 35

S
Sadduceanism, see conversos
Sagunto, 137, 138, 160, 295n55
Sal family of Seville, 184
Salamanca, University of, 47, 48,
   59–63, 67, 92, 93, 96, 108, 164,
   201, 233, 235
Salceda, Franciscan monastery at, 36,
   37, 44
Salinas, Jerónimo, 48
Salinas y Castro, Juan de, 238
Salmerón, Alfonso, 48–49
Salonica, 317n72

Salucio, Fray Agustín, 100, 102, 103, 159, 168, 169, 173, 225–227, 235, 241, 307n135
Sánchez, Jaime, 284n28
Sánchez-Albornoz, Claudio, 230, 231, 239, 326n14, 326n15, 326n18
Sánchez de Arévalo, Rodrigo, 249n19
Sánchez de Cepeda, Alonso, 97
Sánchez de Cepeda, Juan, 96, 97
Sánchez de las Brozas, Francisco (El Brocense), 92, 164, 229, 241, 280n1
Sánchez de Licona, Marina, 41
Sánchez de Oropesa, Francisco, 116, 146
Sánchez de Villanueva, Fernán, 280n3
Sancho Panza, 245n13
Sandoval y Rojas, Bernardo de, 100, 169, 175
Sandoval y Rojas, Francisco, Duke of Lerma, 173, 202, 209–211
Sanlúcar de Barrameda, 54, 187, 329n34
Santaella, Rodrigo de (Maese Rodrigo), 76, 77
Santiago (Saint James the Greater), 203, 204, 315n51
Santiago de Compostela, 46, 263n101
Santiago, Military Order of, *see* Military Orders
San Plácido convent, 204–206
Sarmiento, Pedro, 12, 13
 See also *Sentencia-Estatuto* of Toledo
Scholasticism, 16
Segovia, 35, 42, 45, 48, 328n22
Segura de León, 163, 305n125, 305n126
Seneca, 18, 25, 55, 109, 117, 161, 179, 216
 See also Neostoicism

Sentencia-Estatuto of Toledo, 3, 4, 12, 17, 25, 254n44, 259n81
Serrano, Juana, 44
Servetus, Miguel, 275n94
Seso, Carlos de, 85, 86
Seville, viii, 2, 6, 9, 10, 20–22, 39, 52, 54, 62, 68, 69, 75–84, 86–88, 94, 95, 100–102, 108, 116, 118–121, 136, 141, 144–147, 148, 149, 150, 159, 176, 177, 180–193, 201–203, 214, 218, 228, 232, 233, 236–238, 273n74, 311n18
Sigüenza, Fray José de, 131, 143, 144, 147
Silíceo, Juan Martínez de, 49, 60, 62, 157, 269n32, 274n84, 283n24
Simancas, Diego de, 158, 159, 302n110
Simancas, Juan de, 158, 302n111
skepticism, 23, 25, 165, 166
Solomon, King of Israel, 9, 26, 37, 93, 103–105, 107–109, 111, 112, 132–140, 160, 172, 293n42, 295n55, 313n38
Solomon's Temple, 10, 107, 111, 112, 132–139, 160, 162
Song of Songs, 93, 244n4
Soria, 328n22
spirituali, 82, 86, 87, 109
Stoicism, *see* Neostoicism

T
Tacitus, Publius Cornelius, 117, 179
Talavera, Hernando de, 21, 25, 229, 241, 252n31
Tarazona, 108, 284n28
Tarifa, 330n34
Tendilla, Count of, *see* Mendoza, Iñigo López de

INDEX 369

Teresa of Ávila, xi, 36, 96–101, 103, 119, 191, 203, 204, 229, 233, 234, 241, 281n9, 281n13
Tesiphon, 139, 140
Titian, 179, 214, 218, 323n108
Tizón de la nobleza de España, 60, 263n99, 269n26, 278n115
Toledo, vii, 3, 12–14, 17, 19, 22, 25, 33, 35, 46, 47, 49, 51, 79, 80, 95, 96, 97, 98, 100, 119, 137, 138, 157, 158, 180, 206, 232, 248n16, 259n81, 328n22
Toleration, xii, 10, 65, 111, 165, 172, 254n43, 270n34, 283n25, 286n1
Torre, Felipe de la, 108–112, 133, 284n26, 284n28, 285n29
Institución de un Rey Cristiano, 108, 109–111
Torre, María de la, 157
Torre Turpiana manuscript, 141, 176
See *also* Lead Books of Granada
Torreblanco Villalpando, Francisco de, 294n47
Torrejoncillo, Francisco de, *Centinela contra judíos*, 270n36, 323n110
Torrelaguna, 86
Trent, Council of, 75, 82, 86, 87, 91, 92, 96, 100, 118, 122, 180, 232
Túbal, 17, 137, 248n16
Tudela, Julián de, 284n26

U
Úbeda, 52
Ulloa, Ana de, 316n62
Ulloa family of Toro, 46, 98, 263n99
Ulloa, Guiomar de, 98, 281n13
Ulloa, María de, 47
Ulloa, Pedro de, 281n12
Ulloa Pereira, Juan de, 98, 201
Ulloa, Rodrigo de, 277n104
Ulloa de Fonseca, Alonso, 263n99

Unamuno, Miguel, 229–231
Uncastillo, 109
Urban VIII, Pope, 205

V
Valdés, Alfonso de, xi, 30–32, 43, 241, 290n21
Diálogo de Mercurio y Caron, 30
Valdés, Andrés de, 257n63
Valdés, Fernando de, 80, 86, 88, 102, 279n117
Valdés, Hernando de, 257n63, 263n99
Valdés, Juan de, xi, 9, 31–32, 34, 43, 82, 86, 87, 241
Valencia, 27, 28, 57, 112, 118
Valencia, Pedro de, xiii, 116, 118, 142, 146, 147, 163–177, 210, 241
Academica, 165–167
comentary on Saint Paul's 'Epistle to the Galatians,' 167–170
family background, 163–164
Tratado acerca de los moriscos de España, 172–173
Valera, Cipriano de, 241
Valera, Diego de, 12, 13, 17, 249n19, 265n2
Valladolid, 30, 35, 36, 41–43, 47, 72, 87, 88, 92, 94, 95, 97, 98, 120, 159
Protestant cell in, 75, 82, 84–88, 98, 99, 125, 201
Valladolid debate (1527), *see* Erasmus, Desiderius
Valladolid Laws (1413), 246n1
Valladolid, University of, 92, 93, 269n26, 270n36, 271n50
Valtanás, Doming. de, 68, 69, 271n53
Velasco, Antonio de, 60
Velasco, Catalina de, 43, 47

Velasco, María de, 261n89
Velázquez, Diego, xiii, 1–3, 6–8, 10, 171, 172, 177, 180–224, 309n5
  Adoration of the Magi, 197
  An Old Woman Cooking Eggs, 197–199
  Caravaggio influence on, 194, 209, 218
  Christ after the Flagellation contemplated by the Christian Soul, 207–209
  at the court of Philip IV, 202–224
  family background, 180–186
  investigation for entry into the Order of Santiago, 181–184
  Kitchen Maid with Supper at Emmaus, 196–197
  Kitchen Scene with Christ in the House of Martha and Mary, 194–196
  Las Meninas, 1–2, 213, 221–224
  Los Borrachos, 211–214
  Titian influence on, 218
  The Waterseller, 197, 199–201
Velázquez, Fernando, 186, 310n16
Velázquez, Gerónima, 180, 182, 186, 313n33
Velázquez Moreno, Juan, 183, 186
Velázquez de Cuéllar, Juan, xi, 42, 43, 45, 47, 48, 60, 260n85, 261n89
Vélez, Gaspar, 289n12
Vélez, Isabel, 119, 120, 146, 298n84
Vélez de Guevara, Pedro, 119, 120, 146, 148, 151, 153, 298n84
Vergara, Juan de, xi, 22, 23, 27, 32, 79, 157, 241
Villalón, Cristóbal, *El Scholastico*, 60–61, 269n26
Villalpando, Juan Bautista, 134–139, 160, 162

Villanueva, Jerónimo de, 204, 205
  See also San Plácido convent
Villasevil de los Pachecos, 6, 148
Villena, Marquis of, *see* López Pacheco, Diego, 2nd Marquis of Villena; Pacheco, Juan, 1st Marquis of Villena
Viterbo, Annio da, 249n19
Vitoria, Francisco de, 235
Vivero, Leonor de, 84, 261n89, 269n26, 277n102
Vives, Juan Luis, xi, 22, 23, 27–30, 43, 112, 233, 234, 241, 256n53, 256n55
  De concordia discordia, 29–30
  De veritate fidei christiannae, 28
  Introductio ad sepientiam, 29
Vizcaya, *see* conversos
Vulgate, 93, 113, 126, 127, 174, 292n27
vulgo, 3, 5, 28, 65, 93, 152, 153, 175, 204, 211, 212, 244n5, 248n13

W
Woverius, Johannes, 166, 216

Z
Zafra, 72, 73, 118, 163, 164, 272n65, 304n124, 305n126, 329n34
Zamora, 86, 135, 137, 281n12
Zamora, Gaspar, 78, 313n38
Zapata, Cardinal Antonio de, 206, 207
Zapata, Gaspar, 78, 316n58
Zayas, Catalina de, 180, 183
Zayas, Gabriel de, 124–127, 130, 146, 289n19, 290n23
Zurbarán, Francisco de, 181

The manufacturer's authorised representative in the EU is Springer Nature Customer Service Centre GmbH, Europaplatz 3, 69115 Heidelberg, Germany. If you have any concerns regarding our products, please contact ProductSafety@springernature.com

Printed and bound by CPI Group (UK) Ltd, Croydon, CR0 4YY

23/03/2026

02076745-0003